TEACHING THE SHORT STORY

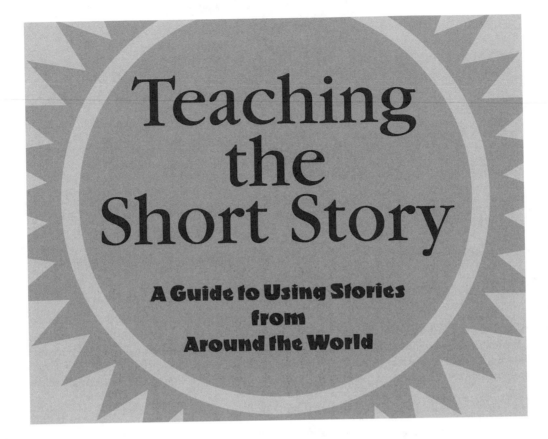

Teaching the Short Story

A Guide to Using Stories from Around the World

Bonnie H. Neumann

Editor

Helen M. McDonnell

Associate Editor

National Council of Teachers of English
1111 W. Kenyon Road, Urbana, Illinois 61801-1096

Manuscript Editor: Michael Himick

Production Editors: Michelle Sanden Johlas, Kurt Austin

Cover and Interior Design: Doug Burnett

NCTE Stock Number: 19476-3050

Library of Congress Cataloging-in-Publication Data

Teaching the short story: a guide to using stories from around the world / Bonnie H. Neumann, editor;
    Helen M. McDonnell, associate editor.
    p. cm.
    Includes indexes.
    ISBN 0-8141-1947-6
    1. Short story. 2. Short stories—Study and teaching. 3. Short stories. I. Neumann, Bonnie H.,
1942-   . II. McDonnell, Helen M.
PN3373.T43 1996
808.83'1—dc20

            96-12993
            CIP

CONTENTS

CONTENTS

CONTENTS

CONTENTS

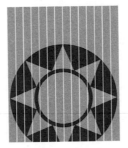

INTRODUCTION

Teaching the Short Story: A Guide to Using Stories from Around the World is a unique resource for teaching the short story at all levels of education. Its format is designed to help teachers select appropriate short works of fiction for study and to identify universal experiences as they are variously expressed in that genre throughout the world. The text emphasizes the importance of recognizing national similarities, of distinguishing unique differences, and of realizing that through the study of great literature one can come to understand and respect systems and ideologies different from one's own. The art of the short story, like all art, reflects the values, basic assumptions, problems, ideals, and philosophical, social, and political climates of the world that created it. Certainly, if we are to have world peace in its most comprehensive sense, it has to come with the tolerance, appreciation, and respect founded on an exposure to, and an understanding of, the experiences of others. Ultimately, we can see in the lowest common denominators the universality of humanity's most basic concerns and of the human condition for which each story serves as a basic metaphor. At no time in the history of art has such an enterprise had more crucial consequences.

The short stories annotated in this text have been carefully selected to represent the best stories from as many countries as possible, excluding the English-speaking countries, since their stories are frequently anthologized and fully discussed in readily available textbooks. Most of the stories included were thus originally written in languages other than English. Generally, we have listed the translator of the English-language version used in our discussions. If no translator is listed, either none was identified in our English-language source or the story was originally written in English. Although we have selected the finest translations available, we have been forced to recognize their uneven quality, especially when there is only one translation available and the translator's knowledge of English is obviously limited.

Because all great art combines the universal and the particular specific to an individual culture, we have attempted to identify themes that are universally expressed, especially those regarding the human condition, and to suggest in the biographical sketch and again in the synopsis of the story those aspects that reflect the particular world from which the story originated. Similarly, our discussions attempt to provide a clear idea of the styles as well as the distinctive qualities of various representative writers from around the world.

The comparisons that we have suggested for each story offer opportunities to enrich the experience of studying it. In addition to identifying and evaluating the various characteristics of a story, it is useful to develop analytical skills through comparison-contrast study. Teachers and students alike can engage in both critical analysis and interdisciplinary thinking. Ultimately, one can appreciate the value of extensive reading when one realizes that the experience of any story is enhanced by its juxtaposition to another and by its comparison or contrast with works in other genres, the visual arts, film, and music. This comparative methodology also demonstrates the universality of particular thematic content or techniques and provides a basis for contrast by which one can see why, how, and to what extent the different milieu, genre, or underlying assumptions account for the particular angle of vision or form of expression manifested in each work.

The biographical material we include is designed to provide succinct information regarding the fundamental conditions of life, thought, and various religious, economic, and social experiences that have shaped the literary expression of the author. Particular attention is given to those writers whose biographical data may be limited or difficult to locate.

We have organized the text by author and have included several indexes to enable teachers to select stories by title, country, English-language source, thematic and literary similarities, or comparable study with frequently anthologized and readily available literary and artistic works. To make *Teaching the Short Story* still more helpful to its readers, titles of works annotated in the text are capitalized wherever they appear.

Ultimately, *Teaching the Short Story* is designed to entice teachers to work with the short stories represented here by providing a superior multicultural and comprehensive selection, presenting sufficient biographical background to enrich the stories, and suggesting comparative approaches both to the more familiar short stories of England and North America and to comparable works of art in other genres, all intended to suggest viable and creative avenues by which stories can be made relevant to each student's educational and personal experience.

One of the most rewarding experiences in teaching the short story is discovering language with students, the language of symbol and metaphor capable of transmitting the human experience of the writer to the mind of a receptive reader. Selected to reflect the experience of its creator, it is a language capable of eliciting a fresh response from the reader and of making specific experiences in another time and place—or even a world—stand for a universal experience that can be shared with the immediacy and intensity of the original. The means of achieving success in this joint venture we leave to the individual instructor, who, according to the requirements of the world of the story and the abilities of the students, will analyze character, plot, point of view, setting, style, other narrative techniques, imagery, or tone with the primary goal of making students aware of both the universality of the message and the distinctive features and implications of various cultural backgrounds, backgrounds that are at once very different from our own, but at the same time an expression of a human experience that the reader can share. — R H M

ANNOTATIONS

Abrahams, Peter. Episode in Malay Camp.

South Africa

Of Time and Place: Comparative World Literature in Translation. Glenview, IL: ScottForesman, 1976.

Author: Peter Abrahams (1919–) grew up in the black quarters around Johannesburg. He experienced poverty and the tensions of apartheid, frequent subjects in his fiction. After graduating from St. Peter's in 1938, he worked in Cape Town as a teacher and magazine editor. After two years of travel as a ship's stoker, he settled in England. He has become South Africa's most prolific writer, penning poetry, novels, many shorter pieces of fiction, and his autobiography, *Tell Freedom* (1954). He has lived in Jamaica since 1959, where he has been editor of the *West Indian Economist.*

Story: EPISODE IN MALAY CAMP illuminates the social structure of South Africa, with poignant insight into the ways in which personal relationships reflect unrelenting racial awareness and tension.

Xuma, a new resident of Malay Camp, a black community on the outskirts of Johannesburg, walks into the heart of the city. The areas through which he passes are increasingly dominated by whites. "They did not walk or look like his people, and it was as if they were not really there." The evolving scene, from barefoot, cold, poorly dressed people to glimpses into bright, warm restaurants, offers contrasts between the lives of the two races occupying different sections of the same city. Xuma, stopped by a policeman and made to show his pass, realizes that only at his job in the mines are men treated as individuals, not judged by their color. There "he was the *boss-boy.* He gave the orders to the other mine boys.... And underground his white man respected him and asked him for his opinion before he did anything."

Returning to his own neighborhood ("It was all right here"), he joins a crowd in time to see a man in flight from the police fall from a roof. Xuma is amazed by the scene and by the sudden appearance of Dr. Mini, who is "dressed in the clothes of the white people and behaved like the white people." Xuma helps Dr. Mini defy the police in order to carry the injured man into the doctor's house, which is "like the white people's place" and makes him uncomfortable, as does the doctor's wife, who is "almost white and ... was dressed like the white people." But Xuma stays for tea; the doctor wants him as a witness when the police arrive. In spite of the doctor's apparent friendliness, Xuma cannot rid himself of the feeling that "he did not belong there and it was wrong for him to be there." His instincts are right. When the injured man escapes, the doctor harshly dismisses him.

Xuma is lonely. In Malay Camp "everywhere he saw couples ... and they all seemed so happy." In city restaurants he sees "white people ... eating, talking and smoking and laughing at each other." His closest approach to others takes place in his neighborhood, where he "rubbed against people and did not step out of the way. He bumped against them, and felt their warmth and softness." Even from these Xuma feels isolated, for they "drank and they fought and they gambled. And there were so many like that in the city." In Dr. Mini he recognizes someone who could have been a hero. "No one Xuma knew could have done what this one had done. And yet this was one of his people." But remembering how Dr. Mini had dismissed him when Xuma was no longer of use, he realizes that the doctor has adopted not only the white man's clothes and furniture, but his attitudes as well.

Comparison: The theme of isolation makes a rich contribution to literature, whether it is encountered in the face of death ("The Open Boat" by Stephen Crane) or in confronting a personal choice (THE GUEST by Albert Camus). It can be imposed

from without (*Invisible Man* by Ralph Ellison), or be a product of imagination ("The Secret Life of Walter Mitty" by James Thurber), or be induced by guilt ("Markheim" by Robert Louis Stevenson).

Often associated with isolation is a search for identity. Camus and Ellison, for example, suggest that to make meaningful contact with others, one must find one's natural place in the world. Confusion between reality and façade is central to the theme of EPISODE IN MALAY CAMP. When supposed opposites come together, neither side prevails, perhaps because the "opposites" are not opposite at all. Perhaps Dr. Mini and his wife are as much the victims of social circumstance as is Xuma. — B H N

ACHEBE, CHINUA. GIRLS AT WAR.

Nigeria
Girls at War and Other Stories. Greenwich, CT: Fawcett, 1972.

Author: Chinua Achebe (1930–) was born in eastern Nigeria. He was reared in the large village of Ogidi, one of the first centers of Anglican missionary work in eastern Nigeria, where his father taught school under the Church Missionary Society. He received his B.A. from Ibadan University. He has held many important posts in the Nigerian Broadcasting Corporation, including director of its external service. He joined the Biafran Ministry of Information and represented Biafra on diplomatic and fundraising missions. In 1972, he was awarded an honorary Doctor of Letters from Dartmouth College. He has been senior research fellow at the Institute of African Studies at the University of Nigeria at Nsukka.

He has published novels, short stories, essays, poetry, and children's books. Among his major works are *Christmas in Biafra* (joint winner of the first Commonwealth Poetry Prize), *Arrow of God* (winner of the New Statesman–Jock Campbell Award), *Anthills of the Savannah* (a finalist for the 1987 English Booker), *No Longer at Ease* (winner of the Nigerian National Trophy), and *Things Fall Apart* (awarded the Margaret Wrong Prize). He is also a recipient of Nigeria's highest award for intel-

lectual achievement, the National Merit Award. Achebe lives with his wife and four children in Nigeria.

Story: At a checkpoint on the road to Awkea, Minister of Justice Reginald Nwakwo is stopped by a pretty girl with a somewhat defiant look. She is vaguely familiar and finally introduces herself as the girl to whom he had offered a ride when she left school to join the militia.

More than a year later, Nwakwo is on the road again, this time to take food from a war distribution center operated by an old friend. As his driver loads the car with food, Nwakwo is embarrassed by the wasted bodies and sunken eyes of the starving crowd that jeers at him and shouts remarks. To clear his conscience, Nwakwo agrees to share his supplies with the driver.

On his way home, he comes upon a beautiful girl standing by the roadway and waving for a ride. When Nwakwo stops to pick her up, he is surprised to encounter, again, the girl "you gave a lift to join the militia." Although Gladys claims to be on her way to visit a girlfriend, when she discovers that her friend is not home, she is perfectly willing to stay the night with Nwakwo. Although Nwakwo's first impulse is to dismiss Gladys as no more than a prostitute, he eventually becomes more understanding. "Gladys was just a mirror reflecting a society that had gone completely rotten and maggoty at the centre. The mirror itself was intact; a lot of smudge but no more. All that was needed was a clean duster. 'I have a duty to her,' he told himself."

The next day, on the road to return Gladys to her home, Nwakwo's car is caught in an air raid. Gladys, Nwakwo, and the driver are all killed.

Comparison: GIRLS AT WAR is exemplary of the breakdown of family life and the position of women in Nigerian society. For those characteristics, it can be compared to Bessie Head's "The Collector of Treasures." — M J J

Achebe, Chinua. Vengeful Creditor.

Nigeria
Girls at War and Other Stories. Greenwich, CT: Fawcett, 1972.

Author: See GIRLS AT WAR.

Story: Mrs. Emenike, a social service officer and wife of a minor civil servant, bemoans the recent introduction into the country of free primary education. She has personally felt the impact of the new law: within the last few weeks, she has lost three servants, including her baby's nurse, to the lure of education. Children in their early teens who had migrated to the city in search of work, a source of cheap labor for professional people like the Emenikes, were returning to the villages to register for school. The Education Ministry had estimated that 800,000 children would take advantage of free education; 1,500,000 attended schools the first day.

Mr. and Mrs. Emenike, well able to pay for their own children's education, are among those relatively affluent citizens who suspect that free education for the masses could well be a communist plot, but their primary concern is for their own comfort. For example, when the only "boy" available to carry her groceries to her Mercedes is a forty-year-old cripple, Mrs. Emenike hands him an insultingly small tip and thinks that she "never cared for these old men running little boys' errands. . . . That was what free primary education had brought."

After one term, the support for free public education is withdrawn. The popularity of the program made it so expensive that politicians saw no means of supporting it without raising taxes, a move which

would have cost them their positions. The politicians rationalize about the man who is again unable to send his children to school, "The worst that can happen is that his child stays at home which he probably doesn't mind at all." The impact that the withdrawal of educational opportunity might have on the children is, of course, never considered.

It is against this background that ten-year-old Veronica goes to work for the Emenikes. The daughter of Martha, a poor village widow, Vero had loved the one term of school she had been able to attend. While negotiating for Vero's service, Mr. Emenike points out to Vero's mother that if Vero "'is obedient and good in my house what stops my wife and me sending her to school when the baby is big enough to go about on his own? Nothing' . . . . He knew that the part about sending her to school was only a manner of speaking. And Martha knew too. But Vero, who had been listening to everything from a dark corner of the adjoining room, did not."

Vero goes happily to the city and works well for the Emenikes, every morning sending their older children off to school while her envy of them grows. In the context of her impatience, the baby seems to grow very slowly. One day, Vero plays at being an adult and covers her lips and fingernails with red ink. To impress her, Mrs. Emenike warns Vero that red ink is poisonous. A week later, Vero feeds ink to the baby. Mrs. Emenike beats Vero, and Mr. Emenike dumps her at her mother's doorstep.

When Martha understands that Vero has tried to kill the baby, she too threatens to beat Vero. Remembering Mr. Emenike's statement, "I have always known that the craze for education in this country will one day ruin all of us. Now even children will commit murder in order to go to school," stops her. A "slow revolt, vague, undirected, began to well up at first slowly inside her. 'And that thing that calls himself a man talks to me about the craze for education. All his children go to school, even the one that is only two years; but that is not craze. Rich people have no craze. It is only when the children of poor widows like me want to go with the rest that it becomes a craze.'" In the end, "she threw away the whip and with her freed hand wiped her tears." Veronica has been spared a second whipping, but her dreams have ended; she has been returned to her life of hopeless poverty.

Comparison: VENGEFUL CREDITOR is a story of initiation, the innocence of childhood encountering, and being forever tainted by, the prejudices and closed minds of adulthood. In that respect, the story resembles such popular stories as Willa Cather's "Paul's Case" and Ralph Ellison's "Battle Royal."

It is also a political story, one in which the author uses the medium of fiction to express a personal opinion about a controversial issue or to introduce an unpopular idea. In this case, Achebe attacks the Nigerian caste system, perpetuated because greed and power have blinded those in control to the humanity of those from a different background. Achebe's weaving of a moral judgment into the fabric of his story is similar to Hawthorne's use of the same technique in stories such as "Young Goodman Brown" and novels such as *The Scarlet Letter.* A contrast can be drawn, however, between Hawthorne's works and VENGEFUL CREDITOR based on the complexity of the characters' motivations. Hawthorne's characters tend to be contrivances for his moral themes, whereas the Emenikes, insensitive as they are, have good reason to wish Vero out of their house.

Finally, VENGEFUL CREDITOR raises questions about the future of a society in which people, especially children, dare not dream. A village without hope becomes a society without hope, one in which the children of the future might be like those in Graham Greene's "The Destructors," taught by the world around them that destruction is the only form of creation. — B H N

ACHEBE, CHINUA. THE VOTER.

Nigeria
World Writers Today. Glenview, IL: ScottForesman, 1995.

Author: See GIRLS AT WAR.

Story: In order to ensure his re-election, Minister of Culture Marcus Ibe gives his campaign staff a bag of shillings to distribute to prospective voters. Rufus (Roof) Okeke, "a very popular man" in Ibe's home village, works vigorously on the Honorable Minister's behalf. Shortly after Rufus meets with the tribal elders to negotiate a price of three shillings each for their votes, members of the opposition party visit Roof late one night, offering him a five-pound bribe to vote for Maduka, Ibe's rival. Believing in Marcus's certain victory and the secrecy of the ballot system, Roof agrees. As soon as he takes the money, the men uncover an *iyi,* "a fearsome little affair contained in a clay pot with feathers stuck into it." They declare that the *iyi* will know if Rufus does not keep his word.

On the day of the election, Roof joins other organizers enthusiastically promoting Marcus Ibe's candidacy. When Rufus enters the polling booth, however, his fear of the *iyi* proves too much for him. He carefully tears his ballot paper in two, depositing the first half into Maduka's box and saying, "I vote for Maduka," before putting the other half in Ibe's box.

Comparison: Corruption in politics and the conflict between native and colonial values and customs are central themes in much of Achebe's writing. In both his second and fourth novels, *No Longer at Ease* and *Man of the People*, a civil servant takes bribes. *Man of the People*, published a year after THE VOTER, presents a more fully developed portrait of the crooked politician seen here. M. A. Nanga, like Marcus Ibe, is a "not too successful" village schoolteacher who rises quickly in national politics, becoming the Minister of Culture. Achebe contrasts the opulent lifestyle of the elected official with that of his impoverished constituents as an ironic comment on the villagers' belief that despite his success, the Minister has remained "a man of the people," a phrase found in both works. Characteristically, however, Achebe does not idealize the local tribal people in THE VOTER. They are just as anxious to accept bribes as the national campaign workers are to offer them.

Parallels in characterization and theme can be seen in works by two contemporary Nigerian writers. In Wole Soyinka's novel *The Interpreter*, Chief Winsala, an old rogue, takes petty bribes as he fronts for a supposedly incorruptible judge. Cyprian Ekwensi, in his novel *Jagua Nana*, portrays Uncle Taiwo as a jovial but completely dishonest politician with whom Jagua, the heroine, becomes involved.

Many Nigerian writers use village proverbs and variations in language to represent a hybrid culture, as does Achebe. In THE VOTER, proverbs that reflect the tribal culture make wry comments on the action, and characters switch from English to Pidgin in their conversations. Ibo words such as *iyi* and *ozo* are not given an English translation. Humor underscores the mixture and adulteration of languages. For example, the villagers say "corngrass" for "congrats" to the winner.

The corrupting power of greed is a basic theme of many well-known literary works. Several prime examples are Ibsen's play *An Enemy of the People* and Twain's short story "The Man That Corrupted Hadleyburg." In Ibsen's play, public officials value making money more than they value the health of the visitors to the town's famous, but polluted, baths. In Twain's "The Man That Corrupted Hadleyburg," the townspeople's belief in the honesty of their prominent citizens proves to be a travesty when they lie in order to gain a bag of gold. Ironically, the villagers in THE VOTER believe that "the people exercised power" in the national election, even though they sold their votes to the highest bidder. — M A F

Agnon, S. Y. The Document.

Israel

Twenty-One Stories. New York: Schocken Books, 1970. Translated by Joseph Moses.

Author: S. Y. Agnon (1888–1970) was born in Buczaca, Galicia, then part of the Austro-Hungarian Empire. Agnon wrote in Hebrew, and from the beginning his stories were deeply imbued with the traditions of Jewish thought and scholarship. At the age of nineteen, he emigrated to Palestine, where he lived for six years before returning to Europe. Over the next eleven years, he participated in the intellectual and cultural life of Germany. In 1924, he made his permanent home in Jerusalem. Partially under the influence of the powerful trends in contemporary European literature during and after the First World War, Agnon's later writing grew more universal, demonstrating a concern for many of the spiritual issues that burden modern individuals. His short stories, novels, and novellas evoke the basic elements of human destiny: the language of the common people, plots evolving from darkness to light, and characters controlled on one side by nature and on the other by laws and conventions. His international reputation grew, and in 1966 he received the Nobel Prize for Literature. Agnon continued to live and write in Israel until his death.

Story: In this brief, dreamlike story, a man receives a letter from a distant relative asking him to go to a certain office and obtain a document on which the relative's life depends. The man is ill, but he nevertheless undertakes to fulfill the task. He arrives early at the office, but soon finds himself pushed about by hordes of people, standing in long lines, and being sent from one room to another without result. This goes on for three straight days as the man becomes increasingly ill.

On the third day, things seem to start going a little better. By this time, however, the man has forgotten why he has come, why he is standing there, why he is running from room to room. A man sitting behind one of the desks turns out to be an old acquaintance, a druggist he knew before the war. The druggist offers him a bar of chocolate. He meets a professor who, for no apparent reason, engages him in a discussion about the etymology of a word. Finally, as the story ends, the man finds himself shoved by a mass of people onto an outside balcony floating on an endless ocean.

Comparison: Agnon's dream narrative must be seen in the context of a tradition that includes Talmudic scholarship on the one hand and the stories of Franz Kafka on the other. The "document" may be the text we are reading. At any rate, it cries out for interpretation, both as a dream and as a parable of life. As such, it may be fruitfully compared with other dreams and parables in American and European literature, from Kafka to Borges to John Barth and beyond.

The thematic threads of the story include the search for meaning in a confusing, bureaucratic, and impersonal world; the role of human compassion and scholarship; the decline of the body in the course of life; the inevitability of death; and the freedom of the spirit. Because the dream represents a link between the inner mind and the external world, the form of the tale suggests as well that life's meaning cannot be restricted to purely rational analysis.

Melville's "Bartleby the Scrivener" also deals with the inevitability of death and freedom of the spirit, as Bartleby goes through life apparently aware of some great truth that eludes everyone around him. He cannot act on that truth, however, because he is a mere mortal trapped in a human body. But his spirit is so much more; it *knows.* A sense of relief is felt at the end when Bartleby dies in prison, for his spirit is now free. Whatever lies beyond, if anything, only Bartleby knows.

THE DOCUMENT is a parable of life in much the same way as Kafka's THE METAMORPHOSIS. Gregor's symbolic and literal decline of body and spirit and the nightmarish existence he leads both before and after his metamorphosis reveal the absurd repetition inherent in everyday human life. The latter concept is also expressed in Thomas Wolfe's "For What Is Man?" from *You Can't Go Home Again,* an essay on the glory of human existence amid "the senseless nihilism of the universe" and "a million idiot repetitions." — B M

AGNON, S. Y. A WHOLE LOAF.

Israel
A Whole Loaf: Stories from Israel. New York: Vanguard Press, 1962. Translated by I. M. Lask.

Author: See THE DOCUMENT.

Story: The narrator, whose wife and children are traveling abroad, sets out for a restaurant dinner. Passing through Jerusalem's old quarter, he meets Dr. Ne'eman (No Man), a "very considerable sage" who criticizes the narrator for not working harder to help his family overcome the bureaucratic delay that has been keeping them out of Israel. Feeling guilty and ashamed, the narrator agrees to mail some letters for the old man to get back in his favor. Oppressed by hunger and sorely tempted to stop for food, the narrator carries on a lively debate with himself over his priorities. "It is easy to understand the state of a man who has two courses in front of him: if he takes one, it seems to him that he has to follow the other; and if he takes the other, it seems to him that he ought to go along the first one. But at length to his joy he takes the course that he ought to take." The narrator decides that complying with Ne'eman's request is more important than eating.

In front of the post office, the narrator sees Mr. Gressler, whom he has known since childhood. Flattered to be given special notice by this important man, the narrator climbs into Gressler's carriage and forgets "all about the letters and the hunger." Suddenly, the carriage overturns, and, when he finally extricates himself from the ruins, the narrator heads straight for the nearest restaurant.

The restaurant is crowded. When a waiter finally stops at his table, the narrator is so hungry that he notes, "I showed him the bill of fare and told him to fetch anything he wanted. And in order that he should not think me the kind of boor who eats anything without selecting it, I added to him gravely, 'But I want a whole loaf.'" One guest after another is served, but not the narrator. Each time he passes the table, the waiter apologizes and promises him that "the whole loaf" will be right there. Desperate, the narrator barely restrains himself from grabbing food from other people's tables. New customers are served, and still the narrator sits before an empty table. He notes, "I began rebuking myself for asking for a whole loaf, when I would have been satisfied even with a small slice."

Suddenly, the narrator remembers the letters in his pocket. He jumps up to run to the post office. As he does so, he butts into a waiter carrying a tray loaded with food and drink, and the tray and the waiter tumble to the floor. The tray had been intended for the narrator. Again, he waits. All the customers leave. The lights are extinguished. Still the narrator sits patiently. The waiters leave. The outer door is locked. A rat appears and nibbles bones. A cat appears and ignores the rat. The narrator falls fatigued to the floor between them. "The cat's eyes shone with a greenish light that filled all the room." He lies there until dawn. When the door

is unlocked by the cleaners, he goes home, washes, and goes out "to get myself some food." In his pocket are the letters, but "that day was Sunday, when the post office was closed for things that the clerk did not consider important."

Comparison: Agnon's narrator can be viewed on the fundamental level as the Good Man, on the philosophical level as the Existential Man, and on the theological level as a modern Moses. Like Archibald MacLeish's J. B., the Good Man rails against the demands laid on him by God and surrounds himself with self-doubt. Yet the narrator as the Good Man possesses a self-confidence inherited from God's covenant. Just as in the medieval play *Everyman,* when the hero confronts vice, he is sure of the inevitable triumph of virtue through God's mercy.

From another perspective, the meeting of a multiplicity of characters who define a country's moral and ethical structure vividly suggests James Joyce's *Dubliners.* The same use of choice to define existential integrity is evident in Agnon's narrator. The narrator realizes that if he does not choose God's strictures, he, and thus Israel, will become the cat with green eyes, just as the young wife in Rosario Ferre's "The Youngest Doll" became a grotesque doll with eyes oozing prawns. If the narrator chooses the green-eyed monster oozing capitalist envy—illustrated in the story in the character Hopni—the choice could destroy his nation. This same symbol appears in Kafka's A HUNGER ARTIST, where a panther replaces the starving artist in his cage. Agnon's green-eyed cat, however, would surely devour the narrator without God's letters—symbolized by the letters Ne'eman asked the narrator to mail—sealed next to his heart.

Finally, this wandering Moses portends a new Jerusalem rich in possibilities and alive to the Book that God has entrusted to His people. Like successive images within a Dali painting, each moment along the narrator's path elicits another part of Jerusalem's surreal growth in a materialistic twentieth century. — D V D

9

AHMAD, RAZIA FASIH. PAPER IS MONEY.

Pakistan
Short Story International. April 1982.

Author: Razia Fasih Ahmad (1934–) is a leading Urdu fiction writer, known for her novels as well as her short stories. She writes for both children and adult audiences and occasionally writes in English. She has received numerous literary awards, including Pakistan's highest, the Adamji Prize for Literature.

Story: This tale, subtitled "Values of a Manuscript," is the story of a first-person narrator, a writer with education and no belief in superstition. He rents a supposedly haunted house with the intention of writing a novel in the manner of Thomas Wolfe. The house is cleaned by a Hindi woman, Shanti, who is unable to count or read. She and her sickly husband are described by the narrator as "both old and ugly. They were both poor and stupid, and only had each other."

Over the next two years, the narrator's novel grows, beginning as a series of recorded memories and recollections, "a large bulk of papers increasing day by day." At the peak of enjoyment in structuring these recollections into novel form, the narrator is perplexed by the sudden disappearance of the manuscript. Looking everywhere, he notes that the manuscript was "the most precious thing" he had: "Yes, it was precious to me. For others it would be a bundle of papers but for me it was everything—my life." He becomes aware that some books and magazines have also disappeared. The neighbors, of course, believe the disappearance of the manuscript to be the work of spirits somehow annoyed by the writer's living in their midst.

Dejected, frustrated, and miserable, the writer becomes physically and mentally exhausted. Then, one day, he notices Shanti's husband "ransacking the garbage in the back lane." Aside from the food scraps, which Shanti and her husband eat, the old couple sell the other rubbish for five paisas, an amount equivalent to practically nothing. The awareness of his employee's desperate situation causes the writer to raise Shanti's salary.

Returning to his house, the narrator comes upon several sacks of trash representing Shanti's garbage collection for the past week. Operating on a desperate hunch, he empties the sacks and finds the pieces of his magazines, books, and beloved manuscript. They were "not in one of the sacks but in all four, torn to pieces and smeared with all sorts of refuse." Shanti and her husband had seen the papers as useless and had "torn them to make them still more useless so that nobody could suspect them of stealing." The narrator realizes that "my manuscript for which I was hoping to get a lot of money had no value for them as such, but as a torn and dirty pack of paper it meant money to them."

Comparison: Severe poverty produces extraordinary, often perplexing, behavior, and writers attempt to evoke compassion through understanding for those in such dire circumstances. This is the case in PAPER IS MONEY and in the German märchen "Jack and the Beanstalk" and "Hansel and Gretel," collected by the brothers Grimm. In the former, the mother is forced to sell the family's most precious possession—a cow. In the latter, the woodcutter's children are given over to their fate in the woods with the hope of their being adopted by a new, more affluent family. In PAPER IS MONEY, the narrator's precious manuscript becomes the means of survival for the impoverished elderly couple. When the writer reconciles himself to the loss of his book at the end of the story ("And that is how the novel which was to be the greatest of the century got lost forever"), the manuscript, like the cow and Hansel and Gretel, is sacrificed to survival.

In each case, the sacrifice is noble, like that in the film classic *Stella Dallas,* starring Barbara Stanwyck, and its recent remake *Stella,* starring Bette Midler. Such is also true of O. Henry's classic short story "The Gift of the Magi." — J A G

AICHINGER, ILSE. THE BOUND MAN.

Germany
Continental Short Stories: The Modern Tradition. New York: Norton, 1968.
Translated by Eric Mosbacher.

Author: Ilse Aichinger (1921–) was born in Vienna and spent her childhood there and in Linz. Because of her Jewish ancestry, she was not permitted to continue her education, so she worked in a factory during the war. After the war, she studied medicine for several semesters and then became a reader for a publishing firm. Her novels include *Herod's Children* (1963) and several others that have not been translated into English. She published *The Bound Man and Other Stories* in 1953 and one translated miscellany, *Selected Short Stories and Dialogues,* in 1966. In recent years, she has lived in Upper Bavaria with her husband, German poet Gunter Eich. She has won several literary prizes, including election to the prestigious P.E.N. Club. In 1952, she won the prize of the "Group 47," an association of young writers representing the best among the postwar talents.

Story: A man suddenly becomes aware that he is bound by ropes cutting into his flesh. Trying to free himself, he finds that he is able to move, but only with great restriction and considerable pain. A circus animal tamer watches the Bound Man as he tries to cut his ropes with a broken bottle. Intrigued as the Bound Man "knelt, stood up, jumped, and turned cartwheels," the animal tamer decides to present the Bound Man as an act in his circus. There, the audience too "found it astonishing as if they had seen a bird which voluntarily remained earthbound, and confined itself to hopping." People are fascinated that he is always bound, even when he is not performing; he seems to be helpless. Other performers are jealous and try to free him, but the proprietor prevents them. "He could have freed himself if he had wanted to whenever he liked, but perhaps he wanted to learn a few new jumps first." There are even times when he does not seem to be aware that he is bound.

One day, a young wolf escapes and confronts the Bound Man, who is able to hurl his body against

it and kill it. Unfortunately, no one believes that he is capable of this feat, and they force him to repeat the performance in a cage. The proprietor's wife, in an attempt to save him, frees him from his ropes, but realizing that his real freedom is now gone, he uses a gun to shoot the wolf and takes flight. Alone, hiding from his pursuers, he realizes that all life is frozen within him. Even the memory of the experience has disappeared.

Comparison: The Bound Man is clearly an artist, but as soon as his art comes under question, he is forced to live according to the rules of society and his art is destroyed. The theme of a man finding his freedom within the restrictions imposed on him by the human condition and by meeting the challenges of transcending those restrictions is also found in Kafka's story A HUNGER ARTIST. Kafka's Hunger Artist achieves a certain kind of freedom by starving himself before an audience, thus gaining a peculiar liberty from those restricting forces affecting everyone else. His hunger strikes are essentially his will to power. But the crowd becomes dissatisfied with this subtle art in favor of more blatant circus acts, just as the Bound Man's audiences become uninterested in his artful manipulations. They cannot believe that these artist figures can transcend traditional notions of freedom, so the art of both heroes is destroyed because the audience is unable to understand or appreciate it on its own terms. Unauthentic people cannot share the experiences of the creative artist and must destroy what they cannot understand. The Bound Man loses his reason for existence when he loses his freedom, and the new kind of freedom he gains is an insufficient substitute. So we see him at the end, frozen within himself, under a moon that resembles death.

One is also reminded of Camus's Sisyphus, whose freedom is removed and whose will is frustrated. He too is devoted to an absurd cause, but like the Bound Man, he finds freedom within the restrictions that have been imposed on him. Although he accepts these restrictions as part of his existence, he knows that he need not be destroyed by them. Sisyphus's freedom exists in his mind, which his punishment cannot destroy. In fact, he gains a sense of freedom in the very act of pushing a boulder up a mountain in spite of the inevitability that it will forever roll down again. The Bound Man and the Hunger Artist, however, are both destroyed by society at the point when they are able to bring their art to perfection and achieve a degree of creativity beyond the understanding and emotional sophistication of the very audiences that once encouraged and admired them.

The technique of the story is one used by many surrealist artists who portray nature as a reflection of the interior world of consciousness. Giorgio de Chirico and René Magritte, for example, emphasized the inexplicable character of human experience by juxtaposing familiar and unfamiliar objects and environments in an unexpected or dreamlike manner, resulting in a kind of irrational horror that we cannot escape. One also thinks of the paintings of Francis Bacon, such as *Lying Figure* (1959), which invariably portray people and animals trapped within very strict limitations of movement. — R H M

AIDOO, AMA ATA. NO SWEETNESS HERE.

Ghana

African Rhythms: Selected Stories and Poems. New York: Washington Square Press, 1974.

Author: Ama Ata Aidoo (1942–) was born in Ghana and educated at the University of Ghana. She received her A.B. degree in 1964 while serving as research fellow at the Institute of African Studies. That year, she completed her first play, *Dilemma of a Ghost,* which won critical recognition. Since that time, she has given seminars at the University Colleges of Dares Salaam and Nairobi. She has published two plays and has been lecturer at the University of Cape Coast. Her first short story collection, *No Sweetness Here,* was published in 1970.

Story: NO SWEETNESS HERE portrays family life in the African village of Baniso, which "is not really a big village." Conflict has arisen between Kodjo Fi, "a selfish and bullying man," and his wife, Maami Ama, who are parents of one son, Kwesi. The story is told from the point of view of Chicha, a schoolteacher and friend of Kodjo Fi. As marital discord mounts, the reader comes to understand a great deal about the family's everyday life.

Contrary to tradition in Western culture, when divorce is granted to Maami, she and her family must pay. The judge even decrees that Kwesi should go to his father. Just as the formal proceedings are ending, news comes that Kwesi has been bitten by a snake and is desperately ill. Despite many attempts at cures by the villagers and medicine man and prayers to the gods and spirits, Kwesi dies. Ironically, Kodjo Fi cannot get Kwesi after all. Maami Ama has lost everything: her marriage, her material possessions, and her son. The villagers' verdict: "Life is not sweet."

Comparison: Despite its sad ending, this story is a celebration of womanhood. Maami Ama is strong. "Life has taught me to be brave," she says. Her character may be compared with Edzi in Francis Selormey's *The Narrow Path.* In tone, there is the customary morbidness often thought to pervade much of black African literature. — M J J

Akutagawa Ryūnosuke. IN A GROVE.

Japan
Rōshomon and Other Stories by Akutagawa Ryūnosuke. Tokyo: Charles E. Tuttle, 1983.
Translated by Takashi Kojima.

Author: Born in Tokyo to a merchant-class father and a mother of samurai stock who clung to past glory and dying traditions, Akutagawa (1892–1927) showed schizophrenic tendencies early in life. Except for his literary success, the circumstances of his life brought him no comfort or happiness. Even his own theory that the creation of art was the meaning of life did not give him satisfaction. In 1927, he committed suicide by taking an overdose of barbiturates.

Like many literary figures of his era, Akutagawa was well read in contemporary Japanese and European literature. He was particularly fond of Ibsen. In his short career as a short story writer, Akutagawa produced over a hundred stories and a few essays. His observations on the ludicrousness of people unaware of their own contradictions took on a gloomier tone in his later works. Among his best-known stories are "The Handkerchief" (1916), "Rōshomon" (1917), "The Puppeteer" (1919), "Hell Screen" (1927), and "Kappa" (1927). "Rōshomon" was made into a motion picture of the same title.

Story: A man in a bluish silk kimono and a wrinkled Kyoto-style headdress is murdered in a grove. Seven parties are questioned. Each gives a unique account of the event. In the end, the truth does not emerge, as the major renditions differ in essential details.

An old woman tells of her spirited daughter leaving for Waka with her husband. A traveling priest tells of seeing the couple with a horse on the road at noon the same day, the woman in lilac and the man armed with sword, bow, and arrows. A policeman tells of arresting a brigand with sword, bow, arrows, and a horse on a bridge that same night. A woodcutter tells of discovering the body flat on its back in a grove the next morning. Tajomaru, the brigand, tells of tying and later releasing the husband from the root of a cedar, dishonoring the woman, and killing the husband in a sword fight when the woman cries out that one or the other man has to die because both have seen her shame. She runs off during the fight.

The woman tells of the brigand raping her and disappearing with sword, bow, and arrows while she is in a faint. When she sees a look of hatred in her husband's eyes, she decides to kill him and herself. She stabs "through the lilac kimono into his breast" while he is still tied to the tree. After waking from a second faint, she unties him, but does not have the strength to kill herself.

The victim, speaking through a medium, tells of his wife asking the brigand to kill him after the rape. Shocked by the request, the brigand asks whether to kill or save her. She shrieks and runs off. The brigand releases the husband and disappears. The husband then picks up his wife's small sword and stabs himself in the breast.

Comparison: To reconstruct the truth by corroborating evidence and testimony is as difficult in Akutagawa's IN A GROVE as it is in "Twelve Angry Men" by Reginald Rose and in countless mysteries and detective stories. Despite the conviction of one's own integrity, truth emerges as a distinctly individual perspective, as shown in the ancient parable of the blind men and the elephant. Each person describes the whole elephant as an extension of the part he touches. The issue of fidelity, suspicion, and jealousy between husband and wife is a timeless theme, such as depicted in the ancient parable retold by R. K. Narayan in THE MIRROR. — M L

Alexiou, Elli. THEY WERE ALL TO BE PITIED.

Greece

The Charioteer: An Annual Review of Modern Greek Culture. No. 22–23. New York: Parnassos, Greek Cultural Society of New York, 1980/81. Translated by Deborah Tannen.

Author: Distinguished writer Elli Alexiou (1894–1988) was born in Herakleion, Crete, into an extraordinary literary family. Both she and her older sister, Galateia Alexiou, became writers. Elli, a member of the "Generation of the 1930s," wrote in the demotic, or vernacular, of the Greek language and was for a time married to writer Vasos Daskalakis. She divorced him when she was fifty-one years old and went to Paris to study. During her career, she taught at an orphanage school and spent thirteen years supervising Eastern bloc countries' post–Greek Civil War schools for Greek children. Although she was usually occupied with matters of politics and quality of life, she used the insight gained through her teaching to write *Hard Struggles for a Humble Life* (1931) and *The Third Christian Girls' School* (1934). In these works, she portrayed in a nonstereotypical way the vulnerability of children. Alexiou wrote over a hundred short stories, six novels, and numerous articles, plays, translations, and memoirs. She established herself as an outstanding figure in Greek letters and as the center of left-leaning literary activity in Athens. Her acclaimed Thursday evening salons attracted both established and aspiring writers and artists.

Story: Alexiou once said that her stories came from her life experiences. She organized this short story as a flashback to the narrator's childhood; the age of the narrator is not known until the end of the story.

The narrator is thinking of one of her few childhood friends, the sickly daughter of her family's carriage driver, and is remembering herself as a child when the story begins. Her memories are not pleasant. She was, she remembers, a mean child who did and said spiteful and unkind things, one who mocked the maids and her nanny. Yet she believes that her nanny loved her very much and that her parents would have loved her too, except that they were just children themselves. Their marriage had been forced upon them. Her mother finally flees the marriage, unable to take her daughter along and doomed never to see her again, for the father will not allow it. Then an incident happens that appears to typify her childhood. Her little friend, who has a heart condition, falls in love with the narrator's beloved mama-doll, given to her by her father. The narrator's reaction is to tear the doll apart.

At this point, the reader learns that the narrator is sixty years old, that her papa and mama have died, and that she is lonely and helpless, an old woman who realizes that she has never been called "mama" by anyone. She cries for mama and papa, for nanny, and for her little friend; they were all to be pitied. But she cries even more for herself.

Comparison: Alexiou achieves a keenly distressing tone in this brief story even as she comments on a society that arranges marriages and gives absolute control of children to their father. Set in this century, THEY WERE ALL TO BE PITIED presents a picture of entrapment different from, but as clear as, that of the main character in Tillie Olsen's "I Stand Here Ironing." A request she receives from her oldest daughter's teacher, saying that the daughter needs help and that the teacher hopes she will come in, sets Olsen's mother to remembering. The daughter was born when the mother was nineteen, the two of them were deserted by the baby's father, and the girl was brought up with all the horrors of poverty. The mother concludes that her daughter should be "let be." In spite of everything, she still has enough spirit to survive. The best that can be done for her is to let her know that she is not as powerless as the dress on the ironing board.

In Willa Cather's "A Wagner Matinee," a music teacher returns to Boston and hears classical music again for the first time since she exiled herself thirty years earlier to the Nebraska plains and a farm life. As she hears the music, the extent of her years of entrapment and agony burst upon her, and she doesn't ever want to leave.

James Joyce writes in "Eveline" about a young woman who has trouble deciding between what she sees as her only two choices: a marriage and exile to a South American country or continuing to take care of her old and disagreeable father. In the end, she is trapped by the promise her mother extracted from her to stay.

In sharp contrast to Joyce's powerless woman are two good friends, Annabel and Midge, in Dorothy Parker's "The Standard of Living." Although they are trapped in low-paying jobs, they do not recognize their situation, and their solid friendship and delight in being with each other in New York City is as refreshing as their ability to set new rules for their favorite game when the need arises.

The family relationships explored in THEY WERE ALL TO BE PITIED are as dynamic as those explored by William Faulkner in "Barn Burning," where a young boy fights the battle of being loyal to his father even when he knows that his father is doing something wrong. D. H. Lawrence, in "The Rocking Horse Winner," writes of a family that needs money and a son who thinks he can furnish it. Finally, Bobbie Ann Mason's wife-husband team in "Shiloh" set about tackling the problem of a disabled truck-driver husband trapped both at home and in life. — E M

ALLENDE, ISABEL. TWO WORDS.

Chile

Secret Weavers. Fredonia, New York: White Pine Press, 1992. Translated by Alberto Manguel.

Author: Isabel Allende (1942–), the award-winning novelist from Chile, began her career as a journalist for various magazines and as a weekly columnist for *El Naçional.* She continued as a TV interviewer, movie editor, lecturer, and creative writing teacher. In 1973, her uncle, President S. Allende, was assassinated. "In that moment I realized that everything is possible. . . . That violence was a dimension that was always around you." Fleeing to Venezuela, she began a several-year hiatus from writing. Later, she received a letter from her grandfather, who believed that "people died only when you forgot them."

To prove that she had forgotten nothing, she wrote her first novel, *House of Spirits* (1985). Combining Gabriel García Márquez's magical realism with politics, the novel added a touch of humor and a woman's perspective. Her second novel, *Of Love and Shadows* (1987), proved her a master at weaving the political history of Latin America with the lives of everyday characters. She skillfully brought forth the horror of daily existence under a military dictatorship and the subtler terror in the "shadows" of life. By intertwining two stories, a plot hatched from the bizarre switching of two babies,

Allende focused her journalistic skills on a scheme to murder one of the girls. Even though her story inevitably descended to horror, Allende sustained a warm, confiding style essential for blending the magical and the real. In her third novel, *Eva Luna* (1989), the plot traveled from personal to political and from realism to fantasy in combining two coming-of-age stories.

Story: Belisa Crepusculario, a name this peasant girl "dressed herself up in," goes through the countryside selling words. When she first saw "flies legs" drawn on newspaper, she immediately had to know what they meant. Seeing words "fly loose with no master and that anyone with a little cunning could catch them," she paid a priest to teach her how to write. With the skill mastered, she becomes an itinerant wordsmith, setting up her tent and selling poems for five cents, dream elaborations for seven cents, and insults for twelve cents. For fifty cents, she sells two-word secrets for buyers to keep in their heart.

One day, a revolutionary general's mulatto whisks Belisa away to his superior, who asks that she create a speech. He wants to become president by using her words to win the hearts of the people. She composes words that "could reach men's thoughts and women's intuition" and reads them three times. The general buys her work, and, in addition to the speech, Belisa gives him his own two-word secret. With his memorized speech, the general campaigns from village to village, winning the hearts and minds of the people. Yet the two secret words keep ringing in his head. Back and forth the sleepless general paces until his followers fear he will not survive to become president.

To relieve his leader, the mulatto goes in search of Belisa. When she appears before the general, he demands—with rifle at her throat—that he give back the two secret words so his manhood will return. Unless she takes them back, he "would not be rid of the charm of those two cursed words." Yet the general with the bloodthirsty eyes of a puma softens before Belisa as she steps forward to take his proffered hand.

Comparison: "Fantastic" literature has bred magical realism, and one strand of this genre comes out of the Kafkaesque. The "absurd" as "real" in this story resides in the magic of two secret words acting as a mantra upon the mind. Each recipient holds fast to these words like a potion whose charm can drive even the bloodthirsty into becoming tenderhearted. (One wonders whether Belisa's initials, "B.C.," refer to that period out of which words evolved.) Nonetheless, Allende's ending shows how the charm of words has a civilizing effect on people. By referring more than once to the general as a puma, she gives a twist to Kafka's panther in A HUNGER ARTIST. Instead of the general's dissipating into a darkly malevolent beast, however, Allende's puma reaches out to Belisa to become a whole person. The power of words transforms those who choose to claim them.

Like Water for Chocolate presents an interplay between the sexes similar to that in the Allende story. Another depiction of the effect of the sexes upon one another occurs in *How the Garcia Girls Lost Their Accent.* In both stories the power of women develops over time, and their strength alleviates the beast within men. Out of two words can evolve a nascent hope for a more civilized reaction, not only between the sexes, but among various cultures as well. — D V D

AMADO, JORGE. HOW PORCIÚNCULA THE MULATTO GOT THE CORPSE OFF HIS BACK.

Brazil

The Eye of the Heart: Short Stories from Latin America. New York: Bobbs-Merrill, 1973.

Author: The son of well-to-do cocoa farmers, Jorge Amado (1912–) is among the best known of all South American authors in this century. The place of his birth, Ilhéus, Brazil, is the backdrop for many of his stories, including this one. The city is also the setting for *Gabriela, Clove and Cinnamon; The Violent Land; Doña Flor and Her Two Husbands; Tereza Batista;* and *Home from the Wars.*

Amado received his secondary education in Salvador, the capital of Bahia, returning to Ilhéus during the summers to work on his father's plantation. In 1930, he settled in Rio, where he began his literary career and published his first book, *O Pais do Carnaval.*

Amado's life and literature have centered around the concerns of the Brazilian people and their needs. Because of this, he was imprisoned in 1935 for political activities. When the Vargas regime began in Brazil in 1937, he was forced to take refuge in the River Plate countries. From there he traveled to Mexico, the United States, and then back to Brazil, where he was once again imprisoned.

In 1941, Amado went into exile, remaining in Argentina and Uruguay for two years. Returning to São Paulo in 1945, he was elected a federal deputy and took part in the drafting of the existing Brazilian Constitution. Because of his Marxist beliefs, Amado was once again forced into political exile in 1948. He lived in Paris and Czechoslovakia and traveled in western Europe and Asia. For a time, he settled in Rio and in Salvador.

Story: HOW PORCIÚNCULA THE MULATTO GOT THE CORPSE OFF HIS BACK, published in 1962, deals with the common people along the waterfront of Bahia. The main character is a mulatto who is in love with a woman, Maria of the Veil. She is a beautiful young girl whose father, discovering that she had lost her virginity, threw her into the streets, condemning her to the life of a prostitute.

The mulatto, unlike the rest of her acquaintances, never uses her as a whore. Their relationship is purely Platonic. Her one obsession in life is with weddings, the one event truly denied her. She tells the mulatto of her enjoyment at watching each wedding that takes place in the community.

When Maria dies, she is married to the mulatto in a mock wedding ceremony and buried in a wedding gown. When Porciúncula tells his tale in a tavern, he, in effect, unloads the corpse, or weight, from his shoulders.

Comparison: This story hinges on the garrulous, unnamed storyteller, a man who (possibly) completes one tale and provides hints of many others. His technique is that of the spinner of oral tales in preliterate days. Instead of having his audience grouped around a primitive campfire, however, this storyteller's listeners are grouped around kerosene lamps at a local bar.

The garrulous storyteller's technique can be compared with that of Jim Baker in Mark Twain's "Baker's Blue-Jay Yarn" or Simon Wheeler in Twain's "The Celebrated Jumping Frog of Calaveras County." It also lends itself to comparison with the tales of Amos Tutuola, a Nigerian whose style and language are probably the closest we have to those of the ancient storytellers. Tutuola's best-known work is *The Palm-Wine Drinkard.*

Amado's technique of repeating key phrases, evident in the border ballads of English literature, lends itself to comparison with those ballads and a discussion of how these gifted early storytellers managed to memorize so many ballads and stories. The theme of the loss of a loved one through death, present in this story, is a common theme in the literature of all countries. — C W and H M M

Andreyev, Leonid. LAZARUS.

Russia

A Treasury of Russian Literature. New York: Vanguard, 1943. Translated by Avrahm Yamolinsky.

Author: Leonid Andreyev (1871–1919), whose stories are most noted for their morbidity, did most of his writing in prerevolutionary Russia, where he was the product of a bureaucratic family and a hereditary alcoholic disposition. His years at the University of Petersburg and the University of Moscow were marked by broken romances and suicide attempts. He lived his life in a rather haphazard, although extravagant, fashion, at various times practicing law, reporting crime, writing newspaper copy, and editing a reactionary newspaper. His short story, novel, and drama writings were achieved by his writing nonstop for days at a time. He was greatly influenced by Chekhov and Gorki in his early sto-

ries and Dostoevski in his later ones. Although honored in 1905 for his writing, he later fell into governmental disfavor. Due to his reactionary beliefs, his popularity had greatly diminished by 1908. When he died in Finland of a heart attack, caused partly by damage done when he shot himself in the chest in an earlier suicide attempt, he was considered an enemy of the Soviets.

Story: LAZARUS is the macabre story of the life of Lazarus after being raised from the grave by Jesus Christ. Although greeted with cheers, festivity, and celebration, Lazarus is taciturn and gloomy. His deathly appearance—bloated with a "cadaverous lividness" of face, "cadaverously blue" fingertips, long fingernails, and cracked lips "shining as though covered with transparent mica"—contrasts sharply with the rich colors of the garments and decorations around him at his homecoming. A guest asks, "Why dost thou not tell us what happened in the beyond?" He is answered with silence and a "deadly gray weariness," for "through the black disks of the pupils, as through darkened glass, stared the unknowable Beyond." Eventually, no one talks to Lazarus; no one takes care of him. Even his sisters forsake him, and Lazarus is left to spend his days indifferent and passive, walking always directly into the sun. All those who converse with him are labeled "madmen" by others, for they come away prattling about loneliness, eternity, and despair. But "surely, much more could have been told by those who wished not to speak, and died in silence." Such is the case with Aurelius, a Roman sculptor; when others talk of art and beauty, he replies, "But all this is a lie."

One day, the Emperor Augustus, curious about the stories he has heard, summons Lazarus to the imperial palace. First, he commands Lazarus not to look at him, pronouncing Lazarus's imminent execution for being the embodiment of the denial of life. Then he seeks Lazarus's gaze, and, in that gaze, "Time stood still.... The throne of Augustus ... crumbled down and the Void was already in the place of that throne and of Augustus. Noiselessly did Rome itself crumble into dust and a new city stood on its site, and it, too, was swallowed, by the void.... and with utmost indifference did the insatiable black maw of the Infinite swallow them." Augustus realizes, through Lazarus, the transient nature of existence and the fact that, in the final

analysis, nothing has meaning; the absolute does not exist.

Augustus orders Lazarus blinded, and the unfortunate man returns to the desert, falling over rocks where "his black body and outspread hands would form a monstrous likeness to a cross," until, one day, he does not return. He who "had risen miraculously from the dead" has finally been claimed by death, as all the living are ultimately claimed.

Comparison: The surrealism of LAZARUS is much like that of Franz Kafka's THE METAMORPHOSIS and Herman Melville's "Bartleby the Scrivener." In each, the central figure—Lazarus, Gregor, and Bartleby—apparently possesses knowledge of some eternal truth about life's futility that only he knows. Death, for each, becomes a release from the torment of that realization and its resulting alienation.

The theme of life's transience is, of course, a common one, but a distinction can be made between those works, like LAZARUS, dealing with the totality of life's impermanence and those dealing with the impermanence of certain aspects of life, as, for example, youth and beauty. The former are less common, including such works as Benjamin Franklin's "The Ephemera," a didactic, whimsical allegory, and Percy Bysshe Shelley's sonnet "Ozymandias," in which Ramses II fails to realize all that Lazarus does.

Finally, Lazarus is delineated as an unnatural creature, something less than human, fully at odds with the cosmos. Change and death are natural occurrences. To return from the dead breaks the laws of nature. The same premise is the basis of much vampire fiction, particularly the young-adult novel *Silver Kiss* by Annette Curtis Klause. — J A G

Andric, Ivo. THE SCYTHE.

Bosnia-Herzegovina
Nobel Parade. Glenview, IL: ScottForesman, 1975. Translated by Joseph Hitrec.

Author: The first Yugoslav to be awarded the Nobel Prize for Literature, Ivo Andric (1892–1975) was born in Travnik, Bosnia, when Bosnia was still a part of the Austro-Hungarian Empire. During his

youth, ninety percent of the Bosnian population was still illiterate and most literature was orally transmitted. By 1914, Andric had made a reputation for himself as a gifted poet and was president of the

Young Bosnians, a literary club of youthful revolutionaries. At the outbreak of World War I, Andric was arrested; he remained in prison until the war ended. Putting his time in prison to good use, he prepared two volumes of poetic prose for publication shortly after his release. After studying history at Zagreb and Krakow Universities, he finally received his degree from Graz University in Austria. Becoming a member of the Yugoslav diplomatic service, Andric served in many countries; he was the Yugoslav ambassador in Berlin when World War II broke out. Prudently returning to Yugoslavia, he spent the war years in retirement, writing the three novels that make up the Bosnian Trilogy. Largely for one of these, *The Bridge on the Drina,* he received the Nobel Prize for Literature in 1961. His citation reads, "For the epic force with which he has traced themes and depicted human destinies from his country's history."

Andric's works were influenced by the oral literature of his homeland, especially epic folklore and legends. Perhaps from the tumultuous experiences of his lifetime, he often dealt with the absurd, with human isolation, and with humanity's desire for security in an insecure universe.

Story: This quietly humorous short story centers on Vitomir, a peasant who goes to town on market day with the primary objective of buying a new scythe. After carefully selecting a hardware store, he tests an entire bundle of scythes, deliberating lengthily before making a choice. Other peasants offer advice, the store's apprentice hovers around him wearing a knowing grin, and the storekeeper is driven nearly to distraction by his bargaining. As Vitomir rides home, the scythe fastened to the saddle behind him, Andric draws a subtle analogy—for which he has cleverly paved the way throughout the story—to a bridegroom taking his new bride home.

Comparison: As a depiction of the character of the Slav peasant, Andric's Vitomir may be compared with Matryona and Zakhar in Solzhenitsyn's MATRYONA'S HOME and ZAKHAR-THE-POUCH. He can also be compared with soldier Trofim in Sholokhov's THE COLT. De Maupassant's "A Piece of String" offers a similar view of a French villager.

To appreciate the extent of Andric's artistry, this story may be compared with his A SUMMER IN THE SOUTH. In the latter, there are more characters, the setting is totally different, the characters are more sophisticated, and plot is uppermost. Its ending, sudden and puzzling, contrasts with that of THE SCYTHE, which is more a character study and lightly humorous *tour de force* than a gripping, plot-oriented story. — H M M

Andric, Ivo. A Summer in the South.

Bosnia-Herzegovina
Russian and Eastern European Literature. Glenview, IL: ScottForesman, 1970.
Translated by Joseph Hitrec.

Author: See THE SCYTHE.

Story: Set in an unnamed town on the Adriatic coast, this deceptively straightforward story ends in a mystery. On their holiday, Professor Alfred Norgess and his wife Anna are at first disappointed with the town and their lodgings, but soon become enchanted by the natural beauty of the place. Professor Norgess is revising a monograph on Philip II of Spain. While he reads galleys, Anna goes into town to shop. Increasingly, Norgess finds himself becoming lost in reveries induced by his surroundings. He daydreams while intently watching the sea and sky. Soon he begins to question the nature of reality—of time, place, relationships, gravity. At one point, the local fruit vendor, seen in reverie, takes on the appearance of Philip II and invites Norgess to enter into the landscape. Norgess accepts, enters, and feels himself become one with it and its parts—the sea, the shore, the mountains, the sky. He even feels that he can step off the mountain and float. His wife's voice, as she returns, recalls him to reality. One morning, however, his reverie takes over completely, and, feeling himself weightless, he begins walking toward the heights. He is never seen again. The townspeople hope that his body will wash ashore, because without an explanation of his disappearance, none of them can have inner peace.

Comparison: In its mysterious ending, leaving readers to deduce the outcome—if they can—this story may be compared with Stockton's "The Lady, or the Tiger." As a story that may be dealing with the supernatural, however, it lends itself to comparison with more sophisticated works: Hawthorne's "The Artist of the Beautiful," Melville's "Bartleby the Scrivener," Henry James's *The Turn of the Screw,* Poe's "The Fall of the House of Usher," and DuMaurier's "The Blue Lenses."

To show the range of Andric's artistry, the story may be compared with his THE SCYTHE. Language, structure, and setting are simple in the latter, far more complex in A SUMMER IN THE SOUTH. Andric may also be compared with his compatriot, Milovan Djilas, who writes a more bitter and emotion-charged type of fiction.

Finally, in its ability to paint impressionistic landscapes, this story may be compared with Sholokhov's THE FATE OF A MAN and THE COLT, with Solzhenitsyn's MATRYONA'S HOME, and with Aron Tamasi's FLASHES IN THE NIGHT. — H M M

ASTURIAS, MIGUEL. TATUANA'S TALE.

Guatemala
The Eye of the Heart: Short Stories from Latin America. New York: Bobbs-Merrill, 1973.

Author: Born in Guatemala City, Miguel Angel Asturias (1899–1974) ranks among the most noted of twentieth-century South American writers. He received a Doctor of Laws degree from the Universidad de San Carlos de Guatemala in 1923 and studied at the Sorbonne in Paris from 1923 to 1928. Asturias was both a diplomat and writer. He was cofounder of a free evening college (Universidad do Popular de Guatemala) in 1921 and of a Unionist Party group. In 1923, Asturias left Guatemala for political reasons. He journeyed to Paris, where he studied South American cultures and religions.

Asturias was a European correspondent for Central American and Mexican newspapers from 1923 to 1932, when he returned to Guatemala. There he worked as a journalist and founded a periodical, *El Diario del Aire.* Although he was elected deputy to the Guatemalan national congress in 1942, he was later stripped of Guatemalan citizenship and forced into exile during the regime of Colonel Carlos Castillo Armas. This provided the background for his first novel, *El Señor Presidente.*

For eight years, Asturias lived in Argentina and worked as a correspondent for *El Naçional,* during which time he wrote TATUANA'S TALE, published in 1957. In 1966, he returned to Guatemala following the election of a new president. From 1966 to 1970, he served as ambassador to France.

Asturias authored many novels, short stories, and editorials. His numerous awards include the Lenin Peace Prize in 1966 and the Nobel Prize for Literature in 1967.

Story: This story is told primarily by an omniscient author. It deals with Father Almond Tree, who is able to change himself into objects of nature and, with this ability, to thwart the blackness that exists in the world. He is first seen as a tree, having separated his soul among the four roads leading to the four quarters of the sky: Black, Green, Red, and White. The Black road sells his part of the soul to the Merchant of Priceless Jewels.

Upon discovering what has been done, Father Almond Tree returns to human form and goes to the city to retrieve the missing piece of his soul.

The Merchant refuses to sell it back, saying it is to be used to buy the most beautiful slave in the slave market. After he makes his purchase, while returning to the city, the Merchant and all but the newly bought slave are killed in a storm.

Meanwhile, Father Almond Tree has remained in the city, still hoping to reunite the pieces of his soul. When he finally knocks on the Merchant's door, it is answered by the beautiful slave who survived the storm. The two are immediately arrested. He is accused of being a warlock and she his accomplice. They are condemned to be burned alive. On the eve before their death, Father Almond Tree tattoos a boat on the arm of the slave, Tatuana, and tells her to trace the boat anywhere, climb in, and let her spirit go. She does as he says and immediately disappears. The next morning, when the guards come for them, they find only a tree with almond blossoms.

Comparison: This work can best be compared to tales of folklore and mythology. Because of the names and images used, however, the comparisons that work most favorably are those involving Eastern myths. Herman Hesse's short story "Piktor's Metamorphosis" shows a similar Eastern influence and includes the transformation of Piktor into a tree. The original source for both transformations may well be Ovid's famous tale of Daphne and Apollo. TATUANA'S TALE may also be compared to numerous other stories, including Kafka's THE METAMORPHOSIS, that tell how the body may be imprisoned while the mind and spirit remain free.
— C W

Aymé, Marcel. THE MAN WHO WALKED THROUGH WALLS.

France
Harper's Magazine. January 1947. Translated by E. and M. Teichner.

Author: Marcel Aymé (1902–1967), a prolific French author, produced novels, plays, children's books, and short stories. He was also a screenwriter, literary critic, and journalist. His upbringing in rural Burgundy is reflected in much of his early work. A best-seller published in 1933, *The Green Mare,* firmly established his literary career. Despite continued success, he shunned publicity. By then a confirmed Parisian, he lived a bohemian life in Montmartre with his artist friends, some of whom appear as characters in his fiction, including the painter Gen Paul in THE MAN WHO WALKED THROUGH WALLS, published in 1943. In much of his work, sophisticated satire targets people's vices and illusions. Witty humor and the fusion of fantasy with reality are distinctive stylistic features of his short stories.

Story: At the age of forty-three, Dutilleul, a meek civil servant, suddenly finds himself able to walk through walls. Considering this faculty annoying, he visits a doctor who prescribes special medication— two pills annually—and vigorous physical activity. Dutilleul takes only one pill, and since his sedentary habits preclude much exercise, he retains his unusual power. He refrains from using it for a year, until a new boss, Lécuyer, introduces reforms that the clerk finds intolerable. After much tension and humiliation, Dutilleul rebels against M. Lécuyer's tyranny by using his gift to scare his superior into insanity.

This success inspires Dutilleul to undertake a series of spectacular burglaries that he autographs under the pseudonym Garou-Garou. His extraordinary crimes fascinate an admiring public. After hearing his colleagues constantly praising the phantom burglar, he reveals the true identity of Garou-Garou, but is disbelieved and ridiculed. He then allows himself to be captured by the police at the scene of a crime, proving to the world that he is the celebrated thief. He easily escapes through the prison walls, but in order to avoid arrest again, he dons a disguise. While in this role, he meets and falls in love with a beautiful blonde. Two nights of vigorous love making cause Dutilleul to suffer a severe headache. Thinking some pills in a drawer are aspirin, he accidentally takes the special medication prescribed a year earlier. That night, while leaving the tryst, he suddenly loses his power and is trapped inside a wall, lamenting the end of his career and love life.

Comparison: THE MAN WHO WALKED THROUGH WALLS can best be compared with Aymé's other works. Dutilleul's duality is paralleled in Aymé's novel *Aller-Retour* and numerous short stories. In these works, ridiculed characters who escape boredom, mediocrity, and anonymity through either psychological or physical transformations act out humanity's hidden desires and aspirations.

The desire for a second self found in THE MAN WHO WALKED THROUGH WALLS also invites comparisons with "The Secret Life of Walter Mitty" by James Thurber. Dutilleul's wish to be famous and sexually attractive is similar to the protagonist's fantasies in Thurber's story. Mitty's dreamworld disintegrates when his wife's nagging yanks him back to reality; Dutilleul's abrupt loss of his extraordinary power leaves him stranded inside a wall. The humorous tone of each work lightens the effect of the protagonist's final predicament.

Hidden beneath the comedy and magical integration of fantasy and reality in Aymé's story are satiric barbs. Aymé shares these elements and others with the absurdists. THE MAN WHO WALKED THROUGH WALLS and Eugene Ionesco's *Rhinoceros* bear some interesting commonalities. In *Rhinoceros,* Ionesco uses the ridiculous and fantastic to convey a caustic commentary on the absurdity of the human condition, especially people's need to conform. In both works, insensitive bureaucrats impressed with their own importance are mocked, and there are comic scenes that treat the absurd as commonplace reality. — M A F

AYYOUB, DHU'L NUN. FROM BEHIND THE VEIL.

Iraq
World Writers Today. Glenview, IL: ScottForesman, 1995.

Author: One of Iraq's most prominent fiction writers, Dhu'l Nun Ayyoub (1908–) writes stories about the clash of modern and traditional values in the Arab world. His stories deal with personal, religious, and political conflict.

Story: Ihsan is a good-looking eighteen-year-old who loves to flirt, a natural pastime for a young man of his age. He prefers, however, the company of young women who are veiled and thus more mysterious and unattainable.

Siham is a young girl who ventures out for a stroll each evening. She has seen Ihsan and even walked up beside him, protected by the anonymity of her veil. But lately, something has begun to happen when she sees him: her heart pounds and she grows nervous. She trusts that her reaction is concealed by her veil.

Ihsan too feels a spark, and he follows her into a park, where they speak and she raises her veil. She is lovely, breathless, young, and in search of a harmless adventure. They flirt, and Ihsan tells her that he merely wants a companion to share his evening strolls. She is pleased to accompany him, or, as she puts it, he may want "to accompany me on these innocent walks." Yet he must never try to follow her home or ask who she is. Ihsan concludes that she is a virtuous girl from a good family.

Siham is atypical of old-fashioned girls, however. She tells Ihsan in no uncertain terms that she knows they are committing a crime by even sitting together, but she realizes that a strict society like theirs fosters deceptive acts, acts that she is ready to commit in order to "break its shackles." Their relationship grows, but still she conceals her identity from him and does not reveal his existence to anyone.

Siham's father reads to her a newspaper article about a young girl who has abandoned her veil. To please her father, Siham acts indignant; she renounces the girl who breaks with tradition and the conventions of society. Her father is pleased beyond words. Siham goes to her room and bursts into laughter. She has learned to use the veil to "hide faults and scandals." It has provided her with a means to an adventure and a way to experience life that only veiled women can appreciate. She has only contempt for those who use the veil to hide behind. For her, a veil is a means to freedom.

Comparison: FROM BEHIND THE VEIL is a portrait of a young girl growing up in a strict Muslim society. The story suggests that, ironically, the more strict the social rules, the more challenging the bending of those rules becomes. Sandra Cisneros's collection of stories, *House on Mango Street*, contains vignettes dealing with the same theme. Here the narrator, Esperanza, is a young Hispanic girl who dares to want to be a writer. Culturally, everything is against her, but, little by little, she manages to suc-

ceed by using the same kind of quiet rebellion Siham employs.

In Paul Marshall's story "Barbados," the protagonist, Mr. Watford, asserts his masculine possessiveness over his young servant, an unnamed girl. She, like Siham, leads a double life, but, unlike Siham, Marshall's character confronts her male "protector" with the truth about herself. In both stories there is also an element of class division. Although the young girl in "Barbados" is a servant and Siham is a member of the upper class, both are constrained by their place in society.

Two novels dealing with similar themes are *The Color Purple* by Alice Walker and *Their Eyes Were Watching God* by Zora Neale Hurston. The protagonists in both are African American women who will not accept their lot in life and who strive to succeed in areas previously closed to them. Hurston's Janie asserts her independence even though she must deal with more than her share of problems. Walker's Celie succeeds in a business world not usually open to women, and certainly not to women of color. — D G

BALZAC, HONORÉ DE. THE ATHEIST'S MASS.

France
French Stories/Contes Français: A Bantam Dual-Language Book. New York: Bantam, 1960.
Translated by Wallace Fowlie.

Author: Born in Tours, Balzac (1799–1850) lived and wrote during the Romantic Age in France. His ambitions as a writer were not those of a Romantic, however, and he is remembered as the first great realist in fiction, an inspiration to writers from Flaubert to Henry James, who called Balzac "the master of us all."

Balzac's lifetime output as a writer was prodigious. Like the dramatist Lope da Vega and the composer Wolfgang Amadeus Mozart, Balzac spent most of his waking hours creating. He planned to write a broad series of 138 novels and shorter works under the umbrella title *The Human Comedy*, a body of fiction that would comprise a sweeping record of humanity and French society during the second

quarter of the nineteenth century. Although he did not complete the series, he completed close to a hundred of its works, the great majority of them novels. THE ATHEIST'S MASS was published in 1836.

As was the case with Molière, Sir Walter Scott, Mark Twain, and many other writers, Balzac often wrote simply to pay off debts. He was, however, usually sufficiently dissatisfied with what he wrote in haste to spend endless hours revising and polishing, frequently at great expense, since the manuscripts had already been typeset. His legacy at its best is one of good humor and graceful expression, of barbed satire at times, and of solid storytelling. It is also a splendid legacy of highly memorable, sharply drawn characters from all walks of life: the comic but thrifty Big Nanon in *Eugénie Grandet,* the Lear-like old Goriot in *Père Goriot,* the beautiful but scheming and vicious Valérie Marnefe in *Cousin Bette,* and the omnipresent and ever-curious Dr. Horace Bianchon in THE ATHEIST'S MASS.

Story: Dr. Horace Bianchon is the student and assistant of the famed physician Desplein. Knowing Desplein to be an atheist, Bianchon is surprised one day to find his mentor hearing mass. Later, without revealing to Desplein that he had seen him in the chapel, Bianchon tries to solve the puzzle of an atheist attending mass. Instead of providing an answer, Desplein launches into an anti-mass tirade. Bianchon lets the matter rest until, three months later, he overhears another doctor asking Desplein why he had been in church. Desplein's reply is that he was attending a sick priest.

Bianchon decides once and for all to solve the puzzle. A year from the day he saw Desplein in church, he witnesses the renowned physician in church again. He finds out from the sacristan that Desplein comes to church four times a year to hear masses that Desplein himself has ordered.

It isn't until seven years later that Bianchon finally confesses to Desplein that he knows of his mentor's visits to church. When he asks for an explanation, Desplein responds with a story. Back when he was a poor student, he and an old man named Bourgeat had been thrown out of their lodgings. Bourgeat, a devoted Catholic, used all his energy and what little money he had saved as a water-carrier to see Desplein through medical school. Before Bourgeat died, he asked Desplein to do what he could to have the church help him in the afterlife. True to his promise, Desplein paid the church to establish a schedule of masses for the old man, and four times a year he attends to offer his prayers on behalf of his benefactor.

Comparison: THE ATHEIST'S MASS, as a story with the mysterious activity of a character at its core, invites comparison with works like Joseph Conrad's *Heart of Darkness,* Henry James's *Daisy Miller,* F. Scott Fitzgerald's *The Great Gatsby,* and Nathaniel Hawthorne's "The Minister's Black Veil." As a story of friendship and loyalty, THE ATHEIST'S MASS can be compared with Bret Harte's "Tennessee's Partner," Fyodor Dostoevski's THE HONEST THIEF, and Leo Tolstoy's THE DEATH OF IVÁN ILYICH. — R S

BALZAC, HONORÉ DE. LA GRANDE BRETÊCHE.

France

The World in Literature. Rev. ed. Glenview, IL: ScottForesman, 1967. Translated by Clara Bell.

Author: See THE ATHEIST'S MASS.

Story: Dr. Horace Bianchon is persuaded to tell some ladies the story of the Count and Countess of Merret, who lived in a home known as La Grande Bretêche. Bianchon became especially interested in the mystery of that great abandoned home when Regnault, a notary, told him to stop walking in its overgrown garden. Trespassing there was against the will of the deceased owner, the Countess of Merret, who had left explicit instructions that the home remain unapproached and untouched for fifty years following her death.

Bianchon, a romantic, was attracted all the more to the story, and, by interrogating Regnault, the former maid at La Grande Bretêche, and his own landlady, he was gradually able to piece together what had gone on. The Countess had apparently been having a love affair with a Spanish captive named Count Férédia. One evening, her husband, the Count, came home and, hearing a suspicious noise, accused his wife of hiding someone in her closet. She swore there was no one there, but, to test her honesty, he had a mason begin walling up the closet while she watched. Although the Countess was able to talk the mason into breaking a pane of glass on the closet door so the Spaniard would have air, her husband insisted on staying alone with her in the room for twenty days. There was one opportunity for her to help her trapped lover, but her husband reminded her, "You swore on the cross that there was no one in there."

Comparison: LA GRANDE BRETÊCHE is a frame story in which both the telling of the story and the story itself are of importance in understanding the author's purpose. As such, it is linked to frame narratives like *Arabian Nights,* Boccaccio's *Decameron,* Chaucer's *Canterbury Tales,* Melville's *Moby Dick,* and Conrad's *Heart of Darkness.* In Balzac's story,

what we learn of Bianchon's interests, and, later, of the reaction of the ladies who listen to him, marks the frame as realistic, while the interior narrative is Romantic.

The interior narrative, because of the walling-up motif and other features, makes the story worth comparing with Edgar Allan Poe's "The Fall of the House of Usher" and "The Cask of Amontillado." The gothicism of the story and Bianchon's romantic nature will encourage comparison with many gothic tales, not the least among them Henry James's *The Turn of the Screw.* Dr. Horace Bianchon also appears in a number of Balzac's other works, including THE ATHEIST'S MASS, *Cousin Bette,* and *Père Goriot.* — R S

Baykurt, Fakir. FRECKLES.

Turkey
Short Story International. April 1982. Translated by Joseph S. Jacobson.

Author: Fakir Baykurt (1929–) is a well-known Turkish writer of novels and short fiction. Born in Akcha, he writes works of social commentary about the villages and peasants of his home country.

Story: FRECKLES deals with the harshness of village life in Turkey. The narrator, passing through a village, decides to spend a night with Uncle Kadir, an old friend of his father. When he arrives at the gate, the old man comes out to welcome "Our Veli's son." His two wives, however, are not quite so eager for a guest, since poverty is so severe that food is counted by the mouthful. Through the dinner conversation, the reader learns that the narrator is equally poor. Uncle Kadir explains that the summer crop was ruined by hail, that two sons sent to Ankara have not found work, and that three of the girls and one of the boys have been married off. His freckled-faced daughter, Selver, captures the narrator's attention. She had been given to a man in a neighboring village, but she ran away and came back home three times in a year. Her family beat her and heaped the humiliating title "unmarriageable

daughter" on her. Luckily, explains Uncle Kadir, she has been asked for by another family in another village, and Uncle Kadir has given his word that she will behave.

The narrator becomes caught up in sensory perceptions: "the smell of poverty . . . the grass smell . . . Selver's odor." He sees Selver's "flock of partridge freckles" and her sweetness. He reflects that she should have a good, hot bath with soap and "plenty of lather" and romanticizes the effect of the bath, which would make her hair shine "as if dipped in a gold rinse."

Finally, he asks the question: "Is it absolutely certain, Uncle, that you'll give the girl?" He already knows the answer is yes, but again asks, "So they'll take Selver away today?" Uncle Kadir explains how important it is for him to get the 400 lira for her; it will buy sugar, coffee, and tobacco, as well as a coat for himself, some shoes for "the evil wife's feet," and sandals for the other children. The narrator imagines the scene of departure. Maybe he will sleep in Selver's bed and dream that he could have Selver for his own, that he would "grasp Selver by the wrist" and take her home. But of course it is not to be. Reality intrudes as the first dog announces the arrival of Selver's new family.

Comparison: FRECKLES is a slice-of-life story giving the reader a glimpse into Turkish village life. We can compare it perhaps to Nikolai Gogol's "Taras Bulba," which also records the ways of village life. There is a sense of dignity in the characters because, even though they are poor, they have strict values and a strong sense of faith. There is also a certain romanticism that only youth possesses, as found in James Joyce's "Araby." But the disillusionment is not so harsh in FRECKLES, since the narrator already realizes that life is hard and that dreams are just dreams. The two stories also share a great deal of sensory imagery, but "Araby" is more subtle. The boy would never imagine Mangan's sister in a bath, perhaps because he lives in the comparatively civilized society of Dublin. In the Turkish village, life is hard, and there is no time for subtleties. — D G

BJÖRNSON, BJÖRNSTJERNE. THE FATHER.

Norway
Fifty Great European Short Stories. New York: Bantam, 1971. Translated by R. B. Anderson.

Author: Björnstjerne Björnson (1832–1910) was the third winner of the Nobel Prize for Literature. He is known as the first Norwegian writer of international stature. In fact, his many activities as journalist, public speaker, poet, lyricist, dramatist, novelist, and humanitarian earned him respect around the world. Even today he is viewed as the one person most representative of the Norwegian spirit of his time.

Björnson's fame as a writer was initially established with his stories of peasant life. He deplored the formal Danish of the grammar books and deliberately wrote in the language of everyday people. In doing so, he fostered the development of a more distinctly Norwegian literary language. Though in his day critics accused Björnson of using themes and details too crude and lifelike for literature, his insistence on realistic phrases and details stirred in his readers nationalistic feelings of pride and unity. Loved for his poems so much that he became known as the poet of Norway, Björnson was equally revered for his personal and patriotic songs, one of which was declared the Norwegian national anthem.

One persistent trait in his works is an effort to awaken within the reader a sense of self-worth and direction. Ever the social critic, Björnson addressed specific problems in Norway, ranging from the need for greater religious tolerance to the cause for advanced education for women. His best-known novels include *Sunny Hill, A Happy Boy,* and *On God's Paths.* Among his most successful plays are *A Bankruptcy, The King, Between the Battles,* and *Beyond Our Power.*

Björnson died in Paris. Perhaps the Norwegian government's dispatching a warship to bring home his body for a period of national mourning best speaks for the reputation Björnson maintained as a writer, citizen, and international personality.

Story: In this deceptively simple story, Björnson chronicles a father's relationship with his son, from the pride at that son's birth to the grief that overwhelms him at the son's sudden death some years later.

Presented as a series of brief scenes between Thord Overaas, the wealthy and influential father, and Overaas's parish priest, the story offers a richness of character development despite a paucity of details. Whether making plans for the baptism or for the posting of the son's marriage banns, Overaas determines that all matters concerning his son will be handled with exclusivity. His son is always to be recognized as someone special, a son apart from other men's sons.

Years after the son's death and the father's long mourning, a visibly changed Overaas appears again before the priest to offer money from the sale of his estate as a legacy to his son's name. The priest interrupts the silence that follows Overaas's pronouncement with a simple question: "What do you propose to do now, Thord?" The reply, "Something better," reveals Overaas's growth as an individual. In fact, these two words, "Something better," represent a major leitmotif in Björnson's work: the reality of one's obligation to the world and to life. Thord Overaas appears at the end of the story as someone genuinely human, someone who has moved from false pride through grief toward awareness. In the priest's suggestion that Thord's son may have at last brought his father a true blessing, the full implication of Björnson's title becomes clear.

Comparison: Because of its treatment of the father-son relationship, this story works well as a complement to longer works exploring this subject, such as Gunther's *Death Be Not Proud,* Agee's *A Death in the Family,* and Guest's *Ordinary People.* The length of THE FATHER would allow it to be effectively paired in one class period with another brief story, Pirandello's WAR, in which parents speak to fellow passengers on a train about the valiant nature of their late son's life. But when someone inquires as to the son's actual death, the parents dissolve into an awareness of grief they had never before allowed themselves to experience. Djilas's WAR provides yet another point of comparison. Parents try to save their soldier son by putting him in a coffin, only to have their deception discovered and the son killed. All these authors examine the dualities of love and pride in the parent-child relationship. — P G L

Böll, Heinrich. Murke's Collected Silences.

Germany
Great Modern European Short Stories. Greenwich, CT: Fawcett, 1967.
Translated by Leila Vennewitz.

Author: Heinrich Böll (1917–1985) was born in Cologne and served in the German army from 1939 until he was taken prisoner by the Americans in 1945. Two years later, after training as a publisher, he devoted his full time to writing. He was known as a "left-wing" Catholic and a sharp critic of the materialism and hypocrisy of contemporary life and the stupidity of war. In 1951, he received the prize of the "Group 47," an association of writers who started the new German literature after World War II. In 1972, he was awarded the Nobel Prize for Literature. Among his best-known novels are *The Unguarded House* (1954), *Billiards at Half-Past Nine* (1959), and *The Clown* (1963). He also wrote a novella, *The Bread of Our Early Years* (1955), and several volumes of short stories, including *Absent Without Leave and Other Stories* (1958), in which MURKE'S COLLECTED SILENCES appears.

Story: Every morning when Murke arrives for work at the Broadcasting House, he performs an existential exercise. He takes the kind of elevator known as a paternoster—"open cages carried on a conveyor belt, like beads in a rosary" that move up and down and across the top of the elevator shaft. But instead of getting off on his floor, he continues on to experience the terror of moving across the shaft before it makes the descent. "He needed this panic." Without it, he is irritable and restless.

His present job is to edit audiotapes according to instructions given by Bur-Malottke, who had made them on the subject of the nature of art. Bur-Malottke, a professor who converted to Catholicism in 1945, is now concerned that he might be "blamed for contributing to the religious overtones in radio," so he decides to omit God from his lectures and replace Him with the formula "that higher Being Whom we revere." He agrees to tape this formula thirty-five times so that

Murke can splice it into his speeches and make the appropriate substitutions. Murke, however, points out several complications; making the changes will not be simple. While Bur-Malottke repeats the nominative and genitive forms of his formula, Murke realizes that "he hated this great fat, handsome creature," and he tortures him by having him repeat and redo his empty phrase in each correct grammatical form.

Later, as he walks to the coffee shop, Murke is irritated by the lack of anything spiritual in his environment, so he hangs on the wall a sentimental picture of the Sacred Heart that his mother had sent him. In the coffee shop, he is further annoyed when he repeatedly hears the word *art*, which recurred without meaning throughout Bur-Malottke's talks. He yearns for silence. Later, he admits to a friend that he collects scraps of tapes that contain any kind of silence he can find. He even asks his girlfriend to put silences on tapes so that he can play them back at his leisure.

Back at the studio, the Assistant Drama Producer is editing an atheist play, the script for which he has permission to change. He is thrilled to learn that there is a whole box of tapes with "God" that he can use to replace the silences the atheist had inserted, and the silences could happily be given to Murke. At the end, the Assistant Producer takes out of his pocket the crumpled picture he found on his door. It is the picture of the Sacred Heart, on which is written "I prayed for you at St. James's Church." He and the technician think it is funny. Böll clearly feels that modern religion and popular culture have debased spiritual values for material gain.

Comparison: Böll's criticisms of a mechanical world that has deleted God and ignored the spiritual values of art are shared by another Catholic writer of short stories, Graham Greene, in such short stories as "The Destructors," in which he portrays the encroachment of a mechanized, materialistic, insensitive culture on the old order that it destroys.

The substitution of silence for meaningless noise for mass audiences poses an interesting question. Is it Hemingway's "nada" in "A Clean, Well-Lighted Place," or is it an existential nothingness, or is it the essence of spirituality? One thinks of the composer John Cage's preoccupation with the relationship between sound and silence and of his theory that silence is simply "sounds not intended." His piano piece *4'33* (1952) is composed entirely of nonintended sounds and is divided into three movements of silence.

One also thinks of the paintings of the abstract expressionists. Kandinsky said that deliberate silence, deliberate negation, is a major way of sustaining the elusive spiritual atmosphere of the abstract work by ruthlessly reducing the artistic to an absolute minimum. The achievement of silence is the logical conclusion of the process of negation that abstraction represents. And Poggioli said that the purity of silence implies that art can free itself from the prison of things and the noisy sound of reality. To him, silence represents the need for extreme liberty and extreme intensity of feeling, particularly absolute spiritual freedom. That seems to be the meaning it has for Böll. — R H M

BORGES, JORGE LUIS. THE GARDEN OF FORKING PATHS.

Argentina
Labyrinths. New York: New Directions, 1962. Translated by Donald A. Yates.

Author: Jorge Luis Borges (1899–1986) was born in Buenos Aires. He was educated in England and Switzerland. He returned to Argentina in 1921 and became associated with the avant-garde poets of the time. Borges was a professor of English literature and a lecturer and in 1955 became director of the National Library of Argentina. He wrote poetry, essays, and short fiction and is considered the most influential contemporary Spanish-American writer. Borges wrote for an intelligent audience. He created labyrinths for exploring human personality and reality. Some of his best-known works have been translated into English and collected in *Labyrinths* (1961), *Ficciones* (1962), *Dreamtigers* (1964), and *The Aleph and Other Stories* (1970).

Story: THE GARDEN OF FORKING PATHS is a detective story set in England in 1916. The narrator, Dr. Yu Tsun, tries to reach his superiors in the German Reich in order to communicate the site of a British artillery unit. But Dr. Tsun is being closely pursued by an indefatigable British agent, Captain Richard Madden.

This short plot, however, is not the only mystery in the story, which also includes the story of Stephen Albert, an eminent sinologist who has spent his life deciphering the labyrinthine work of a man named Ts'ui Pên. It is to Albert's house that Tsun flees, for Ts'ui Pên is Tsun's great-grandfather. From Albert, Tsun learns of his great-grandfather's attempt to create an infinite labyrinth in a novel called *The Garden of Forking Paths*.

These two interwoven plots are not only mysteries in themselves, but also provide the clues necessary for deciphering the true subject of the story. The first clue is this: "To omit a word always, to resort to inept metaphors and obvious paraphrases, is perhaps the most emphatic way of stressing it." Stephen Albert tells Tsun that in *The Garden of Forking Paths* the word *time* is never used. The book is thus an enormous riddle or parable whose subject is none other than time itself.

The second clue is one spoken to Tsun on his way to Albert's house. He is told, "You won't get lost if you take this road to the left and at every crossroad turn again to your left." Tsun recognizes this as a common method for discovering the "central point of certain labyrinths." It is a procedure for eliminating possibilities. The reader is provided with the two clues essential to understanding the meaning of Borges's story. One must carefully eliminate the possible subjects of the story until coming to the only one left, the one that is never specifically named.

In this manner, the reader does just what Madden is doing and what Tsun has already done. At every crossroad, Tsun has made a choice and eliminated a possibility. Madden then plods after him every step of the way until they meet at

Albert's house, the single remaining possibility. When the reader applies the same clues to the story itself, it is evident that THE GARDEN OF FORKING PATHS is a parable about reality. The word *reality* is never used, but it is the subject of constant allusion and description. Through the story, Borges presents a reality shaped like an hourglass. All innumerable futures meet at the isolated center of the glass, where one grain of sand intersects with time and connects the two. Tsun says, "Everything happens to a man precisely, precisely *now*."

This is the unique Borges view of reality: that one person is all persons, one act is every possible act, one time is all time. The single occurrence is infinite and eternal. In this one story, Borges creates the multiplicity of reality.

Comparison: Borges's subjects and style of writing are often linked with those of Kafka and Nabokov, and he has been called "a mystic Montaigne." But the best comparisons for THE GARDEN OF FORKING PATHS are more of Borges's own material. In each of his works, he continually develops and explores the themes of the infinite, the eternal return, one person's history coinciding with all of history, and his view of the universe as a labyrinth of time and space, variable and ultimately a seamless whole. Some of Borges's most notable stories are "The Lottery in Babylon," "Theme of the Traitor and the Hero," "The Library of Babel," and "Death and the Compass."

Other sources of comparison for Borges are vast because of his broad concepts and the numerous connections he makes in his works to history, literature, philosophy, and religion. The play *Old Times* by Harold Pinter in some ways resembles THE GARDEN OF FORKING PATHS. In the course of the play, Anna, Deeley, and Kate blend into one person and one time—one reality—in much the same way that Dr. Tsun, Madden, and Albert become one at the end of Borges's story.

Another play, *Six Characters in Search of an Author* by Luigi Pirandello, has aspects reminiscent of Borges. The characters in the play want to act out their own drama rather than allowing performers to do it. These characters live their drama perpetually, and that is the basis of their undeniable reality. In the play, the Mother comments, "It's taking place now. It happens all the time." This recalls Dr. Tsun's words: "Everything happens to a man precisely, precisely *now*." Tsun later says, "The future already exists." In Pirandello's play, the Father exclaims, "The eternal moment!"

One last comparison can be made with a passage from *The Book of Certainty* by Abu Bakr Siraj Ed-Din. This book is a brief synthesis of the major themes of Sufism. We can see a similarity between the two works in this passage from the text:

The Self, Which is the Truth of Certainty, is One; but It is not one with the oneness of a single thing among many, but with Oneness Which Eternally annihilates all duality, and nothing can be added to It so as to make more than One, for It is already Infinite. This Infinite Unity is sometimes called . . . the Essence. The Garden of the Essence is therefore the Highest of all Paradises. . . . It is the One Paradise . . . and nothing may enter It since Everything is already there.

— C W

BOROWSKI, TADEUSZ. THE MAN WITH THE PACKAGE.

Poland
This Way for the Gas, Ladies and Gentlemen. Baltimore: Penguin, 1967.
Translated by Barbara Vedder.

Author: Tadeusz Borowski (1922–1951) was born in the Soviet Ukraine. He was sixteen and living in Poland when World War II began. During the German occupation, he studied in underground classes, since formal education was denied to Poles, and began writing poetry and publishing it clandestinely. He was caught and arrested by the Nazis in 1943, spent two months in prison, and was transported to Auschwitz, where he escaped being gassed solely because he was not Jewish. In 1944, he was transferred to Dachau. In May 1945, the camp was liberated by the U.S. Seventh Army. Borowski eventually returned to communist Poland, where his writings were attacked as amoral, decadent, and nihilistic. At the same time, the power of his writing was such that he was considered one of the greatest hopes of Polish literature among his generation. Increasingly depressed by personal and political complications, he committed suicide in 1951. He was twenty-nine years old. THE MAN WITH THE PACKAGE was published in 1948.

Story: This extremely powerful and somber story is set in the concentration camp at Auschwitz. Rather than having to perform heavy physical labor, a Jew from Lublin has been given the excellent position of *Schreiber* in the camp sick bay, where he keeps patients' records, supervises the block's roll-call, and escorts patients in and out of the hospital. He also takes part in the biweekly selection of patients sent to the gas chamber, generally those weakest and most ill.

The *Schreiber* falls ill himself and, as the only Jew in the block, is quickly placed on the list for extermination. He carefully packs a cardboard box with his boots, a spoon, a knife, a pencil, some bacon, rolls, and fruit. He is then escorted to the truck that will take him to Block 14, where he will join the others waiting in line for their fate. Those in the hospital watch from the window, wondering why the *Schreiber* bothers with the box when he must know that within an hour or two he will go to the gas chamber, naked and without the box.

As the story closes, the other characters discuss whether or not they would carry the box. They watch as the men are driven off in the glare of the floodlights.

Comparison: Like all of Borowski's Auschwitz stories, this is a tale of unrelenting somberness, told in a straightforward manner that emphasizes the everyday nature of atrocity, the banality of evil, qualities equally apparent in, for example, Franz Kafka's IN THE PENAL COLONY. Although emotionally difficult to read, the story offers a moving insight into very basic human questions raised by the Holocaust. Its thematic content—humanity's inhumanity, how we may face death, what meaning life can have in a world that seems insane—sounds a common chord with much of post–World War II literature, including in particular Jerzy Kosinski's novel *The Painted Bird* and William Styron's *Sophie's Choice.*

In a narrower sense, the horror of the Jewish fate in the camps raises the issue of racial prejudice in all forms, including the condition of African Americans as traced by major African American writers in such works as Richard Wright's *Native Son* and Ralph Ellison's *Invisible Man.*

At its most universal level, the story asks what we as human beings can hold on to when life seems to have lost all meaning. As one of the characters says, holding the package may be a sign of hope that something might still happen along the way to avert fate. It may offer something solid and real to connect us to life, like holding on to someone's hand. We may all want to take our own package along on that final journey. — B M

BUZZATI, DINO. THE SLAYING OF THE DRAGON.

Italy

Catastrophe: The Strange Stories of Dino Buzzati. London: Calder and Boyars, 1965. Translated by Judith Landry.

Author: Dino Buzzati (1906–1972) was born in Belluno, Italy. He abandoned his preparation for a legal career in favor of journalism and became a prominent member of the staff of Milan's *Corriere della sera.* A writer of novels and short stories as well as a dramatist, his success in the short story led to his being awarded the prestigious Premio Strega in 1958 for his collection *Sessanta racconti.* Among his novels, the best known is *The Tartar Steppe* (1940), a powerfully ironic, essentially nihilistic tale that demonstrates his great indebtedness to Franz Kafka. Its depiction of the ultimate meaninglessness of life as symbolized by the barren desert viewed each day by the main character suggests a reason for Albert Camus's translating Buzzati's work. His translator observed that "Buzzati's realistic treatment of fantasy . . . implies that fantastic action is somehow mimetic, a representation of the reader's reality." THE SLAYING OF THE DRAGON was published in 1954.

Story: In response to repeated reports of "a great ugly beast that seemed to be a dragon" in the mountains of the province, Count Gerol organizes an expedition, in May 1902, to find and kill the evil creature. They set out, as if on an excursion, encountering on their way to the forbidding mountains first an old physician who warns them that nothing good will come of their quest and then a young man bearing a goat, the daily offering of the people of the village to the dragon. The Count buys the goat from the man, who then rushes back to the village to buy another and fulfill his duty.

Coming to "a black hole: the lair of the dragon," the Count directs that the goat be deposited in the customary place. Soon "the monster of the legends . . . emerged to the light," somewhat smaller and less threatening than the viewers had expected: "The whole effect was of great age. If it was a dragon, it was one gone decrepit." Not deterred by that appearance and "taken by a joyous excitement, already tasting the slaughter," the Count directs the attack against the "monster." The obvious suffering of the gravely wounded, defenseless "monster" begins to dishearten all but the Count. He persists, and the dragon is eventually killed despite the warnings of the villager, who has arrived with a second goat. As the Count advances to deliver the final blow, "two little unformed reptiles" emerge from the cave and are immediately dispatched by the Count. "Dragging itself, slow as a snail," the near-dead dragon approaches its dead young and begins licking them all over.

Finally, the dragon emits "an indescribable cry, a voice never yet heard in the world, neither animal nor human, so charged with hate that even Count Gerol stopped stock still, paralyzed with horror." But the cry is not answered: "nothing, neither brute nor spirit, had hastened to avenge the slaughter. It had been man who wiped out that last, residual stain from the earth; it had been man, the astute and powerful, who everywhere establishes wise laws to maintain order, man the blameless who exhausts himself for progress, and may not concede the survival of any dragon, not even in the desolate mountains. It had been man who killed it and recrimination would be stupid."

But the quest ends badly, as the premonitory warnings had suggested it would. Having breathed the smoke issuing from the mouth of the dead dragon, the Count begins coughing, vainly trying to control himself as "a kind of fire was sinking into the depth of his lungs, lower and lower."

Comparison: In its allegorical nature, as well as in its opposition of the notion of progress and the triumph of enlightened humanity (i.e., the Count) over the irrational, fundamental impulses of the human psyche (i.e., the dragon), THE SLAYING OF THE DRAGON reveals Buzzati's debt to Kafka. Kafka's IN THE PENAL COLONY, for example, similarly suggests that "evil" and "cruelty" are more basic than enlightened humanity wishes to admit and that they cannot be destroyed or ignored, but must be addressed, as they are by the people of the village with their daily offering in Buzzati's story. Similarly, Buzzati's story might be compared with Shirley Jackson's "The Lottery" in its use of ritual sacrifice, senseless killing, and in the oppressive sense of fatalism that dominates both stories.

One might also see a similarity between this story and the predominantly narrative poetry of Robinson Jeffers, especially such a poem as "Original Sin" (1948), if the dragon can be seen as a manifestation of the unknown, "neither animal nor human," that we must destroy lest it make us aware of our own insignificance. Or one might think of Stephen Crane's "The Monster" (1898), in which the Negro servant, having been disfigured by acid to the point at which "he had no face," must be ostracized and hidden from sight so that the horror of reality can be avoided. — P T M

CALVINO, ITALO. ALL AT ONE POINT.

Italy
Form in Fiction. New York: St. Martin's Press, 1974. Translated by William Weaver.

Author: Italo Calvino (1923–1985) was born in Cuba and grew up in San Remo, Italy. As a young writer, he took as his mentor Cesare Pavese and thus began as an Italian neo-realist, producing *The Path to the Nest of Spiders* (1947) as a result of his involvement with anti-Fascist partisans during World War II. But such disparate events and influences as Pavese's suicide, the eighteenth-century French *conte,* and Italian fables, of which he produced a definitive collection in 1953, enabled him to develop, through experimentation, his own elegant stylistic mode of dramatizing modern alienation. He is best known as a writer for his short stories and three tales collected as *Our Forefathers* (1960). ALL AT ONE POINT was published in 1965.

Story: ALL AT ONE POINT is an interior monologue or long speech thought or delivered by *old Qfwfq,* in response, presumably, to the text that serves as the epigraph to the story: "Through the calculations begun by Edwin P. Hubble on the galaxies' velocity of recession, we can establish the moment when all the universe's matter was concentrated in a single point, before it began to expand in space." *Old Qfwfq* begins, "Naturally we were all there ... where else could we have been? Nobody knew then that there could be space. Or time either: what use did we have for time, packed in there like sardines?"

He goes on to describe the conditions "there." Though living in close proximity, people had only a limited number of acquaintances. His included Mrs. Ph(i)Nk$_O$, her friend DeXuaeauX, an immigrant family named Z'zu, Mr. Pber^t Pber^d, and a cleaning lady. Their problems were compounded by "all the stuff we had to keep piled up in there." Conflicts naturally arose because of the close quarters and because the Z'zus, being immigrants, were not accepted by the others.

Now, some indeterminate time later, *old Qfwfq* meets his former acquaintances from time to time. They always bring up the old conflicts and, paradoxically, look forward to the time when the old group will be together again, an unlikely possibility since the "theory that the universe, after having reached an extremity of rarefaction, will be condensed again has never convinced me." These conversations always turn to Mrs. Ph(i)Nk$_O$, since all of the former acquaintances remember her with pleasure. As *old Qfwfq* puts it, "The happiness I derived from her was the joy of being concealed, punctiform, in her, and of protecting her, punctiform, in me; it was at the same time vicious contemplation (thanks to the promiscuity of the punctiform convergence of us all in her) and also chastity (given her punctiform impenetrability). . . . She contained and was contained with equal happiness, and she welcomed us and loved and inhabited all equally."

Just at the moment that Mrs. Ph(i)Nk$_O$ offered, if she had some space, to make noodles for them all, causing them to imagine space for the first time, the universe, as if responding to her outburst of a loving impulse, expanded, "making possible billions and billions of suns, and of planets, and fields of wheat, and Mrs. Ph(i)Nk$_O$s, scattered through the continents of the planets, kneading with floury, oil-shiny, generous arms."

Comparison: Calvino has labeled his stories of this sort "cosmicomic," and their relationship to the folktales he collected and published is clear, although the story itself could never be mistaken for one of them. The personalization of creation is a common motif in creation myths and tales, and this story could well be compared to such tales. On the other hand, Calvino's use of scientific knowledge suggests a comparison with a story like John Barth's "Night-Sea Journey," which also uses scientific data metaphorically, deals with creation and procreation, and is both comic and humorous.

Since ALL AT ONE POINT concerns itself centrally with humanity's collective loss of innocence and its consequent desire to return to "the mother," in this case a reconstituted Mrs. Ph(i)Nk$_O$, the story may be compared to any of the multitude of works dealing with that theme. One might consider such disparate examples as Arthur Miller's *After the Fall,* with its concern that humanity accept its fallen state, James Joyce's "Araby," with its central character's ambivalence in the face of the "anguish and anger" his venturing forth into the world has caused him, and Walt Whitman's "Song of Myself," in which he celebrates the "knit of identity" that links "here and hereafter" as well as past and present by creating a mystical unity of all life. In this, the latter work is basically similar to Calvino's conception. It should be noted, however, that none of these writers treats his subject allegorically or humorously. — P T M

Camus, Albert. THE GUEST.

France
English and Western Literature. New York: Macmillan, 1984. Translated by Justin O'Brien.

Author: Albert Camus (1913–1960) was born in Algeria, at that time a French colony, the son of impoverished semiliterate parents. He went to public schools and then to the University of Algiers, where he studied philosophy while working at various jobs. Upon graduation, he became a journalist, traveling throughout Europe. From 1937 to 1941, he wrote three of his most famous works: *The Stranger* (a novel), *The Myth of Sisyphus* (an essay), and *Caligula* (a play). Returning to North Africa, he taught at a private school in Oran for two years. French North Africa is the setting for many of his sketches and two major novels. In 1942, he went to Paris, where he became an intellectual leader of the resistance movement in Nazi-occupied France as the editor of an underground newspaper, *Combat.* He wrote THE GUEST in 1957.

Story: Daru, a French schoolmaster born in Algeria, is stationed on a remote, desolate plateau in French-occupied Algeria. Balducci, a gendarme, arrives unexpectedly with an Arab prisoner who has killed his own cousin. Balducci orders the reluctant Daru to take the Arab to the proper French authorities at Tinquit the next day. After feeding the prisoner and sleeping in the same room with him, Daru finds himself unable to deliver the man to the police. Instead, he takes him part way and gives him food and money. He then points out the road to freedom with the Arab nomads in the west and the road to prison under the French in the east, giving his "guest" the choice. As he returns home, he sees the prisoner in the far distance walking eastward. On the blackboard of his classroom, he finds a message from the Arabs promising revenge: "You handed over our brother. You will pay for this."

Comparison: Daru's actions reflect his individual integrity but result in his alienation from both the French colonists and the native Arabs. In Camus's famous novel *The Stranger,* the protagonist, Meursault, refuses to follow the precepts and conventions of society and also becomes isolated, a stranger in a meaningless world. Parallel emphasis upon individualism, isolation, and the absurdity of the human condition is found in many works by existentialists, such as THE WALL by Jean-Paul Sartre. In THE GUEST and THE WALL, the main characters must create their own morality, as there are no absolute values in their godless universe. The ironic results of their moral decisions reveal the absurdity of life.

An interesting comparison can also be made between THE GUEST and Philip Roth's "The Defender of the Faith." The protagonist of Roth's story, Sergeant Nathan Marx, has recently returned from the war in Europe to an army base in Missouri. Like Daru, he feels isolated from society and initially resists the friendly overtures of three fellow Jewish soldiers in training under him. He recognizes, however, the injustices done to these men, whose religious needs are overlooked by an impersonal army. Conflict arises as he attempts to balance the opposing claims of the military and of religious brotherhood, a conflict similar to that faced by Daru between his duty to the French authorities and his sympathy for his fellow man, the Arab prisoner. Both protagonists follow their humanitarian impulses, only to end up isolated again.

The theme of isolation and alienation is pervasive in modern literature. Franz Kafka's A HUNGER ARTIST is another prime example. — M A F

CHEKHOV, ANTON. THE BET.

Russia
Prentice Hall Literature World Masterpieces. Englewood Cliffs, NJ: Prentice Hall, 1991.
Translated by Ronald Wilds.

Author: Anton Chekhov (1860–1904) is noted equally for his short stories and plays. He was born in Taganrog in the south of Russia, the son of a merchant and the grandson of an ex-serf who had purchased his freedom. In 1879, he enrolled in medical school at the University of Moscow. While there, he began contributing short sketches, stories, and jokes to journals in order to make money to help support his five brothers and sisters. Chekhov used pen names, among them "The Doctor without Patients," which is illustrative of his dry humor. His writing caught the attention of the publisher of the *St.*

Petersburg Daily. With a guaranteed income, Chekhov could focus on quality rather than quantity, and his artistic reputation began to grow.

Chekhov contracted tuberculosis while still a student at the university, and his entire short life was a constant struggle against the ravages of the disease. In 1890, he made a trip to Sakhalin, which weakened his condition even more. Upon his return to Russia, Chekhov bought a small estate at Melikhovo and moved there with his family. During this period, he wrote many short stories and two of his major plays, *The Seagull* and *Uncle Vanya.* The production of *The Seagull* was panned by the critics, and at that point Chekhov was ready to give up playwriting. Luckily, two years later *The Seagull* was performed by the newly established Moscow Art Theatre, and it was so successful that the company adopted the seagull as part of its emblem.

In 1898, failing health forced Chekhov to move to Yalta, where he continued writing. The focus of his endeavors there was drama. He married an actress, Olga Knipper, in 1901, but he remained in Yalta while she stayed in Moscow. It was at this time that he wrote *The Cherry Orchard* and *The Three Sisters.* His failing health forced doctors to send him to Badenweiler, Germany, where he died in 1904.

The theme prevalent in all of Chekhov's writing is life's pathos, caused by humanity's inability to communicate and the sadness and hopelessness that result.

Story: THE BET opens with a flashback, seen through the eyes of a banker who is remembering a gathering fifteen years before at which capital punishment was discussed. The banker argued that capital punishment was far more moral and humane than life imprisonment, but a twenty-five-year-old lawyer disagreed, saying both were equally immoral, but if he were given the choice, he would choose life imprisonment, since "any sort of life's better than none at all." The banker bet the lawyer two million rubles that he could not stay in a cell for five years. The lawyer, being young and poor, accepted, upping the ante to fifteen years.

The conditions of the bet were as follows. The lawyer was to stay in a lodge on the grounds of the banker's estate. For fifteen years, he could not see a living soul, could not hear another human voice,

could not cross the threshold or read newspapers or letters. He was allowed a musical instrument, books, wine, cigars, and any type of food he desired. He could also send notes, but he was to receive no response. The confinement began November 14, 1870, at midnight and was to last until midnight November 14, 1885.

The first year, the young lawyer was stricken with boredom and loneliness. He refused wine and cigars because they gave rise to desire, a prisoner's worst enemy. He played the piano constantly and read light books. The second year, the music ceased, and he asked for classics to read. In the fifth year, he began to play the piano again, and he asked for wine. He did not read, but he wrote page after page, only to tear up all he had written. Often the sounds of weeping came from the lodge. In the sixth year, he began to study languages, philosophy, and history. He read almost six hundred volumes and wrote a letter to the banker in six different languages. After the tenth year, all the lawyer read were the gospels, followed by histories of religion and theology. The last two years, his reading habits were eclectic, from Shakespeare to natural science.

As the story catches up to the present time, the banker is reflecting upon the fact that the very next night the prisoner is to be freed and the banker will have to pay him two million rubles. Over the years, the banker had gambled and speculated heavily, and he is now no more than a small-time financier. The thought of having to come up with a vast amount of money terrifies him, and the thought of the lawyer living well on that money makes him angry. Finally, he decides his only way out is to kill the lawyer.

During the night, he creeps into the prisoner's room. The prisoner has aged, his gaunt appearance making him look older than forty. The banker decides to smother him with a pillow, but before he can do so, his attention is caught by a note nearby. The prisoner has written his credo. Since he has read and studied, he is wiser than "all of you," and he is wise enough to despise the blessings of the world. He sees everything as ultimately without worth, since everyone dies anyway. He renounces the bet and says he will leave five hours early just so he will lose. The banker experiences such a sense of relief that he kisses the lawyer on the head and rushes out of the lodge weeping, feeling absolute contempt for himself. The next morning, the watchmen confirm that the prisoner bolted out of the lodge five hours early. The banker goes back to the lodge and recovers the prisoner's note. Saying he wishes to avoid "unnecessary disputes later," he locks it in his safe.

Comparison: The theme of THE BET is greed, and the reader realizes the extent to which the characters illustrate that theme. The banker is not a sympathetic character. Even at the very end, he has no remorse. Money is more important to him than honor or human life. One is reminded of Mr. Gecko's speech on greed in the movie *Wall Street:* "Greed is good." Both characters expect everyone else to operate by the same principles. Thus, the banker takes the lawyer's written renunciation of the bet and locks it in his safe. It is beyond his scope to understand that the lawyer is so disillusioned by what he has learned that money means little to him.

Another classic study in greed is *McTeague* by Frank Norris. The central character, Mac, is similar to the banker, except that he hoards his money like Silas Marner. Mac's greatest pleasure is rolling around on hard, cold piles of gold coins. Unlike the banker in the Chekhov story, he lives like a pauper and actually commits crimes to keep his pile of money safe, while the banker only contemplates murder. Another difference is that Chekhov's banker enjoys his money by spending it excessively rather than hoarding it.

One can also draw comparisons between THE BET and Leo Tolstoy's HOW MUCH LAND DOES A MAN NEED? The driving force for Pahom is greed: how much land can he stake out before sunset? He literally runs himself to death, perhaps realizing at the last moment that he "needs" just six feet in which to be buried. The lawyer learns the same lesson, but not at the cost of his life. Even though his initial motive for making the bet was greed, he comes to realize how foolish he was to engage in the bet in the first place. He has learned the truth behind his earlier words, that "any sort of life's better than none at all." — D G

Chekhov, Anton. THE DARLING.

Russia
Anton Chekhov's Short Stories. New York: Norton, 1979. Translated by Ralph E. Matlow.

Author: See THE BET.

Story: Olenka is a gentle girl whom everyone calls "the darling" because she captivates everyone with her good nature. She lives with her father and falls in love with Ivan Kukin, who is thin, pale, and no longer young. He runs an outdoor theater and complains constantly about the rain ruining his business and the public's lack of respect for outdoor theaters. When her father dies, Olenka marries Kukin and immediately immerses herself in his personality. His opinions become her opinions, and her conversation becomes a replication of his. She flourishes, grows stouter and more pink, while he grows thinner and paler. After a year, Ivan suddenly dies.

Olenka loses all interest in life, but after three months, she meets Vasili Pustovalov, who works for a timber merchant. The "darling" and Vasili marry, and in no time, Olenka again immerses herself entirely in her husband's personality, believing only what he believes, saying only what he would say. After six years, this husband dies too, and once again Olenka is beset with emptiness.

Within six months, however, Olenka finds another solution. She establishes a relationship with Vladimir Smirnin, an army veterinary surgeon who rents her lodge. He is married and has a son, but is separated from his wife and child. Soon Olenka is happily discussing animal epidemics. When Smirnin is transferred to another post, Olenka is again alone. She languishes, becoming sad, indifferent, and old— and she has no opinions of any kind.

Fortunately for Olenka, Smirnin returns. He has left the service and come back to start a life with his family. Olenka gives her house to the Smirnins and retreats to the lodge. Of course, her life begins again, but this time the man in her life is Smirnin's son, ten-year-old Sasha. The father takes work outside the village, and the mother leaves to live elsewhere. Thus, Olenka is "auntie" to the boy, and she soon begins complaining about teachers and homework. Once again, she has an identity; once again, there is a man in her life to fill the void.

Comparison: It is the sweetness in Olenka's character that makes her different from Emma Bovary in Flaubert's *Madame Bovary.* Emma is a romantic, but she is motivated by a desire for social standing, and thus she is selfish and self-serving. She is a tragic figure in part because she is never happy, and she destroys innocent characters around her. Olenka too is a romantic, in love with love, but she is a "darling" (more correctly translated as "little soul"), accepted and liked by the townsfolk, without a bit

of selfishness and doing no harm to anyone. She does not fall in love for personal or social gain, as does Emma. She falls in love because it gives her an identity, a sense of belonging, of purpose. And while Flaubert's attitude toward Emma is clear, Chekhov's opinion of Olenka is less so. Whether he views her sympathetically and kindly or presents her as an example of shallowness is for the reader to decide.

To be a wife, half of a couple, is Olenka's life. It is a clear and uncomplicated goal, like that of Florentino Ariza in Gabriel García Márquez's *Love in the Time of Cholera.* Florentino's love, however, is specific and directed toward Fermina Daza, while Olenka's is sincerely attached to whoever can give purpose to her life. She adjusts her thoughts with each new association, a mirror for each personality filling her life. Márquez uses a similar symbol. Florentino buys a mirror in which Fermina once gazed at herself so that their reflections can mingle in the memory of the images caught in the glass. — D G

CHEKHOV, ANTON. THE KISS.

Russia
A Doctor's Visit: Short Stories by Anton Chekhov. New York: Bantam, 1988.
Translated by Avraham Yarmolinsky.

Author: See THE BET.

Story: THE KISS is a deceptively simple story about a young soldier, Ryabovich, who meets with "a little adventure." He is "timid, round-shouldered and uninteresting." But on one particular June night, he and his fellow officers are invited to tea at the estate of von Rabbeck, the local wealthy landowner. Soon there is dancing and merriment. Ryabovich, because he neither dances nor plays billiards, is uncomfortable and self-conscious. He wanders from one group to another, becoming lost in a maze of rooms. He wanders into a little, dark room where he suddenly encounters an unknown "feminine voice . . . a rustle of skirts . . . and the sound of a kiss" placed on his mouth. Although the shriek that follows indicates that the kiss had not been intended for him,

he is sharply aware for hours afterwards of the "chilly sensation near his mouth," the memory of the kiss. He looks around the ballroom and tries to determine which of the women may have been responsible, but to no avail.

The evening ends, and the men return to camp. Ryabovich reflects on how the kiss has changed him. He has now shared an experience of every other ordinary man, and, like every other ordinary man, he believes for the first time that he will fall in love, get married, and have a conventional life.

When the brigade returns to the area the following summer, Ryabovich is filled with anticipation and excitement at the prospect before him, but soon a "crushing uneasiness took hold of him." He fears that von Rabbeck will not invite the brigade to tea. He takes a walk and sees that the von Rabbeck house is dark. Suddenly, he realizes "how stupid" it all is and how the accidental kiss led to vague hopes and dreams now bathed in the disappointment of reality. He sees the whole world and life itself as an "aimless jest."

When he returns to his quarters, an orderly tells him that the brigade has been invited to a gathering hosted by a general. At first Ryabovich is excited, but then reality takes hold, and he does not attend.

Comparison: THE KISS is reminiscent of James Joyce's "Araby," which deals with a young man's all-consuming first crush, which also results in disillusion. No one can be as perfect as the image created by the boy in "Araby," and when he realizes that the object of his affection is merely flirting with him, he becomes "a creature derided by vanity." In a sense, Ryabovich has a similar insight, which is why he bitterly decides not to go to the gathering.

Nothing will ever be as wonderful as that mysterious kiss.

One is also reminded of Sammy in "A & P" by John Updike. Sammy perceives himself as a knight in shining armor when he sacrifices his job to defend three young girls in bathing suits. He jumps on his horse, armor clanging, only to discover his sacrifice is for nothing. His "Dulcineas" are not even aware of his charge. But Sammy is not disillusioned, because his purpose is a matter of principle, not mere love. His motive is pure, because he acts from his heart, not for recognition. But it is a bittersweet thing, and one wonders if, on the way home to tell his parents he has lost his job, he does not experience a moment of disappointment that things did not turn out as he had expected. The girls are already gone, and he is left to accept the responsibility for his romantic deed. — D G

CICELLIS, KAY. BRIEF DIALOGUE.

Greece

Eighteen Texts: Writings by Contemporary Greek Authors. Cambridge: Harvard University Press, 1972. Translated by Kay Cicellis.

Author: Kay Cicellis (1926–) was born of Greek parentage in Marseilles. She grew up speaking French and English. She learned Greek at the age of nine when her family moved to Athens, where she received her education. Cicellis has worked as a translator and book reviewer and has authored documentaries, short story collections, and several novels, including *No Name in the Street* (1953) and *Ten Seconds from Now* (1957). Her collection of three long stories, *The Way to Colonus* (1961), is based on ancient Greek myths and has received international acclaim. Cicellis has been translated into French, Spanish, German, and Portuguese, and her writing may be found in prestigious Greek, English, and American periodicals. She published BRIEF DIALOGUE in 1970. At that time, Cicellis was one of a small group of leading Greek writers who spoke out against the oppressive military regime of the Colonels. Understanding the danger, however, she

avoids direct confrontation by setting her story in South America.

Story: The story is a conversation between a taxi driver and his passenger. There is little description of characters or setting, other than that the time is late afternoon. The style is terse, the undercurrents heavy. Traffic is moving slowly as people return to the heart of the city after siesta. In the taxi, the passenger, in Greek fashion, has climbed into the front seat to ride. As they move along, the passenger finds that conversation is difficult and that there are long, unnatural silences. He wishes that he had sat in the back. The driver asks the passenger how he thinks their country is viewed by other nations. The driver is searching for information about attitudes toward the military regime. The passenger responds, "What do you think?" Each is afraid to speak openly. Over and over, they sense that their feelings are shared, but the stark reality of living under a military government startles them back to bland remarks and vacant stares at the passing scene. By the time they arrive at the passenger's destination, they have learned to trust each other a little. But it is too late; the ride is over. The picture created by Cicellis is one of communication distorted by overpowering oppression.

Comparison: Another story that relies primarily on conversation is Ernest Hemingway's "The Killers." Three people in Henry's lunchroom try to fathom the meaning of a conversation they overhear between two strangers who, they finally learn,

have come to town to kill a local man. Oppression is the theme of both stories. Cicellis speaks of oppression of a country; Hemingway, of the individual. In both, the meaning of the conversation is unclear at first, but the truth unfolds as the conversation draws to its close.

BRIEF DIALOGUE, as a slice-of-life story, can also be read along with another Hemingway tale, although depression rather than oppression is the theme of "A Clean, Well-Lighted Place." The older waiter in that story believes deeply that many people who try to avoid the nothingness in their lives have a great need for a pleasant, well-lit cafe that stays open into the night. — E M

Colette. THE LITTLE BOUILLOUX GIRL.

France
By Women: An Anthology of Literature. Boston: Houghton Mifflin, 1976.
Translated by Una Vicenzo Trowbridge and Enid McLeod.

Author: The writings of Colette, the pen name of Sidonie Gabrielle Colette (1873–1954), reflect the author's concern for the fate of women restricted personally and professionally by traditional expectations and roles in a male-dominated society. Brought up in the country, Colette had been easily charmed as a young woman by an older, sophisticated man, the unscrupulous Parisian music critic and novelist Henri Gauthier-Villars. Following their marriage, her initial works, the *Claudine* books, were written in forced collaboration with her husband. He took full credit by publishing them under his pseudonym, Willy. Their relationship failed, and after their divorce, she performed in music halls as a dancer and mime. Remarried twice, she became prominent in Parisian society and continued a successful writing career. Elected to the Goncourt Academy in 1945, Colette was the first woman to receive that honor.

THE LITTLE BOUILLOUX GIRL was published in 1922, and THE PHOTOGRAPHER'S MISSUS in 1944.

Story: As a beautiful, adored child, Nana Bouilloux became accustomed to the constant admiration of the villagers. At the age of thirteen, she left school

to become an apprentice dressmaker. Her haughty manner and provocative behavior won her the adulation of the boys, but aroused the jealousy of the girls. Then, when she was eighteen, she met a visiting sophisticated Parisian at a holiday dance. The compliments accorded her by this worldly traveler during a solitary waltz augmented her already exaggerated sense of worth. This incident initiated a change in her expectations. Proudly anticipating the arrival of a "stranger, a ravisher" who would merit a woman of such rare beauty, she began rejecting all of her rural suitors. Twenty years later, the narrator, who as a young schoolmate had envied the little Bouilloux girl, encounters her on the street. A bitter woman whose beauty has faded, she is still looking anxiously for her "long-awaited ravisher."

Comparison: Emma Bovary in Flaubert's *Madame Bovary* has similar romantic illusions bolstered by an ego inflated by the admiration of others. She rejects the love of her simple but sincere husband, just as Nana Bouilloux rejects the attentions of her rural suitors. The unsophisticated Emma is easily seduced by the empty flattery of worldly men. Her pathetic dreams of romance inspired by the ball at Vaubyessard are dashed as her various lovers abandon her. Both women suffer bitter disillusionment.

Such disillusionment causes Nana Bouilloux's good looks to fade. Similarly, the lovely peasant girl Naïs in Émile Zola's NAÏS MICOULIN ages quickly, losing her beauty after being abandoned by her wealthy lover, who considered her beneath his social class.

Much of Colette's work depicts the sorry plight of women taught by society to value themselves in terms of their appearance. To illustrate the devastating effect of the loss of physical beauty upon a vain person, Ivan Albright's painting *Into the World There Came a Soul Called Ida* could be used. The painting depicts a woman's futile effort to conceal the ravages of time through the use of cosmetics.

Women are often depicted in fiction as trying to avoid harsh reality. In William Faulkner's "A Rose for Emily," Emily Grierson lives a life of illusion. Her Southern pride prevents her from accepting her impoverished status following her father's death. Then a failed romance pushes her into insanity, the ultimate escape from reality. — M A F

COLETTE. THE PHOTOGRAPHER'S MISSUS.

France
The Tender Shoot and Other Stories by Colette of the Academy Goncourt. New York: Farrar, Straus & Cudahy, 1959. Translated by Antonia White.

Author: See THE LITTLE BOUILLOUX GIRL.

Story: The narrator, Madame Colette, begins the story by announcing her joy at the failure of the attempted suicide of a woman referred to as "the photographer's Missus." Colette had met the photographer's wife, Madame Armand, while visiting her neighbor across the hall, Mademoiselle Devoidy, a forty-year-old unmarried pearl-stringer. Mlle. Devoidy's confident outlook, bolstered by her professional competence, contrasts strongly to Mme. Armand's attitude of despair at her inability to help her husband with his job or to escape the boredom associated with domesticity. The pearl-stringer derides the feminine vanity of her neighbor, epitomized by Mme. Armand's wearing stockings at all times to conceal her corns and crooked third toe, even when attempting suicide. Summoned by the worried husband, it is Mlle. Devoidy who rescues Mme. Armand when she swallows poison and locks herself in her room. Ironically, the two women later have a violent argument because the spinster agrees with the attending physician's assertion that the suicide attempt occurred during an attack of neurasthenia. The recuperating victim explains to Madame Colette that it was not neurasthenia, but the triviality of her dull life that motivated her actions. She had envisioned that the slow process of the approach of death would result in sublime thoughts, banishing all pettiness. Yet her "dying" moments were not sublime, but filled with worrisome thoughts of wifely duties and bodily miseries. After some reflection, she vows never to attempt suicide again. The narrator describes her as "sustained by the sheer force of humble, everyday feminine greatness: the unrecognized greatness she had misnamed 'a very trivial life.'"

Comparison: Much of Colette's work depicts the plight of women imprisoned by traditional domestic roles. Many similarities exist between Madame Armand's dilemma and that of Nora Tesman in Henrik Ibsen's *A Doll's House.* The title of Colette's story reflects society's view of the wife as her husband's possession, a position also inflicted upon Nora. The duplicity fostered by such relationships is revealed through Nora's secretly eating forbidden macaroons and the photographer's wife's furtive mild flirtation with a younger man.

The traditional roles of the domineering husband and submissive wife are also seen in Charlotte Perkins Gilman's "The Yellow Wallpaper." In this story, the husband is a doctor who, like the photographer, appears to love his wife but is unable to view her as an equal. His demeaning personal and professional treatment exacerbates his wife's depression, leading to her insanity.

Madame Armand's death wish in THE PHOTOGRAPHER'S MISSUS parallels that of Hedda in Ibsen's *Hedda Gabler* and Emma in Gustave Flaubert's *Madame Bovary.* The three women view suicide as a beautiful act. The desire to escape the boredom of a tedious marriage motivates their

actions. Hedda shoots herself, dying instantly, but Emma's romantic vision of a quick death by poisoning results in a painful, lingering demise. Mme. Armand's suicide attempt is neither successful nor beautiful. Reconsidering her choices, she decides to face life, not end it.

Many counterparts of wives who wish to escape the triviality of dull lives exist in modern fiction, such as Margaret Quest in Doris Lessing's *A Proper Marriage.* — M A F

Condé, Maryse. THREE WOMEN IN MANHATTAN.

Guadeloupe
Green Cane and Juicy Flotsam: Short Stories by Caribbean Women. New Brunswick, NJ: Rutgers University Press, 1991. Translated by Thomas Spear.

Author: One of the best known francophone writers from the Caribbean, Maryse Condé (1937–), also known as Maryse Boucolon, was born in Guadeloupe, her current residence. She has lived in West Africa, the United States, and France, where she earned a doctorate in comparative literature from the Sorbonne in 1975. A playwright, critic, and scholar, she has written short stories and several novels, including *Tree of Life* (1987), *I, Tituba, Black Witch of Salem* (1986), *A Season in Rihata* (1981), and *Heremakhonon* (1976). These works cover a range of subjects, historical periods, and geographic settings. *I, Tituba,* for example, is a fictionalized account of a black woman burnt as a witch in Salem, Massachusetts. Condé's work is recognized for both its popular appeal and literary merit. *Segu* reached the best-seller list in France, while *I, Tituba* won the Grand Prix Litteraire de la Femme.

Story: In THREE WOMEN IN MANHATTAN, the lives of Elinor, Claude, and Vera are intertwined around the theme of emerging consciousness and the power of the written word. Elinor, the commercially successful African American writer, is torn between the white literary establishment that "culled her references to folklore of the Old South and to collective black patrimony" and the black critics who want her to write "about slavery and the slave trade

and racism." Vera is the exiled aging Haitian activist who, on occasion, "put her pen in the service of a great cause," but whose manuscripts remain unpublished, rejected by "editors from France, Belgium, Switzerland, and Canada." Claude, the narrator, links the two women: "an Elinor that the absent-minded sorcerer, destiny, had forgotten to gratify after having wrenched her from nothingness." A domestic, she spends mornings cleaning for Elinor and works for Vera some afternoons, not realizing for several months that "Vera had no need of a cleaning woman" and was, in fact, acting as her protector.

An impressionistic story, THREE WOMEN IN MANHATTAN takes place during two days but glimpses the past of all three women. After a conversation between Claude and a buoyant Elinor enjoying her success, the former recalls her childhood on Guadeloupe and the notebooks in which she recorded her thoughts, prompted by "an uncontrollable force within her." The plot moves with Claude on the bus "ninety streets uptown in the heart of Harlem" to the apartment of Vera, who relives past glories and laments her present inglorious plight. Following the next day's encounter with Elinor, despondent over black critics' verdict on her work, Claude returns to Vera's apartment, where she meets "the materialization of a dread she'd carried with her daily"—an ambulance signaling Vera's death.

What unites the seemingly ordinary events in THREE WOMEN IN MANHATTAN is the attempt of each woman to find her voice and the transforming power of the written word. The contrast between Elinor's widely read works and Vera's ignored ones leads Claude to conclude, "Writing is but a trap, the cruelest of all, a snare, a sham of communication." Nonetheless, she enrolls in night classes to learn English and cannot escape the lure of the "series of arabesques [that] symbolized a thought, communicated an element of the imaginary, which, through them, was more penetrating than reality." Recognizing the physical as well as intellectual activity of writing ("To put her hips, her sex, her heart into motion in order to give birth to a world inscribed in her obscurity"), she defies Vera's death through the power of the written word to "present her not such as she was—an octogenarian in a pitiful wool cardigan, raising her pathetic voice in the tumult of distress—but such as she dreamed her to be: Erzulie Dantor, flaming torch clenched in her fist!"

Comparison: Intriguing comparisons can be made with stories of characters seeking to realize a legitimate voice—and thus identity—in the face of a dominant culture that denies them. In "Lullaby," Native American writer Leslie Marmon Silko presents the destruction of a culture symbolized by the virtual silencing of the central character, Ayah. The short story "Seventeen Syllables," by Hisaye Yamamoto, portrays the resistance of a Japanese woman against her traditional patriarchal culture. Her struggle and defiance take the form of the written word, in this case the forbidden act of writing poetry. Sandra Cisneros takes up a similar theme, though with a positive outcome, in *House on Mango Street,* a series of vignettes tracing the emergence of a developing writer's voice. The feminist perspective in Condé's story, particularly the relationships between and among women, might be explored through comparison with Cisneros's "Woman Hollering Creek" and Tillie Olsen's "I Stand Here Ironing." — R H S

CORTÁZAR, JULIO. END OF THE GAME.

Argentina
The Eye of the Heart: Short Stories from Latin America. New York: Bobbs-Merrill, 1973.
Translated by Eliot Weinberger.

Author: Julio Cortázar (1914–1984) was born in Brussels, Belgium. He grew up in Argentina but left the country in protest of the Juan Peron dictatorship. He emigrated to Paris, where he published his first collection of short stories, *Bestiary,* in 1945. Although France became his home until his death in early 1984, he returned to Argentina periodically throughout his life. During that time, he worked four months a year as a freelance translator of French and English into Spanish for UNESCO. He was also a poet, a novelist, and a short story writer. *Hopscotch,* published in English in 1964, earned him recognition as Latin America's first great novelist. This novel also established him as a master of imaginative and fantastic writing and has been credited with triggering the explosion of modern Latin American literature. His other novels

include *A Manual for Manuel* and *A Certain Lucas.*

Cortázar lived in France at the height of the surrealist and jazz movements, and the "Marvelous" of surrealists became the fantastic in Cortázar's writing. He compared the short story to a photograph that limits a view to a single shot and argued that a fragment of reality forces its viewer to supply all the missing parts. The surrealist influence is also reflected in Cortázar's works in the spontaneity of illogical events intended to reflect an absurd world and humanity's precarious condition in it.

Story: END OF THE GAME is a multilevel short story dealing with the nature of illusion and reality. It is told in a first-person narrative as a "slice of life." Three young girls play a secret game by the railroad tracks and learn a great deal about life. There are actually two secrets. The first is the sneaking of Mamma's things to play a game of "Statues and Attitudes." The second is the physical handicap of one of the girls, Letitia. She is treated by everyone as someone special, with special privileges and exemptions from duties. Her handicap, a physical deformity, is ignored by the family and is like a well-kept secret. The only time Letitia is really pretty is when she is dressed-up in Mamma's things, posing as the Venus de Milo or an Oriental princess for the passengers of the afternoon train. The girls take turns posing as statues until one of the passengers, a young boy, takes a fancy to Letitia and wants to meet her. He drops notes out of the train window. Letitia is delighted by his attention until the reality of meeting him arises. She is faced with letting him keep his illusion of her beautiful self or admitting the reality of her deformity. Cortázar uses the situation to frame his characters, and the story unfolds from it. Although influences of the existentialists are present, he does not give in to despair. Letitia's solution to her dilemma is magnificent, however bittersweet.

Comparison: Successful as a novelist, Cortázar was even more successful as a short story writer. His skill with this form places him with the best of the contemporary short story writers, including Jorge Luis Borges. Borges was a significant influence on Cortázar, as was the classicist Machado de Assis. Cortázar was a great experimenter with form, time, place, and the concept of illusion and reality. He drew heavily from his dreams and believed that good writing must "tap the subconscious." He also believed that novel writing is a craft, but that "one must be born a short story writer." Antonioni's film *Blow-up* was loosely based on a story by Cortázar with the same title. Parallels between Cortázar and the influences of Borges and Kafka have been made. Comparisons have also been made with Huxley and Italo Svevo. Readers often find similarities to Poe, Maupassant, and Camus. Of course, the situation in Edmund Rostand's *Cyrano de Bergerac* comes to mind. Cortázar was dedicated to pushing out the boundaries of his art form, believing that dead forms rob people of their identity. In order for humanity to rediscover itself, it must continually explore new forms. — c w

CORTÁZAR, JULIO. NIGHT FACE UP.

Argentina

End of the Game and Other Stories. New York: Random House, 1967. Translated by Paul Blackburn.

Author: See END OF THE GAME.

Story: NIGHT FACE UP combines many of Cortázar's techniques for confusing fantasy and reality. A young motorcyclist, enjoying the early morning as he rides his metal machine among red and green stoplights, does not see a pedestrian step out in front of him. After the collision, he awakens with what he considers to be minor injuries, but is taken off to the hospital, examined, and wheeled into an operating room. His last sight before losing consciousness is of a man in white standing over him with something gleaming in his right hand.

The young man awakes in a dream, an unusual dream with smells and fear. He is deep in swamps.

He is an Aztec, fleeing from his enemies, surrounded by the smell of bogs and war. He gropes through the dark, clutching his knife and amulet and hearing the drums of sacrifice.

"You're going to fall off the bed," warns the patient in the next bed, and the motorcyclist regains consciousness in his hospital room. For the rest of the night, he moves in and out of the dream, which becomes increasingly more vivid and threatening. He is attacked; he fights his enemies with his knife; he is captured, bound, and carried into a deep passageway in the rocks, where he can see only by the light of torches and bonfires and where he will meet his end. He smells death and sees his blood-soaked executioner standing over him with a stone knife.

Knowing intuitively that he will die in both stages of reality, the motorcyclist enters a dream wherein he rides "through the strange avenues of an astonishing city, with green and red lights that burn without fire or smoke, on an enormous insect that whirred away between his legs." In the instant when reality and dream converge, he sees himself picked off the ground, approached with a knife, and left lying dead, face up among bonfires.

Comparison: Time as a psychological phenomenon has been captured by Chuang Tzu. Referring to himself as Chuang Chou, he relates, "Once I, Chuang Chou, dreamed I was a butterfly and was happy as a butterfly. I was conscious that I was quite pleased with myself, but I did not know that I was Chou. Suddenly I awoke, and there I was, visibly Chou. I do not know whether it was Chou dreaming of being a butterfly or the butterfly dreaming it was Chou" (from Yu-Lan Fung, *History of Chinese Philosophy,* Princeton University Press, 1952). According to Chuang Tzu, time-frames provide different perspectives. His dream presents one frame of reference and his awakening offers another, both of which provide their own scope of reality. Cortázar's ending suggests that the so-called past has a broader range of reality than the present, for it impinges on our view of the present.

Cortázar's manipulation of time has been used effectively by the cinema. Time in *Star Wars* appears drawn out in confrontations with Darth Vader and sped up during Luke Skywalker's bombing run. With the use of flashback similar to Faulkner's *As I Lay Dying,* NIGHT FACE UP elongates terror, both within the slowly dying motorcyclist and through the pursuit, capture, and execution of the Moteca warrior. The final flash forward to the other dream, the "real" world of the fatal accident, further blurs both the concept of time and the distinction between fantasy and reality. As with Chuang Tzu's butterfly, the reader does not know whether events take place in the present and flash back to the Aztec ritual or in the past and flash forward to a man "riding on a bug past fires of red and green."

NIGHT FACE UP, like many of Cortázar's works, makes the point that the ordinary hides what too often is ignored. Wheeling the blood-stained motorcyclist down the hospital corridor appears to be an ordinary moment, just as does the carrying of the Aztec to his sacrifice. As in Shirley Jackson's "The Lottery," the ordinary exposes a kernel of what Conrad's Marlowe saw: "the likeness of one of those misty halos that sometimes are made visible by the spectral illumination of moonshine." — D V D

CUBENA. THE AFRICAN GRANNIE.

Panama
Afro-Hispanic Review. May 1983.

Author: Carlos Guillermo Wilson (1941–), known as Cubena, assumed his pen name in accord with an Ashanti custom of taking the name of the day on which one is born. A decidedly political writer, he has written poems, short stories, novels, and articles, many of which have been censored in his native Panama. His fictional works address the racism against the "chombo," a term considered insulting to black Anglo-Caribbean Panamanians. In stories that are intentionally shocking, he shows how extreme perversity and poverty result from substandard living conditions. Cubena's "chombos"

are thus portrayed as human beings crushed by the abnormality of their environment, whereas the non–West Indians are depicted as grotesque caricatures of depravity harassing the "chombos." He thus suggests that the sickness of racism leads the whites into deviant and contemptible behavior.

His poetry, on the other hand, presents the conventional theme of the quest for identity. His verse projects a positive perspective by firmly asserting his own selfhood and that of his people. Although the aims of his fiction and poetry would seem to be in accord, the two methods of reaching those aims and their comparative impacts differ. His prose revolves around the plight of the Afro-Hispanic, and no one is more disdained than the black Hispanic woman.

Story: "Ninety-three-year-old grannie kills prominent surgeon," shout the headlines, and all the city shouts for her head. No one had cried when grannie was handed over from one slave holder to another. No one wept when she had to give up her baby so that her concern for it would not lessen her affection for her owner's children. And now no one bothers to wonder how such an aged person could commit such a crime.

Grannie worries that she will not have enough money to pay her lawyer. A young, black, female lawyer, hearing about grannie's plight, consents to take the case. She has had almost no trial experience, since her law professor could see no reason why a woman should have such experience. To add to grannie's problems, both the judge and the prosecutor are related to the deceased.

During the trial, the defense lawyer has a dream. An erubinrin (female slave) gives birth to an omobinrin (daughter). She manages to hide the baby for awhile, but finally must pray to her three favorite goddesses and send the baby sailing alone down the river. The goddesses hear the mother's prayers, and the little sailor survives and grows up to be a traveler with wide experiences. Upon returning to Panama, she helps 333 slaves escape, sets fire to thirty-three plantations, and instigates three rebellions. When she encounters her grand-

mother, recently freed, the young woman says, "I speak like a Spaniard, pray like a Christian, sing like an Italian. Why don't you recognize me?"

Meanwhile, at the trial, the jury cries "Let there be justice!" and grannie receives three life terms of ninety-nine years each. No one knows the knowledge that the "criminal" takes to her grave: that her seemingly aristocratic mistress, the dead doctor's wife, was a foul-mouthed drunk and pothead who went to bed every Tuesday with the garbage man, that the doctor was an impotent homosexual, that the wife became pregnant and the doctor found out, and that the doctor's wife killed her own husband in an argument over the pregnancy. During the trial, the doctor's wife miscarries, and she and the baby die.

Comparison: Cubena's language, style, and even numerology suggest shifting patterns of perception. On one level, the reader witnesses the inhumane treatment of grannie. On another level, the reader perceives the reaction of a crowd manipulated by a system controlled by tiers of relatives. The dream sequence, a story within a story, offers still another dimension to illuminate the social dynamics of grannie's behavior. Although revealing the depravity of his grotesque white characters, Cubena leaves the reader wondering whether the novice lawyer might be grannie's granddaughter. Like Richard Wright's *Black Boy,* this story permits the reader to understand various modes of prejudice and to begin to uncover them within one's own surroundings. — D V D

CUMALI, NECATI. IN GOD'S PLAINS.

Turkey
Short Story International. June 1978. Translated by Falat S. Halman.

Author: Necati Cumali (1921–) was born in Florina, now part of Greece, and reared in a small town near Izmir. He received a law degree at the University of Ankara before becoming a leading Turkish poet, playwright, novelist, and essayist. A collection of short stories won him the Sait Falk Award in 1957. In 1969, he won the Poetry Prize of the Turkish Language Society.

Story: IN GOD'S PLAINS begins with a truck winding its way through fields. Hedges of myrtle, Judas trees, and shrubbery narrow the road, which is already crowded with overhanging greenery. It is late May. The meadow scent lies heavy on the air, and the joyful chirp of birds is the only noise that breaks the silence. The beauty of the setting has already been interrupted by violence. A hunter has killed a woodsman. In the truck are the court officials, who have come to examine the scene of the crime and to interrogate the witnesses, young woodcutters who had run into the murderer and the victim on the day of the murder.

Suddenly, the truck comes upon a weeping four-year-old boy. The driver and two young woodsmen approach the sobbing child, tan, chubby, barefoot, with a clean-shaven head and wearing nothing but a long shirt down to his knees. The driver asks the boy who he is, and the child, still convulsed with tears, answers, "Receb's." More questions are put to him, but he cannot answer. Finally, he is asked if he has been beaten, and he merely points to his bottom and begins to cry again. The driver realizes what has happened: "They have raped the poor boy." The court officials are stunned and flustered. They ask an old woman nearby to take the child to his parents. She refuses and says, "They'll come and get him."

The judge, the attorney, and the district attorney realize that a felony has been committed, but they can do nothing unless the boy's father files a formal complaint. The lawyer tells the boy to make sure to tell his father what happened and that he must file a report with the police. As they leave, the little boy, more frightened than before, begins to cry again.

Comparison: IN GOD'S PLAINS is a good example of eastern European writing in that it juxtaposes descriptions of nature with the violence of the human world. There is initially the violence of the murder, but even more significant is the unnatural act done to the child. The theme of child abuse has been dealt with in several recent films. The short story YANKO THE MUSICIAN, by Henryk Sienkiewicz, is similar in its brutal treatment of a child. The novel *Frankenstein,* by Mary Shelley, also uses this contrast, as the beauties of the forest are in direct opposition to the ugliness of the monster, his acts, his existence, and Victor's original act of creation. This work may also be compared to Aron Tamasi's short story FLASHES IN THE NIGHT and Mikhail Sholokhov's THE COLT because of its use of lyrical descriptions of nature as a background for the action. — D G

DANTICAT, EDWIDGE. CHILDREN OF THE SEA.

Haiti
Krik? Krak! New York: Soho Press, 1995.

Author: A promising young author, Edwidge Danticat (1969–) was born in Haiti. She joined her parents in the United States at age twelve and published her first article two years later. With degrees from Barnard College and the Brown University Writing Program, she has published in over twenty periodicals and won numerous awards, including the *Essence Magazine* Fiction Award, the James Michener Caribbean Writing Fellowship, and the American Translators Award. *Breath, Eyes, Memory,* her first novel, published in 1994, is an evocative story told through the eyes of a young woman who, like Danticat, lived with her aunt in Haiti until she was reunited with her parents. *Krik? Krak!,* a collection of short fiction by Danticat, was published in 1995. Danticat describes Haiti as "a rich landscape of memory" that forms the source of her stories, "stories that regularly creep into my head, just when I thought I had forgotten them. These stories come back to me in the reserved pitch of old women's voices, in the blink of their eyes, or in their very breath."

Story: CHILDREN OF THE SEA is purely and simply a love story. Yet the reality these two unnamed lovers face is anything but pure or simple in the setting of Haiti under the military regime that ousted Jean Bertrand Aristide.

A variation on an epistolary narrative, this story is told through alternating journal entries of the two young lovers: a woman in Haiti with her family, who are both terrified of and terrorized by the Tonton Macoutes, and a man aboard one of the crudely made boats bound for the United States. Although the young girl's father seems to disapprove of their alliance, it becomes clear that he fears the repercussions for his daughter as well as for the whole family from her involvement with a political activist—indeed, a subversive radical by the reckoning of those in power.

Youthful passion reigns in the journal entries. The two were apparently childhood sweethearts whose depth of feeling for one another has grown to full-fledged love, though it was evidently not sexually consummated (e.g., he writes, "Sometimes I felt like you wanted to, but I knew you wanted me to respect you. You thought I was testing you, but all I wanted was to be close to you"). In their journals, the two vow their love to one another. He writes, "Maybe the sea is endless, like my love for you." She writes, "i love you until my hair shivers at the thought of anything happening to you." These journals, kept for one another, are lifelines, so vividly expressed that it is difficult at times to realize that only the reader "hears" both voices.

Deceptively simple, the journal entries develop complex and interrelated plots of public and private lives. The young woman recounts incidents of bribery, the death by torture of people who refuse to reveal information, and her own family's persecution by the military regime. The young man's story depicts another world—a world consisting of himself and "36 other deserting souls on this little boat." He describes the physical discomfort, his reflections as he comes to terms with his own death ("I know it might happen"), his dreams, and, most of all, the "subplot" of pregnant Celianne. This fifteen-year-old girl, gang raped by the Tonton Macoutes and then disowned by her family because she is pregnant, and the story of the birth and death of her infant daughter become a symbol for the lost hope of the young lovers. When the young man must give up his notebook to lighten the cargo on the little boat, his life also seems in jeopardy. Does he live? It is not clear, though the young woman's last line, "i will write again soon," attests to the power of love.

Comparison: CHILDREN OF THE SEA suggests comparison with other works in which the personal fate of young lovers (or families), for whom the future should hold endless possibilities, is instead threatened by political conflicts. Danticat herself comments that the story was inspired by her connections with Haitian women who had spent uncertain and sad days on the boats between Haiti and the United States. "I have always been amazed that people can love one another on slave plantations and in death camps," she notes. Slave narratives from the United States and Holocaust literature, such as *The Diary of Anne Frank,* are thus potential comparisons, as is literature on the Middle Passage, such as "Middle Passage" by Robert Hayden. The young man suggests a reversal of the captured slave's journey when he writes, "I feel like we're sailing for Africa. Maybe we'll go to Dahomey and ask for our land back. (Laugh, will you?) They would probably throw us out, too."

On the level of symbol and images, the story suggests comparison with other fiction and poetry in which the ocean symbolizes life or, especially, rebirth. Danticat plays with the traditional notions of heaven when the young man writes, "The other night I dreamt that I died and went to heaven. This heaven was nothing like I expected. It was at the bottom of the sea."

Since this story combines the forms of letters and diaries, comparisons might be made with epistolary novels, such as *The Color Purple* by Alice Walker, and fiction in which journals are prominent, such as *Flowers for Algernon* by Daniel Keyes and *A Lesson Before Dying* by Ernest Gaines.
— R H S

Daudet, Alphonse. THE LAST LESSON.

France
Bedside Book of Famous French Stories. New York: Random House, 1945.
Translated by Marian McIntyre.

Author: Alphonse Daudet (1840–1897), a French novelist, poet, and short story writer, was born in Provence. Because his father's business failed when Alphonse was young, he was unable to complete his formal education. He read widely, though, and at age sixteen, he taught briefly at the College of Alais. He then joined his brother in Paris, where he began his writing career. When the Franco-Prussian War began in 1870, Daudet, due to extreme nearsightedness, was sent to the National Guard rather than to the battlefield with his regiment. Many of his works contain his moving depiction of the suffering he observed during this period. THE LAST LESSON was published in 1873.

One of the masters associated with the naturalist school, Daudet is often compared to Charles Dickens. He presented vivid portraits of life in Provence and of the various social classes in Paris.

Story: An Alsatian, Franz, recollects a childhood experience that took place near the end of the Franco-Prussian War (1870–71). He recalls a morning when he was late and unprepared for school. To his surprise, his tardiness was not punished, and the usually empty back benches were filled with villagers. His stern teacher, Monsieur Hamel, shocked his listeners by announcing the new Prussian interdiction against the teaching of French in the schools of Alsace and Lorraine. That day would be the last day French would be spoken in the classroom and his last day of teaching after forty years. Monsieur Hamel's reproaches to the children, the villagers, and even himself made them all regret their previously negligent attitude toward the value of studying their native tongue. The conscientious approach of both the students and villagers to that final lesson echoed the nationalistic pride of the teacher as he wrote on the board for the last time "Vive la France."

Comparison: In "The Pupil," Henry James explores a similar subject. As the title indicates, however, the focus is different. Daudet emphasizes the importance of the subject being taught and the students' apathy, while James concentrates on the close relationship between Pemberton, the exploited tutor, and Morgan, the gifted pupil. The denouement of both stories is emotionally moving, but the schoolmaster's final action in THE LAST LESSON softens the sense of loss, while the tragedy of Morgan's death in James's work is unrelieved.

The initiation theme of THE LAST LESSON, as represented by the maturing consciousness of Franz, receives modern treatment in Toni Cade Bambara's "The Lesson." Sylvia, a sassy young black girl living in the ghetto, treats education with derision until a concerned college-educated neighbor takes her and her friends on a trip to an expensive toy store. This experience changes Sylvia's perspective, moving her to contemplate at length the lessons presented that day. Bambara's economical style, her directness of presentation, is much like Daudet's in THE LAST LESSON.

The nationalistic pride felt by the villagers in THE LAST LESSON is also seen in Daudet's "The Siege of Berlin." In this story, a chauvinistic retired French officer suffers a heart attack when Prussian troops enter Paris.   — M A F

DESAI, ANITA. A DEVOTED SON.

India
World Writers Today. Glenview, IL: ScottForesman, 1995.

Author: Born of a Bengali father and a German mother in Mussorie, Anita Desai (1937–) knows German, Bengali, Hindi, and English, but prefers to write in English because of the richness, vitality, and suppleness of the language. Her first novel, *Cry the Peacock,* published in 1963, set a new trend in Indian literature by focusing on psychological rather than physical details. Recognized internationally by the time of the publication of her fifth novel, *Fire on the Mountain,* she won many awards in India and was considered for a prestigious British award in English literature. In her short stories as well as her novels, Desai explores the interior world of her characters as they struggle with common human dilemmas in the context of existential predicaments.

Story: Son of poor, illiterate parents, Ravesh gains a reputation as a devoted son when, after he wins academic honors and earns an M.D. degree in the United States, he returns to his small village in India and touches his father's feet in respect. He weds an illiterate girl in an arranged marriage and continues to live at home and serve his parents.

His devotion takes an ironic turn, however, when his father becomes ill. Ravesh sanitizes his father's diet to such a degree that the last remaining pleasure in the old man's life, eating, is taken from him. He suffers unspeakable misery as Ravesh tries to prolong his life by feeding him tonics and pills.

Comparison: What occurs between Ravesh and his father when the son gains control happens frequently as parents age. Yet there are added dimensions when traditional societies are confronted by Westernization. Such complicated intergenerational encounters are depicted in countless stories from around the world, such as GRANDMOTHER TAKES CHARGE by Lao She. The neglect and helplessness felt by Ravesh's father can also be compared with the plight of the old woman in THE GRANDMOTHER by K. Surangkhanang. — M L

DESAI, ANITA. GAMES AT TWILIGHT.

India
Games at Twilight and Other Stories. London: Heinemann, 1978.

Author: See A DEVOTED SON.

Story: After a hot day, the children are eager to play outside. In a game of hide-and-seek, Ravi, determined not to be found, heads for a secret place next to the garage. Sliding through a small gap between the door and walls, he hides in a locked shed stuffed with old household goods. When the person who is "It" comes charging close to him, he is scared at first, but the sheer delight at not having been discovered enables him to endure a long stay in the dark. When at last he gets tired of his confinement, he emerges with a victory cry. As he breaks through the crack, he falls on his knees and chokes with tears of rage and humiliation. His playmates have completely forgotten about him and are concentrating on new games. His mother scolds him for being a baby. He lies down in the grass, "silenced by a terrible sense of his insignificance."

Comparison: The central existential dilemma presented here corresponds with themes of isolation and alienation found in writers classified under the existential school, such as Camus, Sartre, and

Kafka. In Kafka's THE METAMORPHOSIS, for instance, protagonist Gregor Samsa, also "silenced by a terrible sense of his insignificance," finds himself changed into an insectlike creature. Despite his freedom from human pressures in his new state, he is shunned, denigrated, and all but forgotten, even by his own family. In dying, he leaves a light empty shell, which the maid sweeps away.

Ravi's loss of innocence and his initiation into real life, the realization that what occurs does not necessarily match one's own expectations and that one is fundamentally alone in life, parallels the "anguish and anger" expressed by the narrator in James Joyce's "Araby" when he too is disillusioned and disappointed that his experience of the bazaar does not match his dream. This sense of absolute aloneness is also realized by Juliet in Shakespeare's *Romeo and Juliet,* when she realizes that she has no one to trust and must take the sleeping potion alone. — M L

DHLOMO, H. I. E. THE DAUGHTER.

South Africa
H. I. E. Dhlomo: Collected Works. New York: Raven Press, 1985.

Author: Herbert Dhlomo (1903–1956) was born at Siyamu, near Pietermaritzburg, Natal, and died in Durban. He was the second son of parents from prominent families in Johannesburg. Like his older brother, Herbert qualified as a teacher and worked at the Amangimtoti Training Institute in Natal from 1922 to 1924. Later, he became head teacher at the American Board Mission School in Doornfontein.

His early ambition to write prompted him to prepare articles for the South African newspaper. Like many other blacks prominent during that time, he joined the African National Congress and, in 1935, published his first short story, "An Experiment in Colour," and left the teaching profession. He produced many articles and literary works, including short stories, poetry, and plays. He served as librarian at the Ndonyeni Library in the Bantu Social Centre in Durban and then became assistant editor of *Ilanga Lase* in Natal, where his older brother was editor. He held this position until just before his death.

Story: THE DAUGHTER is a romance, a story of love that entangles the lives of four people from the same family. Bursting with exotic imagery, classical allusions, and aphorisms, the story is told from an objective point of view in order to drive home a universal truth: "Absence makes the heart grow fonder"—often, however, fonder of someone else.

The main character is Zodwa Valo, who married Bob Frafa when she was only sixteen and he twenty, a marriage that lasted just fifteen months. After this short time, Bob decides to leave Durban for Johannesburg, the "big city" of excitement and glamour. After Bob leaves, Zodwa gives birth to a girl, Bob's daughter, Rose. When she grows up, Rose too decides to go to Johannesburg, leaving behind both her mother and her lover, Max. In the city, she meets Bob. Neither recognizes the other, of course, and after a number of meetings, they consummate their love.

The story concludes when Bob's work calls him back to Durban. Rose also returns, and the two lovers meet at Rose's mother's house. Just as they begin making introductions, Max enters the room. The reader is kept in suspense as the truth unfolds and the point of the story is revealed: "Absence makes the heart grow fonder."

Comparison: THE DAUGHTER mirrors the culture of the South African people. The story may be reminiscent of Sophocles's *Oedipus Rex,* a reversal disguised within a seemingly innocent but incestuous relationship. — M J J

DIB, MOHAMMED. NAEMA—WHEREABOUTS UNKNOWN.

Algeria

One World of Literature. Boston: Houghton Mifflin, 1993. Translated by Len Ortzen.

Author: Mohammed Dib (1920–) was born in Tlemcen, Algeria, a town near the Moroccan border. He was raised a Muslim, and after receiving his education in Algeria and Morocco, he tried a number of occupations before becoming a full-time writer. But even while working as a primary school teacher, a carpet weaver, a railway worker, and, finally, a journalist, he contributed fiction and articles to Algerian publications. In 1959, he moved from Algeria to France, where he continues to live and where his novels and short stories have been widely acclaimed. Two of his novels, *Omneros* (1978) and *Who Remembers the Sea* (1985), are available in English translations.

Always interested in using his fiction as social commentary, Dib was naturally drawn to the subject of the Algerian war for independence, but his treatment of that struggle often shows evidence of his earlier fascination with surrealist style. NAEMA—WHEREABOUTS UNKNOWN, published in Arabic in 1966, is a case in point, as the style of the diary entries is at times so vivid as to seem surreal.

Story: NAEMA—WHEREABOUTS UNKNOWN opens with the narrator's anguished thoughts about his wife, Naema, who has been taken to prison, or perhaps killed, by French soldiers, presumably as a result of her involvement in the armed struggle for Algerian independence. The reader learns later in the story that the narrator's thoughts are actually entries in a diary, and the first entry continues as he ponders his young son's attitude toward the war and the French. While his son feels that the rebels should "Kill the lot. Keep throwing bombs," the narrator wants only an end to the killing, a personal peace.

This diary entry is followed by one that recounts the narrator's escape from a bomb explosion and the ensuing police violence. Dashing into a cobbler's shop, he suggests that the proprietor lock his door to protect them from the police, who are

seeking the bomb thrower. When a loud pounding comes at the door, he tells the man not to open it, but the police break it down and kill the cobbler. The narrator escapes, returning the next day to find the shop padlocked. Upon inquiring at the neighboring shops, he can find out only that there will be no funeral. All the victims of both the bomb and the police have already been buried by the authorities.

This entry is followed by a page or so of musings on the situation in Algeria. The narrator has come to realize that "While we remain at the mercy of these butchers, bound hand and foot, the real war is taking place elsewhere. So we find our only defense against this daily terror is in disturbances and the breakdown of law and order. We have paid too dearly already, to hesitate or draw back. Something has got underway which is even worse than war."

Following these thoughts come three vignettes, each illustrating the narrator's changing attitude. First, he and the other diners at a popular café are held in silence at gunpoint for over an hour while the police check identity cards. After the incident, he thinks, "My throat was sore from the insults I had swallowed." Next, later that same day, he is ordered by the police to stop, but rather than obey, "looking straight at them, I made the decision to walk towards them. At every moment I expected them to open fire on me. I was quite cool and calm, and filled with disdain." In the final vignette, he describes "the most astounding procession ever seen in the town." Arab women without their veils and barefoot Arab children were "sweeping forward shrieking out the Liberation Anthem," carrying a makeshift rebel flag. "All at once, automatic weapons began to stutter," and the women and children were mowed down.

The final entry is brief. An agent of the rebel forces seeks him out because his earlier inquiries about the dead cobbler led the rebels to believe that he was the cobbler's friend. The cobbler's shop, the narrator is informed, had been used by the rebels, and they now need someone to replace the dead man and to reopen the shop. "I let him deliver his little speech. . . . 'Have you the keys,' I said. . . . He produced a ring with two keys from his trouser pocket. I took it. . . . I am closing this diary now. It was thinking of my wife, the shoemaker and the others which sustained me and helped me to carry on until now. They knew why they died, they did."

Comparison: Especially in light of Dib's earlier work, one can see NAEMA—WHEREABOUTS UNKNOWN as a work of social commentary demonstrating the need for commitment to a socially worthy cause. In that sense, one might compare this story to such socially conscious novels as John Steinbeck's *The Grapes of Wrath* or *In Dubious Battle* or John Dos Passos's massive trilogy *USA*. Dib's story might also indicate that involvement in armed struggle can provide meaning in life. The nar-

rator turns away from the self-involvement of the diary at the end of the story and begins a real involvement with the life of his time. One finds a contrasting view in Stephen Crane's "An Episode of War."

NAEMA—WHEREABOUTS UNKNOWN could also be considered a story of initiation. The narrator moves step by step from a relatively meaningless absorption in his own personal loss to a commitment to a changed life, one of meaningful struggle for a just cause. Just as the narrator of James Joyce's "Araby" must put his childish life of self-involvement behind him, so Dib's narrator must go beyond his great personal loss if he is to find something worth living and dying for. The fact that he achieves his initiation through surmounting situations of grave physical danger suggests a comparison to Doris Lessing's "Through the Tunnel," where Jerry must swim to manhood through a dangerous underwater tunnel.   — P T M

DINESEN, ISAK. THE SAILOR BOY'S TALE.

Denmark
A World of Great Stories. New York: Crown, 1947.

Author: Isak Dinesen was the pen name of Baroness Karen Blixen of Rungstedlund (1885–1962). Born into an old Danish family, she married a cousin, Baron Blixen, in 1914 and spent the next seventeen years of her life in Kenya Colony of British East Africa. For much of that time, she managed a coffee plantation almost single-handedly. Her book *Out of Africa* is an account of those years.

Returning to Denmark in 1931, Dinesen produced two volumes of long short stories in English, *Seven Gothic Tales* and *Winter's Tales.* With their masterful blend of fantasy and reality, these stories established her fame, especially in the United States. Dinesen died in her ancestral home near Elsinore.

Story: The combination of fantasy and reality that characterizes Dinesen's stories is nowhere

more apparent than in THE SAILOR BOY'S TALE. Young Simon rescues a peregrine falcon entangled high in the rigging of his sailing ship. He attempts the dangerous rescue only after much thought: "Through his own experience of life he had come to the conviction that in this world everyone must look after himself, and expect no help from others. But the mute, deadly fight kept him fascinated for more than an hour. . . . He remembered how, many years ago, in his own country and near his home, he had once seen a peregrine falcon quite close, sitting on a stone and flying straight up from it. Perhaps this was the same bird. He thought: That bird is like me. Then she was there, and now she is here." As he reaches the trapped falcon, who looks at him "with a pair of angry, desperate yellow eyes," a bond is formed. Despite the danger of his mission, he feels a sense of unity, "as if the sea and sky, the ship, the bird and himself were all one." Simon climbs down, with the falcon secured inside his jacket, only to endure the laughter of shipmates for risking his life so foolishly. As he releases the bird, though, he thinks proudly, "There flies my falcon."

Years later, the same yellow eyes of a falcon stare out at Simon from the face of an old woman who rescues him from his own entanglement with a band of Russians. Simon has changed greatly from the boy who first saved the falcon. He has killed a man and kissed a girl. More importantly, he has forgotten the unity of all living things that he had once known. But the old woman saves him in every respect, for she restores this harmony and sends Simon on his way again with a blessing. A sense of universal retribution pervades this coming-of-age story that, like all fairy tales, is enjoyable on more than one level.

Comparison: THE SAILOR BOY'S TALE and Coleridge's "The Rime of the Ancient Mariner" underscore reverence for all life, a lesson the mariner and Simon must both learn. Dinesen's suggestion of the mythological element pairs interestingly with Coleridge's emphasis on the religious aspect. Doris Lessing's "A Sunrise on the Veld" and George Orwell's "Shooting an Elephant" are additional choices for comparative reading.   — P G L

DINESEN, ISAK. SORROW-ACRE.

Denmark
Winter's Tales. New York: Random House, 1942.

Author: See THE SAILOR BOY'S TALE.

Story: This strangely compelling tale is a story within a story. On one hand, "Sorrow-Acre" refers literally to the field of rye a widow contracts to mow with a scythe between sunup and sundown on a single day. This extraordinary feat—should she accomplish it—will save her son's life. Should she fail, her son must suffer the punishment for arson, a crime he claims not to have committed. Against this long day of agonizing toil for the widow, Dinesen balances a philosophical struggle between the old lord with whom the widow has struck her bargain and his young nephew and possible heir.

Both contests—one a physical marathon, the other an ideological debate—revolve around the line of a plaintive French tune. Translated, the line suggests that to die for a person one loves is an effort too sweet for words. Such a degree of commitment is on a level of consciousness far higher than Adam, the lord's nephew, can imagine. Yet the cleared field at the end of the day symbolizes more than the greatness of the mother's love. It represents as well the cleared thought, the resolutions Adam has made about the heritage of his homeland and his acceptance of that heritage.

Comparison: In SORROW-ACRE, students should note that the landscape exists more as a principal character than as mere setting. Much in the manner of a Conrad story, the landscape functions as a primal mirror in which the questions of life must be endlessly reflected. Nadine Gordimer's "The Train from Rhodesia" offers a thought-provoking juxtaposition with SORROW-ACRE. The young woman on the train questions the whole nature of human relationships, the valuing of human worth and dignity, against the landscape—and the heritage—of South Africa. Similarly, Sholokhov's THE COLT and Tamasi's FLASHES IN THE NIGHT offer stories set against a lyrically described natural background.   — P G L

DIOP, BIRAGO. THE WAGES OF GOOD.

Senegal
African Writing Today. Harmondsworth, England: Penguin, 1967.
Translated by Robert Baldick.

Author: Born in Dakar, Senegal, Birago Diop (1906–1989) is best known for short stories inspired by the folktales of West Africa. He left Senegal to study in France and received a doctorate in veterinary science from L'École Nationale Vétérinaire de Toulouse in 1933. He served as a veterinary officer in Senegal and in French Sudan and as a nurse in a military hospital in St.-Louis, Senegal. He was employed at L'Institut de Médecine Vétérinaire Exotique in Paris and as head of zoological technical services in Upper Volta. He has also been administrator for a broadcasting company, ambassador from Senegal to Tunisia, vice president of La Confédération Internationale de la Société d'Auteurs et Compositeurs, and an official in the French National Defense Institute. He has won many awards, among them the Grand Prix Littéraire de l'Afrique-Occidentale Française and the Grand Prix Littéraire de l'Afrique Noire from the Association des Écrivains d'Espression Française de la Mer et de l'Outre Mer. He has published several short story collections and a volume of poems. He has also adapted several of his stories for the stage.

Story: THE WAGES OF GOOD is a short, simple folktale with a clear message. Like many traditional folktales, the forces of evil are outsmarted, and the forces of good win in the end. And like many such tales, most of the main characters are animals. In this case, the only human is a child who interacts and speaks with the animals as though all were intellectual and social equals. As a matter of fact, the animals, because of their greater experience, are wiser than the child and serve as both adversary and rescuer.

Diassigue-the-Alligator becomes stranded when the stream in which he lives is drained. He is helped by Goné-the-Child, who rolls the alligator into a mat and carries him to the river. Once he is safe, Diassigue turns his attention to his stomach. He tricks Goné into wading into the water up to his neck and then threatens to eat the child. Yet Goné is able to make a deal with the alligator. They will ask the first three people they see whether "a good deed is repaid with a kindness or with a bad turn." They ask Nagy-the-Cow, who remembers how well she was treated when she was young, how she gave great quantities of milk and mothered many calves, and points out that now that she is old, she must look for her own food. Her good deed, she says, was repaid with a bad turn. Much the same story is told by Fass-the-Horse, who was well treated when he was a young war horse, but now he is hobbled and left to care for himself. He too claims that a good deed is repaid with a bad turn.

The third to approach Diassigue and Goné is Leuk-the-Hare. Instead of simply answering the question, Leuk investigates the source, and he immediately understands the cruel trick the alligator is playing on the child who just saved his life. Leuk, pretending not to believe the story of Goné's rescuing the alligator, has the two reenact the scene: they come out of the water, Diassigue allows himself to be rolled into the rug and tied, and Goné places the bundle on his head. Leuk then advises the child to carry the now helpless alligator home for his own supper, for "that is how to repay those who forget a good deed."

Comparison: This story, told in the tradition of the fable, may be compared with Aesop's fables or with stories derived from or modeled after his fables, such as Fontaine's classic *Fables*. Kafka's parables offer an interesting variation of the fable.
— B H N

DJILAS, MILOVAN. THE OLD MAN AND THE SONG.

Montenegro
The Stone and the Violets. New York: Harcourt Brace Jovanovich, 1971.
Translated by Lovett F. Edwards.

Author: Born in Montenegro, then a Turkish province, Milovan Djilas (1911–1995) distinguished himself throughout his life by his uncompromising love of freedom—even when his principles led to his sacrificing his own personal freedom. Djilas attended Belgrade University, where he won recognition in several areas: for his poetry, short stories, and revolutionary activities. In 1932, he joined the illegal Communist Party and was arrested and imprisoned for three years by the Austro-Hungarian government.

During World War II, Djilas became a partisan leader, fighting against the Italian and German occupation forces. With the end of the war, he rose to high office in the Communist Party and the Yugoslav government. His journalistic criticism of the Communist regime, however, culminating in his comments on the Hungarian uprising, caused him to be expelled from the Communist Central Committee and sentenced to a three-year prison term. Refusing to be silenced, he published *The New Class,* was accused of slandering his country, and had his sentence extended. After his conditional release, he published *Conversations with Stalin* and was rearrested and returned to prison. THE OLD MAN AND THE SONG was written in prison at Sremska Mitrovica in March 1966 and published that same year.

Several themes in Djilas's works reflect his philosophy and experiences: the cosmic struggle between good and evil, the need for the individual to fight evil, and the need for the individual to survive and to preserve freedom in the world.

Story: Set during World War I, at a time when the Turks still occupied much of Montenegro, this story deals with two mountain tribes that in the past had often fought their own small wars over the boundaries of mountain pastures.

Vuk, a young man of the Rovci tribe, has left his mountain home for the first time, with a letter that he hopes will gain him a position in the Montenegran prince's bodyguard. En route, because of danger from the Turks, he finds he must stay overnight at the home of his friend Šćepan, a member of the Piperi tribe. Struck with how much more prosperous Šćepan's family is than his, as well as with their courtesy and hospitality to him and the respect and care they show toward a very old man living with them, Vuk accepts their invitation to play the gusle and sing a song. He decides to sing a folk song about Savić Spasojev, a great Piperi hero. When he finishes, the family and some friends look at one another strangely. After Šćepan's father has thanked Vuk, the others also thank him, and then Šćepan asks if he would like to meet Savić. To Vuk's amazement, the hero of the folk song is the old man whom he had noticed earlier and who is lying on a felt pallet near the fire. The old man, who is ill-humored, listens to the others recite more of his deeds, then asks, "Why are you repeating all that tonight? Let me rest! Then it was easy to be a hero."

Accustomed to the old man's ill humor, the Piperi leave, still praising Vuk and his song. When Šćepan asks Vuk if he is glad to have seen Savić, the disillusioned Vuk, tears in his eyes, responds negatively, saying it would be better if he had never started his journey.

Comparison: Primarily a story dealing with the shattering of a young man's illusions, this story may be compared with Hemingway's "The Killers" or Joyce's "Araby." Its unusual setting amid the mountain tribes of former Yugoslavia permits comparison with other stories of peasants and peasant life, especially with Andric's THE SCYTHE and the peasant parents of Djilas's own WAR. Both of these stories are also set in former Yugoslavia. Savić, as a leader of the Piperi, may be compared with the title character in Steinbeck's "The Leader of the People."
— H M M

DJILAS, MILOVAN. WAR.

Montenegro
Russian and Eastern European Literature. Glenview, IL: ScottForesman, 1970.
Translated by Giovanni Segreto.

Author: See THE OLD MAN AND THE SONG.

Story: In this tragic story, two simple peasants are counterposed against a modern army and its discipline. Djilas carefully avoids naming characters or places, merely setting the story on the banks of a river where fighting has been going on for three months. All means of crossing the river have been destroyed except for a motorized scow run by the army. During the night, when there is no danger of bombing, this scow is used for military purposes. During the day, it ferries the inhabitants, largely peasants, across the water.

As the story opens, two old peasants, a man and a woman, board the scow with a wagon carrying a coffin. They explain that they are returning home with the body of their son, who was killed at the front. Earlier they had lost two sons in the war; in the coffin is their last one. When they reach shore, while papers are being checked, another peasant asks to see the commanding officer, whom he tells that he has heard sounds coming from the coffin. When the coffin is opened, it contains the son, alive and dressed in peasant clothing. The peasant who reported his suspicions is horrified, saying he thought the coffin contained a spy. At the order of the commanding officer, the son is shot through the heart, and the two parents, now mourning in reality, are told to return home with the body.

In the concluding lines of the story, Djilas has something bitter to say about the value of human life: "The lieutenant said:'Strange people, these peasants. Look at them. They're mourning and crying just like they did before.' However, no one heard him. They were all busy with the trucks on the bank of the big river."

Comparison: In its depiction of the character of the Slav peasant, this story may be compared with Solzhenitsyn's MATRYONA'S HOME, Andric's THE SCYTHE, and Sholokhov's THE COLT. As a story dealing with humanity's inhumanity, it may be compared with Solzhenitsyn's THE RIGHT HAND, Sholokhov's THE COLT, and Sienkiewicz's YANKO THE MUSICIAN. The story also lends itself to the broad subgenre of antiwar fiction. In this area, it may be compared with Sholokhov's THE COLT and THE FATE OF A MAN, with Hemingway's "Old Man at the Bridge," and with other antiwar stories written in Europe and America after World War II. — H M M

DOSTOEVSKI, FYODOR. THE DREAM OF A RIDICULOUS MAN.

Russia
Notes from Underground, "White Nights," "The Dream of a Ridiculous Man," and Selections from "The House of the Dead." New York: New American Library, 1961. Translated by Andrew R. MacAndrew.

Author: Fyodor Mikhailovich Dostoevski (1821–1881) was born in Moscow, the second son of a merchant's daughter and a staff doctor at Mariinskaya Hospital for the poor. He attended a Moscow boarding school and, after his mother died, the School of Military Engineers in St. Petersburg, from which he resigned his commission after four years.

Dismayed, indeed revolted, by the grim realities of Russian life, particularly the mistreatment of the common people by government workers and officials, Dostoevski became an active member of a socialist group and, while working on his third novel, *Netochka Nezvanova,* was arrested, tried, and condemned to death for political activities. His death sentence was commuted, however, and he spent four years in a penal colony. This served to reinforce his desire to use his writing to change the society in which he lived. Repeatedly, his works, written under conditions of poverty and personal and emotional trauma, call for freeing the serfs, abolishing censorship, and relaxing the laws governing free discussion of political events.

After receiving full amnesty in 1859 and returning to St. Petersburg with his wife, Dostoevski's philosophy as revealed in his work acquired a more mature attitude, stressing the hope of gaining salvation through degradation and suffering. In his later years, during which he was plagued by epilepsy and financial ruin, he produced his best-known works, which demonstrate a mastery of the psychological novel through insight into abnormal states of mind. These include *Crime and Punishment* (1866), *The Idiot* (1869), *The Possessed* (1872), and *The Brothers Karamazov* (1880). The last novel was published just one year before his death.

Story: The story opens with the narrator's avowal "I'm a ridiculous man," which sets the tone for his attitude toward life and his dream. The dream, a story within a story, is provoked by an incident on a cold, gloomy day, a typical Dostoevski setting, in which a ragged, shivering, terrified little girl, apparently separated from her mother, desperately appeals to the narrator for help. He ignores her and continues on his way to his apartment. Feeling intensely sorry for the child, "so sorry that it hurt," and guilty about not having acted, he resolves to kill himself, partly for guilt and partly for despair ("nothing had happened while I'd been alive").

Before he can lift the gun to his head and fulfill his intent, however, he slips into sleep, "still juggling with the eternal questions," and dreams of shooting himself in the heart. The dream progresses through his burial, after which his consciousness awaits its demise while he begs, "Whoever You are—if You do exist—if there is anything more sensible than what's happening here, make it happen." Suddenly, the grave opens, and he is seized by a "mysterious creature" bearing "a human resemblance."

The creature is part of a duplicate universe in which the inhabitants are truly happy, innocent, and serene, for "this earth had not been desecrated by the Fall of Man; its inhabitants still lived in a paradise such as that of Adam and Eve before they sinned." He moves among them noting the lack of disease and war, the serenity of old age and death, and the absolute belief in eternal life. Then, "the truth is that—well, that I ended up corrupting them all."

Once corrupted, the people have to seek ways to find happiness, to unite society, to live in harmony, to develop systems for universal love. Wars are fought, crimes are undertaken, suicide is committed, and religions are formed that worship "nonbeing and self-annihilation for the sake of an eternal repose in nothingness." When the people grow tired and begin to praise suffering, the narrator comes to love them and their corrupted earth more than he has ever loved before. As the agent of their corruption, he asks for martyrdom at their hands, but they laugh at him as "a feeble-minded fool" and exonerate him instead. Filled with sorrow, he awakens.

As a result of his dream, he preaches to everyone a doctrine of love, unity, and happiness. He reveals his dream and himself as the corrupter, and, just as in his dream, people laugh at him. Still, he continues to preach the golden rule and the belief that if everyone acknowledged that "awareness of life is of a higher order than knowledge of the laws of happiness," then "everything could be arranged immediately."

Comparison: Although the opening lines are reminiscent of those in Edgar Allan Poe's "The Tell-Tale Heart" and "The Black Cat," this story does not follow the opening with the adamant disavowal one finds in Poe's stories. Rather, there is casual, even benign, acceptance of one's absurdity.

Embedded in the story are shades of Camus's existentialism as defined in *The Stranger,* especially when Dostoevski's protagonist avers, "I began to feel with my whole being that nothing had happened while I'd been alive." This echoes the deliberate isolation of Raskolnikov in Dostoevski's own *Crime and Punishment,* an isolation born from egoism and based on pure rationalism—rationalism devoid of feeling. Isolation marks the life of the ridiculous man, a circumstance that sets up a tale in which one learns that there is a reality external to one's own thought. There is an actual world in which love and compassion and giving can solve the problem of human suffering. While this is also an unattainable reality, it gives us purpose. Without it, we have nothing for which to strive, nothing to justify our being. In this sense, the central character is representative of humankind.

Presenting this view is also the role of the title characters in *The Brothers Karamazov,* as it is of Gregor Samsa in Kafka's THE METAMORPHOSIS. Gregor too is isolated from the rest of humanity, just as he is isolated from his feelings about the world and the manner in which he lives. In THE DREAM OF A RIDICULOUS MAN, the dream is just that—a sleeping event. In THE METAMORPHOSIS, it is a nightmare in wakefulness. In both, however, it is

indicative of the state of humanity from Dostoevski's perspective, and, in both, the rest of humanity remains oblivious to the truth of the situation. Such nonrecognition of the truth is also seen in Mark Twain's "The War Prayer," the result of which is a continuation of anguish.

Once the dream has been experienced, the dreamer moves outside himself and begins preaching universal love, the betterment of all humanity, in the manner of Joe in Dalton Trumbo's *Johnny Got His Gun* and the narrator in Upton Sinclair's *The Jungle.* The preaching consists of truths that, if recognized and accepted, could allow humanity to take a small step toward establishing the dream of an earthly paradise, the same sort of paradise depicted by James Hilton in *Lost Horizon.* — J A G

DOSTOEVSKI, FYODOR. THE HONEST THIEF.

Russia
The Best Short Stories of Dostoevski. New York: Modern Library, n.d.
Translated by David Margarshack.

Author: See THE DREAM OF A RIDICULOUS MAN.

Story: As he leaves for work one morning, the narrator is informed that an elderly gentleman is about to become a lodger in the same household. Despite his usual solitude and "boredom of existence," the narrator finds this old soldier, Astafy Ivanovich, quite pleasant, particularly due to his storytelling abilities. When the narrator's coat is stolen, Astafy begins a tale about a thief he had the dubious pleasure of knowing two years earlier.

One evening at a pub, Astafy met a vagabond drunkard for whom he felt overwhelming pity, so Astafy allowed the man to stay the night in his own lodgings. One night turned into two, two into three, and so on, until the drunkard, Yemelyan Ilyich, became a permanent figure in Astafy's life. Yemelyan was quiet and gentle but could not be trusted to spend a single ruble on anything but drink. Although Astafy was "dreadfully sorry for the poor fellow" and could not throw him out into the

street, Astafy himself was quite poor and wanted to rid himself of this obviously dependent creature.

One day, Astafy moved to a single room in an old lady's flat and bade a grateful farewell to Yemelyan, declaring, "You'll never find me now!" Upon arriving at his new room, however, he found Yemelyan waiting for him. Yemelyan again became an integral part of Astafy's life, but this time, instead of running from his guest, Astafy decided "there and then to be his only provider and benefactor."

Astafy tried to teach Yemelyan a trade; none could be found at which he was adept. Astafy tried to make Yemelyan look reputable; his coat remained torn and tattered. Astafy tried to make Yemelyan give up drinking; he "just heaved a sigh" and his "blue lips started quivering all of a sudden and a tear rolled down his pale cheek and trembled on his stubby chin." One day, Astafy casually mentioned a pair of blue checkered riding breeches he hoped to sell for fifteen rubles. That evening, he found Yemelyan extremely drunk and the breeches missing. Both Yemelyan and his landlady denied taking them, and later the sober Yemelyan helped look for them. Astafy finally apologized: "I am sorry if, fool that I am, I've accused you unjustly." Despite his words, however, Astafy developed an intense dislike for Yemelyan. He felt betrayed, but still he pitied the man, whose drinking continued to become worse and for whom sulking had become a habit.

Knowing he wasn't trusted, Yemelyan left. "He wasn't to be found anywhere: gone, vanished!" Astafy was worried until, after five days, Yemelyan returned, obviously driven home by hunger. Feeling more pity than ever before, Astafy offered him a drink, which, to his dismay, Yemelyan refused, declaring that he was ill. Astafy put him to bed and cared for him. As he lay dying, Yemelyan had one last piece of business to take care of: he confessed to the theft of Astafy's breeches—and died.

Comparison: THE HONEST THIEF has a typical Dostoevski character in Yemelyan, who cannot resist temptation under any circumstances. This is his tragedy, as it is the tragedy of Raskolnikov in *Crime and Punishment.* The idea of repentance at the moment of death for fear of retribution is also common in Dostoevski and evident in the character of Svidrigalov in *Crime and Punishment* and in early editions of WHITE NIGHTS: "I am told that the proximity of punishment arouses real repentance in the criminal and sometimes awakens a feeling of genuine remorse in the most hardened heart; I am told this is due to fear."

There is also in THE HONEST THIEF a love of humanity's poor and wretched, which is also evident in the writing of Charles Dickens, one of Dostoevski's favorite authors. And, like Gregor Samsa in Franz Kafka's THE METAMORPHOSIS, Yemelyan seems to have some special knowledge of life's meaning, a meaning of which only the wretched seem conscious. This insight is also evident in the title character in Herman Melville's "Bartleby the Scrivener." Dostoevski's Yemelyan also parallels Melville's Bartleby in the sudden way each arrives on the scene and their tenacious presence. Finally, Astafy parallels Bartleby's employer in their mutual compassion, pity, and desire to understand.   — J A G

DOSTOEVSKI, FYODOR. WHITE NIGHTS.

Russia
Notes from Underground, "White Nights," "The Dream of a Ridiculous Man," and Selections from "The House of the Dead." New York: New American Library, 1961.
Translated by Andrew R. MacAndrew.

Author: See THE DREAM OF A RIDICULOUS MAN.

Story: A young man, the story's narrator, bemoans the state of alienation and isolation in which he finds himself as the people of St. Petersburg vacate the city for the summer. Not realizing that his isolation is self-imposed, he feels a personal sense of betrayal: "Why, they were deserting me for their summer places." During one of his evening walks, he comes upon a young girl, Nastenka, crying as she stands by an embankment. Like him, she is lonely, but hers is a lovelorn loneliness imposed by separation from her love, the young lodger in the attic room of her grandmother's house. Her lover has gone to Moscow for a year to attend to business.

She has agreed to wait, for he promises, "When I come back, if you still love me, I swear we'll be happy." During their nightly meetings to escape their loneliness, Nastenka shares all this with the narrator, along with her hopes, dreams, and desires. He too shares his past and his feelings with her, and, despite her request to the contrary, he falls in love with her.

The narrator reveals this love when Nastenka's young man returns to St. Petersburg and fails to contact her, despite her having sent a letter the narrator unselfishly helped her write. In her moment of despair, she returns the narrator's vow: "I do love him but I'll get over it. . . . I'm already getting over it. . . . I love you. . . . Yes—I love you—I love you the way you love me." He agrees to move into the room vacated by the lodger, and they excitedly make plans for the future.

Suddenly, the lodger appears. Nastenka runs to him, then back to the narrator, then back to the lodger, and, "Still without uttering a word . . . caught his hand, and hurried away with him."

A new morning dawns, appropriately raining and dreary, and the young narrator receives a letter from Nastenka in which she begs forgiveness for hurting him. His reaction is one of great understanding, compassion, and insight: "So may the sky lie cloudless over you, and your smile be bright and carefree; be blessed for the moment of bliss and happiness you gave to another heart, a lonely and a grateful one." More importantly, however, he ends with an affirmation of love and self-sacrifice: "My God, a moment of bliss. Why, isn't that enough for a whole lifetime?"

Comparison: The theme of this story, subtitled "A Sentimental Novel from the Memoirs of a Dreamer," recounts the poignancy and delicate charm of a quixotic state of existence. It is most often sympathetic to the dreamer who would trade all worldly fantasies for a single, fleeting moment of true happiness. The youthful exuberance with which the story opens and sustains itself—"It was a marvelous night, the sort of night one only experiences when one is young"—is most immediately reminiscent of Joseph Conrad's "Youth," in which all that occurs, the most dangerous and life-threatening situations, is adventuresome and exciting. One also hears echoes of Conrad's impressionism in Dostoevski's

depiction of a hazy, dreamlike St. Petersburg, as if it were a fairy tale setting.

The same youthful enthusiasm depicted by Conrad gives rise to passions rooted in unthinking haste and unrestrained outpourings of emotion in WHITE NIGHTS:

> he deceives himself and winds up by believing that he is moved by true, live passion, that there is substance—flesh and blood—to his fancies! And it is quite a deception!! Just look at him and see for yourself. Can you believe looking at him, Nastenka, that he doesn't even know the woman he loved so passionately in his sultry flights of fancy.

This is not unlike the passion portrayed by the nineteenth-century American short story writer Fitz-James O'Brien in "The Diamond Lens," the tale of a young man who goes to emotional and criminal extremes for the love of a girl seen in an idyllic world encased in a drop of water viewed through a powerful microscope lens.

The tone can be likened to that of Edith Wharton's *Ethan Frome,* although without the ultimate despair. Dostoevski's narrator says, "I am reduced to celebrating anniversaries because I no longer have anything with which to replace even these silly, flimsy dreams. For dreams, Nastenka, have to be renewed too." Life offers at the very least celebration of the imagination, of the internal workings of the artist painting and controlling his own existence. Like Ethan Frome's dreams, the narrator's sad dreams also change and fade, leaving only memories.   — J A G

DOVE-DANQUAH, MABEL. THE TORN VEIL.

Ghana
A Selection of African Prose. Oxford: Clarendon Press, 1964.

Author: In 1952, Mabel Dove-Danquah was the first woman elected to the Gold Coast Legislative Assembly. She was educated in Ghana and in England and has been a practicing journalist and editor of the *Accra Evening News.*

Story: THE TORN VEIL is a ghost story in the tradition of Washington Irving. In this case, the innocent victim of the evildoer comes back from the grave to seek, and find, a fitting revenge.

Ten years ago, Kwame Asante married Akosua under the Native Customary law, a civil law that "needs disinfecting, for though it aids the man to gain his desire when it is at its fiercest, it does in no way safeguard the position of the woman when the man's passion abates." Over those past ten years, Kwame has become an important man in the community and is considering entering the town council. A "cloth woman" might have been adequate ten years ago, but now, he convinces himself, he deserves better. He has decided to marry a "frock lady" in a Christian church ceremony.

Kwame confronts Akosua in a bitter scene in which he self-righteously offers her one hundred pounds to go away. "You are only entitled to twenty-five pounds," he reminds her, "and here I am out of kindness offering you a hundred. Show some gratitude, Akosua." She spurns his money and threatens to leave. He cannot allow that. A potential town councilman must keep up appearances. He threatens her: "If you leave this house without my knowledge and permission, I shall claim every penny I have spent on you since I married and lived with you these ten years; and not only that but I shall claim all the presents I have given to your parents and other relatives." In spite of these threats, the next day Akosua leaves with the children. Far from being distressed, Kwame sends his father-in-law a bill for three hundred and fifty pounds and begins scheming how he will marry his "frock lady" and win Akosua back too: "I can then have one wife in Akwapim and another in Accra—after all, monogamy is all humbug."

At this point, the narrator inserts an analysis of Kwame's character: "[He] had foundered in his sense of values; the western impact on his mentality had sent it all askew. He would have been very much surprised if an outspoken friend had told him that he was neither a Christian nor a gentleman, and that Akosua had far finer instincts and culture than he; but fortunately for him his friends could not see farther than himself—so he was happy in his good opinion of himself."

The marriage to the "frock lady" takes place, and Kwame turns Akosua's "desertion" to his own advantage. No one blames a man for marrying again when his first wife has run away. After the wedding guests depart, Kwame steps onto the veranda for a bit of air. Upon returning, he sees a figure in bridal finery resting on the settee: "She lifted her head. Asante blinked rapidly. He rubbed his eyes. Was he drunk or dreaming? Akosua was looking at him shyly. He remembered that look; it had charmed him again and again. . . . Had he really left this cameo in ebony for that other common-place girl? 'I must have been mad.' He stretched out his arms. 'Akosua, forgive me.' She smiled and beckoned to him." In an almost comic scene, Kwame chases Akosua about the room until he trips and falls, hitting his head.

The next morning he is found dead, "a flimsy bit of a torn bridal veil tightly clenched in one fist. Joy was in his countenance." Nearby lies a stack of unread congratulatory messages. Among them is a telegram that reads, "To Kwame Asante, Adabraska. Your wife Akosua died 10 a.m. today."

Comparison: Supernatural forces are often shown interceding in human affairs, not uncommonly by aiding those seeking revenge against great wrongs. Such literature ranges from the comical "The Legend of Sleepy Hollow" to the more serious *Don Giovanni* and Dante's *The Divine Comedy.* This use of divine intervention to aid in the attainment of revenge can be compared with supernatural intervention in other stories for other purposes, as, for example, in "Young Goodman Brown" by Nathaniel Hawthorne and "Markheim" by Robert Louis Stevenson. Those stories of "salvation" can be further compared to stories in which divine intervention appears in the form of "temptation," as in Stephen Vincent Benét's "The Devil and Daniel Webster" and Christopher Marlowe's *Dr. Faustus.*

THE TORN VEIL is also an attack upon a particular social tradition. In this regard, it can be compared to more subtle handling of the same kind of message, such as in "The Lottery" by Shirley Jackson and "Battle Royal" by Ralph Ellison.   — B H N

EKWENSI, CYPRIAN. THE GREAT BEYOND.

Nigeria
Restless City and Christmas Gold. London: Heinemann, 1975.

Author: Cyprian Ekwensi (1921–) was born in northern Nigeria and educated at the School of Forestry in Ibadan, after which he studied pharmacy at London University. He has taught biology, chemistry, and English and has worked as a pharmacist with the Nigerian Medical Corporation. He has also worked for the Nigerian Broadcasting Corporation as head of features and as director of information in the Federal Ministry of Information in Lagos. He resigned his position at the outbreak of war to do the same work in the East. He then returned to his profession as a pharmacist. His stories and novels are set in West Africa between pre-independence in the fifties and modern times. His work includes the novels *Burning Grass, People of the City, Beautiful Feathers,* and *Jagua Nana* and two story collections, *Lokotown* and *Restless City and Christmas Gold.*

Story: THE GREAT BEYOND is a story of the supernatural—the story of Ikolo's sudden return from the dead in the middle of his own funeral procession. The note of lightness struck in the first sentence never falters: "He has always said that on the day of his death he would come back—if only to have his last laugh." When Ikolo begins banging with all his might against his coffin lid, the pastor and the son of the undertaker pry it open. Ikolo, looking "much too young," sits up, sneezes, and asks for Jokeh, his wife. "He looked at her for perhaps half-an-hour, during which time he said not a word." At the end of that time, Ikolo tumbles back into his coffin, the procession continues to the cemetery, and Ikolo is buried.

Two weeks later, Jokeh approaches a stranger and demands the money he was to have paid her husband. No one knew of the debt except Ikolo and the stranger himself. Jokeh takes the money to the pastor, who is surprised by the donation. "'I do not understand this,' the pastor says. 'I mean no harm to your husband's memory . . . but was he all that religious?'" Jokeh does not understand either.

All she knows is that "when my husband looked at me like that, something seemed to happen to me. I was looking at things, pictures before my eyes . . . just like in a cinema. He did not talk to me, but every wish of his I saw before me." The only explanation she can offer is that Ikolo described "a long journey beyond death" leading to "a hall with white clouds" in the midst of which was "some Great Power" that "sent him back to make amends for all he had done wrong." Failure to donate to the church was evidently one of the things he did wrong.

As she speaks, Jokeh, like Ikolo, seems to grow younger, "even younger than Ikolo." She has had a great experience, one all humankind would like to share. She "contacted someone who had been there . . . to the Great Beyond, and who came back to tell." She leaves to prepare for her own anxiously awaited departure to the "Great Beyond."

Comparison: THE GREAT BEYOND is told in the style of a tall tale. The tone is appropriate to the absurdity of the situation. The glimpse of the "Great Beyond" and the "Great Power" is not detailed, but neither is it the point of the story. The theme is a very simple and common one: that there is life after death, during which people will be judged according to the deeds of their life on earth; however, there will also be an opportunity, at least for some, to make retribution for the wrongs they may have committed.

Other "tall tales" of supernatural retribution include the popular "The Legend of Sleepy Hollow" by Washington Irving, *A Christmas Carol* by Charles Dickens, and THE TORN VEIL by Mabel Dove-Danquah. They are told with the same mock-seriousness, and all suggest more than they reveal about supernatural events. A far more serious story dealing with questions of the relationship between death and life is William Faulkner's "A Rose for Emily," in which the "haunting" takes place in recognizable circumstances and with psychological credibility that adds a chill not present in similar themes handled with humor. Students familiar with the works of Stephen King and many modern "horror" movies could probably draw many comparisons and contrasts between the styles of Ekwensi, Irving, Faulkner, Dove-Danquah, and the more modern works.

As a story of repentance, one might compare THE GREAT BEYOND to "Markheim" by Robert Louis Stevenson and to several works by Nathaniel Hawthorne, including *The Scarlet Letter.* Each invites the reader to think about the advantages of mending one's ways while still on earth, rather than taking a chance on beneficent kindness beyond the grave.   — B H N

FENG JICAI. THE MAO BUTTON.

China
World Writers Today. Glenview, IL: ScottForesman, 1995.
Translated by Susan Wilf Chen.

Author: Born and reared in Tianjin, China, Feng Jicai first trained as an athlete, but later worked at the Chinese Traditional Painting Press. Both an artist and a writer, he taught Chinese traditional painting at the Tianjin Workers' College of Decorative Art and later became vice chairman of a branch of the Chinese Writers' Association. Since 1976, he has published three novels: *The Boxers, Magic Light,* and *The Miraculous Pigtail.* THE MAO BUTTON is taken from *Chrysanthemums and Other Stories,* one of his six collections of short stories and novelettes.

Story: In the heyday of Mao, the worker Kong had only one aspiration: he wanted to get the most "stupendous" Mao button, at least a "three-and-a-half." He stops bypassers to ask for the buttons they wear and wanders far in search of button traders. After a near scrape with a man who tries to coerce him into getting a huge novelty button that lights up on battery power, he returns home to find out from his wife that the best supplier lives next door. From this neighbor, he acquires a "five-and-a-half," weighing at least half a pound.

Beaming with pride the next day, he pins the button onto the back of his denim jacket. He is such a sensation that a crowd gathers around him. In squirming his way out, he hears a clank and recognizes it as the sound of the button falling. Frantically looking for it, he steps back and finds himself committing the worst of offenses: stepping on a portrait of Chairman Mao. The consequences he suffers contrast sharply with a subsequent era, when not a single Mao button would be seen across the country.

Comparison: This archetypal story of self-destructive greed is the story of King Midas from Greek mythology. Midas too desires the largest and the most of everything, which for him is symbolized by the golden touch—everything he touches turns to gold. Unfortunately, this gift turns to misfortune when he finds that the food he touches also turns into gold.   — M L

Flaubert, Gustave. A Simple Heart.

France
Literature of the Western World. New York: Macmillan, 1984.
Translated by Arthur McDowall.

Author: Gustave Flaubert (1821–1880) was born in Rouen, in and near which he spent most of his life, although he traveled extensively. He studied law, but his inclination from an early age was the creation of fiction—meticulously written, objectively handled, and well researched.

Following some youthful association with Romantics like Victor Hugo, Flaubert chose to write "realist" fiction and set about honing his craft. *Madame Bovary* (1848) was his first published and most important novel. It also proved to be his most controversial, treating as it does the extramarital affair and eventual suicide of Emma Bovary. Of his other works, some with realistically treated historical subjects, the book called *Three Tales,* published in 1877, remains his most popular. Each of the collection's three stories—"Herodias," "The Legend of St. Julian the Hospitaler," and A SIMPLE HEART—is quite different from the others.

Story: Félicité, whose name in French means "happiness," has had but one "affair of the heart" in her lifetime. At age eighteen, she fell in love with Theodore, but he deceived and deeply hurt her. With all her belongings in a single handkerchief, she left for Pont l'Evêque, where she met and became the servant of Mme. Aubain, a widow with two children.

During her fifty years with the Aubains, Félicité knows happiness—the kind of happiness only one as simple as she and as willing to have as little in life as she does could possibly tolerate. She loves the children, Paul and Virginia, and she loves Mme. Aubain. She also loves Mr. Bourais, a retired lawyer who manages the Aubains' affairs, and she loves her nephew, Victor.

A SIMPLE HEART is a story of loss. All her life, Félicité has lost everyone she loved: her father was killed, her mother died, her sisters went their own ways, her abortive relationship with Theodore alienated her from him, Victor dies while a merchant seaman, Paul leaves home as a young man of the world, and Virginia dies. The lone break in this steady succession of losses over the years has been Félicité's parrot, Loulou. Still, although Félicité attends to the parrot's every need, just as she did the needs of everyone else in her life, Loulou dies too, followed soon by Mme. Aubain.

Fortunately, Félicité had taken Mme. Aubain's advice to have Loulou stuffed. Thus, Félicité is not totally alone. As her eyes begin to fail, she begins confusing the stuffed parrot with the Holy Ghost. Finally, alone in an empty house, with no one to care for her, Félicité becomes very ill. As she dies, she imagines she sees a parrot in the heavens opening above her.

Comparison: A SIMPLE HEART is a moving, sometimes comic, story, arguably Flaubert's best. Félicité's simplicity is both her handicap and her salvation. Hers is a perfect example of a life that would have been miserable had it been lived by anyone else.

The story may be compared with Sherwood Anderson's "Death in the Woods," since that story too has in it a life lived totally in subservience to the needs of others, with no real personal satisfaction except that contrived by a simple mind. Silas, in Robert Frost's "Death of the Hired Man," is another such character.

A SIMPLE HEART can be contrasted with *Madame Bovary,* for what Félicité and Emma do in life and expect of it contains the core of their stories. That the characters are almost total opposites makes for an effective comparison. — R S

FRANCE, ANATOLE. THE PROCURATOR OF JUDEA.

France
Bedside Book of Famous French Stories. New York: Random House, 1945.
Translated by Frederic Chapman.

Author: Anatole France, the pen name of Jacques Anatole François Thibault (1844–1924), French novelist, poet, and critic, was born in Paris. His father had a bookshop, and his mother, a devout Catholic, tutored him, stimulating his imagination with stories from the Bible and legends of saints. At college, he studied the classics. As a young man, he abandoned his faith in Catholicism. His urbane cynicism is reflected in his writing, and his style is sophisticated, subtle, and ironic. A major force in French literature, he produced a prodigious number of works and was elected to the French Academy in 1896, four years after publishing THE PROCURATOR OF JUDEA. A socialist, he risked his literary and academic reputation to defend Zola's position in the Dreyfus affair. He was awarded the Nobel Prize for Literature in 1921.

Story: A Roman patrician, Aelius Lamia, while convalescing at the Baths of Baiae, encounters the ailing Pontius Pilate. Twenty years earlier, Lamia had spent ten years in Jerusalem with Pilate, then Procurator of Judea. The two discuss Rome and its colonies, especially the Procurator's turbulent experiences with the Jews, which led to his early retirement. Pilate's long-standing resentment of the rebellious Hebrews and his insensitivity to their culture are evident as he defends his official actions. Lamia describes a more positive relationship with this sect, especially with an attractive woman who later became a follower of a young Galilean named Jesus. This recollection leads him to ask Pilate for information about the crime resulting in this man's crucifixion. Pontius Pilate searches his memory, then murmurs, "Jesus—of Nazareth? I cannot call him to mind."

Certain pointed references lead the reader to expect a discussion of Christ's crucifixion and the traditional Biblical perspective of Pilate's reluctance to condemn him. The sharp irony of the Procurator's having forgotten an incident leading to the founding of a great religion illustrates the relativity of historical and religious perceptions.

Comparison: The irony of the Procurator's having forgotten Jesus could be compared with that found in Thomas Hardy's poem "God-Forgotten." In a dialogue between God and an inquisitive mortal, God at first is unable to recall ever having created the earth or the human race. This poem, like most of Hardy's work, reflects the author's loss of religious faith.

THE PROCURATOR OF JUDEA has been cited as expressing Anatole France's religious disillusionment. "The Legend of the Grand Inquisitor" from Dostoevski's *The Brothers Karamazov* illustrates a similar theme through a story about a second prosecution of Christ. The intellectual atheist Ivan tells his religious brother Alyosha the legend of Christ's return to earth during the Inquisition. He is put on trial and condemned again, this time by the Catholic Church. Christ responds to the sentence by kissing the prosecutor who, unlike Pilate, releases him, telling him never to return.

The story of Pilate's role in the crucifixion of Jesus is central to Mikhail Bulgakov's novel *The Master and Margarita.* A Mephistophelean character overhears two modern Russians' discussion of Jesus as a mythological, not historical, figure. He disagrees, relating to them the story of Pilate's role in the crucifixion, which he claims to have witnessed. This tale, which parallels the Biblical one in its major points, is also the plot of a novel written by another character, the Master. The emphasis is upon Pilate's desire to save Yeshua (Jesus), as contrasted to his act of condemnation.

In Tintoretto's painting *Christ Before Pilate,* Pilate washes his hands as a symbolic gesture that the decision of Christ's fate belongs to the crowd, not him. It could be used to represent the traditional treatment of Pilate's role. — M A F

65

FUENTES, CARLOS. THE TWO ELENAS.

Mexico
The Eye of the Heart: Short Stories from Latin America. New York: Bobbs-Merrill, 1973.

Author: Carlos Fuentes (1928–) was born in Mexico City. His father, Rafael Fuentes Boettinger, was a career diplomat. Consequently, Fuentes grew up outside Mexico. He learned English at the age of four while his father served in Washington, D.C. He also lived in such diverse cities as Rio de Janeiro, Buenos Aires, Montevideo, and Quito.

Fuentes received excellent schooling throughout his childhood and attended both the Colégio de México and the National University of Mexico, from which he received a law degree. He later studied economics at the Institute of Higher International Studies in Geneva.

Fuentes has served in a number of government posts, including secretary of the Mexican delegation to the International Labor Organization, head of the department of cultural relations for the Ministry of Foreign Affairs, secretary of the Mexican delegation to the International Law Commission of the United Nations, and cultural attaché to the Mexican Embassy in Switzerland.

Fuentes's political career and his political leanings are all reflected in his work. His first novel, *Where the Air Is Clear,* is both a portrait of Mexico City and a portrayal of the things that are wrong in Mexican society. *The Death of Artemio Cruz,* perhaps his best novel, is a panorama of Mexican history. His most controversial novel, *A Change of Skin,* was banned in Spain as "Communistic, pro-Jewish, and anti-German." Fuentes attempts to point out the Mexican identity, and the flaws in that identity, and has been criticized in Mexico and elsewhere for his political views.

His other works include a volume of short stories, *Los Dias Enmascarados;* two plays, *Todos los Gatos Son Pardos* and *El Tuerto Es Rey;* a number of political writings; and an important work on the Latin American novel, *La Nueva Novela Hispanoamericana.* Fuentes continues to write and must be considered one of Mexico's greatest writers.

Story: The story is essentially a study in contrasts, narrated by a man with knowledge of both of the title characters, his wife and his mother-in-law. The story begins at a Sunday luncheon, attended by the narrator and his wife at the home of her parents. The immediate conflict is expressed in the first sentence: the difference in ideology and temperament between mother and daughter. The mother is a typical bourgeois woman, content with the status quo. The daughter is a revolutionary, desperate to break free of the rigid and regimented life to discover all of the world's pleasures.

The narrator regresses to discuss some of the steps his wife has taken to escape the mold, revealing that she has stopped short of a ménage à trois only because society expects her to have an affair. During the luncheon, it becomes clear that mother and daughter cannot communicate, that only the narrator can serve as a bridge between them, understanding both worlds. It also becomes obvious that the relationship between the narrator and his mother-in-law, the older Elena, is not a simple family relationship. The last paragraph reveals that the narrator loves and is loved by *both* Elenas, a surprising end to a story whose narrator has seemingly been against infidelity.

Comparison: The juxtaposition of two characters who represent different values is found in a number of literary works. Even the device of using relatives, such as twins, or people with identical names in such a fashion is standard. Examples include the contrasting characters of Robert Cohn and Pedro Romero in Hemingway's *The Sun Also Rises,* architects Peter Keating and Howard Roark in Ayn Rand's *The Fountainhead,* Frank Shallard and Elmer Gantry in Sinclair Lewis's *Elmer Gantry,* and Charles Darnay and Sydney Carton in Dickens's *A Tale of Two Cities.*

What allows the concept of juxtaposition to work effectively in this story is the irony generated by the affair between the narrator and the older Elena. Although she is conservative and cautious and her daughter is adventuresome and worldly, it is the mother who takes a lover, not her daughter, who only thinks about doing so. The story thus illustrates Fuentes's favorite subjects: the hypocrisy of the Mexican bourgeoisie and the falsity of the revolution trying to change Mexican society.　　— C W

GIDE, ANDRÉ. THE RETURN OF THE PRODIGAL SON.

France

Norton Anthology of World Masterpieces. New York: Norton, 1992. Translated by Wallace Fowlie.

Author:　André Gide (1869–1951) was a French novelist, essayist, critic, playwright, and editor. The only child of a rich but puritanical family, he rebelled against his narrow Protestant upbringing. Although Gide read the gospels regularly, he questioned traditional institutions and rejected conventional ideas and modes of behavior. Because of his homosexuality and his advice to young people to reject established norms and to seek new experiences, his enemies accused him of corrupting youth.

A richly talented author, he produced more than eighty works, publishing THE RETURN OF THE PRODIGAL SON in 1907. Search for self is a major theme in his writing. Founder and editor of the influential literary magazine *La Nouvelle Revue Française,* he achieved a considerable reputation as a writer and thinker. He was awarded the Nobel Prize for Literature in 1947.

Story:　Gide follows the Biblical parable's narrative except for the addition of two characters, the mother and a younger brother. A young man from a wealthy family leaves home to lead a life of adventure and depravity. After spending his inheritance and ending up in menial servitude to a cruel master, he returns home destitute. His father and mother receive him warmly, but his elder brother berates him. The prodigal son responds gratefully to his parents' loving reception. Yet when his younger brother reveals the desire to run away, he encourages the boy to forget the family and go into the world, never to return.

In a monograph on this work, Aldyth Thain explains the origin of the story in detail. It was written as a work of self-justification in response to a campaign to convert Gide to Catholicism. Two distin-guished writers, Francis Jammes and Paul Claudel, had made vigorous but unsuccessful attempts to bring their fellow author into the fold of Catholicism, and Gide felt the need to reply. In a letter to his friend Christian Beck, he explained his feelings that a return to the church, symbolized by the ancestral home in the story, would be a defeat for him as an individual. To Gide, individualism and creative freedom were not possible inside the confining boundaries of religious or intellectual systems. That was the reason he had the prodigal son encourage his younger brother to go out into the world alone and experience life, no matter what the cost.

Comparison:　The motif of the return of the prodigal son found in the Bible is prevalent in the arts. For example, it is the subject and title of a painting by Jean Baptiste Greuze and an oratorio by Arthur Sullivan.

Gide's addition of the two characters expands the meaning of the parable. The mother symbolizes love and security, and the younger son represents the desire for uninhibited experience. Although the prodigal son in both Gide's story and the Bible is penitent, the revision permits Gide to convey his belief that an artist must have complete freedom. The theme of rebellion against any established authority inhibiting individualism permeates modern literature. In James Joyce's novel *A Portrait of the Artist as a Young Man,* Stephen Dedalus rejects family ties, nationalism, and Catholicism in order to assert his identity as an artist. Eugene Gant, the protagonist of Thomas Wolfe's autobiographical novel *Look Homeward, Angel,* also is a rebel as he searches for self and meaning in life. The genre of the

German Bildungsroman, which depicts the personal development of an individual, includes many works with this same theme.

In Eudora Welty's short story "Why I Live at the P.O.," a grown daughter resents the family's joyous reaction to the return of a younger sister after a few years away from home. Much like the elder brother in Gide's story and the Biblical parable, the older sister's jealousy results in animosity directed at her sibling. — M A F

GORDIMER, NADINE. LITTLE WILLIE.

South Africa
Friday's Footprint and Other Stories. New York: Viking, 1960.

Author: Nadine Gordimer was born in South Africa in the 1920s. She was educated in convent schools and at the University of Witwatersrand in Johannesburg. Her first novel, *The Lying Days* (1954), helped establish her international reputation as a writer. Since then, she has become one of the leading voices among white writers in Africa and has received numerous literary prizes, including the Nobel Prize for Literature in 1991. Among the writers who influenced her she acknowledges D. H. Lawrence, Henry James, and Ernest Hemingway. She is best known for her imaginative and compassionate portrayals of the way in which the political situation in her home country affects both past and present human relations. She has traveled widely, and her work appears regularly in American and English periodicals. A prolific short story writer, she is also the author of numerous novels, including *A Guest of Honor* (1970), *The Conservationist* (1974), *Burger's Daughter* (1979), and *July's People* (1981).

Story: LITTLE WILLIE is something of a mystery story. The reader never meets Little Willie, nor finds out for certain whether he exists beyond a social stereotype. Physical child or not, he profoundly affects eight-year-old Denise, whose revulsion toward him turns her into a lifelong snob.

It is Denise's Uncle Basile who first mentions Little Willie. "He knows you," Uncle Basile says. "He never talks about anything else *but* you." Pressed by Denise for more details, Uncle Basile confides that Little Willie lives "in Railroad Avenue," and the horror for Denise begins. "In the gold-mining Transvaal town where her father was town clerk, the poor whites of the town were the railway gangmen and their families who lived in one mean street of corrugated-iron cottages.... The name of the street was not only the synonym of poverty, it was a name-calling epithet for all standards that fell below those of the town clerk's family and the friends who lived and thought as they did."

Uncle Basile continues to insist that Little Willie watches every move Denise makes. He identifies a family trip to a regatta as the first time Little Willie saw Denise. Of a gang of urchins there, she remembers "one of the dirtiest, with round patches of ringworm showing on his head." In despair, she pleads with her uncle, "He doesn't know me! He doesn't!" But Uncle Basile persists. "Sometimes when Uncle Basile took the family out in his car, he would slow down incomprehensibly. When he had crawled along for half a block, someone would say, 'What's the matter?' ... Then ... he would say casually, 'I thought I'd give poor Little Willie a chance to get a look at Denise.'" The fabric of the young girl's life slowly changes. "She tried to remember never to smile in the street; it was her way of showing him his place."

The final betrayal occurs when her mother joins in the teasing. "Denise had thought—or rather accepted—that forever, in everything, her mother would be on her side." Instead of becoming more desperate or vulnerable, however, "the fact that her mother was no longer with her produced a hardening in Denise that became her armor against, and finally defeated Little Willie. She did not care, any more, if he saw her smile in the street. She did not care if he was watching her. She despised him. What a cheek he had, a hopeless cheek, to look at *her.* All her embarrassment fell away; she scarcely thought about him."

An incident at the end of the story establishes her attitude of superiority and snobbery forever. As she is about to leave town with her family, a porter hands her a beautifully wrapped box of candies "from Little Willie." "She thought of a group of ragged children; of a bony-headed boy, looking on at her pleasures and triumphs. A dirty boy without shoes. She was ashamed of him. She would never speak to him or look at him; and he knew this. But the present in her lap was not to be resisted. No one whom she had loved, been kind to, or tried to please had ever rewarded her with something as

fine as this. Earned by scorn and disdain, it was like nothing she had ever been given before . . . and when she peeled the gold paper off the first choco-late and put it in her mouth, the cherry inside was the fruit of knowledge on her tongue."

Comparison: LITTLE WILLIE is a story of child-hood initiation, an initiation into the cruel knowl-edge of adulthood. In that regard, it can be com-pared to VENGEFUL CREDITOR by Chinua Achebe, "Paul's Case" by Willa Cather, and "Battle Royal" by Ralph Ellison. It is also a story of social prejudice, whether based on economic status (as in this story), skin color (as in Abrahams's EPISODE IN MALAY CAMP), or gender (as in Dove-Danquah's THE TORN VEIL). — B H N

GORDIMER, NADINE. A SOLDIER'S EMBRACE.

South Africa
A Soldier's Embrace: Stories. Baltimore: Penguin, 1982.

Author: See LITTLE WILLIE.

Story: A SOLDIER'S EMBRACE, set in an imaginary South Africa, portrays the dilemma faced by a liberal white couple shortly after black South Africans have at last gained political power. As she returns home amid the street celebrations of the cease-fire, a woman is swept into the arms of two soldiers, one white and one black. Without thinking, she kisses each of them on the cheek, exchanges a few unin-telligible words, and passes on.

The woman and her lawyer husband are elated at the political developments. The husband is well known for having defended many black leaders in the past, and he has every reason to expect to be consulted by the new political regime. As the cou-ple watch many of the whites around them sudden-ly try to appear more liberal, they are secure in the knowledge that they have always been on the "right side." Yet many of their former black friends seem strangely reluctant to visit or talk with them now, and their black servant is afraid to visit the market because he works for them. Gradually, it becomes

clear that even this couple doesn't quite fit into the new society. Without ever explicitly admitting to themselves why they are doing so, the lawyer and his wife prepare to move to an adjoining country still controlled by whites. As they leave and wave to their former servant, the right words fail to come.

Comparison: Many of Nadine Gordimer's stories trace with sensitivity and insight the complexity of human relationships in a time of political and racial tension. Although the setting here is clearly South Africa, the themes are much broader, and the story may serve as a useful counterpoint to any tale of race relations. A particularly effective comparison is offered by Flannery O'Connor's "Revelation," set in the American South, in which a white woman comes to terms with her own conflicting emotions about blacks and whites.

The brief embrace between the woman and the two men in the story comes to symbolize the hope for racial harmony, set against an ultimate failure of communication. Gordimer returns to the scene again and again in the course of the story, as the woman continues to recall it in increasingly greater detail. The embrace becomes a subtle but powerful symbol of sexual tensions between the races as well, of power and domination, of the politics of force on a basic human level. Caught up in the moment, the woman allowed herself a freedom she fears her husband might see as license, and so she represses the details in retelling the incident. Here too repression and the failure of communication reflect a larger thematic social tension.   — B M

Grace, Patricia. A Way of Talking.

New Zealand Maori
Selected Stories. Auckland, New Zealand: Penguin, 1991.

Author: Maori author Patricia Grace (1937–) was born in Wellington, New Zealand. She is of Ngati Raukawa, Ngati Toa, and Te Ati Awa descent and is affiliated with Ngati Porou by marriage. After teaching in primary and secondary schools, she published a collection of short stories, *Waiariki,* in 1975, the first collection of stories by a Maori woman writer. *The Dream Sleepers,* her second short story collection, was published in 1980. Her third collection, *Electric City and Other Stories,* was published in 1987. *Selected Stories* appeared in 1991, and her latest collection, *The Sky People,* appeared in 1994. She has also written several children's books: *The Kuia and the Spider* (1981), winner of the Children's Picture Book of the Year Award in 1982; *Watercress Tuna and the Children of Champion Street* (1985); *The Trolley* (1993); and *Areta and the Kahawai* (1994). Her children's stories have appeared in numerous anthologies and journals. She also wrote the text of *Wahine Toa* (1984), which celebrates women in Maori mythology. In addition, she has written several novels: *Mutuwhenua, the Moon Sleeps* (1978); *Potiki* (1986), which won the fiction section of the New Zealand Book Awards; and *Cousins* (1992). She was the international guest speaker at the National Council of Teachers of English's annual convention in 1993. Also in 1993, she and Witi Ihimaera, another Maori writer, participated in the Indigenous Writers Conference in Ottawa, Canada.

The Maori are the indigenous people of New Zealand and make up less than ten percent of the population. Those of European descent are called Pakeha.

Story: Set in the 1950s, A WAY OF TALKING is told from the point of view of Hera, the older sister. The younger sister, Rose, is home from university. While the older sister has been planning her wedding, the younger sister has been involved in university demonstrations for Maori rights. When the two of them go to see Jane Frazer, the Pakeha dressmaker, Rose asserts herself against a subtle form of racial prejudice. Jane does not know the names of the Maori workers because their names are too difficult to pronounce, while the Maoris know her name. Rose insists that they walk out of Frazer's home. The older sister questions her own inability to stand up for herself and her people: "All my life I had been sitting back and letting her do the objecting. . . . And how can the likes of Jane know when we go round pretending all is well. How can Jane know us?" Hera notes that the Maoris, particularly the older people, are equally prejudiced in their behavior. The sister-to-sister discussion about knowing the time and place to use racial terms is poignant and relevant. By the end of the story, Hera finally understands Rose's courage and loneliness in standing up for Maori rights. In fact, Hera finally decides, "But my sister won't have to be alone again. I'll let her know that." Throughout the story, members of this close-knit family tease one another, and Grace uses humor to relieve the tension.

Comparison: Hera's inability to stand up for herself and her naiveté regarding the racial situation is similar to that evident in Liliana Heker's "The Stolen Party." Although one takes place in New Zealand and the other in Argentina, the protagonists in both stories learn a valuable lesson from other family members. Neither wants to believe the obvious about racial or economic prejudice, but both become stronger from their growing insight.

Grace's story may also be compared with Ray Bradbury's "August 2002: Night Meeting." Being able to see an event from two viewpoints, whether Maori–Pakeha, older sister–younger sister, or earthling–Martian, as in Bradbury's story, questions the validity of any one person's view. Indeed, Hera shouts, "We do it too," when Rose accuses others of prejudice. Prejudice and lack of cultural understanding go two ways, then. This is dramatically depicted in Elliott Merrick's "Without Words." In Grace's story as well as Merrick's, there is a lack of communication between the races. In Merrick's story, this failure to understand nearly results in the death of a Native American.

As a story of racial insensitivity and lack of cultural understanding, one might compare Grace's work to Chinua Achebe's African tragedy *Things Fall Apart*. The British District Commissioner clearly lacks any inkling of the richness of Ibo life and relegates Okonkwo's suicide to perhaps a "reasonable paragraph" in his new book. — M J S

Hahn Moo-sook. SHADOW.

Korea

Asian and Pacific Short Stories. Rutland, VT: Charles E. Tuttle, 1974. Translated by Richard Rutt.

Author: Hahn Moo-sook (1918–) was born in Seoul and became a well-known writer of fiction during a period when Western influence became pervasive in Korea. Her first ambition was to paint, but she turned to writing instead. In studying problems of the human condition, she draws from the raw material around her and depicts the pain of children growing up wayward, the sorrows created by war, and the lack of support systems to comfort and help those who suffer. She represented Korea at the International P.E.N. meetings in 1965 and 1969. Her novels that have been translated into English include *In the Depths* (1955) and *Running Water Hermitage* (1966).

Story: Son-hui does not want to go to the funeral of her lover. As she hesitates, the day turns dark, and she lies motionless on the floor.

Her whole life has centered around Yong-ho, whom she met twenty years before, when he was a soldier in a Japanese uniform. They fell in love, but were separated when he planned to desert. She had borrowed clothes for him and arranged to meet him at a crowded train station, but she waited in vain. His battalion was suddenly transferred to another area.

Years later, when they meet again by accident, he has married. Just to be near him, she moves to Seoul and opens a beauty salon. They meet occasionally, but she feels fulfillment only once, when they go to a Buddhist sanctuary. As a result of guilt over his double life, Yong-ho's health steadily deteriorates. Son-hui too lives a shadowy existence. She cannot even attend his funeral without some pretext.

As the day draws to a close, she is left in complete darkness, with nothing in life except private memories and a memento.

Comparison: As in many tales of love, the couple in this story meet with obstacles. The way in which the two meet, separate, and meet again without being able to establish an acceptable relationship resembles the fantasy in the mind of the protagonist in the story ON MEETING MY 100 PERCENT WOMAN ONE FINE APRIL MORNING by Murakami Haruki. In the Japanese story, however, it is the couple's own choice, not an extraneous circumstance like war, that causes the separation. When they meet again many years later, it is their own diminished memories, rather than an external factor such as a marriage, that prevents the relationship from resuming. — M L

HAMSUN, KNUT. THE CALL OF LIFE.

Norway

Great Stories by Nobel Prize Winners. New York: The Noonday Press, 1959.

Author: One of the greatest Norwegian writers of modern times, Knut Hamsun (1859–1952) worked at a variety of jobs—sheriff, teacher, dockhand, and peddler, among others—until he caused a literary scandal with the publication of his book *Hunger* in 1890. As a powerful psychological study of the workings of a starving man's mind, the book was at once realistic, intense, and highly personal. Its appearance marked the beginning of Hamsun's long career as a writer.

His later novels—*Mysteries, Pan,* and *Wanderings*—were all widely read, but a particular trilogy—*Children of the Age, Segelfoss Town,* and *Growth of the Soil*—led to his receipt of the Nobel Prize for Literature in 1920. *Growth of the Soil,* in particular, has been highly praised as the greatest novel of peasant life.

Always interested in the individual and what he believed to be that individual's existential situation, Hamsun deplored the development of an industrialized, consumer-oriented society. His aversion to what he termed "decadence" in his own beloved Scandinavia led him to support Germany's Nazi invaders. After the liberation, he was tried and convicted of treason. Though age enabled him to avoid prison, Hamsun lost all his fortune and was made to undergo involuntary psychiatric examinations. After his release from the sanitarium, he withdrew to a country estate that had not been taken from him, and it was there that he died.

Story: Hamsun's choice of first-person narration succeeds in maintaining a tone of intimacy between speaker and reader throughout this brief story. In fact, the reader feels privy to the details of a confession.

While walking one evening, the narrator encounters a veiled woman who appears to have been waiting for someone, possibly even for the narrator himself. There is a genuine sense of mystery as the woman, who eventually identifies herself as Ellen, leads the narrator to her apartment. Once there, she throws her arms around him, kissing him eagerly—behavior that contrasts sharply with her persistent reticence. Ellen and her newfound companion spend the night together.

The next morning, the narrator's ardor cools dramatically as he witnesses something "which even now strikes me as a gruesome dream. I was at the wash stand. Ellen had some errand or other in the adjoining room, and as she opened the door I turned around and glanced in. A cold draft from the open window in the room rushed in upon me, and in the center of the room I could just make out a corpse stretched out on a table. A corpse, in a coffin, dressed in white, with a gray beard, the corpse of a man."

On her return, Ellen offers no explanations, nor does the narrator question what he has seen. As he rather hurriedly leaves, however, Ellen urges him to return to see her in two days. "Why not tomorrow?" he asks, partly to test her, and she replies, "Not so many questions, dear. I am going to a funeral tomorrow, a relation of mine is dead. Now there—you have it." Later, after some detective work on his own, the narrator learns that the relative is, in fact, Ellen's much older husband, who had died the day before. The narrator's closing lines provide a touch of irony: "A man marries. His wife is thirty years younger than he. He contracts a lingering illness. One fair day he dies. And the young widow breathes a sigh of relief."

Comparison: The details of the story, while not graphic, are realistic enough, and comparison with contemporary novels and television plots and characters is inevitable. Exploring the title of the story itself provides an interesting essay topic that will force readers to define and justify their attitude toward Ellen's behavior.

The story is comparable to Kate Chopin's "The Story of an Hour," in which a wife believes her husband to have been killed and rejoices at her freedom. Sympathetic friends assume her tears are tears of grief, but they are really tears of relief. Yet the joy of that single hour is shattered when her husband walks in the door and the wife dies, not of shock, but of disappointment. — P G L

Haris, Petros. LIGHTS ON THE SEA.

Greece
Introduction to Modern Greek Literature: An Anthology of Fiction, Drama, and Poetry.
New York: Twayne, 1969. Translated by Mary P. Gianos.

Author: Petros Haris, the pen name of Yiannis Marmariadis (1902–), was born in Athens. He studied law, but began his successful literary career in 1924 with the publication of his short story collection *The Last Night on Earth.* Soon his short stories were being published in literary journals, then in book form, including *The Longest Night: Chronicle of a Dead City* (1969), from which the Gianos translation of LIGHTS ON THE SEA is taken. Haris, who has been a major figure in the Greek cultural scene during this century, has served as general secretary of the Fine Arts School in Athens and has presided over the National Society of Greek Writers as well as the Association of Greek Theatre and Music Critics. He has been the long-time editor of the Greek literary journal *Nea Estia* and has published critical essays and travel accounts such as *China Without Walls* (1961). His novel *Days of Rage* deals with the Greek Civil War of 1944.

Story: Haris has tied together his series of prose narratives in *The Longest Night* with a common location in or near Athens and a common time—the World War II German occupation of Greece. Writing of the suffering of forgotten occupation victims, Haris has made the setting a vital element.

The story takes place on a tiny island in the Saronic Gulf, inhabited by only 250 people, cut off from the world and their German conquerors, lacking even radio contact. There is no principal character. Instead, Haris gives the reader a glimpse of the island idiot, the first to observe, far out at sea, the lights of a ship heading for their island harbor. Then, a week later, a young man sees the lights. After ten days, so do two other people. Using the symbolism of a lighted ship as the bearer of free-

dom and of church bells to proclaim the event, Haris has the islanders, one by one, over a period of time, climb the belfry, see the ship, and ring the bell. Each time, however, as people gather in response, the lights at sea disappear. Haris leaves the reader with the idea that, though the desperate isolation rolls on and on, everyone on the island believes that some day all of them will see the lights at sea together. A major work in the area of antiwar literature, this story, like other Haris stories, is presented in a factual way. The author is careful to keep his own opinion in low profile, allowing the full strength of the message to come through.

Comparison: Since starvation ruled Greece during the World War II German occupation, it is significant that the Greeks on this island could feed themselves. But there are other kinds of oppression besides lack of food. The high school boy in Willa Cather's "Paul's Case" is oppressed by what most would consider a normal, everyday life, so he creates an illusionary world for himself in which he can be what he wants to be. In Doris Lessing's "A Woman on a Roof," a woman who wants the basic freedoms of movement and privacy is oppressed by the sex-oriented stares and fantasies of some construction workers. Oppression is real rather than psychological or emotional in Nadine Gordimer's "The Train from Rhodesia," in which the main character's young husband bargains for and then finally buys a carved lion for one-third price from a train station peddler. In LIGHTS ON THE SEA, it is desire for freedom that causes the oppressed to create their comforting illusion. — E M

HAYASHI FUMIKO. BONES.

Japan
The Catch and Other Stories. Tokyo: Kodansha International, 1981.
Translated by T. Takaya.

Author: A postwar writer who reflected the mood of Japan as a result of its defeat and occupation by U.S. forces, Hayashi Fumiko (1904–1951) was born in Shimonoseki. Her life was characterized by constant moves and many changes in jobs and personal relationships. Her tone of pessimism and despondency was typical of the writers of fiction and postwar memoirs of this period. Her novel *The Drifting Cloud,* for example, tells of a young woman who goes to Indo-China to serve as a typist for the Japanese army. The luxurious life and her love affair there, coupled with the realization that Japan is fated to lose the war, thrust her into a *carpe diem* philosophy of life. After years of indulgence, the war having ended, she returns to the drabness, monotony, and poverty of Japan and drags out an existence.

This tone of gloominess persists in Hayashi's works. Her other well-known works include *Diary of Roaming;* "Late Chrysanthemum," which won her the Women Writer's Award in 1948; and *Rice.*

Story: In her husband's empty bone box, Michiko keeps her extra earnings from her life as a prostitute. She has been driven to desperation and prostitution by the death of her husband on Okinawa in the war and by her younger brother's illness, her father's disability, her little daughter's helplessness, and the lack of decent jobs. In betraying her resolution to be faithful to the memory of her husband, she waits several months after her friend suggests that she try prostitution. The first time she has to grit her teeth to undergo the abhorrent experience, but her rationalization, her resolve, and her ability to see her partner as man and herself as woman enable her to accept her degradation. Afterward, she simply sees her body as her means to livelihood.

Her bedridden brother Kanji sees her as the source of little luxuries in life. In postwar Japan, when eggs are scarce, he pesters her with "Buy me two eggs today" and "Buy me everything I ask for." Despondent because, despite his patriotism and hard work, he is reduced to skin and bones by tuberculosis, he asks his sister to lend him money for an uncertain lung operation. While Michiko offers to send him to a sanatorium, she also lets him know that she is miserable in her struggle to keep him and the rest of the family alive. Later, when Kanji dies, Michiko is relieved. Yet the fact that he died alone, choking on his blood, sends a great wave of guilt over her. She takes out her savings from the bone box and spends it on Kanji's funeral and cremation.

Even as she hugs his urn, the wave of emotion that possessed her passes. Like her first experience in prostitution, death becomes remote, "meaningless and even stupid." She walks down the street with her daughter beside her singing "Jesus loves me," and she callously wonders when her father will die.

Comparison: Like any number of stories on a woman's lot or a woman's response to tragedy, BONES shows the protagonist dealing with her available options. Beginning with the archetypical story of Medea's desperate reactions to being abandoned, the woman frequently has little recourse except personal sacrifice or retaliation, all sense of ethics or sentiment having been repressed. Take, for example, William Faulkner's "A Rose for Emily." While Emily suffers no other deprivation, her inability to satisfy her one need, that of getting a man, drives her to unmentionable means. Behind her closed doors and a respectable façade, she lives with her own act until her death. Or compare BONES with "Sorrow Rides a Fast Horse" by Dorothy Gilman Butters, in which a woman is thunderstruck by her husband's sudden death. Not realizing what she is doing, she takes her two young sons on a wild and dangerous tour of the world that almost costs their lives. — M L

HEAD, BESSIE. HEAVEN IS NOT CLOSED.

South Africa
The Collector of Treasures. Portsmouth, NH: Heinemann, 1977.

Author: Bessie Head (1937–1986) was born in South Africa, but most of her writings are set in Botswana, the country to which she fled when she was no longer willing to live with apartheid. In addition to her short stories, her works include a history, *Serowe: Village of the Rain Wind,* and four novels: *When Rain Clouds Gather, Maru, A Question of Power,* and *A Bewitched Crossroads,* her final novel before her death.

Story: Old man Modise has lived in Setswana all his life and is "deep-rooted" in the laws and customs of his village. The story illustrates the conflict between Christianity, represented by Galethebege, and Setswana law and custom, represented by Ralokae.

Ralokae, who suffered the death of his wife just one year after their marriage, has undergone a year of the cleansing ceremony demanded by custom before he can resume the normal life of a man. When he emerges from that process, he announces to Galethebege that he intends to marry her. Startled and pleased, she nevertheless informs him that "I have set God always before me," implying that she wishes he would become a Christian. The matter becomes "a fearful sword" between them, until finally Ralokae wins Galethebege over and she consents. Ralokae reminds her that "I took my first wife according to the old customs. I am going to take my second wife according to the old customs too."

Galethebege had not anticipated that her acquiescence to Ralokae would result in her excommunication from the church. When the villagers hear of it, they begin to question their own participation in the Christian church. "They wanted to know how it was that Ralokae, who was an unbeliever, could have heaven closed to him? Some decided then that if Heaven were closed to Galethebege and Ralokae, for they were highly respected in the village, it might as well be closed to them too, so they all no longer attended church." Thus, tradition wins.

The result is not so clear to Galethebege, however. Even after her excommunication, she sneaks away to private places to pray to the Christian God.

Comparison: The subject of this story has its parallel in a number of works by black African writers and American authors. The conflict between traditional and modern lifestyles is evident in Soyinka's play *The Lion and the Jewel,* in which Baroka, the Lion, and Lakunle, the modern schoolteacher, vie for the hand of Sidi, the Jewel. Chinua Achebe's *Things Fall Apart* also reflects the difficulty of change when traditional social issues are subjected to modern ideas. In Frederick Douglass's autobiography, Christianity and gospel songs are prominent in the lives of slaves, reflecting the positive attitude of many black people toward Christianity.   — M J J

HESSE, HERMANN. THE POET.

Germany
German Stories: Deutsche Novellen. New York: Bantam, 1946. Translated by Harry Steinhauer.

Author: Hermann Hesse (1877–1962) was born in south Germany into a family of missionaries. As an adolescent, he rebelled against his strict parental and school atmosphere by running away, working first as a machinist and then as a bookstore clerk. He went

to Switzerland before World War I, where he remained and became a citizen. He received the Nobel Prize for Literature in 1946. Always in conflict with traditional bourgeois society, he was an outspoken individualist who ardently believed in resisting the pressures of conformity in order to search within oneself with a free mind. He was constantly aware of the conflicting souls that struggle within each of us. He studied throughout his life in many diverse areas of the world's cultures, including Eastern mysticism, psychoanalysis, German Romanticism, and medieval mysticism. He published several volumes of short stories and some Romantic poetry. He is best known for his novels, including *Siddhartha* (1922), *Steppenwolf* (1927), and *Magister Ludi* or *The Glass Bead Game* (1943).

Story: A Chinese poet, Han Fook, wants to "perfect himself in everything that in any way pertained to the art of poetry." He is soon to be married and his life seems fulfilled, but he is not totally content because "his heart was filled with the ambition to become a perfect poet." One evening, he sees reflected in the water a celebration taking place on the other side, and although he wants to join the festivities with his friends, he prefers to remain alone contemplating the scene from afar so that he can incorporate its beauty into a perfect poem. Suddenly, unsure if he is awake or asleep, he sees a stranger who "spoke some verses which contained everything that the young man had just felt." He is the Master of the Perfect Word, and he tells Han Fook how to find him.

The young poet announces to his father that he must leave his bride and family to pursue his dream. He finds the old man, who, although he hardly ever speaks to him, teaches him to obliterate from his mind all that he had written before and to immerse himself in his lute playing, in which he gradually excels. He begins to feel worthless because nature seems to him much more beautiful than his poetry. After two years, the homesick youth returns to his village. Seeing his father and bride from a distance, he realizes that "in the dreams of poets there dwells a beauty and grace which one seeks in vain in the things of reality," and he returns to the old master to study the zither.

For a moment, he hates the old man, who seems to be keeping him from his life, but he is reminded that the choice is his. After mastering several instruments, he turns to poetry and learns "the secret art of saying what seems uncomplicated and simple, yet stirs the listener's soul as the wind stirs the surface of the water." Many years later, the old man disappears, and Han Fook returns to his village, where a celebration is again taking place. Everyone there is fascinated by his music. As he looks at the reflection of the festivities in the water, he notes that the mirrored images and the real ones are inseparable, and he "found no difference in his soul between this feast and that first one."

Comparison: The theme of this parable is comparable to that of many stories of Thomas Mann dealing with the relationship of the artist to society. In TONIO KRÖGER, for example, Tonio recognizes that his art separates him from ordinary society, and at the end he is still standing between those two worlds. In TRISTAN, we see that the world does not permit the artist to return in triumph; instead, the artist is forced to run away in defeat from the vulgarity that triumphs in life. In his very long novel *Joseph and His Brothers,* Mann portrays the kind of artist that we find in this Hesse story, in which Hesse expresses his belief that the artist must separate from society to find and develop creative ability. With that, the artist can return to the world with the beautiful message of truth. Likewise, Joseph learns how to communicate his art to others and returns to the world. The Romantic belief that the artist will triumph is also manifested in such stories as "The Great Stone Face" by Nathaniel Hawthorne, in which the artist is seen as the savior of society.

The fusion of dream and reality is a technique that Hawthorne uses in "Young Goodman Brown" and Chekhov uses in his story THE KISS, in which the whole dream episode of the kiss is used metaphorically to suggest the way an inner vision becomes part of an external reality. E. T. A. Hoffmann's story "The Golden Flower Pot" also provides an interesting comparison, and the dreamlike episode in Mann's story of Tonio Kröger's visit to Copenhagen, in which he reexperiences the earlier episodes with his friends, provides another. What, the artist seems to ask, is the true nature of reality? Is not what is imagined or felt as real as what one sees or touches?

Also comparable is Henry James's story "The Real Thing," which is concerned with the way art departs from literal actuality in the interest of truth.

Many of the surrealist artists, such as Giorgio de Chirico and René Magritte, use this technique as well, and the symbolist Gustave Moreau in his paint-ing *The Apparition* (1875) juxtaposes the image of the head of John the Baptist with reality as it appears in a vision to Salomé.   — R H M

HEYM, GEORG. THE AUTOPSY.

Germany
Great German Short Stories. New York: Dell, 1960.
Translated by Michael Hamburger.

Author: Georg Heym (1887–1912) was born in Hirschberg, Silesia. He was a German expressionist poet and short story writer. He was pathologically shy and seemed to have interests paradoxically in both the "decadent" period and in the beauty of nature. He was influenced by Rimbaud's poem "The Drunken Boat" and the French symbolist models; he wanted to be the Van Gogh of poetry. His works, few of which have been translated, are full of explosive visions of urban ruin with a profound sense of evil and loneliness. He prophesied the Great War in his novels *Der ewige Tag* (1911) and *Umbra vitae* (1912). They and his revealing dream diary were published in the volume *Gesamtausgabe* in 1960. He drowned in a skating accident on the Wannsee.

Story: "The dead man lay naked and alone on a white table" in an operating theater. His body is "like the brilliant calyx of a giant flower," and beautiful colors appear on it. Doctors enter and look at him, and like machines they take out their dissecting instruments, which appear like vultures, and dissect the body as if they were "white cooks drawing a goose."

The dead man sleeps while they perform their gruesome task. A dream, "the remnant of love in him, awoke like a torch shining into his night." He dreams of his loved one, and he pictures her as she walked through poppy fields, expecting to see her again tomorrow and every night at dusk. They will always be together. And so the story ends: "And the dead man trembled softly with bliss on his white mortuary table, while the iron chisel in the doctor's hand broke open the bones of his temple." The point of the story is made clear in this last image: beauty and love in the power of the imagination transcend reality and the fact of mortality.

Comparison: This very short story is full of ter-ror—terrifying beauty as well as ugliness—and can be compared to the paintings of such expressionist artists as Kirchner and Nolde. As the doctors dissect his body, it opens up to reveal the beautiful memory of his life, which becomes a hymn to the beauty of living that transcends the images of mortality.

One can also compare the story to the paint-ings of Géricault, who often sat in mortuaries and painted the bodies of those who were waiting there for interment, as in *Severed Heads* (1818), in which there is a delicate beauty portrayed in the depiction of the dead bodies on the mortuary slab.

James Joyce's much longer and more involved story "The Dead" also comes to mind. Joyce shows us that the world of the dead is stronger and more vital than that of the living. He too indicates that memory and imagination transcend reality and the fact of mortality. The dream sequence also suggests Ambrose Bierce's "An Occurrence at Owl Creek Bridge." Both give us a juxtaposition of death and life; both emphasize the beauty of life with the iron-ic presence of death.   — R H M

HILDESHEIMER, WOLFGANG. A WORLD ENDS.

Germany
Great Modern European Short Stories. Greenwich, CT: Fawcett, 1967.
Translated by Christopher Holme.

Author: Wolfgang Hildesheimer (1916–1991) was born in Hamburg. In 1933, he went to Palestine and from there to England, where he studied painting and graphic design and worked as a stage designer. When World War II began, he was made an officer in the British Intelligence and was stationed in Palestine, where he was both an art critic and a painter, exhibiting his work in Jerusalem and Tel Aviv. He was back in London when the war ended and immediately went to Nuremberg, where he served as an interpreter during the postwar trials of Nazi war criminals. In 1949, he gave up art for a writing career and made his home in Poschiavo, Switzerland. He published many volumes of short stories, several radio plays, and a radio opera. Much of his work has not been translated.

Story: The narrator, Herr Sebald, is invited to one of the famous parties given by Marchesa Montetristo because he had once sold her the bathtub in which Marat was murdered, thus adding to her collection of eighteenth-century washing utensils. She lives on an artificial island that she created because "she could find nothing to suit her in the existing stock of islands." She devotes her life "to the cult of the antique," which she calls "the true and eternal." Her home is an exact replica of the Palazzo Vendramin, and her elite guests, such as the Dombrowska, are involved with activities that have no relationship to real life. In fact, Sebald realizes that he blundered when he even mentioned contemporary art. Even the entertaining musicians "had purposely so arranged themselves—like a picture by Watteau."

During the performance of two forged musical compositions, Sebald "heard a dull reverberation like very distant thunder," and the floor begins to vibrate. While the foundations of the island and the palace are breaking up, the concert continues. The others continue to listen, but the fearful Sebald announces in a quiet voice that he is leaving and proceeds to do so, "as a world, no less, was here sinking beneath the ocean." The guests, holding their hands above their heads to applaud the performers while the water reaches the level of their chins, sit in darkness as the water extinguishes the candles. Sebald looks back; "the sea lay dead calm in the moonlight as if no island had ever stood there."

Comparison: The story, told with a kind of elegance and controlled irony, can be compared to William Faulkner's "A Rose for Emily," which is also the story of an anachronism. The characters in A WORLD ENDS live in isolation from reality with useless and artificial values, which, even if they once did, no longer have meaning in the present. There is a kind of horror in their juxtaposition to reality. It is a dead world; it has long since disappeared. Humanity cannot survive in the present by attempting to escape through recreating the values and environment of past eras. Such is the life Faulkner portrays in "A Rose for Emily." Emily lives in a dead past that becomes repugnant. Both stories are told in a very matter-of-fact way with subtly controlled irony. Neither of the narrators is fully aware of the implications of the stories they tell. In both cases, this use of the innocent narrator provides the tension between what we see and what we feel.

Hildesheimer's story recalls other stories dealing with obsessed individuals and the consequences of that obsession and neglect of the commonplace realities of everyday life, such as we find in Edgar Allan Poe's "The Fall of the House of Usher," in which Roderick Usher's house, like the Marchesa's palace, cracks down the middle and sinks into the tarn. Both stories build up to the time when the obsession reaches the point beyond which the real world of everyday experience can continue to exist.

Also comparable in subject matter is the work of the surrealist Paul Delvaux, particularly his painting *Venus Asleep* (1944), in which he also juxtaposes the past and the present, emphasizing their incongruity as he portrays the contrast between the agitated figures in the background and the languid calm of Venus in the foreground. The agitation, which Delvaux explained was related to the bombing of Brussels in 1944, is muted, and the skeleton and black-clothed dressmaker's dummy, dressed in the style of an earlier period, watch over the sleeping Venus showing no emotion. The dreaming classical town, with its temples lit by the moon, and the building with horses' heads that the artist took from the old Royal Circus at Brussels are sufficiently removed from the real world to show no evidence of its destructive realities. Like the world of the story, this world is one of false environment and escape. But here the agitation of the real world is alluded to, whereas in the story we see only the sterility and superficiality of the dream as it disappears. Hildesheimer's satire with grotesque and surrealistic distortion can be compared to many of George Grosz's paintings, such as *Pillars of Society* (1926), in which we see a town in flames while groups of men fight for their obsessive, destructive ideals. — R H M

HUBER, HEINZ. THE NEW APARTMENT.

Germany
Great Modern European Short Stories. Greenwich, CT: Fawcett, 1967.
Translated by Christopher Holme.

Author: Heinz Huber (1922–) was born in Württemberg and grew up in a village in the Black Forest. He studied applied graphics in Stuttgart and then went into military service, during which he was a prisoner of war. Released in 1947, he took a job as a window decorator for a chain of grocery stores and began writing short stories and radio plays, which were successfully produced. In 1953, Huber became a TV director for documentary features in Stuttgart. In 1963, he published *The Third Reich,* a two-volume work containing his written documentaries and several of his short stories.

Story: The narrator and his wife are invited to the apartment of Marx Messemer and his wife to spend an evening together. The narrator sees this kind of social gathering as "the development of a form of society . . . which is adapted to our changed environment. When we began, there was no social intercourse and no society. Our grandparents were dead, our parents had made a mess of things. . . . A zero-point situation as the literary periodicals called it." Now having started up again, they are busily making money and moving into new apartments.

The narrator admires Messemer's taste, especially the "infallible modernity" that has gone into the details of his apartment. His own is not quite so nice nor in such perfect condition, but he plans to achieve that condition soon. Everything is "carefully matched" here, even to the point of guests' rearranging themselves to sit on a sofa whose color is harmonious with their garments.

Everything is proper, in contrast to the tenants who occupied the apartment when Messemer bought it. They were two elderly women, one a widow of an artist with a great deal of furniture who lived with memories of her past until she died and another whose husband had disappeared in the Third Reich and whose possessions were buried under "a regular mountain of birdseed," with which she fed the birds who constantly flew in and out of the room. They were both quite opposite from the Messemers, who, after sharing the apartment with the latter, arranged to have her removed and sent to an old people's home so that they could take full possession of the apartment. They did everything they could to clean it up, but "only in the one room we simply cannot altogether get rid of the birdseed."

Comparison: The use of the apartment as a metaphor for the new, sterile, industrial Germany that attempted to wipe out and even deny the "mess" created by the previous generation can be compared to Hildesheimer's use of the island in his story A WORLD ENDS. Both the island and the apartment represent isolated societies that have been artificially created in order to avoid the responsibilities of reality. Both are treated with sharp satire, and both, although described as particular places, have clear universal implications. Yet while we see the demise of the island, the apartment has become the model for the future. It is the narrator's ideal, and from that standpoint, it is even more horrifying than its counterpart. In addition, Hildesheimer's ironic humor perhaps eases the impact of his story, whereas Huber's unrelieved portrayal of the inhumanity and sterility of the new society becomes more and more frightening. In spite of the concerted effort to rid the apartment of the birdseed that nourishes nature and helps to sustain life, some of it keeps appearing in the cracks in the floor. But they will keep trying until only the banal and sterile survive and all the "disorder" and reminders of past life and history have disappeared. The narrator's point of view is interesting. He aspires to the same goals as Messemer, but one wonders if he might have the faintest insight that perhaps it isn't all as it might be when he says, "Messemer now had really gone a bit too far, for an ordinary party." In fact, "for some reason or other," he

himself hasn't quite got around to getting himself "properly fixed up."

This story can also be compared to Thomas Mann's DISORDER AND EARLY SORROW, which portrays the conflict involved with a sudden and dramatic change in values and lifestyles. Mann's story focuses on a professor's nostalgia and a yearning for the stability of the past, whereas the characters in THE NEW APARTMENT have attempted to cut themselves completely off from the past. THE NEW APARTMENT shows that by attempting to rid itself of its history, a society becomes superficial and sterile.

This is also a theme in Graham Greene's story "The Destructors," in which a house built by Christopher Wren represents the rational, balanced, elegant, and restrained aspect of the past, "an apt representation of the older English social order" and the product of meticulous and sophisticated craftsmanship. Having withstood a multitude of attacks from the enemy, the house is, after the war, destroyed from within by the new generation of those who worship "things" with no respect for the beauty of the past—the birdseed, so to speak, of THE NEW APARTMENT. The house receives its final blow from a motor vehicle, a product and symbol of the mechanical world. — R H M

IDRIS, YOUSSEF. THE CHEAPEST NIGHT'S ENTERTAINMENT.

Egypt
Modern Arabic Short Stories. New York: Three Continents, 1976.
Translated by Denys Johnson-Davies.

Author: Youssef Idris (1927–) is equally famous in Egypt as a dramatist and short story writer. He first gained attention with THE CHEAPEST NIGHT'S ENTERTAINMENT and published his first collection of stories in August 1954 under that title. Trained as a medical doctor, Idris served as a physician and health inspector in the rural Egyptian region of Sharkyia, the traditional land of Goshen. Many of his stories explore the social reality of modern Egyptian villages, often in an ironic and humorous manner. Briefly a Marxist, Idris retains in his writing a concern with social classes and the effects of the

Egyptian Revolution of 1952 in ordinary people's lives.

Story: Abdel-Karim, the simple, illiterate villager in Idris's story, is an amusing grotesque. His physical appearance is comically grotesque—"long nose, hooked and black-pitted . . . brass-yellow face . . . tips of his moustache ran parallel to the tops of his eyebrows where a few drops of water still hung, left over from his ablutions"—and his blustering anger is absurdly out of proportion to its provocation: his inability to purchase an evening's entertainment

80

because he hasn't a single piastre. The cheapest night's entertainment he does manage to receive is merely a glass of strong tea from the village's night watchman. Throughout the story, Abdel-Karim curses the watchman's hospitality because, as we later discover, the ironic outlet for the tea's stimulation will be Abdel-Karim's reluctant sexual relations with his lethargic wife.

One value of the story is its graphic portrayal of Egyptian village life. We first see Abdel-Karim enraged by the swarm of children in the village's narrow streets. They tease and torment him while he curses the plague of overpopulation in his land, gaining a moment's peace only by thinking of the starvation and cholera that will likely thin the ranks of these brats. Ironically, he is himself the father of six children. Escaping the children, he walks through the village until he reaches its center, a fetid waste ground surrounding a pond—actually an open public latrine—ringed by low, grey, mud huts with heaps of manure stretching before each of them "like long-neglected graves."

While Abdel-Karim stands in this stench, he imagines the village pleasures beyond his means tonight: coffee and a hookah at Abdul-Isaad's shop with card games, gossip, and radio programs; a wedding at Balabsa's farm with "dancing, lute-playing, jollification of every sort." One particularly revealing village pleasure that he regrets missing is an evening's conversation with Sheikh Abdel-Megid, during which the Sheikh might recall the revolution of 1952 ("the nights that had turned his hair grey") and his repentance since then "of his former swindles and robberies and his arsoning of other people's crops." But Abdel-Karim cannot seek out the Sheikh because the day before he had disputed the cost of a water wheel repair with him and pushed him down the well shaft in his anger.

With the village's entertainments beyond his reach, Abdel-Karim fantasizes about a warm welcome by his wife: she lights a lamp for him, toasts bread, and prepares leftovers while he sits complacently "like the greatest sultan of his time." The truth that he must admit, though, is that his wife "slept like a sack of grain with her six offspring strewn around her in a huddle like pups," that any leftovers have long since been eaten, and "that there was nei-

ther helba, nor sugar, nor anything at all at home— praise be to God all the same!"

At story's end, Abdel-Karim walks resignedly into his squalid home and roughly rouses his wife to a half-waking state. Then—after a long passage of time signaled by three asterisks—"the women were congratulating him on the birth of another boy, while he was consoling with himself upon the addition of yet a seventh child."

Comparison: For an American reader, the characters in Idris's stories, exemplified by the central character in THE CHEAPEST NIGHT'S ENTERTAINMENT, resemble the "grotesques" in Sherwood Anderson's *Winesburg, Ohio.* As Anderson explains in his preface, each grotesque is distorted by his obsessive hold on a partial truth, yet "grotesques were not all horrible. Some were amusing, some almost beautiful." From *Winesburg, Ohio,* Anderson's character studies in "Hands," "Adventure," and "Queer" offer especially good comparisons to the sympathetic grotesque Abdel-Karim.

Anderson stands in a long tradition in American literature of humorous portraits of small town and rural oddities, any number of which would be apt comparisons with THE CHEAPEST NIGHT'S ENTERTAINMENT. Flannery O'Connor's "The Life You Save May Be Your Own" and Eudora Welty's "Petrified Man" and "Why I Live at the P.O." are masterpieces in this comic genre. In them, we find the same exaggerations of personal quirks and elaboration of comic obsessions as in the portrait of Abdel-Karim. Less well known than the stories of O'Connor and Welty is the marvelous gallery of village characters in Zora Neale Hurston's *The Eatonville Anthology,* set in a small, isolated black community in rural Florida during the 1910s and 1920s.

Other American village and rural character studies that would make good comparisons with Idris's story are Hamlin Garland's "Mrs. Ripley's Trip," Sarah Orne Jewett's "The Town Poor," and Mary Wilkins Freeman's "A Village Singer." Short stories by Anton Chekhov, Isaac B. Singer, and Bernard Malamud also explore the humanity of odd characters in villages or urban ghettoes. Singer's "Gimpel the Fool" would be a good choice for comparison on the themes of marriage and responsibility.   — J D M

Izgü, Muzaffer. WANTED: A TOWN WITHOUT A CRAZY.

Turkey

Short Story International. February 1993. Translated by Joseph S. Jacobson.

Author: Muzaffer Izgü (1933–) was born into a poor family in Adana, Turkey. After working his way through school and graduating from the Institute of Education, he taught in several different areas of Turkey. He writes both children's stories and stories for adults and also writes plays for stage and radio. His work has gained international recognition and is frequently anthologized. Among the awards he has received are the International Golden Hedgehog Award (Bulgaria, 1978), the Turkish Language Society Short Story Award (1978), and the International Folk Tale Award (Bulgaria, 1978).

Story: "Wanted: A Town Without a Crazy" is the ironic story of a man who pretends to be other than he is in order to find success and happiness. Hilmi Bey has established himself as a town lunatic. He spends his days entertaining the townspeople with inane antics, nonsensical talk, and outlandish garb. The townspeople provide him with food and drink, even allowing him to eat, without paying, in the finest restaurants. He is also supplied with money, expensive cigarettes, clothing, health care, and the mayor's personal attention. Believing in his authenticity, "the people are so happy at finding a loony that they don't even ask who or what he is or even where he comes from." Every month, Hilmi Bey disappears from town for a few days, at which time he visits his wife and children, who live very well on the money and valuable items he frequently sends them.

One day, a visitor recognizes Bey as a former co-worker in the civil service. Bey had resigned the service because it paid so poorly and offered no hope for a better life. His resignation had freed him to search for a town in need of a resident madman.

When he found his present place of residence, he settled in. His former co-worker cannot understand Bey's behavior, asking, "When are you going to put an end to this lunacy?" Bey responds, "Are you nuts?" So, at the story's end, Hilmi Bey has no intention of leaving this wonderfully easy, successful life that he has established for himself and in which he has found such great satisfaction.

Comparison: This story is a social commentary, one that views mundane, repetitive, unfulfilling work as meaningless. The same observation is evident in THE METAMORPHOSIS by Franz Kafka, illustrating the "insectification" of the individual victimized by industrialization. In "For What Is Man?" from Thomas Wolfe's novel *You Can't Go Home Again,* work like Hilmi's civil service job is referred to as "sterile labor," a phrase reminiscent of Thoreau's *Walden,* particularly the chapter entitled "Where I Lived and What I Lived For." Thoreau comments on the nature of work: "We haven't any of any importance." Hilmi Bey appears to have discovered this "truth," an inkling of which the reader perceives not only from Gregor in THE METAMORPHOSIS, but also from Bartleby in Melville's "Bartleby the Scrivener."

The attraction that Bey holds for the people of the town, especially the children who amass as he exits the bus, is akin to that of the title character in *The Pied Piper of Hamelin.* The belief of the townspeople that "he brings good luck" can be likened to the film *Pocketful of Miracles,* in which a gangster, Dave the Dude, refuses to start his day without purchasing an apple from one of the city's derelicts, Apple Annie. In this sense, WANTED: A TOWN WITHOUT A CRAZY provides insight into human reliance on superstition.   — J A G

KAFKA, FRANZ. A HUNGER ARTIST.

Czech Republic
Literature: The Human Experience. 3d ed. New York: St. Martin's Press, 1982.
Translated by Edwin and Willa Muir.

Author: Franz Kafka (1883–1924), the son of a well-to-do middle-class Jewish merchant, was born in Prague, then an important town in the Austro-Hungarian Empire. He studied at the German university in Prague and obtained a law degree in 1906 and then worked for an insurance company. A sense of his own inadequacy in adjusting to life was emphasized by the contrast he continually made with his father's success in both business and his home life. The resulting sense of guilt was further augmented by the social pressures he experienced as a Jew. Although he never married, he lived with Dora Dymant, a Hebrew scholar and successful actress. He wrote several novels, including *The Trial* (1925) and *The Castle* (1926) and many volumes of short stories, the most famous of which are THE METAMOR-PHOSIS (1912), THE JUDGMENT (1913), and IN THE PENAL COLONY (1919). He died of tuberculosis, from which he suffered throughout his life.

Story: People in the town are fascinated by the Hunger Artist, who is kept in a cage for people to marvel at. Watchers are hired to make sure that he does not break his fast, and that suspicion becomes a source of misery for him. Ultimately, he is the only one who could know how religiously he keeps his fast, and he is also the only one who knows how easy it is to keep it. He is allowed to keep it for only forty days. That is as long as people's interest lasts, after which he is made to leave his cage, effect a scene of imminent collapse, and then eat to save himself. The artist would prefer to keep his fast longer to demonstrate both his uniqueness and the full extent of his art, but his impresario, interested only in financial gain, does not allow it. The artist is particularly upset by the perversion of truth when the impresario shows photographs to prove that, although the artist says he can fast beyond the forty days, he is "almost dead from exhaustion." Thus, "what was a consequence of the premature ending of his fast was here presented as the cause of it! To

fight against this lack of understanding, against a whole world of non-understanding, was impossible." Suddenly, however, there seems to be a general revulsion from professional fasting. Too old to find another profession, the Hunger Artist is also "too frantically devoted to fasting" to do anything else.

Finally employed by a large circus, he promises "to astound the world by establishing a record never yet achieved." Requesting that his cage be situated near the animals where the largest crowds come, he is dismayed to find that the animals are a far greater attraction than he is. "He was only an impediment on the way to the menagerie," and gradually no one pays any attention to him. One day, the attendants decide to clean the cage and find him among the straw. He tells them his secret: there is no reason to admire his fasting "because I have to fast. . . . I couldn't find the food I liked. If I had . . . I should have made no fuss and stuffed myself like you or anyone else." After his death, a panther replaces him in his cage and becomes a major attraction because it exudes a passionate joy for physical life.

Comparison: An obvious comparison exists with Aichinger's story THE BOUND MAN, which is also based on an outrageous premise from which everything else follows logically. Both stories are concerned with the artist's relationship to the audience and the commercial exploitation of art. The spiritual and redemptive function of the artist in the twentieth century has been replaced by the empty materialistic values of an insensitive society from which the artist is necessarily alienated.

Like the Bound Man, the Hunger Artist achieves a certain freedom. By starving himself in front of an audience, separated by the bars of his cage, he gains a kind of liberty from those aspects of life that affect everyone else. His hunger strikes, like the ropes of the Bound Man, represent a will to power. Ultimately, in Kafka's story, the spirituality of the artist is replaced by the physical joy and fleshly interests symbolized by the panther, just as that of the Bound Man is destroyed by the imposition of those who do not understand him. The plight of the artist in the modern world is a theme also found in many stories of Thomas Mann, particularly TRISTAN, in which mundane life once again triumphs over art.

Considered as a fable, Kafka's story can also be compared to Ursula K. Le Guin's science-fiction story "The Ones Who Walk Away from Omelas." Although the central character here is not treated as an individual, while Kafka's character is, both fables suggest a lesson: Le Guin's that no society should rest on the misery of the unfortunate and Kafka's that the world must begin to care more for spiritual than for physical values. Both stories center on imprisoned and isolated souls.

One is also reminded of O'Neil's image at the end of his play *The Hairy Ape,* when Yank enters the ape's cage and the ape triumphantly destroys him, reminiscent of the Hunger Artist's being replaced by the panther. Another comparison can be made with Ionesco's play *Rhinoceros,* which also suggests that society turns away from the complexities and philosophical concerns of life to a more bestial level of existence. — R H M

Kafka, Franz. IN THE PENAL COLONY.

Czech Republic

Franz Kafka: The Complete Stories. New York: Schocken, 1948. Translated by Willa and Edwin Muir.

Author: See A HUNGER ARTIST.

Story: IN THE PENAL COLONY is a macabre, gripping story about dedicated devotion to rigid standards, punishment, and execution and change from old ways to new. These themes are developed by concentrating attention on the death machine and the marvels of its operation. The reader, like the explorer, a central character, is told that they do not make machines like this one anymore. But while the aging torture-killing device holds our primary attention, there is also the condemned man and a total lack of consideration for him. He neither speaks nor understands the language spoken here, and he is not aware of having committed any crime. Neither the explorer nor the reader has any reason to consider him a criminal. He has had no trial, not even the suggestion of one, and he is unaware of any sentence. Calmly, he "hears" how the intricate machine will take his life without either understanding what is being said or knowing that he is to be its victim.

The story is told simply and directly. It speaks to the intellect, not to the emotions. Our attention is directed and redirected to the complex machine, with its metal spikes and movable "bed," its innumerable cogs and its precise needles, which will inscribe the punishment on the body of the victim. Will it function properly, as the "old commandant" painstakingly developed it to do, or, in accord with the "new commandant's" way of doing things, will it *not* do its duty? The suspense is measured, muted—and strengthened—by the matter-of-fact telling. No dramatic turn of events saves the prisoner. The machine simply does not work and therefore does not score the prisoner to a bloody death.

Soon another crisis develops. The officer who operated the machine and who took deep pride in its execution of death sentences realizes that the famous explorer opposes this style of execution and will therefore not oppose the methods of the new commandant. There can never be a return to the old style of justice. He looks for the appropriate sheet among the revered parchments that the old commandant had prepared to control the machine. He sets the design to inscribe the words "Be Just." Then he sets the machine to his own measurements. It does its horrible work on the officer's naked body. In doing so, it self-destructs.

Comparison: For the use of the bizarre as commonplace as well as for unusual sentencing and execution, Shirley Jackson's "The Lottery" comes to mind. Both stories are told with a carefully controlled objectivity in the narration. Both stories pass judgment about our society, and both show the conflict between tradition and progress. Both stories build up a considerable suspense, and the black box of the Jackson story can be seen to have some symbolic aspects similar to those of the machine in Kafka's. Both are certainly studies of the blind spots in a society dominated by unexamined tradition. One might compare what changes the stories suggest and how, in each case, those changes would or would not be an improvement. Other Kafka stories, such as THE METAMORPHOSIS, share many of the same storytelling devices, and their allegorical or symbolic suggestions would make interesting comparative studies.

Several surrealist artists have used the symbol of the machine to make a commentary on society. One thinks, for example, of the various works by Marcel Duchamps, particularly "The Big Glass," in which he shows the mechanical world and its accompanying loss of humanity. Fernand Léger's paintings are also filled with the machinery of the city, but he reveals the beauty of the machine as well as the power of the inhuman. For Léger, the machine conveys a feeling of strength and power. The machine in Kafka's story suggests an interesting comparison.   — H J   a n d   R H M

Kafka, Franz. THE JUDGMENT.

Czech Republic

Franz Kafka: The Complete Stories. New York: Schocken, 1948. Translated by Willa and Edwin Muir.

Author: See A HUNGER ARTIST.

Story: THE JUDGMENT is, like Kafka's other stories, strange and compelling. It stimulates the imagination and challenges the reader to accept it, even though— or perhaps because—it is outlandish. At the same time, it reads like a simple, straightforward narrative.

The central figure, Georg, is trapped by forces from which there is no escape: his unnamed friend, his bride-to-be Frieda, his father, and the memory of his mother. The friend, a businessman whose business in St. Petersburg is not doing well, rarely returns home. Georg has found it tactful to write to him only of hometown trivia and avoids telling his friend of his upcoming marriage to Fräulein Frieda Brandenfeld. She insists, however, that she has a right to meet all of his friends, so Georg writes to him of his happiness, taking care that his friend will not feel compelled to return home for the wedding.

With letter in hand, Georg goes to his father's room. Father and son have occupied the house alone since the death of the wife and mother three years ago. Georg has attempted to take care of his father, but he becomes self-recriminating when he notices that his father's underclothing is not as clean as it should be. The two see each other daily in the business his father had established; they even have lunch together. Business, we learn, has increased greatly since Georg took over. Now, upon entering the bedroom, Georg is struck by its darkness. Even the window is closed on this fine day. Knowing that the old man needs rest, Georg proposes that his father change rooms with him. He carries him bodily to bed and covers him, noticing that he is "still a giant of a man."

Then, with no warning, the father accuses the son of really wanting to cover him up. First, he tells Georg that there is no such person as his friend in St. Petersburg, but later acknowledges that he has himself kept in touch with the friend, who he feels has been a better son to him than Georg has been. The father also belittles his son by mimicking Frieda, who, he says, got Georg by lifting her skirts. He says that he, the father, has in his own pocket all the business Georg thought he got. Then the father actually sentences his son to death by drowning. Georg drowns himself, still declaring the constancy of his love for his parents. Traffic moves right along over the bridge from which he fell. The splash of his body goes unnoticed.

Comparison: For other stories in which the commonplace becomes bizarre or the bizarre commonplace, Kafka himself offers the best comparisons, and most of his stories and novels would qualify: for example, THE METAMORPHOSIS, A HUNGER ARTIST, *The Trial,* and *The Castle.* For unusual relations between father and son, there is Prosper Mérimée's "Mateo Falcone," which demonstrates an unhappy relationship between father and son. Of course, the story of the prodigal son in the New Testament and Gide's THE RETURN OF THE PRODIGAL SON tell the most famous of the father-son stories.

Two prominent themes in this story remind one of Willa Cather's "Paul's Case." Each of the stories ends with the death of a sensitive young man who—although for different reasons—cannot live in the world in which he is entrapped. In both stories, the relationship each young man has with his family is vital to the outcome of his life. A focus for comparison is the question of inevitability: to what extent do the suicides seem inevitable from the beginning of the story? The theme of isolation from society is also a focus in both stories. Each of these men is misunderstood, but each is isolated from those around him for different reasons. A comparison of the effects of their deaths on the world they leave behind would be valuable. One might wonder if, in either or both cases, there is evidence that the death is more symbolic than actual. — H J and R H M

KAFKA, FRANZ. THE METAMORPHOSIS.

Czech Republic

Franz Kafka: The Complete Stories. New York: Schocken, 1948. Translated by Willa and Edwin Muir.

Author: See A HUNGER ARTIST.

Story: Gregor Samsa is a commercial salesman and the sole support of his bankrupt, self-pitying, semi-invalid father, his weak mother, and his artistic and refined sister. One morning, Gregor awakens to find himself flat on his hard-shelled back, waving insect legs in the air—metamorphosed. Still able to speak in a near-human voice and to move and think in a semi-human fashion, he tries to approach his parents and sister in despair and grief but meets with misunderstanding, disgust, and hatred. It is as if his metamorphosis disclosed what his family had actually thought of him behind the veil of convention. Gradually, Gregor deteriorates, losing his human faculties and acquiring increasingly those of the insect, yet still pitiably conscious of his plight, still attempting to communicate, still trying to show tact and consideration. Locked in his room and fed the garbage he craves, he crawls on the ceiling, cherishes a few human mementos, and resigns himself. When he inadvertently enters the family living room, his enraged father throws apples at him. One of them penetrates the hard shell of his back, hangs and rots there, and brings on his slow death. One day, the chambermaid pokes him with her broom, finds Gregor dead, and disposes of him in the dustbin. The family, greatly relieved of the embarrassing situation, goes out for a celebrative excursion in the country. While one automatically thinks of the metamorphosis as taking place in Gregor, the changes in the members of his family are equally important.

Comparison: In his play *Rhinoceros,* Ionesco shows an entire community undergoing a transformation in which, as in Kafka's story, a lower order emerges to be compared with the supposedly preferable human level. Other works of modern literature that point out the weaknesses of humans through animal characters are George Orwell's *Animal Farm,* Karel Čapek's *War with the Newts,* and Mikhail Bulgakov's *The Heart of a Dog.* Some older works also use the device of transformation. Ovid's *Metamorphoses* plays on such changes but without the grimness and realism of Kafka's treatment. Apuleius's picaresque *The Golden Ass* jovially recounts the misadventures of a man who is turned into a donkey with all of his mental faculties intact, but he does not suffer the insectival deterioration

that gives Kafka's tale its shuddering poignancy. Kafka's theme of extreme human alienation is also evident in A HUNGER ARTIST and *The Trial*. — taken from *Guide to World Literature* (NCTE, 1980)

Kapadia, Kundanika. PAPER BOAT.

India
Modern Indian Short Stories. New Delhi: Indian Council for Cultural Relations, 1976.
Translated by Usha R. Sheth.

Author: Born in Rampur, Kundanika Kapadia (1927–) studied political science at Baroda University. She published her first collection of short stories in 1954. Her literary output includes three short story collections, two novels, and numerous essays. In addition to editing a monthly journal, she published a journal of her own from 1956 to 1958.

Story: In a pause between heavy rains, two boys go out to collect cow dung. When they see rains coming again, they run. Suddenly, Jeeva feels a bite on his foot. Taniyo, realizing the wound is lethal, hopes Jeeva will not recognize it as a snake bite. As they struggle toward the village to get help, Taniyo tries to keep Jeeva awake. The poison works quickly up his leg to his waist, throat, and eyes. Frantic but not knowing what to do, Taniyo tries to tell stories to keep Jeeva alert, but he cannot think of any story without reference to snakes. Jeeva's eyes turn blank.

In a panic, Taniyo tries to carry him and then begs him to walk, promising they will never go to the forest again for fear of snakes. At the word "snake," a sudden realization comes to Jeeva. With the riddle of his affliction solved, he closes his eyes and dies.

Comparison: Simply and poignantly told, this story can be used in conjunction with any story on death, friendship, realization, and initiation. A realization through some initiatory event that shifts the protagonist's perspective can be found in such stories as "Through the Tunnel" by Doris Lessing and "Araby" by James Joyce. Jerry, in "Through the Tunnel," sheds his childish outlook after he trains himself to do what big boys have done in swimming through a long tunnel, nearly dying in the attempt. In "Araby," the boy narrator "saw himself as a creature driven and derided by vanity" with his disappointing excursion to the bazaar, which he had held as a dream for so long.   — M L

Kariara, Jonathan. HER WARRIOR.

Kenya
Modern African Prose. London: Heinemann, 1964.

Author: Jonathan Kariara is a Kikuyu from Kenya. He attended the University College of Makerere in Uganda, where he received an honors degree in English. He has served on the staff of the East African Literature Bureau in Nairobi.

Story: HER WARRIOR is a simply told story about tribal taboos and the hard times that befall those who violate them. It is told in the first person by a grandson mystified by his grandparents' relationship. His grandmother "was not like other children's grandmothers. . . . Grandmother lived three hills away, which was inexplicable." Even more mysterious to the grandson is the fact that his grandmother "never mentioned her husband. If ever she heard any of us refer to him she would instantly snort and push away any small object near her with an impatient sweep of her long arm. . . . She had been insulted." The story begins near the end: Grandfather is dying, and Grandmother has been summoned. At last, the history of these two people can be told to the younger generation.

Grandfather Wanyoike had been a great Kikuyu warrior. Shortly after his marriage to Grandmother, Wanyoike had led the Kikuyu in a war against the Masai tribe. When the Kikuyu appeared to be losing, Wanyoike "was blind with anger. For days he had fought, never uttering a word, but as the conviction grew that they would lose the battle his anger grew into such a frenzied hatred of the Masai that he would do anything to see them retreat. Next day he did the unexpected, the unprecedented." He did a thing that would ban him from his tribe forever: he chopped the arm off a dead Kikuyu warrior and "waving it aloft, he charged into a group of Masai warriors, striking right and left with the dead man's arm." The reaction was stupendous: "And fear spread among them, a primeval fear of warm blood coming in contact with the disintegrating dead. One after the other they let out a cry, the inhuman cry of a trapped wild animal. It spread like fire with a wind behind it; it echoed in every warrior, Kikuyu or Masai, so that the Kikuyu paused, paralysed with fear, and the Masai, afraid of 'evil-let-loose,' took to flight." The Kikuyu won the war, but never again would Wanyoike be accepted as a member of the tribe, an equal of other men: "Once the victory was won they were all afraid of him. Deadly afraid. Many of them said later that they all wanted to be religiously cleansed after that battle, although they should have been singing victorious. . . . Wanyoike crept back to his young wife, afraid of himself."

Ostracism from society led to arguments and, finally, to bitter quarrels between husband and wife.

Wanyoike hoped to rejoin the tribe; his wife wanted to seek revenge for having been cast out. "Their fights were still and terrible, like quicksands, each keen to destroy the other. Then one day he decided they could not live together and soon after built her a hut where she now lives. He never called her back but something went out of him with her departure." Bitter though their relationship was, it nevertheless gave to the two old people a shared history, a reason for defiance against the rest of the world and each other—a reason to live. When Wanyoike dies at the end of the story, there is no longer a source for Grandmother's proud disdain: "Something, as it were, snapped in the very core of her being. . . . She was no longer a proud old lady. She was a tottering old woman who would from now on sit outside her hut, looking at the horizon."

Comparison: Superstition evoked by proximity to death, or even more strongly by the proximity of the dead, is evident in such popular works of fiction as William Golding's *The Lord of the Flies,* Joseph Conrad's *Heart of Darkness,* and Edgar Allan Poe's "The Masque of the Red Death." In all of these works, as in HER WARRIOR, the presence of death throws living people into fits of ungovernable horror. In many stories, such as *The Lord of the Flies,* people in such a state are shown to revert to a more "natural" state, to become more like hunted—or hunting—animals than like "civilized" humans. Such is not the case in HER WARRIOR, however. Even though the society of the story could be described as primitive, the horror of being touched by the blood of the dead terrifies the warriors into seeking "cleansing" through a "civilized" ritual, much like those that exist in the practices of many modern religions.

Other examples of the power of social ostracism to destroy the human spirit can be found in VENGEFUL CREDITOR by Chinua Achebe, *Black Boy* by Richard Wright, "Paul's Case" by Willa Cather, and "Miss Brill" by Katherine Mansfield.

— B H N

KAWABATA YASUNARI. THE JAY.

Japan

World Writers Today. Glenview, IL: ScottForesman, 1995. Translated by Lanc Dunlop and J. Martin Holman.

Author: Born near Osaka, Kawabata (1899–1972) was orphaned in infancy and lost his grandparents during his student years. His unusually lonely childhood, which taught him to understand sorrow, gave him a view of existence that was to pervade most of his mature works. His early ambition to be a painter was soon abandoned as he began to read Scandinavian and contemporary Japanese literature and become active in literary circles. Shortly after his graduation from Tokyo Imperial University in 1924, he started his own literary magazine. His early works reflected the influence of European writers, especially postwar French literature. His later works drew from the style of traditional Japanese prose and the *renga* (linked verse) of ancient Japan. Like this verse form, the power of his works comes in the links between brief lyrical episodes. Regarded as typically Japanese in tone and style, he nevertheless achieved widespread recognition for the universality of his writing. Some of Kawabata's best-known works include "The Izu Dancer" (1925), "The Mole" (1929), "Snow Country" (1947), "Thousand Cranes" (1959), and THE MOON ON THE WATER (1953). In 1968, he became Japan's first recipient of the Nobel Prize for Literature.

Story: While preparing for her wedding, Yoshiko hears a mother jay sing noisily. Later she finds a baby bird under the bush clover. She takes the weak baby into the house and gives it water. Revived, the baby starts to sing, and the mother responds by flying nearer to the house. Yoshiko places the baby outside on the ground and, from behind the glass door, observes the moment of reunion between mother and chick.

The story of the birds frames the story of Yoshiko, who has not seen her mother since Yoshiko was four, at which time her father had divorced her mother. Yoshiko accepts the marriage arranged for her by her father, and she is moved when her father asks the groom's mother to bring back the happy days of Yoshiko's childhood rather than treating her like a bride. She is also gladdened that her husband's household will become one with hers, for otherwise there would be no one to take care of her brother and grandmother.

Comparison: The metaphor of the mother jay and chick reflects the Asian emphasis on parent-child relationships and family structure. Yoshiko's father is concerned about recapturing the childhood that Yoshiko has missed, while Yoshiko herself wishes to preserve her natural family. This emphasis on the family bond is also seen in A DEVOTED SON by Anita Desai. Unfortunately, in that story, Rakesh's devotion to his father takes an extreme form, resulting in helpless misery for the ailing old man.   — M L

KAWABATA YASUNARI. THE MOON ON THE WATER.

Japan

Modern Japanese Stories: An Anthology. Rutland, VT: Charles E. Tuttle, 1980. Translated by George Saitō.

Author: See THE JAY.

Story: Kyoko's husband, a bedridden invalid, is given new life when Kyoko thinks to let him use her hand mirror to watch her work in the garden.

He had complained about not being able to get her attention to tell her things like "Did you hear the lark?" Sensing his loneliness, she eventually thinks of the mirror. In the reflection, the world is brought to him. He sees the sky, the snow, birds, men, and children. Working in the garden, Kyoko senses him watching every move she makes. Side by side with him, so intimate that he memorizes her fingerprints on the mirror, she shares a reflected world that she comes to regard as the more beautiful, the more perfect world. "The sky shines silver in the mirror," she says, when the sky is actually grey. She wonders how she looks to him in the mirror. Curious, she gazes into the mirror and realizes that one cannot see oneself unless one looks into a mirror. She concludes that one's face is not for oneself, but for others to see. Such is the situation in love. But then a horrible thought strikes her. Since her husband can constantly see his own face in the mirror, "perhaps it was more like seeing death itself. If his death was a psychological suicide by means of a mirror, then Kyoko was the psychological murderer."

The reflected world brims so full of love that in Kyoko's second marriage she has trouble dealing with the real details of life. Terrified by her pregnancy, she is on the verge of a nervous breakdown. Her doctors suggest hospitalization, before which, on the way to visit her parents' home, she stops by her first house. Outside it, she gazes at the real world that had been reflected in her husband's mirror and sees a curtain hung across his window. The ensuing thought that the child might resemble him gives her peace.

Comparison: The archetypal story of seeing oneself by reflection is, of course, the story of Narcissus. Like Narcissus, Kyoko is fascinated by her own image and contemplates the differences between what is reflected and what is real. Narcissus perishes by his inability to tear himself away from the pool, but Kyoko, after her husband dies and the mirror is put away, rejoins the world and deals with it.

In "The Secret Sharer," by Joseph Conrad, the narrator, a young sea captain, helps a naked swimmer on board, an incident that begins a relationship he describes in these words: "It was, in the night, as though I had been faced by my own reflection in the depths of a somber and immense mirror." Because the captain, who feels insecure about himself at the beginning of the story, helps the fugitive with whom he shares the most confidential relationship, he identifies with him and at the end gains self-confidence and mastery of his ship.

The minister in "The Strength of God," from *Winesburg, Ohio* by Sherwood Anderson, sees his own turmoil through a crack in the window at the belltower of his church. As though in a mirror, the world of Kate Swift, which arouses such passion in him, remains an unattainable projection. The only possible resolution for him in the end is to transfer what has been aroused in that world into his own ministry of the word of God.

Perhaps the most famous literary example of twinlike existences mirroring each other occurs in Oscar Wilde's *The Picture of Dorian Gray,* where the portrait reflects intimately the psychological changes in the protagonist. — M L

Kiwon So. THE HEIR.

Korea
Flowers of Fire: Twentieth Century Korean Stories. Honolulu: University of Hawaii Press, 1986.
Translated by Uchang Kim.

Author: Kiwon So (1930–) left the university to fight in the Korean War. In his literary debut in 1956, he graphically presented both the student soldier who failed to inspire a model of commitment and a postwar society teeming with contradictions. His writings about that period show that because the war did not inspire a sense of dedication, it caused a myriad of absurdities within postwar Korean life. These elements provide the psychological nuances within his characters, who live in a society devoid of hopes and dreams. A direct consequence of that societal collapse is the breakdown of the traditional values so cherished by Korean society.

Story: Sogun, a guest in his uncle's home, finishes reading to his middle-school-age cousin, Sokhui. Although Sokhui would like to attend school, she is forbidden to do so by their grandfather. Leaving his room, Sogun listens to his grandfather in conversation with a friend as the two discuss Sogun's father. The young man remembers the force of his father's grip just before he walked off to the gas chamber.

Sogun is keenly aware of his grandfather's hopes for him. He also knows full well that his dissolute life has hindered his studies and that his grandfather is making excuses for him. Stealing out to the barn behind his uncle's house, Sogun opens a paper chest containing a leather case holding trinkets and two milky-colored jade rings. He puts the rings in his pocket—weren't they lawfully his inheritance?—and leaves the barn.

A source of discomfort for Sogun at his uncle's home is his cousin Sokpae's epilepsy. Frightened by the first seizure he witnesses, which occurs at a family meal, Sogun jumps away from the table, but not before witnessing his grandfather's tears. Sokpae's father orders his son to be taken away from the table, but the old man retorts, "Is he not your son, sick as he is?" When Sogun has an opportunity to paint Sokpae's portrait, he marvels how much Sokpae's face resembles his own.

Another source of tension for Sogun is the periodic ritual for the dead that his grandfather, his grandfather's friend, and his family members hold for Sogun's father. As he watches from his place across from his grandfather, he is aware of the bluish incense smoke and the stink of fish and his father's warning not to spend money on such foolishness. When his grandfather ceremoniously hands him the brass wine cup, Sogun feigns a stomach ache and runs from the room. "How like his father," his grandfather murmurs after him.

The crisis occurs when *tori* beads, symbols of high office, are found to be missing. Grandfather blames the absent Sokpae. Search parties arrive and depart, and the monsoon rains begin. Sogun's aunt keens, almost ritualistically, "Oh, that I might be struck dead." In the morning, Sokpae's body is found. Sogun puts his inheritance and the jade rings in his pocket and, with the cries of Sokhui at his back, races down the road.

Comparison: The clash of old and new, city and country, youth and age, and male and female and the ennui stemming from alienation are all embodied in this story. Opening with a foreshadowing, the author suggests the male-female tension prevalent in a restrictive society. Such strictures as kowtowing, the horsehair headgear worn by the grandfather's friend, and, especially, the ceremonial sacrifices to the dead awaken loneliness and alienation in the urbane Sogun. As in Horace's ode about the city mouse and the country mouse, he wonders aloud about his plight. While he is still reeling from his father's death, his feelings of separation are augmented by the strange life in the country. His grandfather's hopes and excuses for his evident failure as a scholar just heighten the gulf. Like Holden Caulfield in *A Catcher in the Rye,* Sogun attempts to rid himself of these feelings by taking to the road. — D V D

KUNDERA, MILAN. NOBODY WILL LAUGH.

Czech Republic
Laughable Loves. New York: Knopf, 1974. Translated by Suzanne Rappaport.

Author: Milan Kundera (1929–), born in Brno, is the best-known Czech writer of his generation. He grew up in an intellectual household, studying literature, music, and film. At the age of forty, he published the first of his works to attract attention outside Poland, a novel entitled *The Joke,* about a student sentenced to hard labor for making a joke about Trotsky. Soon thereafter, his work was banned in his home country and he emigrated to France, where he still lives today. He has continued to write novels dealing with the tension between the political and private spheres of life, among them *Life Is*

Elsewhere (1974) and *The Farewell Party* (1976). His favorite subjects remain art, love, and human relationships. *The Unbearable Lightness of Being* (1984) has enjoyed the greatest popular success of all his novels and appeared as a film that was widely discussed. Kundera has always shown a special interest in the English versions of his works, as indicated most clearly by a reissue of *The Joke* in 1992 in an authorized version by Kundera himself.

Story: NOBODY WILL LAUGH is the comic story of a small white lie that grows to have major and unpleasant consequences. Mr. Klima, an art historian teaching at a college in Prague, has been asked to comment on another scholar's work. Not wanting to hurt the second man's feelings, but convinced that the essay is of no scholarly value, he manages to avoid writing his evaluation while still implying that he likes the work. The second scholar, Mr. Zaturetsky, begins to pester Klima for his report. Indeed, he becomes obsessed with obtaining it.

Klima's life becomes a series of evasive tactics to avoid Mr. Zaturetsky: he hides out in a secret apartment he shares with his girlfriend; he alters his teaching schedule without reporting it to the administration; he involves others in his attempt to escape notice. He falls deeper and deeper into a tissue of lies and misrepresentations, all minor, but increasingly upsetting to his girlfriend, the university administration, and Mr. Zaturetsky. Cornered at last, Klima is forced to admit the truth: that he finds the essay unacceptably bad and unworthy of publication. But it is too late. He is believed by no one.

The administration considers his evaluation to be motivated by envy and a petty desire for revenge, and his girlfriend sees his promises to her as lies as well. As the story ends, he has lost both his job and his girlfriend. His only comfort is the comic nature of his predicament.

Comparison: Milan Kundera is often compared to such international postmodernists as Borges and Calvino and such American writers as Robert Coover and John Barth. His work is humorous, self-reflective, and playful. At the same time, he is interested in deeper philosophical issues. In this story, the comic surface of the events is used as a springboard for brief but intriguing passages dealing with broader questions of the human condition. From exile, he writes stories that deal with a social reality in which the everyday effects of communism, bureaucracy, and class tensions are woven into the background fabric of the narrative. Not surprisingly, this story bears strong thematic similarities to several early twentieth-century works by Franz Kafka. Kafka, who wrote in German but lived all his life in Prague, portrays alienated heroes who, like Klima, gradually find themselves more and more deeply drawn into a web of events they can neither control nor understand. Kundera may also be fruitfully compared to any American author who deals with human alienation and hypocrisy and the way in which the line between the truth and a lie is often blurred. In a larger sense, Kundera's story is a parable of the human condition, where our smallest actions may set off a train of events beyond our control. — B M

LAGERKVIST, PÄR. FATHER AND I.

Sweden
17 from Everywhere: Short Stories by World Authors. New York: Bantam, 1971.

Author: Pär Lagerkvist (1891–1974) achieved fame as a poet, short story writer, novelist, and dramatist. Born in Sweden, he published a collection of poems and a novel, *People,* while still a student at Upsala University. He left the university for a stay in France, where he was deeply influenced by the cubist movement. The rest of his life's work echoes that influence, particularly *The Eternal Smile,* his collection of short stories.

As a poet, Lagerkvist was viewed as the Swedish equivalent to T. S. Eliot. He exerted a visible and lasting effect on Swedish poetry. His influence as a novelist was no less profound. Though he declared himself an atheist, his works are concerned with themes of morality, of good and evil in a changing world. Many of his books and plays are anti-Nazi in outlook and purpose. His novels *Barabbas, The Dwarf,* and *The Sybil* as well as his plays *The Invisible* and *The Man Without a Soul* received high praise, and in 1951 Lagerkvist was awarded the Nobel Prize for Literature.

Story: This dark and symbolic tale begins lightly enough, as a father and son enjoy strolling through sunlit woods, listening to the birds sing on a Sunday afternoon. The narrator is the son, a young boy who calls his father "Daddy" and who attributes to that Daddy all the strength and knowledge and assurance of the adult world. It is, in fact, a perfect day within a perfectly ordered universe.

But the day and mood change at sunset. The journey home must be made through the dark, forbidding forest, and the father seems insensitive to the ominous sounds and sights that the boy cannot ignore. To the son's question, "Why is it so creepy when it's dark?" the father simply counters, "No, child, it isn't creepy." The father then refers to the security of believing in God, but the reference to this mysterious God only increases the child's anxi-

ety: "The thought of God made one feel creepy, too. It was creepy to think that He was everywhere in the darkness, down there under the trees, and the telephone posts that mumbled so."

The boy's terror crescendos, as a phantom train suddenly bears down on them. In a masterful role reversal, however, it is the child who grasps the sense of the ghostly train, the father who hides his fear behind a casual questioning and dismissal of the event. The darkness ahead becomes the child's life ahead, his fate in the unknown future. The father's perfunctory acceptance appears now as blind ignorance, at best only a restatement of past experience. The future belongs to the child, and it is a future for which platitudes can offer little strength.

Comparison: FATHER AND I offers good opportunities for student reaction. In its classic portrayal of a naive narrator who possesses true insight, there are possibilities for comparison with Paul in D. H. Lawrence's "The Rocking Horse Winner" and Laura in Katherine Mansfield's "The Garden Party." Both of these characters hear the explanations and excuses offered by adults around them, yet both perceive the existence of higher truths that they cannot yet completely understand. — P G L

LAGERLÖF, SELMA. THE OUTLAWS.

Sweden

Great Stories by Nobel Prize Winners. New York: The Noonday Press, 1959. Translated by Pauline Bancroft Flach.

Author: Selma Lagerlöf (1858–1940) was the first woman to win the Nobel Prize for Literature. Born in Varmland, Sweden, she was teaching in a grammar school for girls when she decided to enter a writing contest sponsored by the queen. To her surprise, she won with a simple tale of the people and life she had known as a child. She was then inspired to give up her teaching career for a year to work on a collection of stories and folktales about her native province. The result, *Gosta Berling's Saga,* was an instant success. Within a year, she had produced a

second successful collection of stories, *Invisible Links,* based on the daily life of Swedish peasants. Writing thus became Lagerlöf's permanent career.

Lagerlöf is viewed as a storyteller supreme. Her tales are simple, warm, personal, magical, and religious all at once. Her book for children, *The Wonderful Adventures of Mils,* has long been considered a classic. She is equally praised by critics for her novel *Jerusalem,* about Swedish farmers who emigrate to the Holy Land, and for her autobiographical *Memories of My Childhood* and

Marbacka. She died at Marbacka, her childhood home.

Story: Two fugitives from justice—Berg, a rich peasant who has killed a monk to avenge the honor of his beautiful young cousin Unn, and Tord, a fisherboy who had been accused of stealing a herring net—fashion a life together, hidden deep in the woods, away from their pursuers. Sleeping in a cave, hunting for survival, the older man and the boy form an unlikely friendship as they learn the truth of each other's past and struggle to understand the laws of guilt and retribution. Berg becomes the mentor, the father, the hero Tord has missed in his life. But the enforced isolation of their existence drives Tord into delusions of religious paranoia. He will "save" Berg from the ultimate judgment of God by betraying him to the authorities now. Berg can then repent, be punished for his crime, and thus escape eternal damnation.

After the betrayal, even as vengeful peasants pursue an unsuspecting Berg, Tord cries out in his guilt, "For your sin, Death and all his specters follow me.... You have lifted your hand against God himself.... You compel me to betray you.... Save me from that Sin. Go to the priest." To Tord's amaze-

ment, Berg is moved by his young friend's pain: "He was measuring his sin against his friend's anguish, and it grew big and terrible before his soul. He saw himself at variance with the Will which rules the world. Repentance entered his heart." But as Tord then confesses his act of betrayal, Berg cries, "I have trusted you and loved you." As he bends to reach for his axe, Berg is struck and killed by Tord, whom the arriving peasants now honor as a hero. Tord is left to ponder the nature of justice in the world.

Comparison: Within THE OUTLAWS are intricately connected overtones of mythology, religion, and fantasy. Readers of Tolkien and Ursula K. LeGuin will find parallel points of discussion. Hawthorne's "Young Goodman Brown" and "The Minister's Black Veil" are definite suggestions for comparative study. In his pious rejection of the sinners around him, Young Goodman Brown struggles to honor religious principles, yet he fails to acknowledge his own human propensity for sin. He spends the rest of his life in bitterness and disillusionment. "The Minister's Black Veil" similarly addresses the question of physical as opposed to psychological sin. The minister's veil physically portrays the mental and emotional separation that a sinner must endure.   — P G L

La Guma, Alex. Blankets.

South Africa
A Walk in the Night and Other Stories. Evanston, IL: Northwestern University Press, 1967.

Author: Alex La Guma (1923–) was born in Cape Town, South Africa, and attended Trafalgar High School and Cape Technical College. He worked as a clerk, factory hand, bookkeeper, and journalist. Involved in South African politics, he was arrested for treason with 155 others in 1956 and acquitted in 1960. He was again detained, this time for five months, during the "state of emergency" following the Sharpeville massacre. La Guma left South Africa as a refugee in September 1966 and moved to London. He has published several novels, including *And a Threefold Cord.* His primary literary subject is the plight of nonwhites in South Africa.

Story: BLANKETS is a stream-of-consciousness story told from the view of Choker, a South African black man who has been stabbed three times and waits for an ambulance to transport him to a hospital. In three brief vignettes related through their association with blankets, the author conveys a sense of the sordidness of the lives of thousands of Chokers in South Africa's large cities.

The tone is established in the opening description of the lean-to in which Choker lies: "the sagging roof ... the pile of assorted junk in one corner; an ancient motor tire, sundry split and warped boxes, an old enamel display sign.... There was also the smell of dust and chicken droppings and urine." In that setting, the reader is prepared for the first blanket, used to cover Choker as he waits, which "smelled of sweat and having-been-slept-in-unwashed, and . . . torn and threadbare and stained." The statement that "he was used to blankets like this" provides a transition to other blankets remembered through Choker's semiconscious haze. He is reminded of his fumbling, fruitless search for "the thickest and warmest blankets" when he was admitted to prison. He ended up with two that "were filthy and smelly and within their folds vermin waited like irregular troops in ambush." The vision of a prison guard is transformed in his hazy consciousness into that of his older brother, and the memory changes to Choker's childhood and the brothers fighting over the "thin cotton blanket" on the "narrow, cramped, sagging bedstead" while "outside the rain slapped against the cardboard-patched window, and the wind wheezed through cracks and corners like an asthmatic old man." Again the scene changes, this time to Choker awakening with a woman in a bed that "smelled of a mixture of cheap perfume, spilled powder, human bodies and infant urine" to the sound of a baby crying, "its toothless voice rising in a high-pitched wail that grew louder and louder."

Choker regains full consciousness to the realization that the baby's wail is, in fact, the siren of the approaching ambulance. Gravely injured, probably about to die, Choker is treated by the medics with gentleness and dignity for the only time in his life.

As he lies in the ambulance, "his murderous fingers touched the folded edge of the bedding. The sheet around him was white as cocaine, and the blanket was thick and new and warm."

Comparison: The sordidness of Choker's life can be compared to the background of Bigger Thomas in Richard Wright's *Black Boy.* There is a contrast between the two works. La Guma, unlike Wright, does not present the relationship between the races as a contributing factor to the condition of poverty. The people are simply what they are, and La Guma casts no blame. The same contrast can be made between this story and the Achebe story VENGEFUL CREDITOR, in which the author clearly blames politicians for perpetuating the conditions under which the main character is forced to live.

The stream-of-consciousness approach to telling a story is available in several regularly anthologized American short stories, such as "The Jilting of Granny Weatherall" by Katherine Anne Porter. Yet the flashbacks in BLANKETS are easier to follow than those in Porter's more difficult story, which may make BLANKETS a good story to use to introduce the technique.

Finally, the framework narration employed by La Guma is also available in many of Melville's works, including "Billy Budd" and "Bartleby the Scrivener." A more complex application of the framework principle can be found in Salinger's "For Esmé—with Love and Squalor."   — B H N

LANDOLFI, TOMMASO. PASTORAL.

Italy
Form in Fiction. New York: St. Martin's, 1974. Translated by John Longrigg.

Author: Tommaso Landolfi (1908–1979) was born in the small town of Pico, Italy, not far from Rome. He was brought up in a Catholic boarding school. An intensely private man, he earned a Ph.D. in literature from the University of Florence and published his first collection of short stories in 1937. He was jailed as an anti-Fascist in World War II. During his literary career, he translated major works of nine-teenth-century Russian literature into Italian, contributed regularly to leading Italian magazines and was awarded a number of literary prizes. He lived variously in the small town of his birth, in Florence, in Venice, and on the Riviera, where he was able to enjoy his passion for gambling. Such diversity perhaps stems from the same fundamental qualities that made him one of Italy's most experimental and unique writers, often compared to Kafka and Borges, except that his writing is noted for its unusually humorous quality. PASTORAL was published in 1954.

Story: PASTORAL is an epistolary tale made up of five letters from Anne, recently moved from Paris to a castle in the provinces, to her close friend Solange, still in Paris. In the first of the letters, written in early autumn, she sings the praises "of the unsullied joys of country life, of this delicious new world" unmarred by the frenetic pace and expensive luxury of Paris. And she has already met a "young, dashing, romantic" landowner whose acquaintance may well develop into something closer.

The second letter, written in late fall, compares the preparations for hibernation taken in this rural area with those of Paris. Here "there are no *lits embaumés,* no ointments, no purging of blood or vapors, . . . none of the many operations usual at the *maisons de léthargie*" of Paris. Here the people are merely suspended in goatskin bags from the beams of their houses. Here everyone hibernates, whereas in Paris very few, practically no one known to the writer, do so.

The third letter, written during the onset of winter, indicates the repulsiveness of the rural method of hibernation to Anne. During her visits of charity to the peasants, she can "no longer keep count of the bags hanging from the beams." They "give off a foetid odor like bladders of lard, and soot is already gathering on their surfaces, for they are nearly all in the kitchens." Never having seen a hibernating human before, she finds the sight repellent, but concludes from her unsuccessful efforts to keep a young peasant boy from hibernating that the practice is somehow natural to the people among whom she now lives.

In the fourth letter, her tone shifts from repulsion to alarm: "I can no longer hide it either from myself or from you. An unbelievable number of people here have already fallen asleep. Wherever I go, I see nothing but hideous, foetid bags hanging from the ceilings." And to make matters worse, the young, dashing landowner she had mentioned in the first letter, at the very point when "the hour was propitious for our hearts to declare themselves," began falling asleep, indicating the onset of the hibernating impulse. By contrast, she imagines, "everything in Paris lives and trembles with movement."

The fifth and final letter, written in the dead of winter, betrays her genuine terror at everyone's having gone into hibernation. Solange, her friend, must rescue her: "I cannot prepare my food, I cannot do anything, there is nothing in the house, I am frightened of the horses . . . I shall die here if you do not save me."

Comparison: In its ironic opposition of the natural life of the countryside to the life of the city, as seen through the thoroughly citified eyes of a young woman brought up in high society, and in its thematic suggestion that those alienated by urban life from the natural realities of human life ironically find such realities unnatural and revolting, PASTORAL may be compared to J. K. Huysmans's *Against the Grain* (sometimes translated *Against Nature*), which expresses the decadent, *fin de siècle* distaste for things natural and glorifies the artifice associated with society. On the other hand, PASTORAL may be contrasted with the quite different perspective on the opposition of nature to culture offered by D. H. Lawrence's "The Horse Dealer's Daughter." In that story, the relatively urbane Jack Fergusson succumbs to the unconscious, quite natural erotic force of Mabel, despite his intentions to the contrary. That both stories focus on rebirth sharpens the contrast.

In its surrealistically graphic depiction of hibernation, the story may be compared with a number of paintings by René Magritte, such as *The Red Model* (1936), which similarly depict nonexistent "natural" realities, as well as paintings by Paul Delvaux, such as *The Sleeping City* (1938), which contrast the natural and the artificial from the perspective of an urban observer. — P T M

LAO SHE. GRANDMOTHER TAKES CHARGE.

China

Asian and Pacific Stories. Rutland, VT: Charles E. Tuttle, 1974. Translated by George Saitō.

Author: Lao She, pseudonym for Shu Ch'ing-ch'un (1899–1966), was born to a poverty-stricken Manchu family. A brilliant scholar, he taught school for a while and in 1924 went to England to teach Chinese at the University of London. Upon his return to China, he established his reputation as a novelist and wrote various kinds of patriotic literature to bring the nation to social and political awareness. His prolific writings were frequently scathing satires on the parties responsible for the welfare of the people, making him a friend of the Communist initiative. Later, however, he was branded as rightist and reactionary. At the height of the Cultural Revolution in 1966, the official news broadcast declared his death a suicide, but it is widely suspected that he was a victim of the misguided zeal of the Red Guards. His novels, *The City of Cats* and *Camel Hsiang-tzu,* were effective indictments of Chinese society.

Story: Old Mrs. Wang really wants to have a grandson. After all, what other purpose would there be to acquire a daughter-in-law? Unfortunately, both of the first two grandchildren died, so now that the daughter-in-law is pregnant again, Mrs. Wang wants to ensure that the child will be born alive and well. The pregnant mother plays no role except as a vehicle for birth. The young father is not important enough to mention. The maternal grandmother takes a back seat, as her daughter has become the property of the husband's family. So in all matters, Old Mrs. Wang dictates her will.

Her will is the will of mindless tradition and superstition. She stuffs the mother to feed the baby, whereupon the mother is rendered immobile. Then the fetus grows so large that it cannot be born. The crisis comes when it becomes apparent that Old Mrs. Wang has to swallow her pride, abandon tradition, and send the young mother to a hospital. Once there, two persons in charge have to sign a statement absolving the hospital of the responsibility for the fate of both mother and child. Old Mrs. Wang reveals herself to be not only ignorant and illiterate, but almost recalcitrantly resistant to healthy and scientific innovations from the West. Under pressure, she signs a release with an "X" and is temporarily elated to find herself rewarded with a thirteen-pound grandson delivered by Caesarean section.

The young mother is deathly ill. The doctors wish to keep mother and baby in the hospital, but again custom intervenes, and Old Mrs. Wang insists upon taking the baby home immediately. At last the doctors yield, and Old Mrs. Wang carries the baby home—triumphant, but not for long. For in the hospital, Old Mrs. Wang has caught a cold, and in sneezing on the precious bundle she greedily cradles, she overwhelms it with the germs from which it will die in a few days.

The story is a scathing satire on the ignorant Chinese masses in the early decades of the twentieth century, who, despite proof of the superiority of Western science and administrative tactics, adhered blindly to superstition and tradition—to their own detriment.

Comparison: Aside from the satire on the ignorant masses, this story hinges on a woman's almost neurotic sense of possessiveness over her progeny, which she destroys by her overindulgence. A familiar parallel can be found in the classical myth of Apollo and Phaethon, where, to make up for past negligence, Apollo gives his son anything he wants. Phaethon dies as a result of getting his gift.

A contemporary story, "A Visit to Grandmother" by William Kelley, tells of the same preoccupation. Here, a mother's favoritism, either unknown to herself or rationalized by her, causes one son to remain a perpetual child. Even at the age of fifty, he is footloose and irresponsible, sporting the "innocent smile of a five-year-old." The other son, shut out of the limelight, suffers the pain of rejection and feels bitterness and hatred all his life.   — M L

LAXNESS, HALDOR. LILY.

Iceland
Great Stories by Nobel Prize Winners. New York: The Noonday Press, 1959.
Translated by Axel Eyberg and John Watkins.

Author: Haldor Laxness (1902–) was born in Reykjavik. For the first years of his life, he studied music—the piano, particularly—as his parents had determined that their son would enjoy a great musical career. When he turned sixteen, however, Laxness rebelled against their decree and vowed he would become a writer.

His decision was no momentary whim, and his stories of Icelanders and their pride of heritage were immediately successful. Three of his works—the novels *Salka Valka, The Great Weaver of Cashmere,* and *Independent People*—have been translated into English. Laxness's choice of writing over music as a career was clearly vindicated by his acceptance of the Nobel Prize for Literature in 1956 for his trilogy of Icelandic history, *Islandsklukken.*

Story: A medical student, the narrator of LILY, offers the reader a look into the life and death of a man whose real name is either never known or long forgotten. He is a bedraggled, elderly figure who tends the furnace in the student's rooming house and who sits staring into the fire each night, singing some fragment of a melody. When the student asks about the song, the old man claims, "I don't sing . . . I've never been able to sing." This statement of inability best characterizes his life: he is a man haunted by a melody he has never been able to sing.

There are several encounters between the old man and the student in the course of the tale. Each time, some piece of the man's background, some clue to the person he could have been, emerges. For a brief time, the man experiences some happiness. He befriends a young girl who also lives in the apartment house, and the child becomes for him the reincarnation of his beloved Lily from the past. But even this slight respite from isolation is temporary. He loses the child's companionship as well as his old-age pension, his only income, when others judge him to be a menace.

As a rather ingenious twist, Laxness has the student encounter the old man one final time when his aged corpse is sent to the morgue. Through a bizarre but believable involvement in the details of the burial, the student meets Lily, the real Lily of the story's title and of the old man's youth. In her simple admission of her own long years of silent loneliness is an ironic, poignant image of a lost moment and a lost life.

Comparison: Readers familiar with Alan Sillitoe's *The Loneliness of the Long-Distance Runner and Other Stories* will recognize in Haldor Laxness's LILY a perfect companion piece. The old man of LILY and the aging upholsterer in Sillitoe's "Uncle Ernest," especially, should be compared. Both writers achieve in their sketches a level of description that evokes empathy but avoids becoming maudlin. — P G L

LENZ, SIEGFRIED. THE LAUGHINGSTOCK.

Germany
The Selected Stories of Siegfried Lenz. New York: New Directions, 1989. Translated by Breon Mitchell.

Author: Siegfried Lenz (1926–) was born in an East Prussian district that is now part of Poland. Drafted into the navy as a teenager near the end of World War II, he served on submarine combat duty before deserting to Denmark. After subsequent study at the University of Hamburg, he initially embarked on a career as a journalist. He published THE LAUGHINGSTOCK at the age of twenty-four and his first novel at the age of twenty-seven, but his breakthrough to international fame came with the publication of *Deutschstunde* (*The German Lesson*) in 1968, which was hailed throughout Europe and America for its sensitive portrayal of the tensions between duty and human values in wartime Germany. It was followed by a series of novels and short stories that solidified Lenz's reputation as one of the finest living German authors.

Story: Set in the wilds of the far north, this is a tale of a man's struggle with nature and his own sense of inadequacy. Atoq, the son of a famous hunter, is the laughingstock of his tribe. No matter how hard he tries, he finds that fate constantly thwarts him on hunting trips. As the story opens, Atoq is setting out to prove himself once and for all by shooting a fierce musk ox and bringing his sled home piled high with meat.

At first, things seem to go better. Atoq tracks and finally traps a small herd of wild musk ox in a ravine, and in spite of losing his rifle to their trampling hooves, he at last manages to kill the leader, a legendary old bull who has been vainly tracked for years by the best hunters in the tribe. He cuts up the meat and stores it under heavy stones outside the hut where he spends the night. But in the darkness that night, he is forced to watch helplessly as polar bears dig up the meat and carry it away. He has nothing left but his broken rifle, his splintered harpoon, and the horns of the ox. These he loads on the sleigh and returns to the village, prepared to be laughed at once again for having failed. But instead, the villagers stand in respectful and silent awe at the sight of the remnants of his mighty struggle.

Comparison: The stories of Siegfried Lenz are generally light in tone, approaching problems of the human condition with warm compassion and sensitivity. The most interesting comparison here for American readers is with Hemingway's "The Old Man and the Sea." The thematic parallels are striking: the single-handed struggle with nature, the protagonist's attempt to prove himself against the odds, the successful capture of a legendary foe, the loss to natural predators, the return with the bare remnants of the battle. Jack London's stories will also come to mind, both in terms of the wilds of ice and snow and the hand-to-hand struggle with nature for survival.

Because the story also deals in a significant way with a son's attempt to live up to his dead father's image, the tale may be fruitfully compared with other quests or rites of passage by means of which a son enters manhood. Atoq uses his father's rifle, repairs and sleeps in his father's abandoned hunting hut, and, in the end, defeats the animals his father had failed to conquer. His final acceptance by the villagers marks the initial point of his true entry into adult society. — B M

LIM BENG HAP. POONEK.

Malaysia
Asian and Pacific Short Stories. Rutland, VT: Charles E. Tuttle, 1974.

Author: Lim Beng Hap has worked as both a health inspector and author of fiction. He lives in transitional times, when many Asian societies grapple with problems brought about by rapid modernization and Westernization. Lim places his characters in situations where they must struggle with the conflict between traditional ethics and customs and the new social forces.

Story: After ten years of school, Mahsen returns home a scholar, a fact that awes his relatives and neighbors. He soon finds himself the subject of an arranged marriage to a girl who was his childhood playmate. Although she has grown up to be quite attractive, he regards her as a sister and refuses to subject himself to tradition. Mahsen feels that Louisa should also be free from the bonds of tradition. His mother protests that Mahsen, in refusing the good thing offered to him, is "poonek"—subject to bad luck. But her son laughs.

Walking out of the discussion with his mother, he finds Louisa waiting for him at the roadside. She gently accuses him of not observing proper form in not calling on her family after his return, to which Mahsen replies that he is on his way right now. Realizing that he does not have a gift, he stops at a floating shop on a roofed-in boat. As he talks to the owner, Louisa shouts a warning that a crocodile is about to attack. Indeed, the poonek is upon Mahsen. He shoves the old man into the kitchen area of the boat and swiftly jumps onto the bank. Since his original refusal to marry Louisa was based solely on his newly acquired defiance of tradition, he decides to marry her.

Comparison: This story, stereotypical in its description of the traditional Asian family, in which the parental generation knows how to see to the best interests of its children, exemplifies one aspect of filial piety, which is charmingly supported by supernatural laws. It stands in sharp contrast to the myth of Apollo and Phaethon, in which both father and son act rashly. When Apollo finally remembers himself and advises caution, the son refuses to pay heed and brings death to himself and grief and loss to his father. While in the myth, the outcome is final, in real life, as in POONEK, there comes a time when youth either acknowledges the wisdom of the elder generation's position or grows independently into adult maturity. In acquiescing in his parents' arrangement, Mahsen happily yields to their judgment. — M L

LIM, CATHERINE. PAPER.

Singapore
World Writers Today. Glenview, IL: ScottForesman, 1995.

Author: Born in Malaysia (1942–), Catherine Lim observes with a sharp eye and depicts life in the ultra-modern, fast-paced city-nation of Singapore. At one time a teacher and lecturer, she has written one novel and several collections of short stories.

Story: Tay Soon dreams of a house that combines all the best features of all the houses he has seen on estates and in magazines. He and his wife ploddingly save toward his goal, until one day they are enticed to invest in a fast-growing stock. As the stock rises, so do their hopes. But when the stock falls, they at first refuse to acknowledge reality and then they make another bad investment. Their diminishing fortune leads to Tay Soon's declining health and demise.

Upon his death, Tay Soon's mother orders a beautiful paper house to be built, complete with swimming pool and Mercedes. At the funeral, it is set afire at Tay Soon's grave. "It burned brilliantly and in three minutes was a heap of ashes on the grave."

Comparison: In the same way that Tay Soon plays the stock market to make a quick fortune to benefit his family, Paul, in "The Rocking Horse Winner" by D. H. Lawrence, plays the horses to benefit his mother. Both protagonists end up dying in a somewhat demented state.

The burning of the paper house at the end of the story reinforces the theme that everything in life is illusory. Tay Soon lives for an illusion. His means to that goal is, in effect, a nightmare that chases away his dream. Similarly, the main characters in "The Monkey's Paw" by W. W. Jacobs and "The Secret Life of Walter Mitty" by James Thurber are both empowered by their illusions and disabled by them. — M L

LO LIYONG, TABAN. THE OLD MAN OF USUMBURA AND HIS MISERY.

Uganda
Africa Is Thunder and Wonder. New York: Scribner, 1972.

Author: Taban Lo Liyong (1939–) was born in Uganda and attended the Government Teacher Training College and the National Teachers College in Uganda and the University of North Carolina and Georgetown University in the United States. He is recognized as the first African to receive a Master of Fine Arts degree from the Writers Workshop of the University of Iowa. Many of his writings have been published in journals and anthologies. In 1968, he returned to East Africa and has been in the Cultural Division of the Institute for Development Studies at the University of Nairobi, where he is a lecturer in English researching Luo and Masai literature. Among other works, he has published the short story collections *Fixions and Other Stories by a Ugandan Writer* (1968) and *The Uniformed Man* (1971), the novel *Meditations in Limbo* (1970), and the poetry collections *Another Nigger Dead* (1972) and *To Still a Passion* (1977).

Story: THE OLD MAN OF USUMBURA AND HIS MISERY is a tale of contrast between the old man of Usumbura, very rich and knowing nothing of misery, and the old man of Kigali, very poor and "thoroughly sunk in misery." The scene is rural, with families having strong ties and living close to the land.

The story, charmingly told in a rhythmical, parallel prose structure, is entertaining. The very rich man of Usumbura visits his friend, the very poor man of Kigali. The man of Usumbura is struck by his friend's cry of "Oh, my misery!" After much persuasion, he convinces his unhappy friend to share some of his misery with him. Later, the man of Usumbura sends his sons to Kigali to bring back a slice of the old man's misery. The misery is bundled up and given to the sons, with orders not to tamper with "this pregnant egg." Curious and innocent, the sons begin opening the bundle. Each becomes dissatisfied with the contents, and they begin to argue among themselves. The argument escalates into a fight, brother killing brother. Only one son is left to tell his father, the wealthy, heretofore happy old man of Usumbura, of his great loss. Out of breath, he tells his father that misery has escaped. His father strikes him dead.

The old man of Usumbura leaves home that night, taking with him his fifty-five wives, to find his slain forty-nine sons. On their way, the wives kiss their lifeless sons as they pass them. Having no more stomach for misery, the wives return to their parents' homes, taking with them their daughters and their share of wealth. They leave their formerly happy husband alone to enjoy his misery.

Comparison: Illustrative of human frailty, this story focuses on two strata of the human condition: the very rich and the very poor. Ironically, the rich man seeks misery—too much happiness bores him—while the poor man would love some of the wealth of the rich man. There is a note of pathos here, as the rich old man succumbs to what he thought he wanted. This same affiliation of wealth with happiness and poverty with misery is evident in Leo Tolstoy's HOW MUCH LAND DOES A MAN NEED. In that story, a poor man's search for wealth and happiness becomes his undoing.

One may also see this story as a study in good and evil, a reflection of Chaucer's "The Pardoner's Tale," in which the Three Revelers search for Death, whom they meet in a pot of gold, just as the sons of the rich man meet death in their search for misery.
— M J J

Lu Xun. DIARY OF A MADMAN.

China

Selected Stories of Lu Xun. New York: Norton, 1977. Translated by Yang Hsien-yi and Gladys Yang.

Author: Lu Xun (or Lu Hsun), the pseudonym of Chou Shu-jen (1881–1936), is the literary giant of modern China. The eldest son of a declining family from Shaohsing, Chekiang, China, he received a government scholarship to study in Japan. His decision to major in medicine was prompted by his observation of the need for Western medicine to effect scientific cures in China and the need for the same rapid progress in China that Western medicine had brought to Japan. Later, however, he turned to writing as a profession, drawn by such influences as Nietzsche, Darwin, Gogol, and Chekhov. Through his stories, he found the means to awaken China to awareness of the confining traditions and stultifying mentality that had robbed the society of any real life or love among the people. Throughout his career, he held to his goal to serve his country as a spiritual physician. As such, he not only startled his audience with his observations, but also revolutionized the short story in China, which, before his writing, had been considered as nothing more than passing entertainment. DIARY OF A MADMAN was published in 1918.

Story: In an envelope framework, Lu Xun introduces his madman as having completely recovered from a bout of madness. In the selections of his diary written while mad, the protagonist feels victimized by everyone around him, including a rich neighbor's dog, the children on the streets, his brother, his doc-tor, and a young man. He slowly begins to see that all of these belong to a society of cannibals, for which he is to be a savory victim. His outspoken penetration of "truth" beneath the surface of things brands him as a madman. He curses his society for its four-thousand-year savagery of "eating" the weak and hapless and tries unsuccessfully to dissuade his brother from further perpetrating these crimes. Realizing that he too, despite his understanding, is a product of the same society, he ends his diary and his illness with a desperate plea to "save the children."

Comparison: Lu Xun is indebted to Gogol for both the form and title of this story. His compassion for the powerless common man is also echoed in "A Pedestrian Accident," an absurdist tale by Robert Coover, in which the protagonist, Paul, after being struck by a truck, lies in pain amidst the callous comments and gestures of onlookers. Likewise, James Baldwin in "Previous Condition" explores the mind of a black man who is haunted by bad experiences from the past and by the lack of future expectations.

While Lu Xun thinly disguises social criticism in his madman's diary, Conrad Aiken in "Silent Snow, Secret Snow" studies the experience of dream and reality by tracing a boy's descent into madness. Willa Cather in "Paul's Case" shows how the clash between temperament and environment stifles the individual. — M L

Mahfouz, Naguib. THE CONJURER MADE OFF WITH THE DISH.

Egypt

World Writers Today. Glenview, IL: ScottForesman, 1995. Translated by Denys Johnson-Davies.

Author: Naguib Mahfouz (1911–), winner of the Nobel Prize in Literature for 1988, is the outstanding novelist in the Arab world, with a reputation equal to Faulkner's and Hemingway's in the United States. The author of more than twenty volumes of fiction, he has popularized literary prose in the Arab world, traditionally fond only of poetry. Mahfouz is especially noted for his realistic and varied portrayals of Cairo life, his sensitivity to colloquial Egyptian Arabic, and, infusing all his art, his energetic humor. One further quality of Mahfouz's fiction is the cinematic brilliance of his scenes and dialogue, reflecting his deep experience as script writer, director, and executive in the Egyptian movie industry. He long served as the director in the Cinema Institute in the Ministry of Culture under President Nassar. Shortly after he won the Nobel Prize, he was attacked and stabbed by Muslim fundamentalists, but survived.

Story: Told in the first person, THE CONJURER MADE OFF WITH THE DISH is a poignant tale of a young boy just beginning to discover truths in and about the world around him. His mother sends him to town with a coin and a dish to buy beans for breakfast. Three times he returns empty-handed, either not knowing what kind of beans to buy or losing the money with which to buy them. Each time he receives harsh admonitions for his stupidity or carelessness. On his fourth trip, drawn by the merriment of a group of children, he stops to watch the tricks of a conjurer. The conjurer is angry because the boy has no money to give him, and the boy runs away. When he reaches the bean seller to make his purchase, he discovers that the dish in which he is to carry the beans is gone. He confronts the conjurer with accusations of thievery, and the conjurer threatens him.

Delaying the moment he must return home, the boy joins a group of children at a peep show. Enthralled by the story of knights and damsels, he engages in conversation with a young girl watching next to him. Still under the spell of the story, he kisses the girl, who seems to return his kiss and then abruptly leaves to continue on her journey to fetch the midwife for her mother, who is in labor. She promises to meet the boy later in the day.

The boy returns home and is lucky to find his mother out of the house. He takes another dish and a coin from his own savings and sets out again. Unfortunately, this time the bean seller is closing up his shop and refuses to serve the boy. In anger, the boy throws the bowl, which strikes the bean seller in the head.

Again the boy is afraid to return home, only now he is equally afraid to stay on the streets. He sits down to wait for the girl. A man and woman under the stairs capture his attention. He thinks, "a suspicious inner voice told me that their meeting was similar to the one I had," except that he finds "they showed astonishing expertise in the unimaginable things they did." As he watches, he reacts with curiosity, surprise, pleasure, and a certain amount of disquiet. Suddenly, the two begin arguing, the man attacks the woman and kills her, and the boy screams and runs away. When he comes to his senses, he is in an unfamiliar part of town. Now he is lost, confused as to what action to take about the crime he has witnessed, and afraid of the killer as well as the conjurer and the bean seller. Finding his mother, even after having lost two dishes, one coin, and still having no beans, no longer seems like such a bad idea: "Would some miracle come about whereby I would see my mother approaching so that I could eagerly hurry toward her?" As the story closes, the boy says, "I told myself that I should be resolute and make a quick decision. The day was passing, and soon mysterious darkness would descend."

Comparison: The "irresponsible son" characterization, coupled with the opening situation, is reminiscent of the opening of the folktale "Jack and the Beanstalk." But here the adventure related to the beans is merely the beginning of the story. Although this might be considered an "initiation" story, the boy does not seem to become disillusioned, as is the case in many such stories—James Joyce's "Araby," for example. Instead, he seems merely startled by the world he encounters. At the end of the story, even though he is alone and frightened and longs for his mother, he knows he can depend on his own wits and self-reliance to save him. Although he knows full well that "the day" of childhood "was passing, and soon mysterious darkness" of adulthood "would descend," he does not flinch from the prospect. In his reaction to this insight, he can be compared and contrasted with Peter, Wendy, Michael, and John in J. M. Barrie's *Peter Pan,* Dave in Richard Wright's "Almos' a Man," the young man in Joseph Conrad's "Youth," and the Snopes boy in William Faulkner's "Barn Burning." — J A G

MAHFOUZ, NAGUIB. THE PASHA'S DAUGHTER.

Egypt
Modern Arabic Short Stories. New York: Three Continents, 1976.
Translated by Denys Johnson-Davies.

Author: See THE CONJURER MADE OFF WITH THE DISH.

Story: THE PASHA'S DAUGHTER opens quietly with the arrival of a sleek limousine to the gate of a secluded mansion in a rich Cairo suburb. The first notes of social embarrassment are sounded as the chauffeur stands self-consciously beside the opened car door receiving no response to his discreet signals. Glancing inside, he finds the drunken Pasha and his grossly overweight, equally drunken wife slumped together and snoring in the back seat. From that moment until the story's end, the incongruities between the Pasha's lofty status and lowly moral character widen into unbridgeable hypocrisies. We see this minister of state and his vulgar wife exchange insults about their physical absurdities and defects—his outlandishly conspicuous moustache and her grotesque weight—and we discover, finally, that he is merely a creature of nepotism indebted to his wife's father for his position and property.

The catalyst to these revelations is the Pasha's daughter—and her secret lover, who is captured by a policeman as he tries to make his escape from the Pasha's walled villa. The alarm of the criminal's capture arouses the Pasha and his wife from their stupor. When he rushes into their house "calling out his daughter's name, followed by his wife who staggered and stumbled behind him," the daughter boldly confronts them "clad in a white and transparent nightgown."

In the course of the interrogation, awkwardly and loudly carried out in the street, the truth emerges that the young thief is actually Lulu's lover. Groping for a maneuver to excuse the young man for his daughter's sake and yet mollify his indignant chauffeur, the Pasha proposes to smell the man's breath for evidence of drunkenness. The chauffeur, beside himself with frustration, blurts out, "I beg your pardon, Your Excellency, but usually a man cannot smell alcohol in the breath of others if he

himself has been drinking." For his honesty, the chauffeur is angrily dismissed by the Pasha and led away in the custody of the policeman.

The Pasha's wife then proposes to make the situation acceptable by having her husband appoint the young man, a ten-guinea-a-month government clerk with a grammar school education, to the diplomatic service. When the Pasha resists, the final revelations of corruption and complicity are opened: he had been an illicit lover in his youth, similar in circumstances to the young man now before him, and he owed his elevated position in life entirely to his wife's father, who "made him" as she proposes he now make the young man.

The final truths of the story come in a short epilogue, when the chauffeur and policeman, out of sight and sound of their superiors, agree to forget the whole thing. As the chauffeur turns away, the policeman says in parting, "Maleesh, hassan. The truth is, the Pasha has only been successful in the breeding and raising of his own moustache."

Comparison: THE PASHA'S DAUGHTER is a broad satire on class discrimination in prerevolutionary Egypt, which, though democratic in its institutions, was known for the wide gap separating the very rich and the very poor. In his mockery of social pretensions, flagrant nepotism, and lax morality, and in his irreverent delight in awkward sexual situations, Naguib Mahfouz resembles the modern American satirist Philip Roth.

Mahfouz has often been compared with Faulkner, but his irrepressible humor and burlesque characterizations, while evident in some Faulkner stories, for example, "The Auction of the Spotted Horses," are more consistently apparent in the satiric styles of twentieth-century Jewish American writers Roth, Joseph Heller, and Bernard Malamud.

Of all these authors, Roth exhibits the most affinity with Mahfouz. His short story "Epstein" from *Goodbye, Columbus* would make an excellent comparison with THE PASHA'S DAUGHTER. It also exploits for comic effect the conflict between complacent, indulgent parents and their flagrantly sexual daughter, and it builds to the same revelation: the parents see themselves in their daughter and her lover. Both authors expose the hypocrisy of their characters in exuberant public scenes of wild incongruities and awkward, embarrassing behavior. In characterization, Lou and Goldie Epstein are not as exaggerated as the Pasha and his wife. For comparisons in this technique of satire, see Joseph Heller's "tall tale" characterizations in *Catch-22*.

Finally, Mahfouz's sympathetic yet ironically humorous portraits of common people as characters struggling for security and advantage in modern, urban societies—the government clerk, chauffeur, and policeman in this story—are evocative of some stories by Bernard Malamud, though lacking Malamud's astringent irony. The first half of Malamud's "The Magic Barrel" amuses with a burlesque style similar to Mahfouz's. That story's turn to darker, more bitter revelations would offer a revealing contrast in technique to Mahfouz's more good-humored style. — J D M

Mann, Thomas. Disorder and Early Sorrow.

Germany
Death in Venice and Seven Other Stories. New York: Vintage Books, 1936.
Translated by Helen T. Lowe-Porter.

Author: Thomas Mann (1875–1955), a German novelist, short story writer, and essayist, was born in Lübeck. His father and all of his ancestors on his father's side were respectable and prosperous merchants and prominent citizens. His mother, on the other hand, was the daughter of a German planter and his Portuguese-Creole wife. She entertained her children with fascinating stories about her youth in Brazil, and because she was an accomplished pianist, she inspired in them a love of music. The conflict between his upstanding, respectable, somewhat rigid father and his exotic and artistically inclined mother was the single most important influence on Mann's work. His work includes many short stories and novellas, the most famous of which are TONIO KRÖGER (1903), TRISTAN (1903), and "Death in Venice" (1912); essays; and major novels, including *Buddenbrooks* (1910), *The Magic Mountain* (1924), *Joseph and His Brothers* (1933–42), *Dr. Faustus* (1947), and *The Confessions of Felix Krull: Confidence Man* (1954). Supportive at first, Mann became openly critical of German Nationalism. He was awarded the Nobel Prize for Literature in 1929, four years after writing DISORDER AND EARLY SORROW.

Story: Much of this charming, unsentimentally told story is autobiographical, both in general and in its depiction of particular details. Its main character, Abel Cornelius, is a professor of history during the period of economic inflation of the post–World War I 1920s in a defeated Germany. Cornelius's love for the past is predicated on his belief that "the past is immortalized; that is to say, it is dead; and death is the root of all godliness and all abiding significance," whereas in the present, there is only disorder and change and "thus not history at all."

The professor and his wife have four children—two younger ones, "the little folk," Ellie and Snapper, with characteristics similar to those of Mann's own two youngest children, and the "big folk," Ingrid and Bert, who seem to be a composite of Mann's other four children.

The story focuses on a night that the "big folk" are hosting a party, in the course of which the professor is made acutely aware of the generation gap and the changing nature of society that seems to be taking his children away from him, especially his favorite, five-year-old Ellie. At the end of the story, Ellie "falls in love" with the charming and intelligent Max Hergesell, who also represents the materialistic values of the contemporary society from which

Professor Cornelius has tried to separate himself. When Ellie's sorrow, caused by Max's dancing with someone his own age, is assuaged by Max's presence at her cribside at the end of the story, "the father's feelings towards him are a most singular mixture of thankfulness, embarrassment, and hatred." He is forced to realize that the eventual separation from his beloved child, the sorrow that she will meet later in her life, and the loss of the "coherent and disciplined historic past" to the disorder and brashness of the present are inevitable. Yet in spite of the insecurity of the human condition, there is an inescapable sense of the promise of renewed vitality from the younger generation.

Comparison: The details of this story suggest that it can be read as the story of Germany after the war, exploring the problems of coping with the disorder and disillusionment that followed. Böll's story "Christmas Every Day" is also set in a defeated Germany after a war (World War II) and deals with the problems of changing aesthetic and moral values. But unlike Mann's story, it is more deeply concerned with the moral responsibility of the German people for the horrors of the war and the contrast between the comfort of personal life and the atrocities of war. The emphasis on the way the static past impinges on the present and results in the breaking up of the old order is an important theme in both stories. But whereas the character in the Böll story clings to the past, Mann seems to come to the conclusion that life will insist on change.

The conflict between generations and the loss of innocence and resulting hurt that comes from it are basic themes in Sherwood Anderson's "I Want to Know Why," although Ellie's disappointment is not nearly so intense or so disillusioning as the first-person narrator's in the Anderson story, whose idyllic world is tarnished and who is without the protective concern of a loving father. Anderson's use of the first-person narrator enables him to describe the boy's altered perceptions as a result of his coming of age and thereby intensifies the emotional impact of the experience for the reader, while Mann's story focuses more on the professor's reaction to the experience. Therefore, we never really know the ultimate effect Ellie's disappointment might have on her, whereas the boy's experience is a crucial moral one that has clearly destructive implications for him.

John Updike's "Flight," like Mann's story, is concerned with the child-parent relationship and the experience of coming of age. They both make the comparison between the attitudes and values of the older and younger generations.

Many of Picasso's paintings are concerned with the subject of the difficult time of one's facing the painful transformations that take place during the transition from childhood to adulthood. One such painting is his *Bust of a Woman* (1923), in which the figure is, like a child, discovering herself by seeing her hands as larger than life and manifesting a sense of fear at the discovery.   — R H M

MANN, THOMAS. TONIO KRÖGER.

Germany
Introduction to Literature: Stories. 3d ed. New York: Macmillan, 1980.
Translated by Helen T. Lowe-Porter.

Author: See DISORDER AND EARLY SORROW.

Story: TONIO KRÖGER is directly autobiographical in that Tonio's parents manifest the same conflict as Mann's own. His father "had the temperament of the north: solid, reflective, puritanically correct." He was a merchant "with a wild flower in his buttonhole." His mother, "of indeterminate foreign blood, was beautiful, sensuous, naive, passionate and careless at once, ... irregular by instinct," and she played the piano and mandolin wonderfully. Tonio had an artistic bent that made him different from other boys, such as his friend Hans Hansen, who cared only about horses and the girl he loved, Ingeborg Holm. Ingeborg is depicted as a blond, healthy, natural person, who, like Hans, is insensitive to the world of the artist.

All the major characters in the story represent one of these two extremes, either artist or burger, and Tonio, recognizing the artist potential in himself, feels in his isolation from the others "a longing . . . and a gentle envy; a faint contempt, and no little innocent bliss." But as he gets older, Tonio realizes that he can never be like his friends and "live free from the curse of knowledge and the torment of creation . . . in blessed mediocrity. . . . Their speech was not his speech." They cannot understand him, yet he longs for the bliss of the human and the commonplace.

He returns to the north, but his home is now a public building, and no one knows him anymore. In Copenhagen, he has a vision of Hans and Inge and knows that he could never have been happy with their lives. Recognizing that to become a poet he must have his "bourgeois love of the human, the living and usual," because it is "the source of all warmth, goodness, and humor," he sees himself standing "between two worlds" and being "at home in neither." He "suffers in consequence," but he senses that somehow it will be from the relationship of the two conflicting worlds that his creativity will develop and grow.

Comparison: The theme of the artist's isolation from society is a pervasive one in twentieth-century literature and can be found throughout Mann's entire opus in some variation. One also thinks of James Joyce's story "Araby," in which the young boy, the artist-author as a young man, in a moment at a bazaar realizes that he has values that are different from those of the society in which he finds himself. He stands between his ideal and the reality of the commonplace, and he is "at home" in neither. Although he is not seen as a mature person, as is Tonio, the story is told from the point of view of an older man who looks back at the moment in his youth when this epiphany occurred. In both stories, the authors show that the artist is in the paradoxical situation of needing to experience the warmth of the human while being alienated from it in order to retain individuality and devote oneself to creativity.

In Kafka's story THE METAMORPHOSIS, the theme of alienation is developed to a greater extreme. Gregor is metamorphosed into a bug, and thus he is completely alienated from his family and society. He cannot exist in either world for long. Ultimately, he is completely destroyed.

Melville's story "Bartleby the Scrivener" is also concerned with the themes of isolation and the artist's problem with society, but focuses more on the complex question of an individual's obligation to society. Considered as a parable of the alienation of the serious writer in the modern world, Melville's story dramatizes the artist's refusal to write as a commercial enterprise. Unlike Tonio, he remains behind the walls that separate him from society.

In Conrad Aiken's story "Silent Snow, Secret Snow," Paul expresses a conflict similar to Tonio's when he reflects, "It was as if he were trying to lead a double life. . . . But how, then, was he to keep a balance?" Yet Paul's problem is that of a schizophrenic, a divided personality, whereas Tonio's is a more intellectual and less psychological one.

Mann's parodic technique is demonstrated in his description of Herr François Knaak, the dancing master who teaches bourgeois manners to the children of the burger class and dazzles the audience by "suddenly and unexpectedly springing from the ground, whirling his two legs about each other . . . as it were trilling with them, and then, with a subdued bump, which nevertheless shook everything within him to its depths, returned to earth." Such characterization involves the kind of exaggeration and parody one finds in some of the German expressionists, such as George Grosz, who compared himself to Thomas Mann and wrote similarly about the painted images of the "Philistines" who no longer understood his art. — R H M

MANN, THOMAS. TRISTAN.

Germany
Death in Venice and Seven Other Stories. New York: Vintage, 1936.
Translated by Helen T. Lowe-Porter.

Author: See DISORDER AND EARLY SORROW.

Story: TRISTAN is one of Mann's ironically told stories about the artist. Three major characters dramatize a conflict that Mann himself experienced and often expressed in his work. Herr Klöterjahn represents the healthy, domineering, and materialistic burger. His wife, Gabriele Klöterjahn, a very sensitive woman who suffers from tuberculosis, is a patient in a sanitarium. Herr Spinell is also a patient there, only because his "feeling of [the Empire] style" and "the austere simplicity" of the place has the effect on him of "inward purification and rebirth." Finding the atmosphere "morally elevating," this would-be writer represents the sickly, artistic aesthete who is comfortable only in the world of beauty. He is totally separated from ordinary life in every way and is attracted to Gabriele merely as an object of beauty. He encourages Gabriele to play the piano for his pleasure against the advice of her doctor. She plays several Chopin nocturnes, followed by Wagner's "Tristan": "And on they went, into the intoxicated music of the love-mystery."

As a result of the exertion, her health worsens, and the doctor sends for her husband and child, Anton, who is "healthy even to excess" and whose shouts and screams are described in marked contrast to the ethereal beauty of the music. Spinell writes an insulting letter to Herr Klöterjahn in which he tells him, "I hate the life of which you are the representative: cheap, ridiculous, but yet triumphant life." At the end of the story, life—in the form of the screaming, fat child and the practical, healthy businessman, Herr Klöterjahn—triumphs, as Spinell goes out for a walk, realizing that "inwardly, he is running away" from life.

Comparison: The parodic use of Wagner's "Tristan" and "Liebestod" intensifies Mann's satire of the artistic aesthete who neither experiences Tristan's great love nor becomes united in death with his Isolde, since he is at least partly responsible for Gabriele's death. The comparison with Wagner's music thereby heightens the irony. In his confrontation with Klöterjahn, Spinell becomes a pitiful character, and in that regard he can be compared to Walter Mitty in Thurber's story "The Secret Life of Walter Mitty." Mitty retreats into a fantasy world where he can feel undefeated, until the real world interferes and threatens his imaginary vision of what he would like to be. The effect, as in TRISTAN, is a sadly comic one.

Mann's use of the leitmotif, such as the little blue vein that appears on Frau Klöterjahn's temple, a mark of her artistic sensitivity and delicate health, is reminiscent of Wagner's use of the leitmotif in his music and Mann's frequent use of the technique in many of his other works. For example, in his novel *Buddenbrooks,* Hanno also has light and sensitive skin, "with blue shadows under his eyes" like his artistic mother.

The conflict between Spinell, who represents the artistic spirit, which, taken to its extreme, is morbid and destructive, and Klöterjahn and his baby, who represent the triumphant life force, is a conflict frequently found in Mann's work, such as in TONIO KRÖGER, where Tonio stands between the two worlds they represent. In "Death in Venice," Aschenbach moves from one to the other extreme with very complex results indicative of Mann's difficulty in finding a simple solution to the conflict. He realized that the artist separated from life is inextricably involved with death.

Melville's "Bartleby the Scrivener" is also concerned with the themes of isolation and the artist's problem in coping with society. But neither Melville nor Mann in his other stories is as sardonic or as critical of the artist's sickly isolation as in TRISTAN.

One is also reminded of T. S. Eliot's "The Love Song of J. Alfred Prufrock," in which Prufrock, like Spinell, feels defeated by reality: "human voices wake us and we drown." Also, both the Hunger Artist in Kafka's A HUNGER ARTIST and the Bound Man in Ilse Aichinger's THE BOUND MAN are artists who are overcome by the materialistic and brash society around them. Yet whereas the reader develops a very strong identification with these artists, who are victims of a society not capable of appreciating their art, the unsuccessful and self-indulgent Spinell becomes a pitiful caricature of an artist. — R H M

MAUPASSANT, GUY DE. THE NECKLACE.

France

The World in Literature. Rev. ed. Glenview, IL: ScottForesman, 1967. Translated by Jonathan Sturges.

Author: Guy de Maupassant (1850–1893) was born in Normandy to parents whose claims to nobility were apparently not matched by wealth. Before becoming a successful writer of realistic, often naturalistic, fiction based largely on his own life, he tried his hand at verse and spent time in both military and civil service, the latter as a clerk. Although he loved sports and throughout his life showed an interest in physical fitness and the outdoors, he died paralyzed and insane. Some have attributed his early death at the age of forty-three to a genetic disorder, others to dissipation, still others to overwork during the 1880s, when most of his more than three hundred short stories and six novels were written. THE NECKLACE was published in 1884, nine years before de Maupassant's death.

Story: Mathilde Loisel, despite her feeling that she was born to enjoy the luxuries of higher estate, is married to a petty clerk in governmental service. One day, her husband brings home an invitation to an important party. Rather than being happy, Mathilde is upset that she has no dress appropriate for such a gala occasion. Her husband gives her 400 francs he has been saving for a hunting gun, and she buys a dress. Now, however, she has no jewelry to wear with it. Her husband suggests she visit her friend, Mme. Forestier, and borrow jewelry from her. She does—a lovely diamond necklace—and wears it and the new dress to the party, where she is a great hit.

Upon returning to their home on the Rue des Martyrs, Mathilde discovers that she has lost the necklace. Her husband spends most of the night and all the next day trying unsuccessfully to find it.

Desperately, they shop for a similar strand of diamonds and finally locate one priced at 36,000 francs. Using all their meager savings and taking out ruinous loans, they pay cash for the new necklace and deliver it to Mme. Forestier. They move into a cheap apartment and for ten years work night and day to pay off their debts. Mathilde grows old in the process. Her appearance surprises a still youthful Mme. Forestier when the two meet by chance. Mathilde, for the first time, explains all that happened following the party and during the ensuing ten years. "My poor Mathilde," Mme. Forestier says, shocked, "the necklace was a fake. It wasn't worth more than 500 francs!"

Comparison: The influence of Gustave Flaubert and Émile Zola, both of whom welcomed de Maupassant into their circles, is evident in de Maupassant's fiction. Like theirs, his work is characterized by an unflinching interest in the human dilemma. His characters, the situations in his stories, the themes he developed, and his insights are all reminiscent of those found in their works. From Flaubert, whom de Maupassant at twenty-three declared to be his master, he learned the benefit of the well-chosen word, good humor, and crisp irony. From Zola came the naturalist's concern for heredity, environment, and determinism as governing human actions.

In the course of THE NECKLACE, de Maupassant editorializes, "How little a thing is needed for us to be lost or to be saved!" The comment could well describe many of his stories, which turn on the unfortunate mistake or event. Worthwhile comparison can thus be made using THE NECK-

LACE and stories like "Clochette," "A Piece of String," "The Duel," "Minuet," and "Hautot and His Son." Each of these stories is an example too of the economy of structure and masterful irony typical of de Maupassant at his best.

Comparison with many of the works of literary naturalists and realists is also possible. Society's image for success is the source of grief for characters in the stories of O. Henry, Theodore Dreiser, Thomas Hardy, Émile Zola, and Gustave Flaubert. The gifts in O. Henry's "The Gift of the Magi," if given with love, are the result of sacrifices made, judgments blurred by society's version of "presents." In Sherwood Anderson's "The Egg," the narrator's father pays a great price to rise to a better station in life. In William Dean Howells's *A Hazard of New Fortunes,* the elder Dryfoos suffers through the social ambition of his wife and daughter. — R S

Megged, Aharon. THE NAME.

Israel
Short Story International. April 1983. Translated by Minna Givton.

Author: Aharon Megged (1920–), born in Wloclawcek, Poland, emigrated to Israel with his family in 1926. Educated in Tel Aviv, from 1938 to 1950 he was a member of Kibbutz Sdot-Yam, during which time he was sent to the United States and Canada as an exemplary "Young Pioneer." Since 1950, Megged has become well known as a journalist, editor, playwright, and prolific writer of fiction. As a writer of fiction, he began as a naturalist, then experimented with surrealism, moving finally in the early 1970s to the position of a realist. He has won a number of literary prizes, among them the Bialiki and Fichman Prizes in 1973. THE NAME was published in 1960.

Story: THE NAME opens with Raya and her young husband, Yehuda, paying a visit to her grandfather, Grandfather Ziskind, of whom she has always been very fond. The disorder of the house in which he lives alone reveals his "helplessness in running his home," and the particular items enumerated— crumbs from a Sabbath loaf, books with thick leather bindings, and especially the "clock which had long since stopped"—suggest his living in the past, the past of European Jewry before the Holocaust. Raya's first words in the story, "We ought to make Grandfather a present of a clock," indicate a significant difference between the worlds of the grandfather and his granddaughter, a modern Israeli.

This visit follows the usual course of such visits. Grandfather Ziskind offers the young people food, including fermenting preserves. They eat reluctantly, especially Yehuda, who is forced "to taste at least a teaspoonful of the sweet and nauseating stuff." After a period of chatting comes "what Yehuda dreaded most of all." The old man takes from the clock cabinet a cloth bag containing a manuscript, a "lament for Grandfather's native town in the Ukraine which had been destroyed by the Germans," and various other items, among them a photograph of his grandson, Mendele, who had been twelve years old when he and his entire family were killed during the destruction of the town. It is clear that Grandfather Ziskind idolizes his lost grandson.

As usual, Ziskind bemoans the fate of his village and grandson, the young people indicate their sympathy, and Raya remembers the change in her grandfather after the war as he came to understand that his son and grandson had been killed. As usual, the old man asks the younger one to read the manuscript aloud. Yehuda complies, reading mechanically, since, after many readings, Ziskind's manuscript has lost any meaning it might once have had for him.

After a time, Raya becomes pregnant, and her mother finally tells Ziskind, who has failed to notice. After learning of his granddaughter's pregnancy, the old man appears at her home for the first time, animated and happy as she has not seen him since she was a child. From her mother she later learns that Ziskind wishes Raya and Yehuda to name their child after Mendele, his dead grandson, but that he is reluctant to ask them. Through the mother the young couple convey their unwillingness to name their child Mendele, or even Menachem, a compromise proposed by the mother. Their intention is to name the child Elud, if it is a boy, a name they consider an Israeli name, in contrast to the others, which are European, related to the *Golah,* the Diaspora. Finally, Ziskind confronts them with his wish, but they continue to refuse. "O children, children," he says to them, "you don't know what you're doing. You're finishing off the work which the enemies of Israel began. They took the bodies away from the world, and you—the name and the memory."

When the son is born and named Elud, the couple finally visit Ziskind, who acts as if the child is not there, steadfastly refusing to admit his existence. When the old man begins to take the cloth bag from the clock cabinet, the young parents tell him they must go, and he accompanies them to the door. As they leave, Raya realizes that her grandfather is "alone, an orphan in the world."

Comparison: In its theme of the difficulties in understanding caused by generational change, especially when such change is made even more difficult by historical developments, THE NAME may be generally compared to such stories as Thomas Mann's DISORDER AND EARLY SORROW, Heinz Huber's THE NEW APARTMENT, and Alice Walker's "Everyday Use." Like Megged's story, those of Mann and Huber concern themselves with generational difficulties among Europeans, while Walker's deals with African Americans. An even clearer comparison can be seen between a number of stories by Isaac Bashevis Singer, stories such as "Grandfather and Grandson" and "The Old Man," where the generational conflict is played out by members of the Jewish community. — P T M

MELEAGROU, HEBE. MONUMENT.

Greece

The Charioteer: An Annual Review of Modern Greek Culture. No. 7–8. New York: Parnassos, Greek Cultural Society of New York, 1965/66. Translated by Fotine Nicholas.

Author: Hebe Meleagrou (1928–) was born on Cyprus. She writes of universal themes, of the period of Greece between the First and Second World Wars, and of the years since World War II. MONUMENT is part of the large corpus of antiwar literature that comes from Greece, perhaps in part because the glorification of war was at its best in ancient Greece. In fact, MONUMENT goes a step further by being an antihero story as well. It is written with great sensitivity and presents an illuminating portrait of Greek culture and values and of generational differences.

Story: The monument that has just gone up is in honor of the main character's youngest son, who did exactly what his father wanted him to do: to reach for a cause that would lift him above the commonplace—to become a hero. His older brother and sister believed that such teaching would lead to their brother's death, but they were unable to convince their father of the danger. Through a series of revelations beginning with the installation of the monument, the father is slowly led to full understanding.

Comparison: The classical war-and-hero tradition developed in Greece; it was one of the Greeks' major contributions to the Western world (see Venezis's MYCENAE). Greeks of the twentieth century have had plenty of opportunity to seek to be heroes, and there are many hero stories available. In this one, however, the tradition backfires, as it does in Ambrose Bierce's story "An Occurrence at Owl Creek Bridge." In spite of warnings, Peyton Farquhar, a planter and slave owner, attempts to destroy a bridge vital to the Yankee advance. Farquhar, unsuccessful in his attempt, is hanged on the bridge by Northern troops.

The idea of being a hero is also evident in the leading character in Rudyard Kipling's "The Man Who Would Be King." This rugged, active bum is declared a hero, a ruler, by a remote warrior society. He apparently enjoys the status a great deal, up until the end. — E M

Mérimée, Prosper. THE VENUS OF ILLE.

France
The Venus of Ille and Other Stories. London: Oxford University Press, 1966. Translated by Jean Kimber.

Author: Prosper Mérimée (1803–1870), a French novelist and man of wide culture, studied both law and archaeology. He held various diplomatic posts and became inspector general of historical monuments in 1841. His archaeological interests are reflected in many of his tales. He was elected to the French Academy in 1844. In 1853, he became a senator under the Second Empire. Commonly associated with the Romanticists, he portrays violent passions and strong characterizations in his fiction, but there are elements of classical restraint in his ironical, detached style. Among his best works are *La Chronique du Temps de Charles IX,* a historical novel; "Carmen," a nouvelle made into a famous opera by Bizet; and THE VENUS OF ILLE (1837), which Mérimée described as his masterpiece.

Story: The narrator, an unnamed pedantic archaeologist, visits the district of Ille to investigate the area's ruins. His host, the local antiquarian Monsieur de Peyrehorade, invites him to take part in the wedding preparation for his son, Alphonse. Even more interesting to the Parisian is the recent unearthing and placement nearby of a large, antique bronze statue of Venus. The narrator appreciates the generous hospitality of his host, but dislikes the son's dandified appearance, vulgar manner, and blatantly greedy attitude about his fiancée's dowry, especially in view of the delicate girl's charm and beauty.

The morning of the wedding, Alphonse, a tennis player of renown, capriciously joins in a match because the local players are losing to some Spaniards. In order to improve his game, he removes his betrothed's diamond wedding ring from his hand and places it on the third finger of the statue for safekeeping. Forgetting the ring, he proceeds to the ceremony and an afternoon of eating, drinking, and coarse joking. Later that evening, the drunken groom tells the archaeologist that the Venus is his wife because she will not give the ring back. Her finger has contracted, perhaps due to a hidden spring, he speculates. That night, the narrator hears mysterious, heavy footsteps. The next morning, Monsieur Alphonse is found dead in the bridal chamber, crushed to death. The diamond wedding ring lies on the floor. His widow is regarded as mad when she claims to have seen the bronze statue in bed, holding her husband in a murderous embrace and then dropping his dead body as she walked away.

Comparison: Venus, the goddess of love and beauty in Roman mythology and associated with the Greek Aphrodite, has been the subject of major works of literature by famous authors. Mérimée based THE VENUS OF ILLE on an ancient local legend. Through the use of myth, he was able to portray the dual nature of love as symbolized by the seductive beauty and destructive power of the statue. The love-death synthesis is common in Romantic literature. In Mérimée's tale, the retribution for betraying the goddess is extreme, but the work suggests that justice is served by the fate of the vulgar bridegroom. The narrator looks with disdain at arranged marriages, by which "the most innocent of girls may be handed over to the minotaur." Mérimée treats this theme in a less subtle manner in "Lokis," which also involves a slaying on the wedding night. In many tales of horror, inanimate objects play major roles. A salient example is Edgar Allan Poe's "The Fall of the House of Usher." An interdependence exists between the decay of the mansion and the decline of the mental and physical health of its inhabitants.

Parallels to THE VENUS OF ILLE exist in literary and musical adaptations of the Don Juan legend, such as Molière's play *Don Juan,* Mozart's opera *Don Giovanni,* and Pushkin's poetic drama *The Stone Guest.* Don Juan arrogantly invites the statue of the commander he has killed to dine with him, and Alphonse flippantly places his betrothed's ring on the hand of the bronze Venus, neither character expecting the statue to respond. Both meet with disaster when the figures "come to life" and seek revenge.

Mérimée's story may also be viewed as an inversion of the Pygmalion legend. An interesting contrast would be W. S. Gilbert's comedy *Pygmalion and Galatea,* in which a sculptor falls in love with his creation, a statue of Galatea, and his wife becomes very jealous.

Art works depicting Venus-Aphrodite abound. *The Aphrodite at Cnidos* by Praxiteles and the *Venus de Milo* are obvious choices to be used with this work. Tintoretto's painting *Cupid, Venus, and Vulcan* is also appropriate, since the bridegroom's father jokes about Venus and her lover, Vulcan. — M A F

Mishima Yukio. PATRIOTISM.

Japan
Death in Midsummer and Other Stories. New York: New Directions, 1966.
Translated by Geoffrey W. Sargent.

Author: Mishima Yukio, the pen name of Hiraoka Kimitake (1925–1970), was born in Tokyo. His decision to write came as he was watching the bombing and burning of Tokyo one night. His first novel, *The Sound of Waves* (1958), was written after a trip to Europe and established his enormous popularity as a writer. It was made into a movie almost immediately after publication. His best-known works translated into English include *Temple of the Golden Pavilion* (1959) and *The Sailor Who Fell from Grace with the Sea* (1969). PATRIOTISM was published in 1960. His crowning achievement, the tetralogy *The Sea of Fertility,* which includes *Spring Snow, The Runaway Horses, The Temple of Dawn,* and *The Decay of the Angel,* was delivered to the publisher the day before his death.

Besides producing a prolific amount of writing, including twenty novels, thirty-three plays, and innumerable articles on a great variety of subjects, Mishima was also an athlete, karate expert, actor, film maker, and soldier. His activities were so varied and his achievements so remarkable that he was regarded as the Japanese Renaissance man. His suicide by the traditional sword in December 1970 was no less dramatic than the activities of his life.

Story: On the morning of February 26, Lieutenant Shinji Takeyama hears a bugle summoning troops and finds himself in an insoluble conflict. His unquestioned loyalty to the imperial forces is now compromised by his closest colleagues, who have just staged a ten-minute mutiny.

When he returns home to his bride Reiko two days later, his decision is resolute. He is to commit *seppuku* (suicide by sword) in the prescribed manner. Reiko, who has guessed his mind, is ready to accompany him in death. Husband and wife, very much in love, have been living in passionate happiness, but neither questions the necessity of the lieutenant's decision. In fact, Reiko is flattered by her husband's trust in choosing her to be his witness. They dispense with supper, and after each has taken a bath, retire to their bedroom to enjoy embracing a last time. Fully aware that they are looking at love in the face of death, they plan to experience each with the same rigor. The fact that they see both acts as moral and righteous invigorates them.

In the traditional manner, they write their farewell notes, which they lay in the alcove. The lieutenant unbuttons his uniform, tests his sword's cutting edge, thrusts it five or six inches into his abdomen, and pulls it sideways across to the right. In his last moments of consciousness, he directs the blade at his throat and throws his body's weight against it to make it penetrate.

Almost immediately, Reiko prepares to "taste the true bitterness and sweetness of that great moral principle in which her husband believed" and to enter "a realm her husband has already made his own." She draws a dagger from her sash and plunges it into her throat.

Comparison: Suicide as a final statement on issues of loyalty or principle was an honorable, even expected, act in the Japanese samurai tradition. An act equally regarded in Western stories is to die as a martyr for the same kind of reasons, but at another's hand. Stephen Vincent Benét evokes the self-sacrifice of early Christians in the title of his story "The Blood of the Martyrs." When the protagonist, at long last, recognizes that he has to die if he defies the regime, he becomes a hero in facing severe punishment and the firing squad.

Mishima's lieutenant also resembles those Hemingway heroes who choose to die a manful and violent death. Both authors speak through their characters to demand a certain dignity in death. In Hemingway's first book of stories, *In Our Time*, the boy Nick Adams is initiated into the bullfighting ring, an arena in which death always looms as the ultimate challenge and characters face it with finesse and courage.   — M L

MORAVIA, ALBERTO. THE CHASE.

Italy

Literature: The Human Experience. 3d ed. New York: St. Martin's, 1982. Translated by Angus Davidson.

Author: Alberto Moravia is the pseudonym adopted by Alberto Pincherle (1907–1990). Born in Rome, he spent much of his youth in tuberculosis sanitariums, allowing him to read widely and making him introspective, a quality manifested in his fiction, especially in its frequent concern with adolescence and the loss of innocence. A lifelong anti-Fascist, Moravia found his works banned by Mussolini, and he and his wife were forced to flee to the mountains when the Germans occupied Italy. Many of his stories and novels are anti-Fascistic and suggest that relinquishing individual responsibility causes corruption and human anguish. That theme of alienation is generally linked with the sexual anxiety and frustration naturally resulting from people's self-centered, inauthentic existences. Moravia is perhaps best known for the novels *The Woman of Rome* (1947) and *The Conformist* (1951). THE CHASE was published in 1967, and THE FALL in 1956.

Story: A brief reminiscence of an incident in the childhood of the narrator opens the story and functions as an analogy for its action. He remembers going hunting with his father and being struck by the intense vitality of a bird, "rendered more intense by the very fact of my watching it," which his father shot moments later, picked up, and put in the boy's hand. The startling contrast between vitality and death marked "the end of my shooting experience."

Like the bird, his wife, before they married, had been "'wild'—that is, entirely autonomous and unpredictable," but now "she had become 'tame'—that is, predictable and dependent." What once had been a wild bird had become a hen. One day, however, as his wife is leaving their apartment, he notices a gesture that suggests her former wildness "that in the past had made me love her." Intrigued, he decides to follow her. She boards the bus, and he follows in his car. When she gets off the bus, he leaves the car and follows her on foot, only to be shocked to see her accosted by a young man on the street. Rather than rebuffing him, she walks along by his side, their arms around each other's waists, "evidently obeying the rules of some kind of erotic ritual" predetermined by the two of them. After a time, they step into a dark doorway and kiss. As she leans back in the course of the long kiss, her husband "felt at that moment her vitality had reached its diapason," and "I saw that I would have to intervene," he said.

Imagining himself grabbing her hair and pulling her away from her lover, he realizes that this action would be the equivalent of his father's shooting the wild bird: "After the scene of my intervention it might be possible for me to regain control of my wife, but I should find her shattered and lifeless in my arms like the bird that my father placed in my hand." He watches the seemingly interminable "kiss of passion" until its end and then turns back as they walk ahead.

Comparison: The narrator of the story is essentially a voyeur, not only in his watching his wife and her lover, but in his whole relationship to life. He wants to possess the intense vitality of his wife because he lacks it himself, not realizing that human vitality, fundamentally sexual and solitary, cannot survive possession, the theme of this story. In this sense, he may be compared to John Marcher of Henry James's "The Beast in the Jungle" or to T. S.

Eliot's J. Alfred Prufrock, although it must be remembered that neither of them marry, an important fact in this regard. On the other hand, one might contrast his reaction to that of Tom Buchanan in F. Scott Fitzgerald's *The Great Gatsby* when he experiences a comparable revelation. Interestingly, in both cases the knowledge of the wife's infidelity sharpens the husband's basically sexual interest. One might also contrast Moravia's character's reaction to that of Francis Macomber's wife in Ernest Hemingway's "The Short Happy Life of Francis Macomber" when she becomes fully aware of her husband's "intense vitality." She shoots her husband as our narrator's father shot the bird.

The wife of this story might well be compared to Mabel in D. H. Lawrence's "The Horse Dealer's Daughter." Both of them possess an animal sexual vitality that is part of their very nature and that dominates their life and being. Lawrence, however, sees this force as far more powerful—Mabel, after all, dominates the more sophisticated, more rational, but less sexual Jack Fergusson—and more fundamental than does Moravia.   — P T M

MORAVIA, ALBERTO. THE FALL.

Italy
The Continental Short Story: An Existential Approach. New York: Odyssey Press, 1969.
Translated by Bernard Wall.

Author: See THE CHASE.

Story: "On the threshold of his turbid and troubled adolescence" and recovering from a lengthy illness, Tancredi is sent to vacation in a rented villa at the seaside with his mother and the maid. The villa, owned by an antique dealer who uses it to store furniture, with its old musty smell and arbitrarily arranged furnishings, "seemed to rebuff human intrusion" and adds another terror to "the terror of death which had come with his illness and survived his recovery" and the terror "caused by his break from childhood and by the feeling that his strength was not equal to the demands made on it by his new condition."

As he gradually explores the villa, he becomes fascinated by it and its furnishings, especially a copy of a Caravaggio painting depicting St. Paul's fall on the way to Damascus. Struck by lightning, Paul's naked, emaciated body is depicted being hurled backward into the darkness. After this fall into the abyss, Tancredi thinks, "came perfect faith, so that the world which had been simple was now double, for the lightning had laid bare the soul hidden beneath appearances."

Two events then occur that profoundly affect the young man. First, in an "enclosure" within the villa's garden littered with refuse, pitted with holes, and containing a single tree, Tancredi, almost accidentally, puts out one of the eyes of a cat with his slingshot, causing the cat, strangely, to react not with hatred, but with seeming affection. It was "as if with the catapult shot that had blinded it in one eye the cat recognized an unbreakable bond between Tancredi and itself."

Struck with panic, the boy flees to the villa, encounters the cat there, and runs upstairs to an unused room. Sitting on the edge of the bed, safe for the moment from the cat, he hears the voices of a man and woman in the adjoining room, which holds the picture of St. Paul. Hearing the door from that room to the hall close, he looks in and sees the maid resting on the bed. "Why should Veronica go to sleep in a room that wasn't hers? And what was all the chattering and the man's voice?" The whole experience causes him to feel a shame he doesn't understand. Dozing off, he dreams of a hole in the ceiling whose "flaky edges suggested that some vast den lay beyond, so that if the plaster fell, Heaven knew what tunnels might not be disclosed." Seeing a rat in the hole, he hurries to call the maid, who pokes at the hole with a broomstick, dislodging the rat, which "jumps on top" of her as she falls backward "grasping her loins with her hands."

Awakening from this dream, he is asked by his mother to replace a blown fuse in an inaccessible area over the staircase. As he climbs a ladder and reaches toward the fuse box, he sees the one-eyed cat again, but the cat is at that instant electrocuted. The flash from the electrocution hurls Tancredi backward into the room. The boy, however, is not hurt, but has merely fainted.

Comparison: The number of references to falling in the story, from the title to the concluding incident, clearly reinforce the story's theme of the fall from innocence that is accompanied by a haunting sense of shame and anxiety. That theme's sexual dimensions, especially in the dream sequence, could well be compared to the similarly dreamlike fall from innocence of Young Goodman Brown in Nathaniel Hawthorne's story. The anguish resulting from Tancredi's failure to understand the sexual impulse stirring within him is comparable to the narrator's bewilderment in Sherwood Anderson's "I Want to Know Why" and to the "anguish and anger" James Joyce's protagonist in "Araby" feels at the end of that story.

Tancredi's awareness, on the other hand, of his ability to destroy—another form of initiation—can be compared to the similar realization in Arthur Miller's play *After the Fall*, as Quentin says of Holga's realization after experiencing war and the Holocaust, "after the Fall, after many, many deaths," "we are very dangerous." Tancredi's awareness of his destructive potential, however, contrasts sharply with the almost complete lack of a similar awareness on the part of the main character in Luigi Pirandello's CINCI, who kills but feels no responsibility for his action. — P T M

Mphahlele, Es'kia. The Master of Doornvlei.

South Africa
Short Stories, African (English). Winchester, MA: Faber and Faber, 1965.

Author: Es'kia Mphahlele (1919–), a distinguished South African writer and literary scholar, has long been outspoken against the South African government's Banta Education Act. His powerful voice has been heard in the more than seventeen books he has written or edited since he published his first collection of short stories in 1947. Banned from teaching in South Africa in 1952, Mphahlele sought exile in Nigeria, France, and the United States. He has taught in Paris, Nairobi, Denver, Philadelphia, and the University of South Carolina. He returned to South Africa in 1977 when the ban was lifted. He is now first professor of African literature at the University of Witwatersrand in Johannesburg and has held a Fulbright Visiting Professorship at the University of South Carolina.

Story: The story THE MASTER OF DOORNVLEI depicts the relationship between a white farmer,

Sarel Britz, owner of the Doornvlei farm, and his black foreman, Mfukeri. Because it is important to Sarel to establish a favorable working relationship with his laborers, he puts the black Mfukeri in charge of them. As Sarel observes about his workers, "They're fully grown-up; some of them cleverer and wiser than us Whites."

Sarel stresses to Mfukeri the necessity for fairness to all the laborers and warns against beating them, but Mfukeri does not listen. The laborers protest the black foreman's inhumanity when he drives them beyond their physical abilities, as when he forces a ten-year-old boy to work in the rain and the boy later dies of pneumonia. Led by a refugee from Johannesburg, they present Sarel with an ultimatum that, no matter how liberal he may be, he cannot tolerate from a black man. Sarel's fear mounts as the conflict between whites and blacks

climaxes in a symbolic battle between Mfukeri's bull and Sarel's stallion. When the bull gores the stallion, Mfukeri feels victorious. Sarel now knows that Mfukeri must be given a choice—to shoot his bull or to leave. Mfukeri "coaxes his bull off the premises" and walks away.

Comparison: At one point in the story, a bird trapped and caught in the window by the little boy symbolizes the helplessness of blacks entrapped in a labor system that strips them of their human dignity. There can be no redress against wrongs. So it is with Bigger Thomas in Richard Wright's *Native Son.* Alex Haley's *Roots* reflects a similar theme of oppression and abuse, and *The Life of Frederick Douglass* portrays an almost endless account of the abuse and injustices suffered by enslaved people in America. — M J J

Mrozek, Slawomir. CHILDREN.

Poland
Russian and Eastern European Literature. Glenview, IL: ScottForesman, 1970. Translated by Konrad Syrop.

Author: A master of satire in both short fiction and drama, Mrozek (1930–) was born in Borzicin, Poland. After spending several semesters studying architecture, Eastern culture, and painting in Krakow, he opted for a literary career. At the beginning of this career, Mrozek supported himself as a cartoonist specializing in satire and humor. Both of these characteristics have carried over into his writing, and his short stories tend to possess a pictorial element that can probably be attributed to his work as a cartoonist.

After a short stint as a journalist, Mrozek became a full-time writer of fiction and drama. His first collection of short stories, *Slon,* published in 1957, was a best-seller in Poland and has since been translated into many languages (in English as *Elephant*). Most of the stories in this collection satirize the weaknesses of the Polish Communist government and its leaders. Although generally the satire is more humorous than stinging, the cumula-

tive effect of the stories is to make the government appear more than slightly ridiculous.

In 1969, Mrozek fled Poland after his writing involved him in difficulties with the government. After living in Paris for a time, he made his home in Italy.

Story: Innocently, some children build a snowman in the square. It is a typical snowman. The body is made up of three large snowballs, and it has buttons made of coal and a carrot for a nose. Everyone passing by admires it, but that evening there are complaints. The news agent says its carrot nose mimics his red one and calls attention to his drinking. The chairman of the cooperative complains that the three snowballs, one on top of the other, imply that in the cooperative one thief sits on top of another. The president of the local national council claims that placing the snowman outside his window ridicules his authority and, furthermore, its buttons ridicule his walking about his house with his fly undone. The children plead their innocence to all charges, but are punished nevertheless. The next morning, in their own yard, the children decide to make three more snowmen. The one representing the news agent is to have a red nose to call attention to his drinking. The one representing the chairman of the cooperative will have three snowballs arranged just as the original snowman did. And the one representing the president of the local national council will have buttons because his fly is undone.

Comparison: The most obvious comparison for this selection (also translated as "The Snowman") is with other Mrozek works, including ON A JOURNEY. In addition to the ridicule of communism and the communist bureaucracy, the parable-like structure of Mrozek's short satirical pieces can be examined and evaluated. CHILDREN may also be compared with Sienkiewicz's YANKO THE MUSICIAN for a discussion of the ways in which adults are either deliberately or unwittingly cruel to children. — H M M

MROZEK, SLAWOMIR. ON A JOURNEY.

Poland
Russian and Eastern European Literature. Glenview, IL: ScottForesman, 1970.
Translated by Konrad Syrop.

Author: See CHILDREN.

Story: Adopting the persona of the innocent traveler, a satirical device that follows the examples of Jonathan Swift and Mark Twain, Mrozek describes a journey by chaise to an unfamiliar part of Poland. Passing through deserted countryside, he is surprised to see a man dressed in the uniform of the post office standing by the side of the road, then another dressed in the same manner, and still another, and so on. In response to his question, the coachman explains that these men are on state duty; they are the telegraph line. When a message comes through, one man shouts it along to the next. The coachman proudly explains that they constitute a *wireless* telegraph. Originally the area was to have had a true telegraph, but the poles were stolen and there was no wire.

Thus far, the story is more ridiculous than satirical. But the situation changes when the coachman uses what may be termed "totalitarian logic" to justify the system by explaining its advantages: timber is saved, there is no need to repair storm damage, humans are more intelligent than poles and wires. The only problem is that sometimes in the winter the wolves cause interruptions. In response to a question by the narrator, the coachman says he would not prefer a regular telegraph system to this because now there is no shortage of jobs in the district.

Comparison: Unmistakable in the effect of its broad satire, this short story (also translated as "The Telegraph") may be compared with other works critical, to a greater or lesser degree, of the inefficiencies of a totalitarian regime. Students may be asked to comment on the effectiveness of Mrozek's satire as compared with the more realistic and more incidental criticisms contained in Solzhenitsyn's MATRYONA'S HOME, ZAKHAR-THE-POUCH, and THE RIGHT HAND or with the less vituperative, perhaps incidental criticism in Sholokhov's THE FATE OF A MAN. Students might also read Jonathan Swift's "A Modest Proposal" to discuss the effectiveness of satire in effecting change. — H M M

MURAKAMI HARUKI: ON MEETING MY 100 PERCENT WOMAN ONE FINE APRIL MORNING.

Japan
World Writers Today. Glenview, IL: ScottForesman, 1995.
Translated by Kevin Flanagan and Tamotsu Omi.

Author: Born in Tokyo, Murakami Haruki (1949–) attended Waseda University and managed a jazz band in Tokyo from 1974 to 1981. He won the Noma Literary Prize for his novel *Wild Sheep Chase* and the Tanizaki Prize for *The End of the World* and *Hard-Boiled Wonderland.* Two other novels, *Norwegian Wood* and *Dance, Dance, Dance,* have enjoyed enormous popularity.

Story: On one fine April morning, the narrator passes a woman he considers his 100 percent woman. He fantasizes about her and rehearses what to say to her, but she disappears into the crowd. Still dreaming about the encounter, he tells a story he should have tried to tell her. It begins with "Once upon a time" and ends with "Isn't that a sad story?" In the story, a teenage couple part, with the understanding that if they were really the 100 percent perfect persons for each other they would meet again and marry. But, fourteen years later, the memories are weak. They pass without speaking and disappear into the crowd.

Comparison: This story of unrequited love finds parallels in stories from mythology to cinema. For example, in the story of Apollo and Daphne, as told by Ovid in *The Metamorphoses,* Apollo in his chase plans a speech with which to dazzle Daphne, but to no avail. The protagonist in THE DAY THE DANCERS CAME by Bienvenido Santos also rehearses a speech to impress the visiting dancers.   — M L

NAIPAUL, V. S.   B. WORDSWORTH.

Trinidad
World Writers Today. Glenview, IL: ScottForesman, 1995.

Author: V. S. Naipaul (1932–), born in Trinidad of Indian ancestry, has emerged as one of the most intelligent and powerful writers in the English language. His brilliance in school took him to Oxford for further education, and he soon settled in England. His early stories and novels, many set in the country of his birth, are comedies of manners marked by a colorful cast of characters and deep humor. Among these, *The Mystic Masseur* (1957) and *A House for Mr Biswas* (1961) have become classics. The scathing novels of his middle period are set in various locales, including the portrayal of an emerging African nation in *A Bend in the River* (1979), which has elicited comparison with Joseph Conrad. In more recent years, Naipaul has turned to detailed, sensitive, and highly critical book-length essays based on his travels around the world, including three books on India, one on the Muslim world, and one on the southern United States. He has received every major literary prize awarded in England and was knighted by the queen in 1992.

Story: A stranger appears one day at the gate of a young boy's home in Trinidad. The man says he wants to watch the bees circling about the gru-gru palm trees in the yard. The boy's mother is suspicious, but grants his request, telling her son to stay and watch him. What most impresses the boy is the perfection of the man's English, "so good it didn't sound natural." In response to the boy's "What you does do, mister?" the stranger replies, "I am a poet."

In fact, he claims to be the greatest poet in the world, at work on the greatest poem in the world.

He becomes the boy's friend and gently opens the boy's eyes to the miracles of life and the world about him. As they gaze at the stars together, the boy "felt like nothing, and at the same time I had never felt so big and great in all my life." The boy too resolves to be a poet. In their conversations, and in their walks together, the world is transformed for the boy into "a most exciting place." But one day, he finds his friend looking old and weak. The greatest poem in the world is not going well. The poet has lost his power, and in his face the boy sees the marks of coming death. The old man admits that all his talk about poetry and the greatest poem in the world wasn't true. It was just a joke. But his voice breaks as he says this, and the young boy runs home crying, "like a poet, for everything I saw."

Comparison: Although, as a story of the coming of age of a budding poet and the loss of innocence, B. WORDSWORTH may be compared initially with such classic stories as James Joyce's "Araby," Naipaul's story is primarily a powerful and tenderly

moving evocation of poetic hope in a world of harsh realities. B. Wordsworth, who lives in poverty, earning a few pennies by singing calypso in season, says his name is Black Wordsworth, and an effective discussion of the story can begin with a reading of any one of William Wordsworth's shorter poems, focusing on such issues as the tension between poetic beauty and economic necessity. The implied relationship between William and Black Wordsworth may serve as a basis for a discussion of the impact on our lives of those we look up to and admire while young.

The short story "Sally" by the Mexican American writer Sandra Cisneros offers an excellent thematic comparison. Like B. Wordsworth, Sally is a figure parents regard warily. She is far too free, too beautiful—the very traits that attract the nameless young narrator of the story. Sally too is a complex figure, with her own doubts, her own insecurities at her inner-city school, returning home each day to a life far removed from the freedom she seeks. The young girl narrating the story looks up to her, but recognizes in her as well an unfulfilled imaginative and spiritual life with which she deeply sympathizes.   — B M

NAIPAUL, V. S. THE ENEMY.

Trinidad
A Flag on the Island. London: Andre Deutsch, 1967.

Author: See B. WORDSWORTH.

Story: THE ENEMY is a story of a young boy in Trinidad who is torn between his father and his mother when they separate. Out of loyalty to his father, he thinks of his mother as the enemy. The story is told in the first person by the boy, and we learn of the life the family led prior to the breakup. The father was overseeing workers on a sugar estate, treated them harshly, and seemed about to pay for this mistreatment. Threats of physical harm from the workers finally drove the mother from the house. The boy stayed with his father.

His father talks with the boy, imparting what little wisdom he has. In spite of his father's simplicity, the bond between father and son seems solid and

deep. The father's fear of the workers' threats culminates one evening during a thunderstorm in which he believes he hears the workers moving about outside the house. When the storm blows in the window and puts out the lamp, he screams out in terror. We learn the next day that the father died of fear.

The boy now joins his mother and moves to Port-of-Spain. We see their life together through his eyes as he comes to recognize her love for him, her admiration for his success in school, and her concern when he is injured. In his mother's tears, he discovers his own love for her.

Comparison: This story, set in Trinidad, is typical of Naipaul's humor and compassion in treating char-

120

actcrs who seem simple but are far from simple-minded. The tale paints a vivid picture of daily island life, tracing the relationships among father, mother, and son with sensitivity and insight. Several thematic concerns make the story an apt choice for comparison with stories dealing with father-son or mother-son relationships, family breakups, and coming of age. One such story is Bruno Schulz's COCKROACHES.

On a more general level, the humor and regional flavor of the work make it an interesting counterpoint to American literature of the South. Because it is told in the first person by the son, it also may be compared fruitfully with other first-person accounts of the lives of young boys, for example, Eudora Welty's portrayal of family relationships in such short stories as "Kin" and "Why I Live at the P.O."
— B M

NAKOS, LILIKA. THE BROKEN DOLL.

Greece

Life and Letters Today: An International Quarterly of Living Literature. Winter 1936. Translated by Allan Ross Macdougall.

Author: Lilika Nakos (1890–1989), one of the writers of the "Generation of the 1930s," was born in Athens into a wealthy family. Her father was a lawyer and a socialist member of parliament; her mother was involved with social affairs. She spent the first years of her life under the care of, as she put it, "a woman of the people" from Epirus, a region of Greece typified by remote mountain villages. That early association may have helped her develop the wide understanding of people that shows so clearly in her eight novels, approximately twenty-five fictionalized biographies, and many short stories, all written in demotic Greek.

When Lilika was nine years old, her mother left her husband and, with Lilika, took up a new life in Geneva. Because the husband in a Greek family has absolute control, separation from—indeed, any defiance of—the man in the family bore a risk of retaliation. Because Lilika was a girl, her father was violently opposed to her education. Yet her mother saw to it that Lilika attended high school in Geneva and took advanced degrees. When Nakos's first story was published in Paris in 1928, her father threatened the publisher with a lawsuit if he published any more of her work, and he threatened to cut off Lilika's hands if she continued to write. She was twenty-nine years old at the time. She continued to write, but her father's attitude was a lifelong source of deep pain.

She lived in Paris for a number of years and wrote in French, but in 1930, after her father's death, she moved back to Greece. There she supported herself and her mother by working as a high school teacher and journalist. She wrote *The Children's Inferno: Stories of the Great Famine in Greece* while working as a volunteer at a makeshift hospital during the German occupation of Greece in 1941–42. The stories were smuggled out of Athens by a foreign nurse. When they were immediately published in Switzerland, they brought to the rest of the world's attention the terrible famine in Greece. During that winter, 300,000 people starved to death. The Red Cross and others immediately began sending international aid. Nakos, who believed that important writing affects people in definite ways, considered these stories her finest works.

Her first novel, *The Lost,* created a great stir because it dared to probe the life of a woman who searched endlessly for love without ever coming to terms with sex. Her short stories, including HELENITSA (1944), were published in the United States as *The Children's Inferno* in 1946. Nakos died, after an extended illness, in May 1989.

Story: Nakos draws upon her own experiences in her writing, and this very brief, heartbreaking story is a good example. The father of the family drives his wife and small daughter out of his house. The mother takes Photini to Marseille, where she gets a job and they begin life anew, much as Nakos and her own mother began a new life in Geneva. The fictional family, like the real one, must cope with the threat of retribution. In Nakos's case, she met only threats. In this story, however, the father's henchmen kidnap Photini from her mother.

The characters and the situation are dynamically drawn in a clear style, and the situation is instantly understandable. The story's title comes from a compelling picture at the end of the story: Photini is being driven away, looking out the back and seeing her mother running, crying, after the kidnapper's car, holding out the doll that has been knocked from Photini's arms.

Comparison: One important American short story that shares the theme of the legally sanctioned violence of one family member against another is Charlotte Perkins Gilman's "The Yellow Wallpaper." In it, a husband, in the name of caring, drives his wife mad by cutting her off from her child and refusing to allow her to engage in her work. The family relationships of the safari couple in Hemingway's "The Short Happy Life of Francis Macomber" put forth the premise that a wife who rejects her normal state of being dominated by her husband cannot tolerate that husband's becoming a real man. Truman Capote's "A Christmas Memory" also explores the relationships within a family, as does Katherine Mansfield's slice-of-life tale "The Garden Party." — E M

NAKOS, LILIKA. HELENITSA.

Greece

The Children's Inferno: Stories of the Great Famine in Greece. Hollywood, CA: Gateway Books, 1946. Translated by Allan Ross Macdougall.

Author: See THE BROKEN DOLL.

Story: Two children, six-year-old Helenitsa and her older brother, are brought, half-frozen and starved, to the hospital. There is no room for them there; each bed holds five patients already. The police officer who found them huddled in the subway begs the nurse to take the girl, at least, and she finally agrees. The boy, Dino, says that there are seven children in the family—Helenitsa is the youngest—and that the children's mother is sick in bed. Their father, a mason, has pleurisy and cannot work. The other children leave and return home as hunger dictates. Helenitsa is the one who keeps all the family's spirits up, making them laugh and not crying from her hunger.

After Dino leaves the hospital, Helenitsa smiles at the nurse, and the nurse is so startled and pleased that she automatically asks the child what she would like to have. Helenitsa answers in her weak voice, "I would like some French fried potatoes." The child's simple request, in a city where the population is dying of hunger, is astonishing. Everyone becomes involved in the search for potatoes as the child grows weaker and weaker. They finally find some, fry them, and offer them to her. She dies clutching them in her hand.

Comparison: French fries in this story are survival objects. For all the people involved in the search, they become a symbol of life free from oppression.

In another story concerned with death, Jack London's "To Build a Fire," the main character fails to recognize building a fire as a possibility until it is too late for fire to save his life. In Stephen Crane's "The Open Boat," death is more than a possibility for the four survivors of a shipwreck. It is a probability that must be faced with the violent cresting of each huge wave.

As Sarah Orne Jewett's "Miss Tempy's Watchers" begins, Temperance Dent is dead. Before she died, however, she asked two of her old friends, one very poor and one quite wealthy, to watch over her after her death. During the afternoon and night before Miss Tempy's funeral, the two women are inspired by their shared memories of the generous, loving, simple woman who lies dead. Like Helenitsa, Miss Tempy kept up the spirits of all those around her. — E M

NARAYAN, R. K. FATHER'S HELP.

India

World Writers Today. Glenview, IL: ScottForesman, 1995.

Author: R. K. Narayan (1906–), born in Madras and educated in Mysore in south India, learned Tamil as his mother tongue but writes in English. He first worked as a journalist, then began a career as a creative writer. *Swami and Friend* (1935) was the first of a series of novels set in the imaginary village of Malgudi. His writing is marked by humor, quiet irony, a cast of colorful characters, and the enduring conflict between the Indian and colonial cultures. His first novel was recommended for publication in England by Graham Greene. Narayan has enjoyed a positive critical reception both in England and America, and his prolific output has included ten novels, five collections of short stories, three collections of essays, three books on Indian epics, and memoirs. He is considered the foremost Indian novelist of his generation and won India's highest literary honor for his novel *The Guide* in 1958. In 1980, he was awarded the distinguished A. C. Benson Medal by the Royal Society of London. *The Vendor of Sweets* (1967) and *The Painter of Signs* (1977) are among the best of his later novels. FATHER'S HELP was published in 1972, and A HORSE AND TWO GOATS in 1985.

Story: Swaminathan complains of a headache in order to stay home from school. When his father insists that he go, he complains that the teacher would beat him for arriving so late. Swaminathan's father writes a letter complaining about the teacher and asks Swaminathan to deliver it to the headmaster.

Because Swaminathan knows the teacher is not as mean as he has made him out to be, he delays the delivery of the letter and tries all day to tempt the teacher into beating him. Finally, toward the end of the day, the teacher slaps his palms for repeated insolence. Swaminathan runs to deliver the letter, only to find that the headmaster has left for the day.

Back at home, the father accuses the son of being a coward for not delivering the letter. He also suggests that Swaminathan is lying about the headmaster's absence. In disgust, he tears up the letter and says that his son deserves a mean and violent teacher.

Comparison: By the end of the story, Swami learns a major lesson that is sure to affect him for life. The relationship between father and son in a subtle contest of will and wit to ensure that the son grows up right is a universal theme. Likewise, Swami's plight in getting caught between parent and teacher as he tries to cover up his own reluctance to go to school resonates with young students worldwide. His daylong preoccupation with getting his teacher into trouble is the kind of mischief that Mark Twain's Tom Sawyer and Huckleberry Finn would plot. The relationship between teacher and student might have been a scene in a French classroom in the short story THE LAST LESSON by Alphonse Daudet. Until the boy, Franz, discovered that this day was the last day his native language would be taught in that school, he had dreaded the daily language lesson. — M L

NARAYAN, R. K. A HORSE AND TWO GOATS.

India

Under the Banyan Tree and Other Stories. New York: Viking, 1985.

Author: See FATHER'S HELP.

Story: In this simple tale, the confrontation of two cultures is symbolized by mutual misunderstanding.

An inhabitant of the tiniest village on the huge continent of India, an old man named Muni is left with little in life except his wife and two goats. Once the owner of a flock of forty sheep, he has seen his fortunes gradually decline to the point where he cannot even get credit for food at the local shop. While he waits for the day to pass in the hope that his wife will be able to earn a little money at odd jobs, he whiles away his time sitting on the pedestal of the statue of a clay horse, his two goats grazing nearby.

The sudden appearance of an American tourist in a stationwagon sets the story in motion. The American is attracted to the clay statue and longs to buy it. He launches into a discussion aimed at obtaining the horse from Muni, whom he mistakenly believes to be the owner. Unfortunately, Muni is unable to speak or understand English, with the exception of the words *yes* and *no,* which he uses interchangeably.

In the ensuing discussion, Muni and the American tourist talk past each other in English and Tamil respectively, the former rambling on about a recent murder, his childhood, and the Hindu religion, while the latter is discussing his business, his home, and his hope to add the horse to his art collection. In the end, Muni thinks he has sold his two goats to the man, takes the man's money, and departs. The American loads the statue of the horse into his car. The mystification of Muni and his wife is complete when the two goats wander back to their house.

Comparison: Narayan's gentle comic tone has often been compared to that of Chekhov, and the mutual confusion in the confrontation of two cultures in this story makes a useful comparison for any tale in which misunderstandings are based on linguistic or cultural differences—for example, Paul Bowles's amusing short story of an American in Thailand, "You Have Left Your Lotus Pods on the Bus." It is also reminiscent of a number of American and European stories in which a simple-minded farmer or peasant winds up "outwitting" a more sophisticated city dweller, although in this case the farmer is equally baffled. Examples for comparison here include Siegfried Lenz's stories "A Grand Day in Schissomir" and "Fresh Fish."

The theme of the difficulty of human communication, shown here in its most elemental form as two completely different languages, is interwoven with a broader common literary theme: the conflict of spiritual and material values. For Muni, the horse is the incarnation of powerful legends from Hindu mythology. The redeemer will come in the shape of a horse called Kalki, who will trample all bad men. For the American, the horse is a commodity to be purchased and displayed in his home, something to show off at cocktail parties. Narayan's story ends ambiguously, with the seeming triumph of the material over the spiritual. Yet what the future holds for both cultures is left in doubt. — B M

NARAYAN, R. K. THE MIRROR.

India
A Story-Teller's World. London: Penguin, 1989.

Author: See A HORSE AND TWO GOATS.

Story: "Thousands of years ago, a peasant and his wife were living happily," that is, until a wayfarer gives the man a talisman, a square piece of glass that he is never to take out of its pouch or trouble will follow. Had the peasant not revealed the secret to his wife, all would have been well. When the wife cannot overcome her suspicion and takes the glass out and stares at it, she finds that it is the picture of a woman. Crazed with jealousy, she attacks her husband. He in turn locks her up in a room.

Remembering that the talisman might be put to good use, he takes it out and sees in the glass a picture of a man. Angry at his wife's infidelity, he smashes the glass. In interpreting this gesture as the end to a passing fancy, the wife's attitude improves. In seeing her recover, the husband too gets over his anguish. The two live in harmony thereafter, never mentioning the portraits in the mirror again.

Comparison: Rich with themes, this little parable is reminiscent of the snake's temptation of Eve in the Garden of Eden, but with a happy ending. A

Greek myth, captured as a short story in verse in *The Metamorphoses* by Ovid, a first-century Roman poet, tells the woeful tale of suspicion between husband and wife. Cephalus, seduced by the goddess Aurora while he is away, returns home to test his wife's fidelity. When she hesitates for an instant under his heavy interrogation, he accuses her of having been unfaithful. Now that the seeds of doubt are sown, she wonders about her husband. She follows him while he hunts. His cry "Aura, Aura," a plea for the wind to cool him, sounds like the passionate call for another woman. Upset, his wife stirs. The movement in the bushes alerts Cephalus to his prey. He throws his javelin and kills his wife.

The credulous fascination with a talisman, with the talisman inviting itself to resolve the trouble it has caused, is reminiscent of "The Monkey's Paw" by W. W. Jacobs. In this story, the first wish is accompanied by a death. The second wish is intended to cancel the first by bringing the dead person back to life. The third wish cancels the second, for the presence of a live but mangled body is too great a burden to bear. — M L

Nexø, Martin Andersen. BIRDS OF PASSAGE.

Denmark

A World of Great Stories. New York: Crown, 1947. Translated by Lida Siboni Hanson.

Author: Martin Andersen Nexø (1869–1954) was born into a poor family of eleven children and spent his early years first as a shoemaker's apprentice, then as a schoolteacher. He was nearly thirty years old before he began to write, though he soon completed *Shadows*, a collection of short stories, followed two years later by his first novel, *The Frank Family.*

The reciprocal relationship of work, human dignity, and justice forms a major theme in his writing. In perhaps his best-known works, the four-volume *Pelle the Conqueror* and his trilogy *Ditte,* Nexø successfully idealizes his view of the proletarian struggle to survive and live fully. Both works reveal an attraction to communism.

After World War I, Nexø settled in Germany and later traveled throughout the Soviet Union. He recounted those experiences in the U.S.S.R. in *Toward Dawn,* published in 1923. His return to Denmark was followed by *In God's Land,* a novel about Danish farmers; *A Small Child,* the first volume of his memoirs; and *Under the Open Sky,* his last work. With the publication of these books, Nexø became widely known as one of the strongest critics of Nazism. He was, in fact, imprisoned by the Nazi forces for his sharp attacks on them. Nexø survived the experience, though he wrote no other books.

Story: Nexø's BIRDS OF PASSAGE is an unconventional love story about two highly unconventional lovers. But it is primarily a vivid character sketch of Peter Nikolai Ferdinand Baltasar Rasmussen Djong, who styles himself King Nebuchadnezzar—a shoemaker by trade, a "wandering journeyman" by nature, for whom "the desire to set out for the unknown was the moving power of his life; and he knew nothing finer than to break away, no matter from what."

As an aging yet still incurable vagrant, King Nebuchadnezzar wanders back to his native Denmark, where he is unable to find any temporary work and thus resolves to "accept what great men in antiquity had accepted before him: meals at the cost of the community." He enters the public workhouse and determines to end his days there, free of his urge to roam. His resolution is forgotten the afternoon he spies Malvina, "his lady, his last and only great—but also unhappy—love," the only woman "who, like him, had some of the rotation of the universe in her blood." Malvina too has succumbed to life in the workhouse, where the male and female inmates are strictly segregated. King Nebuchadnezzar determines, no matter what the cost, to have one final day of freedom with her, one final tour of the city.

Their short time of escape and reunion proves both romantic and sadly comic—a bittersweet coda to their relationship over the years. Ultimately, the day is one of awareness for King Nebuchadnezzar, who at last admits that "it was all over. He was absolutely good for nothing. He had grown old . . . life could no longer be snatched in passing." But at the same time, he revels in the fact that "he had had his day. He had been no common trash. Gosh almighty, he had made things hum! What precious memories he had!"

Early the next morning, King Nebuchadnezzar and Malvina are found by the authorities, and both are returned to the workhouse. This final trip, in an open carriage no less, becomes the grandest of adventures: "They had received permission to have the top down, and were now leaning elegantly back in their seats. . . . King Nebuchadnezzar waved his hand condescendingly at the passers-by, and Malvina threw kisses at them with her fingers. Then they both laughed, and the policeman pretended not to notice."

Malvina, who caught cold during the night of freedom, dies shortly afterward. King Nebuchadnezzar "never again had the courage to compete by himself with the big world" and preferred instead to "live in his memories of the glorious days in which he had held his own so valiantly."

Comparison: BIRDS OF PASSAGE is both lyrically sad and humorous, with a descriptive style particularly reminiscent of O. Henry. An interesting counterpoint for the King Nebuchadnezzar–Malvina pairing can be found in the lifelong commitment and final day together of Jeff and Jennie in Arna Bontemps's "A Summer Tragedy." Both Nexø and Bontemps endow their characters with a charm that allows some inherent sense of dignity to triumph over poverty and shabbiness. Both stories are about accepting old age, poverty, and death, yet there is humor amid the pathos.
— P G L

NGUGI, JAMES. THE MARTYR.

Kenya
Modern African Prose. London: Heinemann, 1964.

Author: James Ngugi, pen name of Ngũgĩ wa Thiong'o (1938–), East Africa's most prominent writer, was born in Limuru, Kenya, and graduated with honors in English from Makerere University College in Uganda and the University of Leeds. He has taught in East African schools and in the United States as visiting lecturer at Northwestern University. He is currently senior lecturer and chairman of the department of literature at the University of Nairobi. He has written numerous short stories and essay collections as well as a novel, *Weep Not, Child,* which won the Dakar Festival of Negro Arts. A play he authored has been produced at the National Theatre in Uganda.

Story: Mrs. Hill feels herself drawn into the kind of blind panic that spreads through a community threatened by forces it can neither understand nor control. Mr. and Mrs. Garstone have been murdered in their home by "unknown gangsters." The prevalent rumor is that the murderers were let into the house by the Garstones' own native houseboy.

Mrs. Hill, a widow who lives alone in a house set among large tea plantations, finds temporary solace in the belief that her liberal attitudes and fine treatment of her servants will certainly protect her from such betrayal: "'That's all they need. *Treat them kindly.* They will take kindly to you. Look at my boys. They all love me'. . . . Mrs. Hill had done some liberal things to her 'boys.' Not only had she built some brick quarters (*brick,* mind you) but had also put up a school for the children. It did not matter if the school had not enough teachers or if the children learnt only half a day and worked in the plantations for the other half; it was more than most other settlers had the courage to do!" Her friend

126

Mrs. Smiles expresses the other popular view: "How could they do it? We've brought 'em civilization. We stopped slavery and tribal wars. Were they not all leading savage miserable lives? . . . But I've always said they'll never be civilized, simply can't take it."

Both attitudes are, of course, equally offensive to those to whom they are applied. Mrs. Hill's own houseboy understands both: "He had worked with cruel types like Mrs. Smiles and Mrs. Hardy. But he always knew where he stood with such. But Mrs. Hill! Her liberalism was almost smothering. Njoroge hated all settlers. He hated above all what he thought was their hypocrisy and self-satisfaction. He knew that Mrs. Hill was no exception. She was like all the others, only she loved paternalism. It convinced her she was better than the others. But she was worse. You did not know exactly where you stood with her."

Njoroge seems hardly the "gangster" type: "He was a tall, broad-shouldered person nearing middle age. He had been in the Hills' service for more than ten years." When the plantation quiets down for the night, Njoroge assumes a different persona. Walking to his quarters, he allows his anger to surface: "You. You. I've lived with you so long. And you've reduced me to this! In my own land! What have I got from you in return?" Njoroge's bitterness goes far beyond his personal treatment at the hands of Mrs. Hill. He had once owned the land on which the Hills built their thriving plantation. His father had left during a temporary famine; when he returned, he found the Hills occupying his land. Then he had been killed when police fired upon a peaceful demonstration. As Njoroge remembers the past, "a grim satisfaction came over him. Tonight, anyway, Mrs. Hill would die—pay for her own smug liberalism or paternalism and pay for all the sins of her settlers' race. It would be one settler less."

As the story builds to a climax, Njoroge begins to remember Mrs. Hill with her husband and her children and to see her not as a symbol of her race, but rather an individual person. He realizes he cannot go through with the murder. Even as his accomplices arrive, he sneaks into the bush and runs to warn Mrs. Hill, knocking on her door and calling her name to awaken her to danger. She, meanwhile, has become terrified. She is sitting with her husband's pistol in her hand trying to argue herself out of her fear. For the first time, she thinks of Njoroge not as her servant, but as a husband and father. Surely, she thinks, she has nothing to fear from him. Suddenly, he is at her door, calling her name. She remembers the circumstances of the Garstones' murder. Determined to die bravely, she opens the door and fires.

Comparison: Revenge is a well-known plot mechanism. "The Cask of Amontillado" by Edgar Allan Poe is a classic example of the revenge motif. Both stories also use irony to raise questions about the relative guilt or innocence of the victim.

Also a predominant idea in THE MARTYR is that people frequently see one another not as individuals, but rather as extensions of the larger social group of which they happen to be a member. In that regard, Ngugi's story can be compared to Ralph Ellison's *Invisible Man,* to Willa Cather's "Paul's Case," and to Katherine Mansfield's "Miss Brill." — B H N

Nhat-Tien. AN UNSOUND SLEEP.

Vietnam

Asian and Pacific Short Stories. Rutland, VT: Charles E. Tuttle, 1974. Translated by Le Van Hoan.

Author: A member of the International P.E.N., a society of writers, editors, and literary people, Nhat-Tien is a novelist and writer of short stories. He has also worked as a journalist and a teacher. Nhat-Tien draws his themes from his observations about the rapid changes in Vietnamese society brought about by new political movements and by Westernization and modernization.

Story: Old Phan's peaceful routine and daily indulgence are rudely interrupted by new political movements and by the new independence of young women. One day, returning from his favorite spot at the marketplace where he enjoys a drink in the company of other men, he notices a certain change in his daughter. He guesses correctly that she is in love. He hopes that she is not any more seriously involved, for it is considered "ill-bred" for a girl to form relationships with men that the family knows nothing about. He is disheartened and worried upon discovering that the young man, Su, works for the underground struggle against the government. When he meets him, however, old Phan comes to like Su. Unfortunately, the young man is arrested, and Miss Phan disappears. The old man visits Su at the prison, and the two become good friends as they share their concern over Miss Phan's fate.

After the revolution breaks out, Miss Phan is released and comes home. She marries Su. Both unemployed, they live with her father, who gives up his old pleasures to support them. When Su finds a job in a distant place, they leave old Phan reluctantly. He insists he can take care of himself. When a letter informs him that Su's job has not worked out after all, the old man tries to work harder. But the weakness brought about by age and indulgence

causes his dismissal. His rent unpaid, he is evicted. He leaves his house with only a knapsack. After a while, he looks like the bums he used to laugh at. He carries with him a treasured packet of letters from Su and a picture of the young couple on their wedding day. The wrapper around these, ironically, advertises "tiger balm," an Asian panacea, and features revolution as the main topic.

Comparison: Even though a family tries to stay together, political changes and other elements in society can threaten its unity. Old Phan's peace in his advanced years is threatened by the changing role of women, which separates him from his daughter, and by the changes in the political and economic structures around him. Without the traditional support that can be expected from children and without any type of financial security from the new government, old Phan ends up homeless and lonely. This effect of the evolution of societies upon individuals is also depicted in THE GRANDMOTHER by K. Surangkhanang of Thailand and GRANDMOTHER TAKES CHARGE by Lao She of China. — M L

NICOL, ABIOSETH. AS THE NIGHT THE DAY.

Sierra Leone
Modern African Prose. London: Heinemann, 1964.

Author: Abioseth Nicol, pen name for Davidson Nicol (1924–), was born in Freetown, Sierra Leone, and educated in Nigeria, Sierra Leone, and at Christ's College, Cambridge. He earned an M.D. degree as well as a Ph.D. in religion. He has served as senior pathologist for the Sierra Leone government, ambassador from Sierra Leone to the United Nations, high commissioner of the Republic of Sierra Leone to the United Kingdom, and ambassador to Denmark, Norway, Sweden, and Finland. Although most of his career has been dedicated to medicine and government service, he is nevertheless considered in the forefront of African short story writers. His poems and short stories have been broadcast by the British Broadcasting

Corporation and have appeared in a number of English and American magazines.

Story: Two boys, Kojo and Bandele, wait in the laboratory for their science class to begin. The only other person in the room is a club-footed Syrian boy, Basu, looking out the window with his back to them. Bored with waiting, Kojo and Bandele use a thermometer to measure the temperature of the inner flame of a Bunsen burner. Naturally, the thermometer bursts. The boys just have time to clean up the mercury and dump the broken glass into the waste bin before the rest of the boys enter the room. Before class is dismissed, the broken thermometer is found, and the rest of the story deals with Kojo's agony of guilt, tempered by his fear of being caught.

First the entire class is made to stay an hour after school, even though many of the boys, whom Kojo knows to be innocent, will miss an important soccer match. Then a laboratory attendant tries to test the boys' honesty using a "Bible and Key" method, but Kojo is saved from disclosure by the appearance of the laboratory master, who does not believe in the exercise. So the class continues to sit in silence. Time drags on until Kojo can no longer endure it. As he rises to his feet to confess, Bandele quickly volunteers the information that Basu was in the room ahead of the other boys. Basu denies guilt. When the adults leave the room, the boys all turn on him with accusations and begin throwing books at him. Basu cowers against the wall, bleeding from a small cut on his temple. At first Kojo watches, then "he turned round and picked up a book and flung it with desperate force at Basu, and then another. He felt somehow that there was an awful swelling of guilt which he could only shed by punishing himself through hurting someone. . . . He felt that somehow Basu was in the wrong, must be in the wrong, and if he hurt him hard enough he would convince the others and therefore himself that he had not broken the thermometer and that he had never done anything wrong." When the fight is broken up and the boys are dismissed, Bandele and Kojo skulk behind the door and overhear the master explain to Basu that "men are punished not always for what they do, but often for what people think they will do, or for what they are."

Kojo puts in a night filled with tears and the agony of anticipating the beating he would receive if he were to confess. Nevertheless, he heads out bravely the next morning determined to tell the truth. He is too late. The class bully has forced Basu to make a false confession. The matter is settled, explains the master, for, after all, "you cannot hope for too much from a Syrian boy."

Comparison: The story is told in a straightforward manner, the situation one with which young people can easily identify. The two major themes, suffering from secret guilt and relief from finding a scapegoat, are closely interwoven as they are in many stories. For example, what happens to Kojo in the attack on Basu is similar to the attack on Piggy in *Lord of the Flies.* The character of Bandele is revealed in a few sketchy details that make him immediately recognizable. Kojo is more fully developed and becomes a sympathetic and totally believable character. Thus, the story is particularly effective in demonstrating those human characteristics that all people share, regardless of cultural differences.

An interesting comparison can be made between AS THE NIGHT THE DAY and "The Lottery" by Shirley Jackson. Through its character development, AS THE NIGHT THE DAY provides a psychological framework for the stark Jackson story. The fight scene in Ralph Ellison's "Battle Royal" is another statement about how the operation of group pressure can turn seemingly reasonable people to violence. The harboring of secret guilt as a destructive force is a major theme in such works as Hawthorne's *The Scarlet Letter* and Dostoevski's *Crime and Punishment.* — B H N

O Yong-su. SEASIDE VILLAGE.

Korea
Asian and Pacific Short Stories. Rutland, VT: Charles E. Tuttle, 1974. Translated by Kim Dae-yun.

Author: O Yong-su (1914–) was born in Kyong-sang Nam-do in Korea. Educated in Japan, he taught secondary school, then turned to writing. His favorite subject was the little man in modern cities, whom he captured with a simple lyricism that is distinctly Korean. Exclusively a short story writer, some ninety of his works have been published in a five-volume *Collected Works* (1968). In 1955, he won the Korean Writers Award, and in 1958, the Asian Freedom Literature Award.

Other stories by O Yong-su that have been translated into English include "The Mountain Pass," "Migratory Bird," "Wild Grapes," "Birds of Passage," and "Echoes."

Story: Hae-sun, a young widow, has lived all her life in a small seaside village named "H." After her husband drowns with seven other fishermen, their boat lost in a storm, she continues to live with her mother-in-law and to work with the villagers to catch eels and fish, gather seaweed, and dig for clams. When Sung-su makes advances to her, she at first resists the idea of remarriage, but with her mother-in-law's approval and encouragement and her own sense of obligation to a man who has touched her, she at last decides to go with Sung-su to his farmland home.

The village is not the same without her, nor is she the same person outside her native village. Removed from the sand, wind, and sea that are the basic constituents of her own true self, she becomes distracted and miserable. With her husband away as a conscript laborer, she decides to go back to her native home, just as her mother had returned to her own home as soon as Hae-sun was married. Back again in the salt air of the seashore, she feels whole and alive again.

Comparison: Lyrical in its images, this story describes poignantly the bond Koreans feel with nature. Despite losing her first husband to the sea, Hae-sun never treats nature as an obstacle or enemy with whom she might have a struggle. Instead, she feels herself to be so much a part of the circuitry of nature that until she returns to those particular natural elements that constitute part of her early nurturing, she does not feel like a complete human being. This same participation in nature functions as a background in *The Sound of Waves* by Mishima Yukio. In this novella, the story of young lovers is interspersed among many lyrical passages describing the island, the sun, and the sea. Even though both earn their living in what might be considered a struggle against the sea, with Shinji proving his mettle in a storm, nature is felt to be as much a part of them as their own breath and blood.   — M L

PAPADIAMANTIS, ALEXANDROS. THE BEWITCHING OF THE AGA.

Greece
Tales from a Greek Island. Baltimore: Johns Hopkins University Press, 1987.
Translated by Elizabeth Constantinides.

Author: Alexandros Papadiamantis (1851–1911) was born on the island of Skiathos. This tiny Aegean island, sixteen square miles in size with a population of around four thousand people, became the setting for the majority of his 170 short stories and sketches. The remainder were set in Athens.

Papadiamantis grew up in an austere, religious atmosphere. His father was a priest. Orthodox Christianity, as well as older Greek religious beliefs, played a large role in his writings. As the family's eldest son, Alexandros was expected to take responsibility for his four sisters and one brother; priests like his father received no pay. Alexandros did not accept that responsibility. Although he attended school, he often stayed out due to rebelliousness, ill health, or lack of funds, and he did not take examinations to be a grammar school teacher, even though he qualified for them.

He lived alone in rundown boarding houses in Athens for most of his life, escaping to the island as often as he could. At the age of fifty-eight, too ill and homesick to remain in Athens, he returned to Skiathos, where his sisters took care of him for the last two-and-a-half years of his life.

Papadiamantis's stories, featuring myriad islands and Athenian characters, along with his careful observation of daily life and customs and his preference for the lowly, were popular with the public during his lifetime. The stories usually appeared in serial form in newspapers and magazines. THE

BEWITCHING OF THE AGA was published in 1896. Collections have appeared since his death on Skiathos in 1911.

Papadiamantis often wrote of social ills, such as the enslavement of women in "The Murderess," but he did not believe in change and often spoke out against the emancipation of women. More evidence of his dislike for change is seen in his use of the purist language Katharevousa. Yet he sometimes modified it, as he did in THE BEWITCHING OF THE AGA, with phrases taken from the islanders' talk.

Story: Papadiamantis begins this island story with a description of a deserted village that stands on the slope of a mountain. These ruins were once an occupied Greek village under Turkish rule, and its ruler was the last of the Ottoman Empire. The current Aga is quiet and mild-mannered. He speaks Greek and lives peacefully. To the villagers, however, he looks like a "charmed serpent whose teeth had been removed." One day, Auntie Siraino Pantousa, a soothsayer who possesses mysterious powers, announces to the other villagers that she will kill the Aga within a month's time. Soon she passes the Aga on the street and comments upon how sickly he looks and how unhealthy the village is for him. "You must be careful not to be done in so far from your home, poor soul," she says. From that day on, the Aga's health falters. Auntie Siraino goes into hiding. Although everyone in the village tells the Aga that he looks well, he grows weaker and weaker, and within one month he is dead. At the close of the story, the author asks, "And that sick man with his chronic disease, now four hundred and forty-four years old—who will bewitch him?" The "sick man" to whom the author refers is the Ottoman Empire.

Comparison: The Turks at the time of the story had occupied Greece for almost four hundred years. Agas like this one, living in a Greek community as an absolute ruler, suffered from the hatred directed at Turks and their country by the Greek people. It is clear that Auntie Siraino's powers exist, for the story presents several examples. Furthermore, she is courageous, speaking as she does to an official who could have her put to death on the spot. The question is whether Auntie causes the Aga's death by the power of her suggestion or whether he just happens to die of unknown causes at that particular time. In short, what is reality and what is illusion?

Edith Wharton wrote of reality and illusion in her story "Roman Fever." It tells of two women who happen across each other in a favorite city of their youth. As they explore the events of a particular evening long ago, one woman's illusion, with which she has lived for years, is overtaken by reality. In Kate Chopin's "The Story of an Hour," Louise Mallard, ill with a weak heart, takes the incorrect news of her husband's untimely death in an unexpected way. Although she loved him, she is now ecstatic at the thought of gaining her freedom. It is the reality of his subsequent appearance, alive, that kills her. In Charlotte Perkins Gilman's "The Yellow Wallpaper," a woman retreats from reality into madness because everything she values is taken from her in the name of love.

Illusion and reality are dealt with in a more lighthearted fashion in "The Secret Life of Walter Mitty" by James Thurber and "The Open Window" by H. H. Munro (Saki). Oppression and rebellion, two other compelling themes of this Papadiamantis tale, spring from life in a conquered country. For whatever reason, at the time of this story Auntie Siraino has had enough of the Aga and she does something about it—she rebels. Pearl S. Buck presents another character who rebels in "The Old Demon." Mrs. Wang knows that there is a war and that Japanese are killing Chinese, but the violence has not touched her village, and, besides, she does not even know what a Japanese looks like. She is more concerned with the rising river, for she understands well the danger it poses. But as the days go on, Mrs. Wang's village is bombed by airplanes and she is told of her brother's death at the hands of the Japanese. She thinks long and hard on these things, and when the enemy appears marching across the plains toward her village, she knows what she will do. When the villagers run away to higher land, she says she will follow. Instead, she opens a sluice gate in the tall dike and lets the old Yellow River demon sweep the enemy away. — E M

PAVESE, CESARE. SUICIDES.

Italy
Continental Short Stories: The Modern Tradition. New York: Norton, 1968.
Translated by A. E. Murch.

Author: Cesare Pavese (1908–1950) was born in Piedmont, but lived most of his life in Turin, where he attended and subsequently taught at the university before becoming editor of *La Cultura.* His anti-Fascist activities and writing caused his arrest and imprisonment for ten months in 1935. Following his release until his death by suicide in 1950, he wrote the novels, short stories, and poetry on which his present reputation depends and which made him a leader of the Italian neo-realist school of the time. His best novel is probably his last one, *The Moon and the Bonfire,* published in the year of his death. In addition, he translated the work of Melville, Defoe, Joyce, and Faulkner into Italian. According to one critic, "his *Moby Dick* is one of the great translations of a classic." His posthumously published diary, *This Business of Living,* details the intellectual and personal loneliness that led to his suicide at the age of forty-two. SUICIDES was published in 1938.

Story: SUICIDES details in retrospect the relationship between its male narrator and Carlotta, a relationship that ends in her suicide. The first of the story's four parts uses an interior monologue to describe the narrator, an extremely introspective, alienated man who asserts that he "asks nothing more of life than being allowed to watch," but who realizes that he suffers from "a vast, inept lack of confidence," causing him "to react against other people, when I come into contact with them, with stupid cruelty." Carlotta is his opposite, a remarkably timid woman, willing to accept his cruel treatment because of her desperate need for affection. Not surprisingly, the narrator "had caused her a lot of unhappiness in the short time we had known each other; she didn't know why, but all the men treated her like that." Their first sexual encounters conclude the first part of the story, and each ends with his abrupt departure after telling Carlotta that he prefers "to be alone afterwards."

The second part of the story focuses on the affair between the two as characterized through two typical encounters. In the first, the narrator allows himself to be beguiled by Carlotta (and a few drinks) into responding affectionately, drawing Carlotta into an evening of excited happiness, and staying the whole night with her. "On these occasions," he thinks, "Carlotta drew from me a tenderness that I reproached myself for the moment I was alone again." The other typical encounter shows the narrator making Carlotta "spend an evening of anguish by sitting coldly beside her on the divan," rebuffing all her advances, calling all her tenderness nonsense, and telling her "we are a man and woman who bore each other, but we get on all right in bed."

The story's third and fourth parts describe the narrator's growing boredom with Carlotta and the relationship and her descent into depression ending in suicide, a suicide suggested to her by a story the narrator tells her of the suicide of a friend. Carlotta's final depression is provoked by the narrator's leaving her, again, after a sexual encounter following a period of separation. He does not discover she has taken her own life until a month later, when he is moved to seek her out.

Comparison: SUICIDES, finally, is a story of the almost complete isolation of both the narrator and Carlotta, an isolation broken by a few moments of shared tenderness serving to make their isolation more difficult to endure. As a story of isolation and alienation, it might be compared with Melville's "Bartleby the Scrivener" or Richard Wright's "The Man Who Lived Underground," both of which lack, however, the concern with love. In that concern, SUICIDES may be compared with Hawthorne's "Wakefield," whose main character also isolates himself from the woman who cares for him, though in a far less "realistic" manner.

Both Doris Lessing's "To Room Nineteen" and Charlotte Perkins Gilman's "The Yellow Wallpaper" deal with relationships in which men fail to understand the inner lives and needs of their wives, failures that lead in both cases to the wives' seemingly inexorable movement from love to isolation to madness or suicide. But these two stories differ from SUICIDES in that the husbands' motivation is not conscious—they *think* they love their wives—and in their description of deteriorating relationships. The relationship in SUICIDES is destructive from the beginning. — P T M

Paz, Octavio. MY LIFE WITH THE WAVE.

Mexico
The Eye of the Heart: Short Stories from Latin America. New York: Bobbs-Merrill, 1973.
Translated by Eliot Weinberger.

Author: Octavio Paz (1914–) was born in Mexico City. He was educated at the National University of Mexico. Traveling extensively, he was a Marxist during the Civil War, lived in San Francisco and New York in the early 1940s, and during the postwar years went to Paris, where he was influenced by surrealism. In 1952, he went to India, where he returned in 1962 as his country's ambassador. Throughout the 1970s, he taught in universities across the United States. He was awarded a Guggenheim Fellowship in 1944 and the Grand Prix International de Poésie in 1963. Octavio Paz is known not only as Latin America's foremost living poet, but also as a critic and social philosopher. MY LIFE WITH THE WAVE was published in 1949.

Story: MY LIFE WITH THE WAVE is a surrealist portrayal of an unnamed man's relationship with a wave. It begins with the difficulties of smuggling the wave into the water tank of a train, which leads to the man's imprisonment for trying to poison the passengers. Because of the lack of victims, he serves a short sentence and returns to his apartment to find it occupied by the wave. At first the wave's presence changes his life, and their love becomes "a game, a perpetual creation." Yet he soon realizes that the wave has a dark and destructive side that shows when she begins to miss her solitude. In order to pacify her, he installs a colony of fish in the apartment. The wave's growing attention to these fish makes the man increasingly jealous. One day, he attacks the fish and is almost beaten to death by the wave. After this incident, the man's love for the wave turns to hate. He stays away more and more from his apartment and finally goes to the mountains. It is winter, and when he returns to the apartment, he finds the wave frozen into a block of ice. He takes her to a restaurant and sells her to a waiter friend, who chops her into little pieces and uses her to chill beverages.

Comparison: The complexity and range of Octavio Paz's imagination in MY LIFE WITH THE WAVE allows many comparisons, but few that match his own vibrant imagery. For example, the story of the wave, as a relationship between nature and man, can be compared with Shel Silverstein's "The Giving Tree," in which a boy's love for a tree leads to its destruction.

Philosophically, one may see the wave as a representation of spirit in conflict with and finding consummation in the body. This interpretation is reminiscent of Whitman's "mystic evolution" through the integration of body and spirit. The importance that Paz places on sexual imagery and erotic experience is Whitmanesque as well.

In a story as general and imaginative as MY LIFE WITH THE WAVE, one is led to an inexhaustible number of themes. It is the story of the cycle of love, or possibly it represents the conflict between reality and the eternal, or intellect and intuition. Perhaps this is a story about the artist's relationship with the revolution or the poet's relationship to his art. In MY LIFE WITH THE WAVE, the protagonist's confinement to the city and the wave's loss of solitude bring on the destruction of creativity. Whatever the theme of Paz's story, this reconstruction of reality through the use of imaginative language and symbols can be found as well in Carlos Fuentes's work. Paz, like Fuentes, presents a study in the untraditional concepts of time, reality, and consciousness, where "the world dissolves and transparency is all that remains." — C W

PHIÊN VÕ. THE KEY.

Vietnam
One World of Literature. Boston: Houghton Mifflin, 1993. Translated by Phan Phan.

Author: Phiên Võ, who is also known as Doan The Nhon, was born in Binh Dinh, Vietnam. He came to the United States in 1975 as a refugee. In Vietnam, he was a noted writer and journalist and professor of literature. He is still writing and publishing in California, where he founded and edits *Van Hoc Nghe Thuat,* a Vietnamese-language literary journal.

Story: The story opens with the narrator's remembering having taken a shower, a shower that works in the story both as a symbol and as a reality for the nine thousand Vietnamese refugees landing on the island of Guam. Separating himself from the group and moving from the point of view of "we" to "I," he explains that in Vietnam taking a shower is part of the ritualistic process of "rubbing off the dirt" when welcoming someone home from a long journey. In their new country, however, it is a practical, sanitary process that the refugees are forced to experience. This contrast quickly becomes a symbol of the differences between the two cultures, between social interaction and social sanitation. Yet the shower in the new country also becomes a place for socializing and for sharing the experiences of their lives with each other. Thus, it serves to link the attitudes of the two cultures.

It is in the shower that the narrator hears the confession of a shy man in his mid-fifties, who loses his shyness momentarily in the freedom of being naked in the shower. His story, told within the larger frame story, expresses his guilt at having left his ninety-three-year-old father in Vietnam. Although the son left provisions locked in a closet, he forgot to leave the key so that the dying old man could have access to the closet's contents. The narrator notices that the shy man wears that key on a string around his neck, "where a Christian typically wears a picture of his God."

With the narration returning to the outer frame of the story, the main character points out that he too, like many refugees, has a key that he keeps in his pocket. It represents "something he would feel sorry for the rest of his wandering life."

Comparison: In spite of its brevity, THE KEY contains a story within a frame story, each with a different thematic focus. Another such story is Mark Twain's "The Celebrated Jumping Frog of Calaveras County." Both stories have two first-person narrators, but in THE KEY each narrator is talking about an entirely different event, and neither narration has the humor found in Twain's story.

The main story in THE KEY deals with the theme of acculturation, closely related to that of alienation, in which the problem of integration is dominant. A similar theme is found in Stephen Crane's "The Bride Comes to Yellow Sky," which is concerned with the intermingling of the cultures of the eastern and western parts of the United States.

The internal story in THE KEY moves from the United States back to Vietnam, and it involves the problems, the responsibilities, and the heritage the refugees abandoned when they fled their country. They feel a terrible guilt as a result of having done so. Symbolically, the refugees, by taking the "key" away, have taken away the means by which their country—as symbolized by the old man—can survive. They wear the key around their necks like a Christian cross as a symbol of both their guilt and their atonement. That aspect of the story can be compared to Hawthorne's "The Minister's Black Veil," in which the minister insists on wearing his veil for reasons he chooses not to disclose, although there is a strong suggestion that he wears it as a symbol of his guilt. A comparison of the two stories reveals that although the old man is anxious to tell his story, the minister is not, and while those around the minister are tormented by the veil, the other refugees around the shy man are able to identify his symbol as representative of their own guilt.

Another aspect of the key as a symbol is evident in the fact that it is useless in the new country. Wearing it around his neck in his new life serves only to remind the man of his guilt in abandoning his country and his responsibility to return. It also reminds the reader of the difficulties in assimilating into the new environment with something that cannot "fit," something that works only in another time and another place.

Many of the major twentieth-century Mexican artists, such as Diego Rivera, Sequieros, and Orozco, are also relevant here, in that they are concerned with the acculturation of the Mexican Indian into the society of the Spanish-Christian that has come to dominate the indigenous people.
— R H M

PIRANDELLO, LUIGI. CINCI.

Italy
The Continental Short Story: An Existential Approach. New York: Odyssey Press, 1969.
Translated by Lily Duplaix.

Author: Luigi Pirandello (1867–1936) was born in Girgenti, Sicily, to a wealthy family. His studies at the University of Rome and Bonn University, where he received a Ph.D., were turned to good account when his family's loss of its fortune forced him to teach Italian literature in Rome to support himself. In 1894, he married, but by 1904 his wife had lost her reason and remained insane until her death in 1918. His early fiction was characterized by a penetrating naturalism and a skeptical attitude toward social conventions. But during the period after World War I, he began to write the plays for which he is best known today, such as *Right You Are If You Think You Are* (1917), *Six Characters in Search of an Author* (1920), and *Henry IV* (1922), and to develop his characteristic attitude toward life as a succession of illusions beneath which his characters could not penetrate; what they see as "truth" is merely some combination of those illusions. He was awarded the Nobel Prize for Literature in 1934. He published WAR in 1939 and CINCI in 1969.

Story: Returning from school with nothing to do, Cinci kicks the locked door of his house and his waiting dog and then makes a game of throwing his schoolbooks at the door. Tiring of this violent activity, he plops down on the curb: "He was bored. Above all, he was bored." Deciding to take a walk, he goes off with his dog down the road toward the countryside. Thinking resentfully of his mother, his boring daily life, and his lack of a father, Cinci enters a little church and purposely drops his schoolbooks, causing a thunderous clap that disturbs the worshippers.

Leaving the church, he continues on, still bored, but soon tires of the walk and sits down on a wall. Suddenly, hearing shrill laughter beneath him, he jumps down to discover a country boy trapping a lizard. Catching it and perhaps fearing Cinci will take it, the boy swings it around in the air and brings it down on a stone, killing it instantly. Angered by this because he thought to examine the lizard, Cinci shoves the boy, who responds by throwing dirt in Cinci's face. Pelted with accurately aimed clod after clod, Cinci fights back desperately, finally picking up and hurling a rock at the boy.

"All of a sudden, where before everything had been spinning around, striking his eyes, now nothing moved. . . . It was as if time itself had stopped in stupefied amazement at sight of the boy stretched on the ground. Still panting, his heart pounding . . . Cinci foundered in a backwash of man's eternal solitude from which he wanted to flee." Discovering that the boy, like the lizard, is dead, Cinci runs in terror, deciding finally to return home and tell his mother, when she finally returns, that he had spent the afternoon waiting for her. "And this—which would be true for his mother—became the truth for him too." Thus, Pirandello suggests the story's theme: for many people, life is an essentially meaningless series of episodes characterized by alienation and loneliness, alternating between periods of boredom and violent attempts to dispel the malaise.

Comparison: The deliberate equating of actions we normally would not equate (i.e., the killings of the lizard and the boy), the detachment of Cinci from his actions, his lack of a sense of moral responsibility for those actions, and his inability to see himself as vitally involved in life all invite comparison to Meursault in *The Stranger* (1942) by Albert Camus. Meursault is also involved in a killing, and his relationship with his mother is central to the story. The "frozen moment" of the killing and the lack of human warmth also suggest a fundamental similarity between this story and Ernest Hemingway's "The Short Happy Life of Francis Macomber." It must be realized, however, that the motivations for the killings, specifically, and the conception of the possibility of purposeful action in the world, generally, are quite different in the two stories.

Cinci's momentary panic at the reality of death might be compared to that in Stephen Crane's "The

Upturned Face" (1900). A more detailed comparison of that motif could be worked out with Richard Wright's *Native Son,* in which Bigger inadvertently kills and then panics at the result of his action. Unlike Cinci, however, Bigger is unable to avoid that action's consequences.

Mishima Yukio's PATRIOTISM (1966) provides a stark contrast to CINCI, since the death in PATRIOTISM can be understood only in terms of a life lived with a sense of wholeness and continuity provided by tradition and ritual, precisely what is lacking in Cinci's world. That tradition makes the death in the story an act of the highest responsibility, while the death in CINCI is enveloped in layers of irresponsibility. Interestingly, however, the two deaths probably seem equally pointless to the Western reader. — P T M

PIRANDELLO, LUIGI. WAR.

Italy
Reading Modern Short Stories. Glenview, IL: ScottForesman, 1955. Translated by Michael Pettinati.

Author: See CINCI.

Story: The plot of WAR is slight. At dawn, two new passengers join those already on the night express. One, "a bulky woman in deep mourning," is "hoisted" into the carriage, followed by her thin, weak husband, "his face death-white." He explains to their fellow passengers that his wife is distraught because their only son is due to leave in three days for the front. One responds that his own son has been at the front since the beginning of the war and another that he has three sons and two nephews there. When the husband answers that their case is different since this is their only son, the other passengers point out that an only son is neither more loved nor more needed than any other son.

Taking another tack, a third passenger suggests that children have a life and ideas of their own and that at twenty the love of country will probably be stronger in them than the love of parents. If they must die for their country, "they die inflamed and happy." His own son, in fact, has died at the front, but sent him a message before his death that he was

"dying satisfied." For this reason, he does not even wear mourning.

The bulky wife, "amazed and almost stunned" by this speech and its revelation to her of a way she might bear her own suffering, speaks for the first time. "Then . . . is your son really dead?" she asks. The traveler "looked and looked at her, almost as if only then—at that silly incongruous question—he had suddenly realized at last that his son was really dead—gone for ever—for ever. . . . To the amazement of everyone, [he] broke into harrowing, heart-rending, uncontrollable sobs."

Comparison: Like CINCI, this story succeeds in penetrating what Pirandello saw as the façade of meaning constructed by people to make their lives bearable. Here, the piercing of that façade by the wife's simple question lays bare for the couple an almost intolerably meaningless reality containing not only their son's mortality, but their own. This fundamentally existential theme links WAR to Jean-Paul Sartre's THE WALL, although the latter story suggests that the realization of one's mortality and life's essential meaninglessness confers a sense of freedom on the initiate, a sense not found in Pirandello's story.

But this theme is not peculiar to existential literature. The sudden awareness, through a sense of one's own mortality, of the inscrutability of life can be found in such diverse writers as Herman Melville, Emily Dickinson, James Joyce, and Ernest Hemingway. Melville, in the chapter of *Moby Dick* (1851) entitled "The Whiteness of the Whale," suggests that whiteness in nature "by its indefiniteness ... shadows forth the heartless voids and immensities of the universe and thus stabs us from behind with the thought of annihilation when beholding the white depths of the Milky Way." Similarly, Dickinson indicates:

> There's a certain Slant of light,
> Winter Afternoons—
> That oppresses, like the Heft
> of Cathedral Tunes—
>
> Heavenly Hurt, it gives us—
> We can find no scar,
> But internal difference,
> Where the Meanings, are—

This "imperial affliction," as the poem goes on to call it, is intimately related to the revelation of mortality, and the poem's "internal difference / Where the Meanings, are" seems a precise description of the changed mental states of Pirandello's travelers.

James Joyce's story "The Dead" (1916) depicts Gabriel Conroy's realization of a similar undercurrent of reality. Through a sudden awareness, occurring on a snowy winter night, of the depth and meaning of his wife's earlier love of the now-dead Michael Furey, Gabriel feels "his soul had approached that region where dwell the vast hosts of the dead. He was conscious of, but could not apprehend, their wayward and flickering existence. His own identity was fading out into a grey impalpable world; the solid world itself ... was dissolving and dwindling." Ernest Hemingway's "A Clean, Well-Lighted Place," with the old waiter's acceptance of the nothingness at the heart of things, reveals a similar response to an awareness of mortality. — P T M

PONTOPPIDAN, HENRIK. A FISHER NEST.

Denmark
Great Stories by Nobel Prize Winners. New York: The Noonday Press, 1959.
Translated by Juliane Sarauw.

Author: Henrik Pontoppidan (1857–1943), born the son of a clergyman, was teaching in a high school run by his brother when he decided that writing was his real interest. He began to observe the villagers about him and to put down the details of their daily life. Two collections of stories were the result of his consistently close observations: *Village Pictures* and *From the Cottages.* These stories serve as verbal photographs of the generally drab, restricted life led by the peasants. Though he was always proud of his native Denmark, Pontoppidan never attempted to soften or romanticize the uglier details of the lives he depicted, and he became known as the true realist of Danish writers.

Though Pontoppidan's short stories were widely read, three novel cycles—*The Promised Land,*

Lucky-Per, and *The Kingdom of the Dead*—confirmed his status as a respected writer. For the quality and volume of his work, Pontoppidan was awarded the Nobel Prize for Literature in 1917. He shared the honor that year with Karl Gjellerup, a fellow Danish writer. Pontoppidan continued to write until his death.

Story: Deceptively titled A FISHER NEST, Pontoppidan's story begins as a realistic description of life among the poor inhabitants of a remote Danish fishing village. But reality quickly dissolves into the macabre as the villagers celebrate their most highly prized species of catch: a ship lured in the dark storm onto the deadly shoals by cruelly expert use of a torchlight. The scavengers gleefully gather on shore to await the incoming wreckage—and the occasional survivor who must be killed to prevent any testimony. There is nothing soft or pleasant in this exposé of human nature's darkest side.

The author's assurance that his account is from the long-ago history of the village leads the unwitting reader into the second part of the tale, which is actually a modern-day version of that ancient scene, complete with stranded ship and smiling scavengers. In daylight, an English cargo steamer has run aground several hundred yards from shore. Salvage company officials and villagers alike rejoice in the exorbitant sum that they will demand to free the ship from the shoals. Once again, a ship's crew is at the mercy of enterprising villains.

Readers should especially note the appearance in this second half of a young prostitute, Mary, a stowaway of sorts, whose survival and only hope for a decent life depend daily on the particular mood of the ship's captain. Mary, sensing the captain's ultimate disregard, kills herself. Pontoppidan's essential theme of victimization crystallizes in young Mary's suicide.

Comparison: Humanity's inhumanity emerges as the major message in this story, and A FISHER NEST can be grouped effectively with any number of stories that mirror this concept. As a moment of subtle surprise, Mary's death compares interestingly with the ending of L. P. Hartley's "The Island," in which an army officer learns not only that his lover, the beautiful Mrs. Santander, is dead, but that he is the victim of her deviously vindictive husband. Richard Connell's "The Most Dangerous Game," John Russell's "The Price of the Head," and Shirley Jackson's "The Lottery" further illustrate the horror of discovering human nature at its worst. — P G L

P'u Sung-Ling. THE FIGHTING CRICKET.

China

Strange Stories from a Chinese Studio. Hong Kong: Kelly & Walsh, 1968. Translated by Herbert A. Giles.

Author: Born into modest circumstances, P'u Sung-Ling (1640–1715), under his father's tutelage, strove to become a scholar. He spent most of his life in poverty and ill health and did not pass the official examinations until an advanced age. P'u was known to his contemporaries as a writer of poems and fiction. His best-known work, published in 1679 and still popular today, is variously titled in English as *Records of the Strange, Strange Stories from a Chinese Studio,* or a similar phrase. For this collection, P'u combed every part of China for folktales of the bizarre, the mysterious, and the supernatural. He retold each in rigorous language and polished style and did not spare any opportunity to satirize the gentry and the bureaucracy.

Story: Ch'eng's son, a nine-year-old boy who loves crickets, is asked by his stern and reserved father to help him find a champion fighter cricket. When, after some difficulty, he coaxes a stalwart one from a small hole and readies it for combat in the imperial palace, he accidentally lets it loose. Afraid of his father but filial toward him, the boy, after a fall into a well, languishes in a coma, during which his spirit and consciousness are transferred to a small cricket. The cricket proves to be a dauntless fighter and wins all combats. The cricket becomes a favorite at the imperial palace, and for his contribution Ch'eng's father is highly rewarded by the court. When the boy regains consciousness, he recounts his feats as a fighter cricket. In a gentle and entertaining manner, P'u Sung-Ling thus satirizes the preoccupation of princes and officials and the arbitrary conferring of honorary degrees for favors done.

Comparison: A light story, this cricket tale (also translated as "The Cricket Boy") recalls the adventures of Jonathan Swift's Gulliver, who, as either a giant or a palm-sized human, observes and partakes of life at court. The descriptions of the people observed reveal the foibles of human nature and the inequities of life. A more ponderous statement on society is made in "The Jewbird." Author Bernard Malamud begins the story with a skinny bird flying through the open window, landing at Harry Cohen's dinner table, and speaking in Yiddish about anti-Semitism. — M L

RAY, SATYAJIT. ASHAMANJA BABU'S DOG.

India
World Writers Today. Glenview, IL: ScottForesman, 1995.

Author: Prize-winning film maker Satyajit Ray (1921–1992) was born in Calcutta and studied economics, physics, painting, and art history. He attended a university owned by the Hindu poet Rabindranath Tagore, an old friend of the family. Beginning his career as an art director in a British advertising firm, he also illustrated books. His first film, *Pather Panchali,* an enormous success at the 1956 Cannes Film Festival, launched a distinguished career during which many of his films won international prizes. He wrote all of his own scripts and sometimes composed the music; he was also involved in costume design. In 1961, he wrote stories and did illustrations for a children's magazine.

Story: Ashamanja Babu, a postal clerk, has longed for a dog, but not only for its love and companionship. Dogs belong to the English race, and by giving orders to the dog in English, he would feel a sense of power. He buys a puppy that wags its tail at him. He gives it an English name, Brownie.

Three months later, Ashamanja Babu breaks a stool and falls to the floor, and he hears Brownie giggle. When Brownie laughs on other occasions, Ashamanja Babu tries to borrow a dog encyclopedia from his neighbor, a retired professor, who dismisses him condescendingly.

The first time Brownie laughs at a stranger is when a gentleman's umbrella snaps in the rain. The man spreads the story in Calcutta, and a reporter visits Ashamanja Babu. The reporter stutters, and Brownie laughs.

Brownie's fame reaches an American dealer of old Rolls-Royce cars, who offers to pay up to twenty thousand dollars to hear Brownie laugh. Brownie laughs, long and loud, but with no seeming instigation. As the American is about to write out the check, Ashamanja Babu realizes that Brownie is laughing because "the gentleman thinks money can buy everything." The American leaves, and Brownie "chuckles in assent" with his master's reasoning.

Comparison: The theme that money can buy everything has recurred in many stories since the story of King Midas. In Charles Dickens's *A Christmas Carol,* Scrooge learns eventually that some things are more important than money. In "The Rocking Horse Winner" by D. H. Lawrence, an entire family is haunted by the need for more money. Paul loses his life for race track winnings so he can give his mother money in exchange for her love. In PAPER by Catherine Lim, a man's greed leads to his loss of fortune and eventually to his death. — M L

RIFAAT, ALIFA. ANOTHER EVENING AT THE CLUB.

Egypt
World Writers Today. Glenview, IL: ScottForesman, 1995. Translated by Denys Johnson-Davies.

Author: Alifa Rifaat, the pen name of Fatma Abdullah Rifaat (1930–), grew up in a traditional Muslim family in which her father insisted she get married rather than attend a university. Although her husband disapproved of her writing, she wrote under a pseudonym from 1955 to 1960, then stopped writing for fifteen years while she reared three children, studied religion, and read world literature. Rifaat is a faithful Muslim who writes about women.

Story: A young wife, Samia, is apprehensive about her husband's return, for she has something to tell him. Rifaat uses a flashback to tell of the circumstances of the marriage "only a few years ago." Samia was still in secondary school when she was promised to Abboud Bey, a successful man almost forty years old, well-dressed, and very aware that his social position is above that of his bride's family. He tells her on their wedding night how lucky she is to be marrying someone with a successful career ahead and stresses to her that the most important thing to be concerned about is what others, particularly your equals and seniors, think of you. As he pats her cheeks in a "fatherly, reassuring gesture," he urges her to tell people that her father is a judge.

The day on which the story opens, Samia had arisen after an evening with her husband and a glass of wine "at the club" to discover that an emerald ring, a gift from her husband, is missing. The only person besides Samia and Abboud Bey to have entered the bedroom is Gazia, a young servant girl. When Abboud Bey arrives home and hears about the missing ring, he questions Gazia. When she denies knowing anything about it, Abboud Bey slaps her. She begins to cry from fear and humiliation. Abboud Bey calls the police, assuring Samia that there is nothing more to worry about, for the police have ways of getting confessions.

The next day, Samia finds the ring stuck between the wall and a table leg. She is panic-stricken, even thinking of throwing the ring into the river to avoid having to admit her mistake to her husband. When he returns that evening, she holds up her finger, displaying the ring, and asks him what they must now do for Gazia. "Nothing, of course," is his reply. Abboud Bey explains that the police can keep Gazia only forty-eight hours if they have neither a confession nor evidence. He decides that Gazia can take a few more hours of beatings. His main concern is what everyone else in town would think if they knew about their having accused an innocent girl. To cover their mistake, he decides to take the ring to Cairo and exchange it for something else.

Samia reluctantly gives him the ring, but she cannot look him in the eye. He pats her cheeks, and she realizes her position in society and in life: the man has the responsibilities; the woman's job is to be happy and obedient. She resigns herself to her fate.

Comparison: The easiest comparison is to Guy de Maupassant's THE NECKLACE. The wives in both stories feel the same immediate horror when they discover the missing jewelry. Yet the Maupassant story turns on irony, whereas the Rifaat story is pervaded by a sense of helplessness and hopelessness.

Miss Emily in William Faulkner's "A Rose for Emily" is excused for her eccentric behavior because of her social position, reflected in the town's calling her "Miss Emily." She appears to be a harmless old woman, which makes her crime, when discovered, especially shocking. Abboud Bey also appears to be the model citizen, yet he allows an innocent servant girl to be brutalized for a crime she did not commit. Homer is betrayed by the seemingly innocent Miss Emily; Samia is betrayed by the superficial social graces of her husband, who will sacrifice anything to save his reputation.

In Alice Walker's novel *The Color Purple*, Celie's first husband is a man similar to Abboud Bey. Celie is treated like a possession because that is what he believes her to be. He is as immoral as Abboud Bey, a fact that shocks Celie as profoundly as Samia is shocked. — D G

RIFAAT, ALIFA. AN INCIDENT IN THE GHOBASHI HOUSEHOLD.

Egypt
World Writers Today. Glenview, IL: ScottForesman, 1995. Translated by Denys Johnson-Davies.

Author: See ANOTHER EVENING AT THE CLUB.

Story: The story deals with a contemporary problem: teenage pregnancy. Ni'ma is the eldest daughter in a Muslim family. Zeinat, her mother, is a good woman who says her prayers and does her rituals. Ni'ma's father is working in Libya for a year, so Zeinat must manage the household, the land, and the livestock, as well as the family. When Ni'ma discovers she is pregnant, she tells her mother that she must drown herself by appearing to fall accidentally into a canal. Zeinat is horrified and assures her daughter that they will find a solution to the problem before her father returns.

The plan Zeinat develops comes as a surprise to Ni'ma. When a neighbor comes to take Ni'ma to market as usual, Zeinat says the girl has gone to visit relatives. Ni'ma is perplexed. "What relatives are you talking about?" she asks. Zeinat responds by giving the girl her "life savings" and telling her to take the train to Cairo, where she'll find protection and a way to make a living until the baby's birth. Zeinat goes on to tell Ni'ma that, after the baby is born, she is to return home in the middle of the night and to let no one see her or the child. After giving Ni'ma these instructions, Zeinat begins winding clothes around her own waist, under her djellaba. To Ni'ma she explains simply, "Isn't it better . . . for your father to find himself with a legitimate son than an illegitimate grandson?"

Comparison: Stories dealing with sacrifice are numerous. In O. Henry's "The Gift of the Magi," a young man and woman each sacrifice something most dear to ensure the happiness of the other. The narrator in John Updike's "A & P" sacrifices not only his job, but also his youthful idealism to save the honor of three young girls.

Another popular plot illustrated in this story is thwarting social restraint. In "The Lake Which Took People In" from *The Tale of Genji,* a couple involved in a liaison frowned upon by their feudal society pretend to commit suicide. The ploy is elaborately planned, ultimately fooling the right people, and the two can start their life together anew. The movie *Ju Dou* tells a similar story of deception. Two young people are deeply in love, but the woman has been promised to her lover's much older brother. While she marries the older man, she becomes pregnant by his younger sibling. She decides to try to convince her husband that he is the father of the child, not the uncle. The true father, then, must content himself with being an uncle, not a father.

The theme of family pride is also important. The lengths to which Zeinat will go to protect her family and her daughter from scandal can be compared to the sense of pride that the boy in William Faulkner's "Barn Burning" must summon in order to tell a lie to protect his father. — D G

Roufos, Rodis. THE CANDIDATE.

Greece

Eighteen Texts: Writings by Contemporary Greek Authors. Cambridge: Harvard University Press, 1972. Translated by Rodis Roufos and Sarah Kafatou.

Author: Rodis Roufos (1924–1972) was born in Athens. He wrote, under the pseudonym Rodis Provelenghio, a trilogy: *Chronicle of a Crusade* (1954), *March in the Darkness* (1955), and *The Other Shore* (1958). Under his own name, he published two novels and a play and completed several translations from the ancient Greek. The story THE CANDIDATE is taken from a collection published in Athens in 1970 and two years later in the United States under the title *Eighteen Texts.* The collection was published immediately after the lifting of censorship imposed by the military government during the "Occupation of the Colonels" (1967–74). On the one hand, Roufos and other writers of the literary-political opposition who published in *Eighteen Texts* understood that it would not be prudent to challenge the Colonels' policies on freedom of thought and the press. On the other hand, they knew that if the intellectuals did not publish, the government's "re-education" of the Greek people would go unopposed. Thus, they decided to publish, taking only the precaution of setting their stories, poems, and essays in other countries.

Story: Although Roufos sets his story in South America, the reader can easily transpose it to

Greece during the military occupation of the Colonels. The main character, Juan, is a professor who concentrates on his chemistry, stays out of politics, and tries to cooperate with the reigning authorities. He is rather proud of his ability to stay in his university and a bit disdainful of his many colleagues who leave or have been driven away. At the time of this story, Juan hopes to obtain the university's chair in organic chemistry. During the loyalty interview, one of the last stages of screening, Juan learns about the government and himself. Roufos describes in detail the official questioning to make certain that the candidate understands that the role of the chair will be to support the power structure and to spy for the authorities. Finally, when Juan is asked to accept or decline the position, he declines. Exhausted, he makes his way to a bar, and, as he sits there, he reads a note from a former colleague who has joined the revolutionaries.

As he reads, his exhaustion and bitterness disappear. When he finishes the note, he makes his way, with deep satisfaction, to the meeting of the illegal opposition.

Comparison: The professor in this story wants desperately to believe that his academic work cuts him off from the political sphere. In John Steinbeck's "The Chrysanthemums," a lonely housewife exhibits the same intensity of desire to believe against all odds. Both are devastated when they face the truth they had probably known all along: that dictators use citizens and that the word of a traveling salesman is often not to be believed. In "I'm a Fool," Sherwood Anderson writes about a young man whose enlightenment comes from himself. He has lied about himself once too often, knowing that he should not do so, but doing it anyway. Now, devastated, he must live with the consequences. — E M

RUSHDI, RASHAD. ANGUISH.

Egypt
Arabic Writing Today. New York: Three Continents, 1976.
Translated by Louis Morcos.

Author: Rashad Rushdi (1915–1981) was professor of English language and literature at Cairo University. During his active academic career, he was Egypt's premier scholar, critic, and translator of English literature, noted especially for his championship of the poetry of T. S. Eliot and the fiction and drama in English translation of Anton Chekhov. As a literary artist, he is as noted for his creations in drama as in the short story, producing many plays for the UAR broadcasting service and the Cairo stages. He also served as President Sadat's advisor on cultural affairs.

Story: While professor of English language and literature at Cairo University, Rashad Rushdi promoted the study of Robert Browning and T. S. Eliot for their command of the dramatic monologue. It is this technique that he employs exclusively in the short story ANGUISH, wherein we hear a man address a nonresponding Mr. Salah, much as Fra Lippo Lippi and J. Alfred Prufrock addressed their silent interlocutors.

The revelations that the narrator of ANGUISH makes are shameful: he so fears women, their capacity to injure him and his incapacity to control or manipulate them, that he confesses his deliberate abuse of two wives. Yet his abuse of them is more stupid than injurious. We understand easily that he harmed himself more than the attractive and decent women whom he beat, alienated, and finally divorced. By the story's end, we see Ismail exposed as the foolish victim of his own delusions of jealousy and paranoia.

Ismail's first marriage is a traditional, arranged marriage to "a relative"; the second is his marriage of choice and defiance to "a girl from the city." The first lasts one year; the second three months. During his first marriage ("one long, endless torment"),

Ismail imagines his young, naive wife as easy prey for seducers, particularly "one of these dandified barbers living in the same house," who arouses suspicion by sending his sister to keep the young wife company. After a year of mounting suspicions—all projections onto the wife of Ismail's own suppressed sexual fantasies—he rushes from his shop one night in a fury of jealousy and assaults his wife while she is "singing in the bathroom":

> —What did I do? Si Ismail? Just what did I do?
> —To take a bath at ten o'clock, you shameless
>   woman!
> —What's wrong with that?
> —What about the bed? Why is the bed messy?
> —I was having a rest after I'd finished cooking.

Ismail's quick association of an evening bath and messy bed is not wholly unreasonable. Following Islamic teachings on ablutions, most Arabs take showers or baths after sexual relations.

Waiting for no further explanation, Ismail quickly divorces this woman and soon marries Halima: "She was dark, tall and lusty, and so jolly." Playful Halima soon arouses his suspicions by her jokes and fun. His fantasies of her daytime jollity center on "the manly figure of Saad the carpenter in his tight blue trousers and rubber belt," a projection of desire that suggests Ismail's suppressed homosexuality. After three months, Halima leaves on an innocent journey to her village for the funeral of her father, and Ismail seizes this opportunity to divorce her by mail: "No sooner had she gone to the village . . . than I sent her the divorce paper and got rid of her, and delivered myself from this agony."

Ismail completes his monologue on woman's perfidy by telling Mr. Salah several anecdotes of immoral women, each an obvious projection of his own lusts. The first is of a "beautiful woman, white-skinned, with green eyes and blond hair"—a damning portrait of Ismail's sexual, class, and racial fantasies—who tempted an important civil servant to abandon his wife and family only to betray him three months later in the arms of her servant. Another is a physician's wife whom he has observed in assignations "in a huge Buick with a strange man." Yet another is the wife of his friend and neighbor who tries to seduce him and then falsely accuses him when spurned. And finally even his landlady is a Jezebel of this general type, "bulging out of her tight blue dress!"

The long-suffering and self-righteous Ismail ends his narration by declaring himself well rid of women, but, in so doing, he reveals how much he has lost in his narrow life of jealousy: "Give in? Not on your life! When I was married I used to look at my wife lying beside me, fair, blooming, lovely. I was unable to sleep after that and spent the rest of the night tossing and turning in such agony."

Comparison: Rushdi's short stories can be compared with the poetry of Browning and Eliot. Since ANGUISH explores marriage and sexual anxiety, "My Last Duchess" and "The Love Song of J. Alfred Prufrock" would be good choices. The comparisons should reveal poetry's greater resources of figurative expression and fiction's greater power of drama. Though silent, Mr. Salah emerges as a dramatic personality in the pauses, turns, and inflections of Ismail's responses to the body language and facial expressions the reader can imagine him making.

Rushdi's psychological probing of neurotic characters could also be compared to similar efforts by Russian authors Nikolai Gogol, Anton Chekhov, Fyodor Dostoevski, Yuri Olesha, and Vladimir Nabokov, though Rushdi's exploration is more shallow than theirs. He is more interested in the neurosis than the psyche and exploits the neurotic symptoms for their comic and satiric value. In this respect, his deftly comic portrait of Ismail's petulance and debilitating self-consciousness bears striking resemblance to the style of the American comic writer John Barth, particularly in his ironic autobiographical sketch "Life-Story" from *Lost in the Funhouse.* — J D M

SAND, GEORGE. THE MARQUISE.

France
Bedside Book of Famous French Stories. New York: Random House, 1945.

Author: George Sand, the pen name of Armandine Lucile Aurore Dupin, Baroness Dudevant (1804–1876), was born in Paris and lived there sporadically with her mother, but most of her childhood was spent with her aristocratic grandmother in the little village of Nohant. At fourteen, she began her formal education at a Parisian convent. A marriage of convenience in 1822 to a country squire, Casimir Dudevant, produced two children. When their marriage failed, she moved to Paris, where she collaborated with Jules Sandeau, launching her literary career. Her many love affairs with famous men, most notably Frederick Chopin and Alfred de Musset, and her habit of smoking cigars and wearing men's attire in public resulted in much notoriety. Her pronounced individualism and her belief in political and sexual freedom were reflected in her prolific writing. She produced sixty novels, twenty-five plays, and volumes of essays, correspondence, and memoirs. THE MARQUISE was published in 1832.

Story: Sand uses a conversation between a young man and an elderly beauty, the Marquise de R____, as a frame for the story. The Marquise tells him of the past, recalling the one time she really fell in love. A disastrous early marriage had made her bitter toward all men, alienating her many suitors. Surprisingly, she found herself becoming infatuated with an Italian actor, Lelio, in the Comédie Française as she admired him from afar in his performances.

Since actors were considered beneath her social class, she began attending the theater disguised as a man so that her friends would not recognize her. One night, she followed Lelio to a café and was shocked to see how withered, old, and vulgar he looked without stage makeup and a handsome costume. Disillusioned, she refrained from going to the theater for several days. When she did return to see him perform, however, she fell so desperately in love that she continued to attend his plays. Lelio, becoming aware of her adulation, began directing

amorous glances and lines to her. Despite her intense feelings, the Marquise realized that her passion was intellectual, that she was in love with a fictitious being who did not exist outside the theater.

After five years, Lelio was replaced in the Comédie Française. Before he left France, he wrote a frantic letter, begging the Marquise for one meeting before he departed. When he arrived at the rendezvous, dressed as the character Don Juan, she was mesmerized by his youthful, romantic appearance. At first, they embraced and vowed eternal love, but soon the Marquise insisted that they separate forever. Lelio, crushed by despair, transformed before her eyes into a wretched old man, "the shadow of a lover and a prince." She ends her story by saying that she never saw him again.

Comparison: The artist's role in society and the problem of class distinctions are common literary subjects. Sand treats art and the artist's life in a number of works, must notably *Consuelo,* a novel about a gypsy girl who becomes an opera star.

Thomas Mann in *Confessions of Felix Krull: Confidence Man* depicts a protagonist's reactions to seeing an actor performing on stage and then seeing him later without the illusion created by makeup and costume. Both Felix and the Marquise are shocked by the change in each actor's appearance.

The main theme of THE MARQUISE, the disparity between the visions of the imagination and the sordidness of reality, is a pervasive one in literature. Certainly Ibsen's *Hedda Gabler,* Tolstoy's *Anna Karenina,* and Flaubert's *Madame Bovary* come to mind as works depicting women seeking love that will live up to their dreams. A specific incident in *Madame Bovary* parallels closely the situation in THE MARQUISE. Emma Bovary attends the opera one night and finds herself intensely attracted to the leading actor because of the role he is playing. Emma is easily taken in by illusion, be it the magic spell of the theater or the empty promises of her lovers. Unlike

Emma, however, who attempts to turn her dreams into reality through affairs, the Marquise realizes the necessity of preserving the illusion. She keeps her love idealized by refusing to consummate it.

The need for illusion in people's lives is a major theme in many works. Dr. Relling's life-lie concept in Ibsen's *Wild Duck* provides a prime example. — M A F

SANTOS, BIENVENIDO N. THE DAY THE DANCERS CAME.

Philippines
Asian and Pacific Short Stories. Rutland, VT: Charles E. Tuttle, 1974.

Author: Born in Manila, Bienvenido N. Santos (1911–) was educated both in the Philippines and the United States and has lived and worked in both countries. He was president of Legazpi College, now Aquinas University, and the University of Nueva Caceres in the Philippines. He was also Fulbright professor of English and a lecturer at the Writers Workshop at the University of Iowa and distinguished writer in residence at Wichita State University.

Having spent much of his life outside of his native Philippines, Santos writes about Filipinos who find themselves in foreign lands. He himself was forced to leave his country in the 1970s by Philippine martial law following a serialization of his novel *The Praying Man*.

Santos has won a long list of awards and honors, among them first prize in the *New York Herald Tribune*'s international short story contest, a Rockefeller Foundation fellowship, a Guggenheim fellowship, the Republic Cultural Heritage Award in Literature, the American Book Award from the Before Columbus Association Foundation, a National Endowment for the Arts fellowship, and several honorary doctoral degrees. His works include the short story collections *You Lovely People* (1955), *Brother My Brother* (1960), and *Scent of Apples* (1979); the novels *Villa Magdalena* (1965), *The Volcano* (1965), *The Praying Man* (1982) and *What the Hell for You Left Your Heart in San Francisco* (1987); and the poetry collections *The Wounded Stag* (1956) and *Distances in Time* (1983).

Story: Set in Chicago, the plot centers around two naturalized U.S. citizens who share an apartment. Filemon Acaya anxiously awaits the arrival of

dancers from the Philippines and fantasizes how he will greet them and host them in his home. He anticipates their excitement over their first experience with snow. He cleans his car and apartment and plans to be most attentive in his service to them. He buys front-row tickets to their performance, but his roommate is too worried over an undiagnosed illness to be in the same spirit.

Fil first goes to the hotel and tries to mingle among the dancers. Even as he admires the beauty of the girls and rehearses his introductory comments, the dancers are in their own world and acknowledge him in a cursory manner. He rehearses a grandiose speech, but knows he would be foolish delivering it. He approaches two of the boy dancers and invites them to his apartment, but they too move away. When finally someone touches his shoulder, he finds that he is in the way of a camera.

Later that evening, he goes to the theater and records the performance on his "magic sound mirror," his prized tape recorder. Back at the apartment, he turns on the machine to evoke the dancers in his living room. His sick roommate interrupts his fantasy by asking him to turn the sound off. By accident, he hits the erase button and loses the memory.

The story is a poignant recreation of the plight of immigrant Americans, who have their feet in neither world. The poignancy is doubled by the generation gap, where the glittering world of youth cannot admit even the most hospitable intrusion of older compatriots.

Comparison: Countless numbers of characters have borne the brunt of being victims of alienation, whether in circumstances where they should have felt at home or where they have been thrust into a foreign environment. This sense of not belonging is probably best captured by Franz Kafka in THE METAMORPHOSIS, where Gregor Samsa sees himself as a bug in the midst of a familiar and what should be comfortable world.

Another parallel can be found in Willa Cather's "A Wagner Matinee." A Nebraska farmer's wife goes to a concert in Boston, bursts into tears, and does not want to leave. Like Fil, she finds herself far more at home there than in the tough, real life that she faces day after day. Fil's being bypassed because of an age gap is captured in Hemingway's "A Clean, Well-Lighted Place," in which an older waiter describes the plight of an old customer who has recently attempted suicide. — M L

SARANG, VILAS. THE TERRORIST.

India
Short Story International. October 1983.
Translated by the author in collaboration with Breon Mitchell.

Author: Vilas Sarang (1942–) is one of the most gifted and creative Indian writers of his generation. Born in Bombay, he studied English and comparative literature in both India and the United States, earning two doctorates. A fine scholar and prolific literary translator both from and into Marathi, his native language, Sarang taught for some time at the University of Basra in Iraq before returning home to head the English department at the University of Bombay. He has since founded a literary magazine, continued his scholarly career, and achieved bestseller status with a collection of short stories entitled *Fair Tree of the Void,* published in 1990. Sarang has also provided an important bridge between the literatures of India and the rest of the world. His translations of Ezra Pound, W. H. Auden, Samuel Beckett, T. S. Eliot, and others have contributed a major impetus to young Marathi writers, while his own stories offer concrete examples of a highly creative blend of traditional Indian and European modernist and postmodernist concerns.

Story: The "terrorist" has recently arrived in a strange city in the Middle East on an apparent mission. He finds an apartment, arranges for a post office box, and settles in to wait for further instructions. A package wrapped in brown paper rests at the bottom of his suitcase. He begins to receive letters from a person calling himself "Joseph George." Their carefully guarded exchanges include pages of extraneous, banal information seemingly intended to cover up the true messages. While he is waiting, he fantasizes about a young woman named Dolores who works behind the wall of mailboxes at the post office. Their relationship seems to be developing toward some end when a curfew is suddenly announced, security in the city is tightened, and the "terrorist" is forced to hide in his apartment, awaiting the possibility of arrest. As the story ends, we learn that the line between reality and fantasy may have been blurred for the "terrorist" as well as for the reader. His package is harmless, his letters almost nonexistent, his life a confused dream of love and freedom.

Comparison: The unnamed protagonist of this story appears to be a cross between Dostoevski's "underground man" and James Thurber's Walter Mitty, although the tale is marked more strongly by a sense of menace than by humor. Paul Bowles's enigmatic story "If I Should Open My Mouth," set in New York and written in diary form, offers an excellent American comparison. Sarang has studied modernist and postmodernist literature carefully, and his own work bears traces of the writers he reveres: Kafka, Beckett, and Borges, among others. Beneath the carefully observed realistic detail lie deeper fundamental questions of a philosophical nature. For example, the dividing line between truth and fantasy in this story is a function of the loneliness and alienation of the protagonist.

Sarang's tale may be compared thematically to tales in which the protagonist is a single young man trying to come to grips with his own life. In THE TERRORIST, the political dimensions of revolution and terrorism, as well as the setting in a socialist country, offer parallels to stories of a more overtly ideological nature. In this case, ideology and political revolution are mere dreams in a world where the human condition is one of fundamental and inescapable alienation and where perception is inexorably conditioned and limited by our fantasies and desires.   — B M

Saranti, Galatea. SUNLIGHT.

Greece

The Charioteer: A Review of Modern Greek Culture. No. 9. New York: Parnassos, Greek Cultural Society of New York, 1967. Translated by Katherine Hortis.

Author: Galatea Saranti (1920–) was born in Patras. She studied at the Arsakeion School for Girls and the University of Athens School of Law. Her short stories have been published in the most important literary magazines of Greece. She has won numerous prestigious awards, such as the 1960 State Prize for the novel *Our Old House* and the 1959 Kostas Ouranis Prize for *The Return*. In addition to several novels, she has also published *Paints You Can Trust* (1962), a collection of short stories that includes SUNLIGHT, and "The Boundaries" (1966), about an unsatisfied man who withdraws from his family and departs for foreign lands. Saranti is noted for her inward-looking narrative technique and for her tendency toward surrealism. She is an important Greek literary figure whose works have been highly acclaimed by critics in Athens and internationally.

Story: The story is told from the viewpoint of an old man who is examining the vagaries of life. Saranti makes it clear that the old man likes living in Athens. He enjoys the sunlight and his good friends there. But now he is thinking of his birth village and a man from the village who visited his family when he was a boy. This man, frustrated because his wife gave birth to a daughter rather than a son, had killed his wife so that he could marry a young woman who might give birth to a boy. She had done so, but the child had died. The old man then remembers what his mother, his grandmother, and his aunt had told him about why the murderer's son had died. He examines their perception that the death of a son is a punishment, and he tries vainly to reconcile their position with his own situation. I am not a murderer, the old man thinks in deep sorrow. Why did my son die?

Comparison: Aging affects people differently. This story presents the old man with an opportunity to ponder past events. For Phoenix Jackson in Eudora Welty's "A Worn Path," the infirmities of age are simply barriers that must be overcome as she travels for medicine to ease her grandson's recurring pain. The aging of the church choir soloist in Mary E. Wilkins Freeman's story "A Village Singer" is brought home to her by the sudden and cruel loss of her job. And for Washington Irving's lazy "Rip Van Winkle," aging on a high magic mountain enables him to return to a better world in which everyone who had expected responsible action from him is now dead. In John Steinbeck's "The Leader of the People," an old man's constant recounting of the high points of his life is brought to a halt by his son-in-law's impatience. The other topic of this Saranti story, punishment, is examined in numerous short stories, such as Nathaniel Hawthorne's "The Minister's Black Veil."   — E M

SARTRE, JEAN-PAUL. THE WALL.

France

Introduction to Literature: Stories. New York: Macmillan, 1963. Translated by Maria Jolas.

Author: A leading existentialist philosopher and writer, Jean-Paul Sartre (1905–1980) was born in Paris, where, except for his travels, he spent most of his life. Following his schooling, he taught, traveled, studied further in Berlin, was a journalist, and at the start of World War II enlisted in the army as a private. He was soon captured and imprisoned for nine months before escaping and joining the French underground. After the war, he founded a journal, *Les Temps Modernes,* and was its editor for many years. His career as a writer—which included some philosophical books and essays but mainly dramas, novels, and short stories—reached its peak in 1964, when he was awarded, but refused to accept, the Nobel Prize for Literature. THE WALL was first published in 1939.

Sartre's admiration for detective stories is evident in the dialogue and interrogation scenes found in much of his fiction, and the influence of literary naturalists shows up in the types of detail used, the apparent determinism, and the power of circumstance.

Existentialism, though, is the strong force behind the plots, characters, and general situations found in Sartre's fiction. As is the case in THE WALL, characters are put in situations in which their only resort is to their own inner strength, courage, and conviction. In his dramas *No Exit, The Flies,* and *The Victors* or *Deaths without Burial,* principal characters must go through a process of soul-searching to find the strength that will lead to responsible action. There is no help otherwise, since for Sartre, there is no God.

Story: Set in the basement of a hospital, THE WALL is the story of three men awaiting death: Juan Mirbal, Tom Steinbock, and Pablo Ibbieta. The time is the Spanish Civil War, and the three are prisoners. Their presumption is that they will be shot. As Tom says, "Somebody will shout 'Shoulder arms!' and I'll see all eight rifles aimed at me. I'm sure I'm going to feel like going through the wall. I'll push against the wall as hard as I can with my back, and the wall won't give in."

The three must wait, think about their fate, and face the knowledge that their lives will end in a matter of hours. Each suffers his own kind of weakness, made all the worse by the presence of a Belgian doctor who, unlike the three captives, can "plan for tomorrow." Juan, the youngest, begins to lose his dignity early—except, perhaps, when he bites the doctor's hand extended in sympathy. Tom wets his pants. Pablo, the narrator, reveals to the reader his every tremor.

Finally, Juan and Tom are removed from the cell and shot. Pablo is taken out and interrogated about the hiding place of Ramon Gris. Sure that Ramon is in a farmhouse, Pablo tells his captors that Ramon is in the cemetery. Later, in the hospital courtyard, he finds out from another prisoner that Ramon Gris is dead. He had just been found in the cemetery and shot.

Comparison: Sartre's play *Deaths without Burial* compares with THE WALL in that the situation, the small number and types of characters, and Sartre's purpose are very nearly the same. His *No Exit* and "The Room" may also be compared, particularly for bringing the existentialist perspective into sharp relief.

Other existentialist works where the characters are forced to search for their own "being" and to find meaning in a godless universe are Albert Camus's THE GUEST, Miguel Unamuno's "Saint Emmanuel the Good Martyr," and Friedrich Dürrenmatt's "The Tunnel."

With existentialist fiction at times coming very close in overall "look" to the fiction of literary naturalists, further comparison of THE WALL with Maxim Gorky's story "Twenty-Six Men and a Girl" and his play *The Lower Depths* will be useful. The situation, the activities and fears of the characters, and the general absence of help—from God or otherwise—in all three works are remarkably similar. — R S

Schulz, Bruno. COCKROACHES.

Poland
The Complete Fiction of Bruno Schulz. New York: Walker, 1989.
Translated by Celina Wieniewska.

Author: Bruno Schulz (1892–1942) is considered one of the greatest Polish writers of this century, yet during his lifetime his work was largely unknown. An art teacher at a secondary school for boys in a small village in the countryside, he wrote in his spare time for his own pleasure. He was forty years old before his stories were finally published with the help of a well-known novelist in Warsaw, and they won critical acclaim. His first collection, in which COCKROACHES appeared, bore the title *Cinnamon Shops* and was published in 1934. This was followed three years later by *Sanatorium under the Sign of the Hourglass.* Along with a novella that appeared in a contemporary literary journal, these works represent the sum total of his published writing.

Even after his work had achieved a certain measure of success, Schulz continued to live in the small village where he taught school. At the outbreak of World War II, he was confined to a ghetto along with other Jews. It is said that he was supposedly "protected" by an officer of the Gestapo who liked his drawings. In 1942, he ventured outside the ghetto with what he believed to be a safe pass. He was spotted by another S.S. officer and shot dead in the street. In the late fifties, his work was at last rediscovered, translated into several languages, and accorded worldwide recognition.

Story: A boy questions his mother about the disappearance of his father. On the shelf in the drawing room, only one specimen remains from his father's collection of stuffed birds: a condor, its eyes fallen out, its coat of feathers moth-eaten. The boy's hidden resentment of his mother for the ease with which she seems to have recovered from his father's loss results in a strange question: has his father returned in the form of the condor?

His mother assures him otherwise. She reminds him about the cockroaches. He remembers the invasion of the cockroaches, how they flowed across the floor, his father's screams of horror as he leaped up on a chair, spearing the insects with a javelin. But gradually his father's fascination with and horror of the insects began to drive him mad. Black spots like the scales of a cockroach began to appear on his nails and skin. At night, the obsession took control; he lay on the floor, moving like an insect. The boy's father was given up for lost; he was being transformed into a cockroach. He disappeared for weeks on end. His family ceased to recognize him; he merged completely with that black uncanny tribe.

And yet the boy is sure the condor is his father. As the story ends, his mother assures him that his father is simply on a trip. He has a job as a commercial traveler and comes home only at night.

Comparison: The stories of Bruno Schulz are a unique mixture of poetry and the grotesque, a cross between Proust and Kafka. In the present story, the relationship to Kafka's famous THE METAMORPHOSIS, in which Gregor Samsa is transformed into a gigantic insect, is self-evident, but the comparison is particularly rich in overtones because of the way in which the story interweaves another thematic concern: that of a son's search for his lost father. In this search, the mother may be seen as an antagonist, much like the mother in V. S. Naipaul's story THE ENEMY.

As in Kafka, the theme of alienation is strong: a human being so obsessed with horror that he literally becomes the object of his own loathing. For the sensitive child, however, the ultimate source of authority and security is undermined as well, and the world becomes a mysterious and threatening place, a sort of waking nightmare. In this world, a young man's passage into manhood becomes a dangerous one, a passage in which his own sense of worth is constantly undermined. Only the child's sensitivity, the power of his poetic vision, seems to offer some form of escape.   — B M

SHOLOKHOV, MIKHAIL. THE COLT.

Russia
Nobel Parade. Glenview, IL: ScottForesman, 1975. Translated by Miriam Morton.

Author: Although his fame is overshadowed, at least in the Western world, by that of his exiled compatriot Alexander Solzhenitsyn, Mikhail Sholokhov (1905–1984) is nevertheless known for his masterful portrayal of the life of the Cossacks of the Don River region of southern Russia. In 1965, this achievement was recognized when he received the Nobel Prize for Literature, chiefly for his epic novel *And Quiet Flows the Don.* His Nobel citation reads, "For the artistic power and integrity with which, in his epic of the Don, he has given expression to a historic phase in the life of the Russian people."

Born of middle-class parents in the Cossack village of Kroujiline, Sholokhov learned to love the majestic Don River and the vast steppes through which it flows. Except for brief periods, Sholokhov always lived in the Don region. His works reveal an almost poetic appreciation of the natural beauty of the area. Sholokhov portrays the Don Cossacks— sometimes described as half-warrior, half-farmer— three-dimensionally, using his acute ear to record the nuances of their dialect. Ordinarily, he chose to write about the period in Russian history beginning just before World War I and ending after World War II.

When, after the Russian Revolution of 1917, civil war broke out, Sholokhov joined the Communist revolutionaries. He became a Communist Party member in 1932 and remained loyal to it, some critics think at the expense of his literary output.

Between 1924 and 1926 appeared the stories later collected in *Tales from the Don.* Sholokhov then spent fourteen years on his masterpiece *And Quiet Flows the Don.* Although some chapters were published serially in 1926, the fourth and last part was not completed until 1940. By this time, the work was so famous that crowds of Russians stood in line at bookstores to obtain a copy. From 1932 to 1959, Sholokhov worked on *Virgin Soil Upturned,* a novel about the collectivization of the Don region. These three remain his major works. Though his output is small, his work has been translated into at least thirty-two languages.

Story: Set in the area of the Don during the civil war that followed the Russian Revolution, this story opens with a contrast between death, symbolized by shellfire and the sound of machine guns, and life, signified by the birth of a colt to soldier Trofim's mare. The contrast is accentuated by describing this initial scene from the viewpoint of the colt. Then Trofim enters, and the story shifts to his viewpoint. A basic conflict emerges between the necessities of war and the memories of home and peacetime brought back by the appearance and antics of the colt. Though Trofim is directed several times to shoot him, he cannot bring himself to do this. In an encounter between the Red forces, to which Trofim belongs, and the Cossacks, who are their enemies, the Red troops must swim the fast-flowing Don River under enemy fire. Assigned to a canoe carrying the troopers' saddles, Trofim sees the colt caught in a whirlpool and hears its desperate neighs. Jumping out of the canoe, he swims to it. The enemy commander, seeing what is happening, orders his men to cease fire. Trofim succeeds in rescuing the colt and getting it to shore, where its mother is waiting. Then, just as he is about to rise, he is shot in the back and killed by the enemy commander.

Throughout the story, the life-giving force, exemplified by the colt and by the evocative descriptions of the natural world, is opposed to the death-giving force, exemplified by the war and its agents, the soldiers. Though the ending of the story is a surprise, Sholokhov has laid the foundation for it: it is easier for a soldier to kill another soldier, his enemy, than it is to kill the colt, who reminds him of peacetime and life. Students may question the enemy commander's motive and may identify strongly with Trofim, but they should also be aware that in another minute Trofim would be attempting to kill the Cossacks. Certainly the author's respect for life is uppermost among the many emotions this story evokes and the many messages it carries. It thus becomes a surprisingly strong antiwar piece.

Comparison: Sholokhov has written a story in which an animal provides readers with a better understanding of human nature. From this standpoint, his work may be compared with Faulkner's "The Bear" or Steinbeck's *The Red Pony*. From the structural standpoint, Sholokhov's ironical surprise ending has much in common with those of Ambrose Bierce, especially in Bierce's stories of the American Civil War, most notably "An Occurrence at Owl Creek Bridge" and "The Coup de Grace." Obviously, this story deals with the adverse effect of war. It therefore lends itself to comparison with the many selections in this subgenre, among them Milovan Djilas's WAR. — H M M

SHOLOKHOV, MIKHAIL. THE FATE OF A MAN.

Russia
Russian and Eastern European Literature. Glenview, IL: ScottForesman, 1970.
Translated by Miriam Morton.

Author: See THE COLT.

Story: This, the most famous of Sholokhov's short stories, is set in the Upper Don region as spring arrives in the first year after World War II. Sholokhov uses a first-person frame story told by an unnamed narrator to recount the tragic history of Andrei Sokolov, evidently the victim of an unsympathetic, almost vindictive fate. The narrator describes Sokolov as a weary, middle-aged man wearing patched clothes, accompanied by Vanya, a little boy of five or six, whose bright blue eyes and natural friendliness make him unforgettable.

Sokolov's mother, father, and sister died of hunger in the famine of 1922, leaving him without relatives. After marrying and having three children—a boy and two girls—Sokolov was called up as soon as World War II broke out. He became a driver, but was captured by the Germans while trying to deliver a load of shells to his hard-pressed division. After a number of years at hard labor in prison camps, Sokolov managed to escape and return to the Russians, only to discover that his wife and daughters had been killed two years earlier by a German bomb. Learning of the tragedy, his son, who was away at the time it occurred, immediately enlisted and rose to the rank of captain. Just as Sokolov was expecting to be reunited with him, he received word that his son had been killed by a sniper's bullet—on May 9, Victory Day.

While working in Uryupinsk, Sokolov encountered Vanya, a homeless waif whose mother and father had been killed in the war. After convincing Vanya that he was the boy's father, Sokolov "adopted" him. When the narrator encounters Sokolov, he has just lost his job and is on his way to Kashary in search of another. At the end of the story, when Vanya looks back and waves to the narrator, the narrator must turn away for, as he explains, "The most important thing is not to wound a child's heart, not to let him see the unwilling hot tear that runs down the cheek of a man."

Comparison: From the structural standpoint, Sholokhov's use of the frame story may be compared with Conrad's use of it in *Heart of Darkness*. Likewise, the lyrical descriptions of nature, which form an essential background for the story and which are intensified by Sholokhov's eye for fine detail, may be compared with those of Conrad or of such modern American authors as Eudora Welty.

The tragic events in Sokolov's life may be compared with those of Matryona in Solzhenitsyn's MATRYONA'S HOME. This comparison will be particularly effective if the opposed political viewpoints of the two authors are considered, especially with regard to the endings of the two stories.

Sholokhov's tale may also be considered an antiwar story. As such, it bears comparison with all of that subgenre, including his own THE COLT.

Russian literature often deals with the concept of the "superfluous man," the person whose lifetime means nothing, without whose existence the world would remain totally unchanged. Students might like to discuss why Sokolov was, or was not, a superfluous man. Melville's "Bartleby the Scrivener" makes for good comparison in this area. — H M M

Siddiqi, Shaukat. A Man of Honor.

Pakistan
Short Story International. April 1978.

Author: A native of Punjab, Shaukat Siddiqi is renowned in Pakistan as a journalist, novelist, and short story writer. He is the recipient of several Pakistani literary awards.

Story: A MAN OF HONOR is a social commentary concerning the struggles of the poor to obtain the basic needs for physical survival. It is also an ironic tale of the metamorphosis of human pride under the emotional pressures of the struggle to survive.

The story opens when Farzand Ali, a schoolteacher, has been unemployed for an entire month. This "Masterji," who is "going through hard times," has friends and neighbors willing to help. One, Abdullah, offers to employ the Masterji's wife as cook and household manager for his family. The Masterji's pride, however, provokes him into a rage: "It's perhaps God's wish that we should be disgraced like this."

Farzand Ali's wife shares his views. When told of the job offer, she remarks angrily, "If father ever comes to know of this, he will blame us for bartering away our pride, our honor and dignity and the worthy name of our family to scoundrels." This attitude prevails, despite their great hunger. "Hunger. Eternal Hunger. Unbearable Hunger." Farzand Ali's children too are hungry.

He eventually lies to his wife about future employment prospects. When he tries to purchase kerosene oil on credit, the grocer makes him return it. Farzand Ali even resorts to stealing money from Pahalwan, the milkman. He is caught and publicly humiliated. When he learns that his wife has taken food from the trash behind the town's club building to feed herself and her children, he thrashes her violently and beats his own head against a wall until he knocks himself out. Finally, he walks to the clubhouse himself, where "the smell of cooked food maddened him." Finding the dustbin, he forsakes his pride and eats the scraps of bread he finds scattered there. As he eats, his wife emerges from the bin's other side, and, together, they eat the bin's offerings.

Comparison: The detrimental effect of pride as an overriding theme is not uncommon in the short story genre. It appears in Sally Benson's "The Overcoat" and in Guy de Maupassant's THE NECKLACE. Siddiqi's tale is most like de Maupassant's in that the pride displayed by the protagonists causes undue hardship. In the latter, the borrower of the necklace, a woman forever desiring more than her station in life allows, fails to admit the loss of the necklace to its owner. She toils at menial tasks for a lifetime to repay the debt for having a duplicate necklace made, only to find out that the original necklace was a fake. Playing the martyr makes her cynical, bitter, and old.

In none of these stories, however, does pride reach the tragic proportions of Chinua Achebe's novel *Things Fall Apart,* in which Okonkwo, of the Nigerian Ubi tribe, strives to achieve all that his father, a lazy man, did not. Okonkwo spends his entire life trying to compensate for the fact that he is the only man of the Ubi not to have inherited any possessions or titles. His pride, emanating from a sometimes haughty sense of individual achievement, coupled with his tribal rigidity and inability to adapt to change, culminates in his suicide, a taboo in Ubi culture that ultimately causes his very memory to be disdained forever. The novel, like A MAN OF HONOR, truly demonstrates the adage "Pride goeth before a fall." — J A G

Sienkiewicz, Henryk. THE LIGHTHOUSE-KEEPER.

Poland

Nobel Prize Library: Giorgis Seferis, Mikhail Sholokhov, Henryk Sienkiewicz, Carl Spitteler. New York: Helvetica Press, 1971. Translated by Monica M. Gardner.

Author: A national hero to the Poles, Henryk Sienkiewicz (1846–1916) was born into a wealthy family that lived just outside Warsaw. After being tutored at home, he entered the University of Warsaw and later traveled extensively throughout Europe and the United States. A prolific writer, he produced many novels and short stories, including THE LIGHTHOUSE-KEEPER in 1882 and YANKO THE MUSICIAN in 1879. Most of his novels are epical, based on history. The most famous of these is *Quo Vadis?* (1895–96), a history of the persecution of early Christians under Nero, translated into English under the same title and as *Whither Goest Thou?*

In 1905, Sienkiewicz was awarded the Nobel Prize for Literature. His citation reads, "Because of his outstanding merits as an epic writer." The Nobel Presentation Address refers to "the moving story of Yanko the Musician" and "the brilliant portrait of the Lighthouse Keeper." In 1900, to celebrate Sienkiewicz's twenty-fifth anniversary as a writer, the Polish people took up a subscription and presented him with an estate where he could relax and meditate. At the outbreak of World War I, Sienkiewicz fled to Vevey, Switzerland, where he busied himself organizing help for his country. There he died unexpectedly in 1916. Eight years later, in 1924, after a state funeral, his remains were interred in a place of honor in Warsaw Cathedral.

Story: Sienkiewicz manages to evoke in the mind of his reader the total isolation of life in a lighthouse, with its extended vistas of sea and sky. Skawinski, a seventy-year-old Pole, has been hired as the lighthouse-keeper of Aspinwall, near Panama. The loneliness of the post, which the keeper may leave only on Sundays, means that finding a keeper is difficult. Thus, despite his age, Skawinski has been taken on, near the end of an adventurous life that has carried him to all quarters of the globe, but somehow has managed to thwart all his attempts at finding security. Skawinski is tired and glad to settle down in his lighthouse. He comes to love it and the acre of island on which it stands. Soon he begins to withdraw more and more, becoming somewhat of a mystic, not leaving his tower even to meet the boat that brings him his daily provisions. One afternoon, he finds beside the provisions a small package of Polish books, sent to him by the Polish Society in New York, to which he had sometime earlier sent a sizeable donation. Picking up a book of poetry, he becomes so absorbed in it and his memories of Poland that he neglects to light the lantern. The next day, he loses his post, and shortly thereafter, much aged physically, he must take up his wanderings again. On a ship to New York, he carries against his breast the book of poetry, grasping it from time to time in fear that it too will be taken from him.

Comparison: An unusual story of human isolation, in this case caused by a combination of old age and weariness, THE LIGHTHOUSE-KEEPER lends itself to comparison with other stories of human isolation. In Thomas Mann's "Tobias Mindernickel," Tobias's isolation is also the result of old age, but results in the mistreatment of his dog. In Ivo Andric's THE SCYTHE, Vitomar's isolation is geographic, because of the sparsely populated area in which he lives. In Solzhenitsyn's THE RIGHT HAND, the narrator's social isolation is caused by a combination of his illness and his earlier prisoner status. In Andric's A SUMMER IN THE SOUTH, Professor Norgess's isolation is psychological, perhaps even psychotic, caused by his losing touch with reality. In D. H. Lawrence's "The Island," the protagonist's isolation is voluntary and progressive. And in Kafka's THE METAMORPHOSIS, Gregor Samsa's isolation, an exaggeration of the way his family had treated him, is caused by his being transformed into a giant insect.

Finally, Ray Bradbury's "The Fog-Horn," a blend of science fiction and psychology, is set in a lighthouse and recreates vividly the immense loneliness of the keeper's life—and that of a gigantic prehistoric creature, the sole survivor of its species. — H M M

SIENKIEWICZ, HENRYK. YANKO THE MUSICIAN.

Poland
Nobel Parade. Glenview, IL: ScottForesman, 1975. Translated by Jeremiah Curtin.

Author: See THE LIGHTHOUSE-KEEPER.

Story: Kept from being overly sentimental by its ending, this story deals with a boy who nearly died at birth but lived to grow up in a hostile world. Often hungry, frequently beaten, forced to work when scarcely past the toddler stage, Yanko has a head that is filled with music. He hears it in the forest, in the wind, in the fields, in the shrubbery. His mother cannot take him to church because he is overly affected by the organ music and the singing of the choir. Eventually, he tries to make a fiddle out of a shingle and some horsehair, but its sound is poor. Often he hides in the bushes outside the village mansion to listen to a servant play the fiddle. One day, the fiddle is hanging on the wall, but no one is around. Overcome by temptation, the boy sneaks into the house to steal the fiddle, but he is

caught. He is arrested and sentenced to be flogged. The cruel beating is too much for his frail frame, and he dies after asking his mother if he will be able to have a real fiddle in heaven. The owners of the mansion return from Italy, praising the musicians there and bemoaning the absence of talent at home.

Comparison: This tragic story of a boy whose passion for music leads to his death may be compared with Thomas Mann's "The Infant Prodigy," in its own way equally tragic because of the exploitation of its young protagonist's musical talent. Yanko's harsh, often cruel treatment at the hands of well-meaning adults may be compared with Mrozek's treatment of a similar theme in CHILDREN. But because Mrozek's intent is satiric, his children are from affluent backgrounds, and the ending is not sentimentally tragic but ironic.   — H M M

SIWERTZ, SIGFRID. IN SPITE OF EVERYTHING.

Sweden
A World of Great Stories. New York: Crown, 1947.

Author: Sigfrid Siwertz (1882–1970) was born in Stockholm. His primary success as a writer was always in the realm of the short story. *A Handful of Feathers* and *Old People* are his best-known collections, though the novel *Downstream* was also well received by critics and readers. Siwertz typically portrays the lives of lonely, disillusioned beings whose paths cross those of other solitary souls, yet who converge only in brief, illusory moments of happiness.

Story: Eric, a sensitive, idealistic student, is physically attracted to the sensuous Agda. Later on in the affair, however, he is morally repulsed by the callous manner in which she reacts to her pregnancy. Agda

coolly plans to leave for America and have the baby adopted by wealthy, childless relatives living there. Her ability to move ahead so resolutely with her plans confounds Eric, whose rights as the child's father Agda never considers. He becomes lost in an emotional and psychological quagmire, powerless to stop Agda or to claim his child.

Years later, Agda returns to visit Eric. Their reunion only intensifies the symbiotic misery they seem destined to share. Forced to acknowledge to himself that he has not managed to overcome his addiction to Agda, Eric laments, "I know your failings, your deceit, your hardness when you think yourself secure, your heavy and helpless emptiness when you are alone; and yet I live only in you, all my dreams are in you.... I hate you." They are together, yet still apart, as the story ends.

Comparison: Despite the temptation to view IN SPITE OF EVERYTHING as a somewhat sordid melodrama, students will find many beautifully phrased passages in the story. There are strong echoes of Emily Brontë's *Wuthering Heights,* particularly in Agda's plea to Eric:"My life has been so restless and confused.... You must help me, talk with me. You know more about me than I do about myself." Of primary comparative importance is Somerset Maugham's *Of Human Bondage,* though the astute reader may find in Siwertz's ending the suggestion of a chance for progress that Eric and Agda may yet make together. — P G L

SOLZHENITSYN, ALEXANDER. MATRYONA'S HOME.

Russia
Russian and Eastern European Literature. Glenview, IL: ScottForesman, 1970.
Translated by H. T. Willette.

Author: Among the most famous of all twentieth-century authors is Alexander Solzhenitsyn (1918–), the son of Cossack intellectuals. He was born six months after his father's death, grew up in Rostov-on-the-Don, and graduated from Rostov University with a degree in mathematics. He also took correspondence courses in philology.

Solzhenitsyn served in the army as an artillery officer until February 1945, when he was arrested by the secret police because of unfavorable comments about Stalin made in correspondence with a friend. When Solzhenitsyn's belongings were searched, notes for some short stories were found in his mapcase, adding to official suspicion. In July 1945, he was sentenced to eight years of imprisonment in corrective labor camps. Because of his knowledge of mathematics, he spent four years of this time in a research institute. In March 1953, he was released from prison but sentenced to perpetual exile in Kazakhstan. In 1954, he underwent successful treatment for cancer. These experiences formed the basis for the nonfictional *Gulag Archipelago* and for three of his novels—*One Day in the Life of Ivan Denisovich* (penal camps), *The First Circle* (prison research institute), and *The Cancer Ward* (cancer hospital in Tashkent)—and also for a number of short stories.

Released from exile in 1957, Solzhenitsyn was cleared of all charges a year later. He became a mathematics teacher in Ryazan, in central Russia, an area that formed the setting for MATRYONA'S HOME. After *One Day in the Life of Ivan Denisovich* was published in *Novy Mir* in November 1962, during the "thaw" that followed the Stalinist regime, Solzhenitsyn became famous. Shortly thereafter, he was able to give up teaching to spend all his time writing. MATRYONA'S HOME was published during this period, in 1963. In 1964, however, he came under serious and continuing attack. His works were banned in Russia, and he was excluded from the Soviet Writers' Union. ZAKHAR-THE-POUCH was published in 1966.

In 1970, Solzhenitsyn's greatness was given international recognition when he received the Nobel Prize for Literature. His citation reads, "For the ethical force with which he has pursued the indispensable traditions of Russian literature." Though Solzhenitsyn accepted the prize, he did not travel to Sweden for the ceremony, afraid that if he left Russia he would not be permitted to re-enter. Finally, in 1975, after a brief imprisonment, Solzhenitsyn was forced into exile, eventually settling in the United States. In 1994, after the dissolution of the Soviet Union, Solzhenitsyn returned to Russia.

Story: This first-person narrative is told by Ignatich, who, like Solzhenitsyn, spent a number of years in Russian prison camps. Recently released, Ignatich is searching for the "Old Russia" he remembers as being simple and good. His search takes him to Torfoprodukt, where he teaches mathematics and boards with Matryona.

The story itself, however, is primarily that of Matryona, whom Solzhenitsyn evidently intends to represent Mother Russia. Even her name contributes to this impression. Aging, of unfailing good nature, Matryona is always willing to help others, who are equally willing to take advantage of her. To provide lumber for her niece to build a house, Matryona sacrifices a part of her own home, an act that ironically results in her death. As a tractor is pulling a sledge loaded with the lumber from Matryona's home, the tow rope breaks, leaving the sledge stranded on the railroad tracks. Two unlighted engines, backing out of the Torfoprodukt station, plow into it, killing Matryona. After her funeral, Ignatich realizes that Matryona was the "righteous person" referred to in the Russian proverb "No village can exist without one righteous person."

Comparison: This story may be compared to two others by Solzhenitsyn: ZAKHAR-THE-POUCH,

which, like it, was published in Russia, and THE RIGHT HAND, which was not published there. MATRYONA'S HOME is, in fact, one of only four Solzhenitsyn short stories ever published in Russia.

Because of its depth and complexity, MATRYONA'S HOME lends itself to comparison in several areas. As an analysis of the character of the Slav peasant, it may be compared with Solzhenitsyn's ZAKHAR-THE-POUCH, Sholokhov's THE COLT, Andric's THE SCYTHE, Djilas's WAR and THE OLD MAN AND THE SONG, Sienkiewicz's YANKO THE MUSICIAN, and Mrozek's ON A JOURNEY. It may also be related to the theme of the superfluous man—in this case, the superfluous woman—the person whose life and death presumably mean nothing to the world. Here it may be compared with Sholokhov's THE FATE OF A MAN or Sienkiewicz's YANKO THE MUSICIAN.

The ironic ending of this story may be compared with those of Sienkiewicz's YANKO THE MUSICIAN, Sholokhov's THE COLT, Djilas's WAR, or Mrozek's CHILDREN.   — H M M

SOLZHENITSYN, ALEXANDER. THE RIGHT HAND.

Russia
Stories and Prose Poems of Alexander Solzhenitsyn. New York: Bantam, 1972.
Translated by Michael Glenny.

Author: See MATRYONA'S HOME.

Story: Much of this story appears to be autobiographical. It is obviously related to *The Cancer Ward,* for its setting is the same—the hospital in Tashkent, the same hospital in which Solzhenitsyn himself was cured of cancer. Told by an unnamed narrator, who may be Solzhenitsyn, the story deals in its early part with the impression spring makes on the narrator, who is beginning to realize that he is recovering. Everything around him takes on new meaning—the park, the girls, even the fresh new grass.

In the park, the narrator sees a small, poorly dressed man, evidently ill and weakly asking passers-by for help. The narrator helps him to a bench near the reception office for the hospital.

Though he is dreadfully emaciated and weak, the stomach of the sick man is enormous and hangs down, obviously dropsical.

Going to the counter in the reception office, the narrator encounters a very young, snub-nosed nurse, who is wearing violet lipstick and nail polish. She is engaged in reading a spy comic book and refuses to do anything about admitting the sick man, saying he must wait until morning. During the ensuing argument, the sick man tries with his right hand, which he is scarcely able to move, to take a tattered piece of paper from his wallet. When the narrator helps him, the paper turns out to be a commendation for "personally eliminating large numbers of counterrevolutionary terrorists." The narrator mentally compares the man's now almost useless right hand with the strength it once had when he was swinging a sabre to chop off enemy heads. Unable to persuade the nurse to listen, the narrator quietly lays the commendation on her comic book and leaves.

Comparison: Since this short story could not be published in Russia, it is probably best contrasted with Solzhenitsyn's MATRYONA'S HOME and ZAKHAR-THE-POUCH, which were published there. Probably the best area for comparison is the criticism each story contains of the Communist bureaucracy. What about THE RIGHT HAND would make it unwelcome in Russia? In this respect, how does it differ from MATRYONA'S HOME and ZAKHAR-THE-POUCH? Is Solzhenitsyn criticizing the Communist

regime because he dislikes it or because he wants it to improve in certain areas?

Solzhenitsyn has said that the writer's task is "to treat universal and eternal themes: the mysteries of the heart and conscience, the collision between life and death, the triumph over spiritual anguish." How well does THE RIGHT HAND carry out the aims described in this statement? How does it compare with the other two short stories in this connection?

The theme of humanity's inhumanity, evident in this story, can also be seen in Djilas's WAR, Sienkiewicz's YANKO THE MUSICIAN, and to a lesser degree in Mrozek's CHILDREN. The stories may be analyzed to see what may lie at the base of that inhumanity.   — H M M

Solzhenitsyn, Alexander. Zakhar-the-Pouch.

Russia
Stories and Prose Poems of Alexander Solzhenitsyn. New York: Bantam, 1972.
Translated by Michael Glenny.

Author: See MATRYONA'S HOME.

Story: Probably owing something to Turgenev's *Hunting Sketches,* this almost plotless short story is set in the Don River region, specifically at Kulikova Field, the site of an important battle fought in 1380 between Russians and an invading Tartar army. The Russians were victorious, but ninety percent of them were killed in battle. As Solzhenitsyn remarks during the story, so many died that it took eight days to bury the dead.

The site, now a Russian historical monument, is visited on a summer cycling holiday by the first-person narrator and some companions. Interested in the historical background, they are attempting to reconstruct in their own minds the progress of the battle. During the day, they encounter several other tourists and the keeper of Kulikova Field, Zakhar Dmitrich, who becomes the focus of interest. Tall, red-haired, unshaven, wearing a long overcoat of indeterminate color, he carries a peasant's sack from which comes the sound of clinking bottles. At first curt and unfriendly, he later thaws and becomes almost pleasant. He is dubbed Zakhar-the-Pouch by

the narrator because inside one flap of his overcoat is sewn a pouch just the right size to hold the visitors' book for the monument.

As the sketch progresses, it is possible to see how carefully Solzhenitsyn has intermingled the isolated, natural beauty of Kulikova Field, accounts of the damage done by vandals and local peasants to the iron monument and the church that stands beside it, and historical detail. In the midst of all this, the character of Zakhar emerges detail by detail. He is devoted to his job and to the historical site. His sack contains bottles and jelly jars left by picnicking tourists, and he gives up his shelter, a shed, so the narrator and his companions can spend the night in it. Solzhenitsyn ends his sketch, which has included some incidental criticism of the way the government maintains the site, with the following words:

> That was two years ago. Perhaps the place is tidier now and better cared for. I have been a bit slow about writing this, but I haven't forgotten the Field of Kulikova, or its Keeper, its red-haired tutelary spirit.
>
> And let it be said that we Russians would be very foolish to neglect that place.

Comparison: This is the last of Solzhenitsyn's short stories to be published in Russia. The most immediate comparison is, therefore, with later stories like THE RIGHT HAND, which were banned there.

For technique, ZAKHAR-THE-POUCH may be compared with some of Turgenev's *Hunting Sketches.* Zakhar himself, as a representative of the Russian peasantry, may be compared with Matryona in Solzhenitsyn's MATRYONA'S HOME or with Trofim in Sholokhov's THE COLT.

The reverence for past history that Solzhenitsyn shows in this piece may be compared with Benét's treatment of history in such familiar short stories as "The Devil and Daniel Webster" and "A Tooth for Paul Revere."

Weaknesses of the Communist bureaucracy that appear in this selection may be compared with those Solzhenitsyn touches on in MATRYONA'S HOME and THE RIGHT HAND and also with those Sholokhov mentions in THE FATE OF A MAN. — H M M

SURANGKHANANG, K. THE GRANDMOTHER.

Thailand
Asian and Pacific Short Stories. Rutland, VT: Charles E. Tuttle, 1974.
Translated by the Thailand P.E.N. Club.

Author: A novelist and short story writer, K. Surangkhanang depicts the plight of the poor and the weak. When traditional social structures erode and new structures have not yet matured, the poor, the weak, and the elderly are victims without support systems. Surangkhanang observes with a sharp eye how, in the struggle for survival, people tend to serve their own interests. As a result, the elderly are cast aside and left to fend for themselves, sometimes living lives that have no direction or meaning.

Story: An old woman who lives with her married daughter and family buys tapioca dumplings from a wholesale dealer and sells them on the streets each day. On the day before she dies, a whole morning passes before anyone expresses any interest in her wares. The customer complains because the old woman has forgotten the parsley, but buys some dumplings anyway because the child on her waist demands them. Other potential customers complain that the vendor is old and dirty.

When at last she comes home from a long day, her daughter urges the grandchildren to snatch whatever has been left over for the day. The grandmother yields, but saves two pieces as her offering to monks, her deed of charity that might ensure a better life when she is reborn. The mother pretends to scold the children for their behavior and, in the meantime, asks the old woman for money. By now the grandmother has learned to defend herself by claiming that she has money only for the next supply of dumplings, for the children have eaten the profit. Embarrassed, the mother berates the children, while the grandmother, going to the kitchen to eat the meager leftovers of thinned rice, remembers that none of her other children would even take her in. Later in the evening when the father comes home with sweets, no one thinks to invite the old woman to partake in the joy of the family gathering.

The next day, after she has made an offering to the monks, she goes about her daily routine. At a bridge, she feels faint and falls into the water. A few bubbles disturb the water, but all that remains of the old woman are a few banana leaves from her basket floating on the surface.

Comparison: Katherine Mansfield's vivid depiction of "Miss Brill" brilliantly captures the separateness of the world of the aging and aged, even as it coexists with the world of youth. Hemingway's "The Old Man and the Sea" portrays the determination of the old fisherman to function as he did in his prime. In Flannery O'Connor's "A Good Man Is Hard to Find," when the grandmother leans forward as if to touch the Misfit and murmurs, "Why, you're one of my babies. You're one of my own children," the Misfit recoils "as if a snake had bitten him and shot her three times through the chest. Then he put his gun down on the ground and took off his glasses and began to clean them."   — M L

Svevo, Italo. IN MY INDOLENCE.

Italy

Short Fiction: A Critical Collection. 2d ed. Englewood Cliffs, NJ: Prentice Hall, 1969. Translated by Ben Jonson.

Author: Born Ettore Schmitz (1861–1928) in Trieste of Italian-Austrian Jewish parents, Svevo chose a pseudonym reflecting his background. Translated, it means "Italo the Swabian." Brought up and educated to be a businessman, he began writing in his twenties, but the poor reception of his first novels persuaded him to return to his career in business. Paradoxically, however, that decision led to literary success, since making business his career led him to seek instruction in English, and the instructor he chose happened to be James Joyce. Joyce read his early novels, liked them, and encouraged him to write more. His next novel, *Confessions of Zeno* (1923), completed only after the First World War, was praised by Joyce and the influential critic to whom he passed it on. But Svevo was unable to capitalize on the "overnight" success this review brought, as he was killed in an automobile accident two years later. IN MY INDOLENCE was published posthumously in 1928.

Story: IN MY INDOLENCE is an interior monologue containing the reflections of its narrator on the period of his life following his retirement from business. Convinced that his life is best viewed now as a "struggle against disease," he doses himself with a variety of medicines, since "it has to be understood that every one of my organs cannot help feeling fagged out after so many years of work." In addition to his medicines, he attempts, without much success, to lose weight and gives up eating meat as a substitute for abstaining from smoking, a task that is too difficult for him. But these measures are not sufficient. Mother Nature will only "maintain life within an organism so long as there is hope of its

reproducing itself." Thus, to "hoodwink Mother Nature into believing that I was still fit for reproduction," he takes a mistress, an act "equivalent," he feels, "to entering a pharmacy."

His affair with Felicita, as ironically named as is his wife, Augusta, is a remarkably commercial and passionless undertaking. The proprietress of the small tobacco shop, she and her brother live together and are both extremely concerned with providing themselves a sound financial future. The note of a business arrangement in the "love affair" is clear: "At the beginning—rather, before drawing up terms, and to encourage me to do it—she threw her arms around me and said, 'I assure you, I don't find you repulsive.'"

As the affair goes on, the narrator attempts to persuade himself that Felicita genuinely cares for him, but the closest she comes to expressing affection is to remark frequently, "Isn't it curious! I don't find you repulsive." She is primarily concerned with getting more money from him, supposedly for clothes and furs, leading him to conclude that "she was certainly the most costly woman I have known in my life." But until he finds another elderly "lover" in her apartment, he is willing to be "plundered" as the price of his continued hoodwinking of Mother Nature. That discovery leads to her reprimanding him for appearing on a day when he was not expected and to his feeling offended: "It was disgusting to see myself limited to fixed days at the price I was paying."

After the discovery, the two elderly gentlemen leave Felicita's apartment together, each pretending he was there only to order cigarettes. But as they talk, the truth comes out. The other man, Miscela, admits he will return to Felicita, since at his age "there's no harm in making love occasionally; but we mustn't become jealous, because we easily come to look ludicrous." Resolving not to return, the narrator regards the affair as over, but Felicita's brother comes to his home to deliver the cigarettes he had ordered and demands payment for the rest of the month. Thinking that since he has paid for the time, he should use it, the narrator returns one evening to Felicita's apartment. Surprised by his arrival and not seeing him clearly, Felicita utters a name that is neither his nor Miscela's. When she recognizes her visitor, she rejects him, saying, "You might return on the first of the month, if you wish. I'll see. I'll think about it." Angered, he leaves for good, and after a time realizes that "she was my last love." Condemned now "to the career of an old man," he realizes that "in the field of love, I am worth no more than I pay."

Now his attempts to hoodwink Mother Nature have been reduced to sidelong glances at attractive young women, a recent glance drawing the comment from a watching older woman, "Old lecher." He thinks, "She called me old. She was summoning death. I said to her: 'You old fool.'"

Comparison: On the surface a humorous story of man's rationalizations and almost absurd fear of aging and death, IN MY INDOLENCE also suggests, on a somewhat more profound level, the alienation of a man unable to feel love since he is incapable of getting beyond himself and his own fears. In its concern with death, the story might be compared to James Joyce's "The Dead" or Eudora Welty's "A Curtain of Green," although neither of these stories deals with alienation and in both of them the mystery of death confronts the characters on a far more profound level. In its ironic theme of love's growing out of the biological nature of its characters—Mother Nature in the story—Svevo's story can be contrasted with D. H. Lawrence's "The Horse Dealer's Daughter," which treats that theme seriously. — P T M

Tagore, Rabindranath. Kabuliwallah.

India
Selected Short Stories. London: Penguin, 1991. Translated by William Redice.

Author: First to write short stories in Bengali, Rabindranath Tagore (1861–1941) was also a poet, novelist, dramatist, philosopher, educator, actor, musician, painter, editor, and reformer. Winner of the Nobel Prize for Literature in 1913, Tagore was revered as a great man and a prophet of enlightened humanism. The poetic flash of insight into the truth of the nature of things that runs through the vast collection of his works earned him the reputation of *gurudev* or *risi* (sage) in his native India. His career as a short story writer began with material for a journal that he and his family ran, his subject matter frequently drawn from his observations of Indian life as he expanded his contacts beyond his aristocratic background while managing his family estates. From 1891 to 1895, he wrote forty-four stories, half of his total output in this genre, before switching his interest to the psychological novella.

Though he wrote mostly in Bengali, he translated many of his own works into English.

Story: The narrator, a Bengali gentleman, watches as his little daughter Mini develops a friendship with Rahamut the Kabuliwallah, an itinerant trader from Afghanistan. As Rahamut makes his rounds, busy though he might be, he always stops to visit Mini, the two of them so enchanted by each other that they develop private jokes and routines at which they laugh heartily. For instance, when Rahamut would say, "Little one, don't ever go off to your *svasur-bari*," Mini, not understanding that *svasur-bari* refers to the home of a woman's in-laws, would respond, "Are you going to your *svasur-bari?*" Rahamut would then shake a huge fist at an imaginary father-in-law, and Mini would burst into laughter at this encounter with an unknown creature.

Mini's mother's fears and suspicions of the relationship end when one day Rahamut is jailed for assaulting a customer who refused to pay him.

Years later, on Mini's wedding day, Rahamut happens to drop by to renew his friendship. At first the narrator refuses to admit him. He learns, however, that years ago, Rahamut had left his own daughter, the same age as Mini, behind in his native country and that he always carries a small handprint of her. The narrator is so moved by the Kabuliwallah's story that he diverts part of the funds for the wedding banquet to enable Rahamut to go home. In facing each other at last, Mini and Rahamut hardly recognize each other, but Rahamut's reference to one of their old jokes brings past and present poignantly to focus: "Are you going to your *svasur-bari?*"

Comparison: The intergenerational, interclass friendship that develops between man and girl is commonly depicted in stories of same-sex relationships, such as the relationship between Jim and Huck in *Huckleberry Finn* by Mark Twain, between Juliet and her nurse in Shakespeare's *Romeo and Juliet,* and between Paul and the butler Basil in "The Rocking Horse Winner" by D. H. Lawrence. In each case, the older friend, of lower social class, serves as intimate companion and confidante in such a way as to touch the heart of the younger friend. This intergenerational bond sharply contrasts with the lack of communication in "A Visit of Charity" by Eudora Welty, in which a fourteen-year-old girl is stunned and frightened and runs from the old women in the nursing home she visits.

The underlying theme of love of parents for children, which motivates the actions of Rahamut and the narrator, can be found in many stories in which parental concern constellates as context or instigates the action of the plot. *Romeo and Juliet* and "The Rocking Horse Winner" are two examples.
— M L

TAMASI, ARON. FLASHES IN THE NIGHT.

Hungary
Russian and Eastern European Literature. Glenview, IL: ScottForesman, 1970. Translated by Alexander Harsanyi.

Author: Aron Tamasi (1897–1966) was born in Transylvania. In 1920, Transylvania, formerly a part of Hungary, was annexed by Romania. Like other authors who shared his background, Tamasi feared that his national culture would be destroyed by the annexation. Drawing upon his peasant background, he became a regionalist, writing about the countryside and the sturdy peasants who inhabited it. Lyrical in style, his works often contain elements of folklore and ballads. FLASHES IN THE NIGHT is eminently a regional piece, rich in descriptions of nature and the isolated countryside, yet surprisingly sophisticated in its ability to combine and interrelate a fierce spring storm, the birth of a child, and a strong but subtle antiwar message. In 1923, Tamasi emigrated to the United States, but returned to his homeland in 1925, fearing that he would lose his national identification if he remained here. A novel dealing with the adventures of a peasant lad, *Abel in America* (1934), and some of his short stories are based on his American experience. FLASHES IN THE NIGHT was published in 1958.

Story: Set in a remote mountain district of Hungary, this story is narrated against the background of a fierce storm marking "the birthpangs of spring." Paralleling the storm, increasing in intensity as it does, are the labor pains of Aniska, the wife of Benke Ku. Nature descriptions of the sky and mountains before the storm are lyrical and peaceful, rich in imagery and figurative language. The mood is broken by a single event, a flight of nine fighter planes across the sky, directing attention to the fact that World War II is not yet over, that men are still killing and being killed.

As the story opens, Benke, who is a carpenter, is working at his trade, and his dog Mop is keeping him company. Because Benke is slightly lame, he has not

161

been drafted. When he and Mop go into the house for dinner, they find that Aniska is going into labor a month early and many miles over the mountains from the midwife. They decide to take Aniska to the midwife, and Benke puts her into a farm cart, drawn by a half-broken colt. Mop leads the way down the mountain through the darkness, which falls early because of the storm. The storm is punctuated by constant flashes of lightning, accounting for the story's title.

Just as the storm seems about to overwhelm them, Benke sees the light of Marton Zadog's sheepfold, and they find shelter with him and his wife. The two men sit outdoors by a fire, sheltered from the rain by the roof of the hut, waiting for the birth. When Benke says he would like a boy, the old farmer responds dubiously that a boy may be better for the parents, to which Benke asks, "Doesn't the child belong to the parents?" The old man does not quite agree and replies, "In a way of speaking, for the child belongs to the world and the world is full of trouble, much trouble, all of it caused by men who want the sun and stars; and under their striving feet, the earth is ravaged. Yet we live here on this earth, man's home, and if it is to be a home, we need a blessing on it: warmth, joy and smiling fruit."

After a moment of silence, the old man says, tears in his eyes, "Girls are what the world needs."

By the time he has finished, the storm is over, "and the moon, like a young girl growing up, smiles." Word comes from the house that a baby girl has been born. Overjoyed, Benke runs into the house, and the old man looks at the dawn, "his heart alight with a faith that joy may yet come to the world after all."

Comparison: The vivid descriptions of nature and the delineation of the peasant characters are typical of eastern European writing. Especially good comparisons may be made with Solzhenitsyn's MATRYONA'S HOME and Sholokhov's THE COLT, which deal with both topics, and Andric's SUMMER IN THE SOUTH, in which nature descriptions are important but the characters are not peasants. FLASHES IN THE NIGHT also lends itself to a contrast with Andric's THE SCYTHE in the character of the peasant and the unstated implications of the story. In essence, however, FLASHES IN THE NIGHT is a subtle antiwar story, with a strong current of rebirth and more than a hint of parallels to the Christian Nativity. — H M M

Tanizaki Junichiro. Tattoo.

Japan
Modern Japanese Stories: An Anthology. Rutland, VT: Charles E. Tuttle, 1980.
Translated by Ivan Morris.

Author: Tanizaki (1886–1965) was a major figure in Japanese literature. His life spanned the period of "growing pains" Japan experienced during the period of Westernization that began with the Meiji Restoration. Born in Tokyo to merchant-class parents, Tanizaki displayed his brilliance as a writer early. For a while, he lived a bohemian lifestyle and was infatuated with the West. The aesthetic and epicurean "diabolism" of his early works was the direct result of his immersion in the works of Poe, Wilde, and Baudelaire. The publication of his first story, TATTOO, in 1910 brought him sudden fame.

Later, he shed the superficial veneer of Western ways and became absorbed in the Japanese past. In this period, he produced *The Makioka Sisters.* In the last period of his career, Tanizaki seems to have been obsessed by human sexual perversity and the effect of Western literature and film on the Japanese mind. Two novels, *The Key* and *The Diary of a Mad Old Man,* both done in diary form, depict perverted streaks in men as they record their thoughts and observations.

Story: The great ambition of the famed tattoo artist, Seikishi, is to "have under his needle the lustrous skin of some beautiful girl, on which he

162

dreamed of tattooing, as it were, his very soul." He first recognizes his fantasy girl by the beauty of her foot as she mounts a palanquin. A year later, she happens to be sent to him on an errand by a geisha friend of his, who also asks him to do what he can to help launch the girl in her career as a geisha.

Fascinated by her as he studies her face and recognizes her foot, he leads her upstairs and shows her two pictures: one of the lovely Chinese imperial princess Mo Hsi languidly watching the execution of a prisoner and the other of a young woman with an expression of "pride and satisfaction" leaning against a cherry tree and gazing at the corpses of men laid at her feet. In comparing the present state of the girl to the pictures, Seikishi foretells that she will become a "femme fatale," declaring that he alone has the power to make her into a beautiful woman.

After drugging her with an injection, he works all through the day and night on his masterpiece. The design of an enormous spider spreads across the girl's back. When in the morning the girl regains consciousness and asks to see this work of art, he tells her to take a bath first to bring out the colors. The look on her face as she emerges is that of an experienced woman rather than that of the innocent girl of the day before. She announces that she is now free of all fear and that he will be her first victim. As he asks to see her tattoo, the rays of the morning sun "seemed to set fire to the spider."

Comparison: The theme of the artist creating from the depths of his soul and being ruled or destroyed by his own creation has its prototype in the myth of Daedalus, who, at least twice, was his own victim: his incarceration in the labyrinth he built and losing his son Icarus after fitting him with the wings he made. In "The Real Thing," Henry James uses a variation of the Pygmalion theme with a painter who hopes to become a great artist by choosing flawless models for his works. In "Secret Miracle" by Jorge Luis Borges, the main character creates a play, but finds not only that the creative effort has devoured him, but also that he is his sole audience.

The theme of the transition from innocence to experience is explored in great variety in all types of literature. One starkly different story, Ernest Hemingway's "The Killers," studies an inexperienced and idealistic youth as he discovers the dark power of evil in his life. In John Steinbeck's "The Chrysanthemums," a lonely farm wife is suddenly possessed by powerful feelings that she needs to hide after she is disappointed by a man who has manipulated her emotions. — M L

TANIZAKI JUNICHIRO. THE THIEF.

Japan
World Writers Today. Glenview, IL: ScottForesman, 1995. Translated by H. Hibbett.

Author: See TATTOO.

Story: The narrator, huddling over a candle with his three roommates at a college preparatory school, hears about recent thefts in the dormitory. Because the thief was seen in a jacket with a wisteria emblem, which happens to be his family crest, he begins to sense the suspicion around him. Both his lack of ease and the gulf between him and others grow until one roommate, a good friend, confesses his trust in the narrator despite what the rest of the school thinks.

As it happens, the narrator is the thief. He is caught stealing checks from another roommate, Hirata, who has disliked him from the beginning. The episode ends with the narrator telling the two trusting roommates, "So be on your guard! You two made friends with a thief because of your gullibility. You're likely to run into trouble when you go out into the world. Maybe you get better grades in school, but Hirata is a better man. You can't fool Hirata!"

The story ends with the narrator's testimony to the reader that the entire account is true, but perhaps the reader cannot believe him unless the reader happens to belong to the thief's "own species."

Comparison: The aura of doubt created when one person suspects another can lead to many psychological and actual consequences. In the Greek myth of Cephalus and Procris, told by Ovid in *The Metamorphoses,* the goddess Aurora leads Cephalus to doubt his wife, Procris. Although Procris is unquestionably faithful to him, his doubt of her engenders her suspicion of him. The division that comes between the two is similar to that depicted by R. K. Narayan as he retells an old Hindu myth in THE MIRROR.

In suggesting that the thief is a special species, with a point of view that is perfectly natural to the thief, Tanizaki draws attention to a perspective that is at odds with what might be considered the norm in society. In the same way, the Russian writer Gogol and the Chinese writer Lu Xun create the perspective of the madman in stories by the same title, DIARY OF A MADMAN. — M L

TAYLOR, APIRANA. THE CARVING.

New Zealand Maori
He Rau Aroha: A Hundred Leaves of Love. Auckland, New Zealand: Penguin, 1986.

Author: Born in Wellington, New Zealand, Apirana Taylor (1955–), a Maori writer, is descended from Te Whanau-a-Apanui, Ngati Porou, and Taranaki. He spent some of his childhood in Bangkok. He was educated at Te Aute College and Massey University. Over the years, he has been a laborer, journalist, carpenter, fisherman, and actor. He is a member of the Te Ohu Whakaari, a Maori theater that dramatizes myths, songs, poetry, and street theater and also presents significant productions by Maori authors. He has been described as a stunning actor. Taylor's poetry has been anthologized in *The Penguin Book of New Zealand Verse* (1985), *Eyes of the Ruru* (1979), and *Three Shades* (1981). His short stories are collected in *He Rau Aroha* (1986), which was runner-up in the Pegasus Book Awards, and *Ki Te Ao* (1990). In 1993, his first novel, *He Tangi Aroha,* was released. A modern love story, it tells the tale of young urban Maori. Within this context are issues with which New Zealanders are grappling: race, violence, and work. Taylor currently participates in the Writers in Schools project and makes audio cassettes in Maori for educational institutions.

The Maori are the indigenous people of New Zealand and comprise less than ten percent of the population. Those of European descent are called Pakeha.

Story: The act of carving is sacred for the Maori, who are well known for their work in this art form. Willy Paraha, a laborer, spends his spare time carving figures. Before starting a figure, he makes a spiritual connection with the piece of wood: "he'd seen hidden in the Kahikatea the shape that was this feeling." The figure he is working on begins to take a militant stance, with upraised arm, "gaping mouth with a flicking tongue that stuck out and curved," the Maori representation of war. The figure, named Te Toa, also has in his eyes "the strong warmth of a man who loved." To complete this figure, Paraha tattoos the wooden man in imitation of the ancient Maori tradition of decorating bodies with spirals. "Willy did not realize it but something in the figure made the carving look like him."

Months go by, and Te Toa stands behind boxes in the corner of Paraha's workshop. One day, Willy sees on television scenes of Maori marches to protest the loss of their land. Overcome with emotion, he rushes to his workshop. There he grabs Te Toa and cuts out his tongue because the Maori language has almost disappeared. Then, he cuts off his legs because the wooden figure has no land to stand on. Finally, he cuts off the arms, chops a hole in Te Toa's stomach, and puts a beer bottle in its mouth. Paraha moans, "Perhaps your own weakness caused this, Te Toa. But that's not just it. Pakeha, you did this." Now that Te Toa is dead, his creator feels the same way. But it is time for a new creation. Paraha sets out to create a "man/woman warrior of this day. One that could not be killed. He wanted the Maori to be like that." And so the cycle of creation and death begins again, but this time with more self-knowledge and cultural understanding.

Comparison: As anyone who has lost a homeland or been displaced knows, the grief one feels in this situation is overwhelming. The connection to the land that many indigenous people feel, including the Australian Aborigine, the African tribal member, and the Amerindians in Latin America, is profound. When they lose this connection, their identity is lost.

Nadine Gordimer's "Home" examines the political significance of being a black person in the former apartheid society of South Africa. There is fear, betrayal, and mistrust between Nils, a Swede, and Teresa, his "colored" wife. They have both been displaced from their respective lands, emotionally as well as politically. To be cut off from one's heritage, to feel alienated where one lives, to believe oneself without a voice is a kind of living death. This was true in South Africa and in New Zealand until political movements during the last decades began making progress to correct the situation.

In much of Australian Aboriginal writing, the Land is a central, living character. Indeed, it is the umbilical cord that connects present to past and future. Maoris see the Land as a sacred place where their ancestors once walked. For Paraha, then, his carved warrior has been displaced and literally has nowhere to stand.

In Ngũgĩ wa Thiong'o's novel *Weep Not Child,* the Gĩkũyũ of Kenya saw their land taken by the British. Just as the Maori land protestors were on a march for their rights, so too the Gĩkũyũ sought justice. The question that the son asks the father is relevant to THE CARVING: "How could these people have let the white man occupy the land without acting?" The Africans have chosen to act and have gained their independence. The Maoris are continuing to fight for their rights under the Treaty of Waitangi. — M J S

THEOTOKIS, KONSTANTINOS. VILLAGE LIFE.

Greece

Introduction to Modern Greek Literature: An Anthology of Fiction, Drama, and Poetry. New York: Twayne, 1969. Translated by Mary P. Gianos.

Author: Konstantinos Theotokis (1872–1923) was born into a literary family on the Ionian Island of Zakinthos (Zante). He studied in Paris and traveled widely in Europe, returning to Zakinthos at the age of nineteen with his wife, the Baroness Ernestine von Mallowitz. They lived at the family castle on the island, where he devoted himself to writing and to translating foreign authors into modern Greek. A socialist for a time, he reflected that view in his story "Honor and Money" (1914). Besides his collections of short stories, Theotokis wrote several novels. Among them was one of the first social novels in Greece, *Slaves and Their Bonds* (1922), published a year before his death in 1923. A realist, he wrote carefully and critically in demotic Greek.

Story: Theotokis based his short stories primarily on historical events or on examinations of the inflexible customs and morals of Greek village provincials. This is, as the title indicates, a village tale. The author presents characters who are totally controlled by their jealousies, hatreds, and petty deceits—characters, customs, and attitudes that have not totally disappeared from Greek villages.

As the story begins, a landowner waits in his remote village for an old man, a matchmaker, to arrive with the good news that Margaro, a young woman whom the landowner has selected to be the bride of his only son, Demetris, has accepted the offer. But the news the matchmaker brings is not good. While the family has been pleased with the landowner's offer, their daughter has scorned

Demetris, even going so far as to say that he resembles a monkey. From that moment on, the landowner has but one thought: how he will make Margaro and her family pay for such an insult. Although the women in Greece are under the control of their husbands, they nevertheless carry the family honor. Thus, the landowner knows where and how to strike. By the time he is finished, Margaro's father is cursing her, and the landowner is satisfied. "She will never be able to marry," he says. "She will always live in sin." Theotokis has filled the story with details about life in a Greek village and about Greek Orthodox Christian family relationships.

Comparison: The main character of this story knows that he can accomplish his goal of revenge against the young woman because the harsh realities of life under a severe patriarchal system give him all the benefit of doubt. By contrast, in James Thurber's "The Catbird Seat," the main character, though also living in a patriarchal system, finds it necessary to get what he wants by using the techniques of powerless people. He

fights for his revenge in an indirect, instead of direct, way.

Anna, the principal character of Laura Furman's "Watch Time Fly," has an opportunity to make up for some of the insulting treatment she has received from her soon-to-be-ex-husband and his new woman. After letting the chance go by several times, she accepts it with some satisfaction. The revenge in Edgar Allan Poe's "The Cask of Amontillado" is of a more serious order.

Two stories that center on family relationships are Eudora Welty's "Why I Live at the P.O." and Susan Glaspell's "A Jury of Her Peers." In the Welty story, a family member who cannot tolerate the bad treatment she receives at home moves out and lives in the building where her job is located. In the Glaspell story, two small-town women, wives laughed at and discounted by their husbands, learn the horrible truth about the oppressive life of one of their friends. Without talking about it directly, and under the clear impression that murder is sometimes justified, they withhold evidence that might have proven that the friend killed her husband. — E M

TOLSTOY, LEO. THE DEATH OF IVÁN ILYICH.

Russia
The Continental Edition of World Masterpieces. New York: Norton, 1986.
Translated by Louise and Aylmer Maude.

Author: Leo Nikolaevich Tolstoy (1828–1910), Russian short story writer and novelist, was born at Yásnaya Polyána, about 130 miles south of Moscow. He was able to trace his ancestry back to distinguished nobility. Although he was an aristocrat, he sympathized with the plight of the peasants in his homeland. In 1847, after studying Eastern languages and law briefly at Kazan University, he returned to his inherited family estate. In 1851, he entered the military and served in the Crimean War. Shortly after his marriage to Sofya Andreyevna Bers in 1862, he wrote *War and Peace,* a realistic historical war novel based on the Crimean War, and *Anna Karenina,* two of the great masterpieces of Russian fiction. His wife managed the estate and family mat-

ters, including the rearing of thirteen children, to free Tolstoy to pursue his literary endeavors.

In the 1880s, Tolstoy developed a mystical approach to Christianity that eventually separated him from the Orthodox church. He spoke openly against religious ritual, church organization, priesthood, and the evils of materialism, emphasizing the need for spiritual awareness. Moral lessons and ethical issues became the focus of his short stories. THE DEATH OF IVÁN ILYICH was written after his conversion and expresses his belief that man needs to reform, to return to nature and the basic essentials. HOW MUCH LAND DOES A MAN NEED illustrates his belief that private ownership of land engenders greed, the root of all evil. In 1861, he freed his serfs, many of whom became suspicious of his intentions. Nevertheless, he was dedicated to teaching them and to instituting land reforms on their behalf. In 1901, he was excommunicated from the church.

After a quarrel with his wife concerning the chaos caused by his vision of reform, he left her and died alone in a stationmaster's house while on a religious pilgrimage. Tolstoy was an important force in Russia at the time of its emergence from feudalism.

Story: The story begins after the death of Iván Ilyich Golovin, revealing a world in which Ilyich was never a real person to anyone, nor were other people real to him. His funeral is a cliché, just as his life had been.

A flashback illustrates that, despite the depressing quality of his funeral, he had lived a pleasant life. He had been a judge and always acted out of a sense of propriety, an "Everyman" enjoying superficial pleasures and concerned primarily with advancing his career. Suddenly, he was plagued by a recurring pain that struck as a result of something as insignificant as fixing a curtain. He tried to ignore the pain, but it persisted relentlessly throughout a slow and painful movement toward death.

During that time, he was forced to examine the events of his past life. He came to recognize how false and empty a life he had led, having been cut off from meaningful human contact and emotion. He realized that only a few incidents in his childhood appeared to have been truly happy. Even as he was dying, his only meaningful human contact was with his servant, Gerásim, whose proximity to nature and patient and simple devotion to his master showed Iván how his life should have been lived. He recognized the contrast between that ideal and the coldness and deceit of those who surrounded him and pretended to care about his comfort. And like Everyman in the middle of the journey of his life, finding himself confronted with disease and death, he was forced to face the reality of something he knew as *it*, his own mortality.

In the last moments before his death, Iván found the light and joy of faith and an intense belief in a personal God, and thus he was able to defeat and transcend death, the supreme antagonist of his life. He could declare finally that "Death is finished," but the reader recognizes the horror of carrying out a revealing self-examination too late to reverse life's course.

Comparison: The idea of finding happiness through human contact and in living for others is found throughout Tolstoy's work, particularly in *Anna Karenina* and in his novellas *Family Happiness* and *Master and Man*. Chekhov's "A Dreary Story" also deals with the reminiscence of a man who dies realizing that he has led a spiritually bankrupt life. The Chekhov story, however, does not share Tolstoy's hint of an optimistic ending.

The strong existential base of the story suggests many works of literature, from Camus's *The Myth of Sisyphus* to Sartre's play *No Exit,* in which there is the need to confront death in the midst of life. The difference is that the existentialist insists upon meeting the challenge without a spiritual *deus ex machina*, whereas Tolstoy finds an answer in Iván's leap to faith.

One is also reminded of Eliot's "The Love Song of J. Alfred Prufrock" insofar as both Prufrock and Iván come to realize that they have "measured out [their lives] in coffee spoons." But once again, Tolstoy expresses a kind of romantic spirituality to which Eliot and many writers of the twentieth century do not subscribe. Tolstoy's faith in nature and the goodness of natural humanity is far more akin to Thoreau's thinking than to Sartre's or Camus's.

Although there are many aspects of Edgar Allan Poe's "The Cask of Amontillado" that are very different from those in Tolstoy's story, the suspense and the horrendous and chilling experience of moving toward a slow and inevitable death are common denominators in both stories and provide an interesting basis for comparison and contrast.

Böll's story MURKE'S COLLECTED SILENCES also makes a plea for spiritual values and points up the hypocrisy of the masses of people who have chosen to delete God from their lives, leaving them nothing in its stead. — R H M

Tolstoy, Leo. HOW MUCH LAND DOES A MAN NEED.

Russia
Classics in World Literature. Glenview, IL: ScottForesman, 1989.
Translated by Louise and Aylmer Maude.

Author: See THE DEATH OF IVÁN ILYICH.

Story: In a Russian country village, the devil over-hears a poor peasant, Pahom, boast "that if he had plenty of land he would not fear the Devil himself." The devil arranges a series of opportunities for Pahom to obtain land, each time increasing the amount gained. Pahom becomes more acquisitive and keeps moving his family to new areas where he can obtain more rich acreage. One day, a passing dealer advises Pahom that far away in the area roamed by the Bashkers, land is plentiful and cheap. Planning to take advantage of the simple tribesmen, Pahom travels to their camp. The Bashkers agree to sell him all the land he can circle on foot in one day for just one thousand rubles, providing he returns to his starting place before sunset. Pahom's greed gets the better of him, and he realizes he has "grasped too much" when he has to run a long dis-tance to get back to his initial spot as the day ends. He reaches his goal but collapses and dies. He then receives all the land a man needs—"six feet," enough for his grave.

Comparison: The theme of the evil engendered by greed is common throughout world literature. The moral lesson of Tolstoy's story is similar to that in the biblical parable found in the gospel of St. Luke about the wealthy fool who tears down his barns to build bigger ones to store all he harvests. He ignores his spiritual side as he greedily amasses his earthly treasures, thereby remaining unprepared when God comes to claim his soul. In the short story "Where Love Is, God Is," Tolstoy directly incor-porates several verses from the gospel of Luke into the plot.

Pacts with the devil, such as the one in HOW MUCH LAND DOES A MAN NEED, abound in folk-lore and literary works. In Christopher Marlowe's play *Dr. Faustus* and Goethe's drama *Faust,* the main character enters into a contract with the devil, but his quest for all knowledge and experience is more idealistic than Pahom's purely materialistic aim to gain more land.

The purpose for the pact with the devil is dif-ferent in Oscar Wilde's *The Picture of Dorian Gray,* but the outcome is the same. Dorian too wants more than life ordinarily offers. He wants eternal youth and beauty. To obtain them, he inadvertently deals with the devil. Only with the passing of time and the acquisition of wisdom does he come to know that outward appearances and other people's opinions are not important when compared to the benefits of leading a natural—flawed but uncorrupt-ed—life. The destruction of the devilishly defiled painting, the symbol for Dorian's soul, is equivalent to Tolstoy's six-foot grave.

Washington Irving's short story "The Devil and Tom Walker" offers a satirical treatment on the evil of greed. In this humorous tale, the avaricious Tom Walker sells his soul to the devil in exchange for great wealth and later tries to cheat the devil of his due but is unsuccessful. Stephen Vincent Benét's short story "The Devil and Daniel Webster" and the one-act opera based on it also portray the bargain with the devil in a comic manner.   — M A F

TURGENEV, IVAN. YERMOLAY AND THE MILLER'S WIFE.

Russia

Sketches from a Hunter's Album. London: Penguin, 1990. Translated by Richard Freeborn.

Author: Born in Oryol, Ivan Turgenev (1818–1883) was a member of the gentry and the first Russian writer to enjoy an international reputation. He was ruled by a tyrannical mother and was against serfdom from his youngest years. He studied in Moscow and St. Petersburg, then traveled to Berlin, where he was introduced to German Liberalism. Upon his return to Russia, he became a liberal and a "Westernist." His fame came with his brilliant pictures of peasant life. Turgenev's writings are known for their poetic settings, pictures of country atmosphere, the contrast between hero and heroine, and heroes representing stages of the developing intelligentsia during the period from 1840 to 1870. He was so sorely disillusioned at the criticism of his *Fathers and Sons* that he spent the rest of his life in Europe, where he wrote *Smoke* (1867) and *Virgin Soil* (1877). His greatest work is *Sportsman's Sketches* or *Sketches from a Hunter's Album.*

Story: YERMOLAY AND THE MILLER'S WIFE is written in first person, as are all the stories in *Sketches from a Hunter's Album.* The narrator sets off on a hunting expedition with Yermolay, his hunting partner.

The two hunters seek shelter for the night at a miller's farm. They ask for some straw for a bed, for which they will gladly pay. The miller's workman agrees, and soon straw and hay are brought out to them, along with a samovar. The miller's wife brings out some milk, eggs, potatoes, and bread. The story then shifts to a revelation of her past.

Arina Timofeyevna is about thirty, but thin and haggard. Yet her face "still contains traces of a remarkable beauty." The narrator remembers that she was once a serf belonging to Mr. Zverkhov. Luckily, she became his wife's chambermaid, and thus she lived in the house and was taught to read and write. Unfortunately, Arina fell in love with Petrushka, another servant of Zverkhov's. She asked permission of her master to marry. She was denied on the grounds that she was a chambermaid and could remain in that position only as long as she was single.

Arina was devastated, and six months later she asked Mrs. Zverkhov for permission to marry. Of course, she was again refused, but this time Zverkhov realized the seriousness of her intentions and decided to take drastic action. Arina's hair was cut and she was banished to the country.

The narrator wonders how she happened to become the miller's wife. He looks at her sympathetically and asks how long she has been married. "Two years," she replies. Puzzled by why her master had a change of heart and allowed her to marry the miller, he asks her how this came about. The answer is simple: the miller bought her freedom on the condition that she would marry him.

"It seems that she is not well, is that so?" the narrator asks of Yermolay. But Yermolay dismisses the question and advises that they should get some sleep before the hunt the next day.

Comparison: The story is so rich with character and descriptions that it lends itself to many comparisons. For example, the work opens with the universal anticipation of the hunt. One can compare this to the boys in Ernest Hemingway's "Big Two-Hearted River" or William Faulkner's description of men getting ready to hunt in "The Bear."

The characters in the story are typically Russian, with little quirks like those in Anton Chekhov's *The Cherry Orchard.* Yermolay and his dog have a relationship like James Thurber's character did with his Airedale, Muggs, in "The Dog That Bit People." Both dogs are eccentric, much like their masters, but Yermolay's Valetka possesses a remarkable sense of loyalty. He is also indifferent to everything, while Muggs is indiscriminate in whom he chooses to nip.

The bittersweet life of the miller's wife is but a small part of the story. One can compare it to Alice Walker's *The Color Purple,* except that at the end of that novel, Celie has hope and has made a life for herself. The life of the miller's wife is hopeless, but, as the narrator insists, "You see why I feel sympathy for her." — D G

VALENZUELA, LUISA. I'M YOUR HORSE IN THE NIGHT.

Argentina

Other Weapons. Hanover: Ediciones del Norte, 1985. Translated by Deborah Bonner.

Author: Luisa Valenzuela (1938–) was born in Buenos Aires and has become the most translated Latin American woman author. Her work includes four novels and five collections of short stories and novellas, including *Strange Things Happen Here.* She has contributed to various magazines and newspapers and has written radio programs. She participated in the International Writers Program at the University of Iowa, received a grant from the National Arts Foundation of Argentina to research North American literature, and has accrued many awards. She now lives primarily in the United States.

In the best tradition of contemporary Latin American fiction, her prose is both critical and revolutionary. Central to her criticism is the parody of the conventions of bourgeois society and the fatuous nature of the art of writing itself. She aims her critical barbs at social structures that allow poverty, hunger, and humiliation to exist.

Poking fun at the well-known adage "Absence makes the heart grow fonder" and the sacrosanct tradition of "courtly love," for example, her "Cat-O-Nine-Deaths" portrays a couple who must be far apart in order to make love to each other. When the man begins to gyrate in a theater, seeking contact with his beloved, those about him join in until all experience universal love.

However humorous her parodies, the revolutionary element in her prose links violence and death to metamorphosis, eroticism, ritual, and myth. Fertility and primordial vitality can issue forth only from dispersion, destruction, and cataclysm. This protean "becoming" evolves in characters assuming disguises and undergoing physical mutations. Through surrealistic and dreamlike sequences inside transformational realities, her eroticism infuses repression, torture, and disappearance with mystical realism. A very tangible reality of authoritarian power and its consequences lie within the short story I'M YOUR HORSE IN THE NIGHT.

Story: The story is told from the point of view of a woman rejoining her lover, "Betó," which, she notes, is "not his real name but one I can say out loud." They meet passionately, and the mystery surrounding him deepens. "I poured out one question after another, revealing how I never stopped thinking about him. 'You're much better off not knowing what I've been up to,'" he replies. As they drink cachaca, talk, and make love, they play a Gal Costa record and discuss the lyrics of one of the songs: "'I'm your horse in the night.' It's a saint's song . . . someone in a trance saying she's the horse of the spirit riding her."

Suddenly, the phone rings, and the woman is dragged from sleep. A voice informs her that "They found Betó dead floating down the river." Fifteen minutes later, the police arrive to search her house. "My real possession was a dream, and they can't deprive me of that. But their questions demand the tangible, the kind I couldn't begin to give them. I haven't heard from him in months, he's abandoned me, I hate him." They torture her, and she tells them nothing. "I know I dreamed you last night; but if by chance there's a bottle of cachaca and a Gal Costa record in my house, I will them out of existence."

Comparison: The movie *Official Story* brought to the screen the atrocity of the "Disappeared." Within that context, Valenzuela's story illustrates through passion the female acceptance of the male and through torture the male dominance of the female. This endurance of both passion and torture creates the interplay between the surreal imaginary and the real. The main character can endure because the surreal has greater power than the real. As in a Dali or Magritte painting, or even a Cartier-Bresson photograph, the tangible, ever so slightly distorted or out of focus, reveals how the subconscious controls motives and actions. Like the movie *Missing,* which portrays the American wife and father of an American "Disappeared,"

Valenzuela's depiction of a lover caught up in her beloved's ordeal captures the intensity felt by those personally surrounded by that atrocity. Julio Cortázar's *Manual for Manuel* employs the surreal to depict the "Disappeared" from a male point of view, while I'M YOUR HORSE IN THE NIGHT depicts the same situation from a female perspective. —DVD

VEGA, ANA LYDIA. CLOUD COVER CARIBBEAN.

Puerto Rico

Her True-True Name: An Anthology of Women's Writing from the Caribbean. Portsmouth, NH: Heinemann, 1990. Translated by Mark McCaffrey.

Author: Ana Lydia Vega (1946–), born in Puerto Rico, is a prize-winning writer of fiction whose audience outside Latin America is growing rapidly. She is currently professor of French and Caribbean literature at the University of Puerto Rico, where she received her undergraduate education. She holds a doctorate in comparative literature from the University of Provence. Vega has written film scripts, reviews, scholarly and critical essays, and textbooks, but is best known for her fiction. Named author of the year by the Casa del Auto Puertorriqueno in 1985, Vega has received other awards for her short story collections *Virgins and Martyrs* (coauthored with Carmen Lugo Fillipi in 1981), *Cloud Cover and Other Stories of Shipwreck* (1982), and *Pasion de Historia y Otras Historias de Pasion* (1987).

Story: This brief short story depicts the adventures and interactions of three characters from different Caribbean countries—Haiti, the Dominican Republic, and Cuba—as they try to make their escape by boat to the United States. Antenor, the Haitian, reluctantly rescues Diogenes, a Dominican, from shipwreck, and the two of them rescue Carmelo, "the restless Cuban," whom they find "bobbing along beside the proverbial plank of the shipwrecked sailor." Unwitting comrades, the three banter, vie for the scant food and rum on board, and imagine the better lives awaiting them in America. When they capsize, they are picked up by the United States Navy. Thrust into the ship's hold, they are initially grateful to hear Spanish being spoken. But—just as "the parched lips of each of the trio were curving upwards into a smile . . . a Puerto Rican voice growled through the gloom: 'If you want to feed your bellies here you're going to have to work, and I mean work. A gringo don't give nothing away. Not to his own mother.' Then a black arm thrust through the crates to hand them dry clothes."

Comparison: CLOUD COVER CARIBBEAN is a political satire written with irreverent humor and a scathing criticism of so-called Caribbean, even pan-African, solidarity. It may be interpreted as an allegory, with the three men representing different countries, literally and figuratively adrift in a sea of uncertain political, economic, and social conditions. Vega's language is particularly exciting as she combines colloquial tropes, classical allusion, and popular metaphors. The opening paragraph serves as an example: "September, the *agent provocateur* of hurricanes, has declared war, filling the seas with urchins and men o'war. A suspicious breeze swells the guayabera, makeshift sail for this makeshift vessel. The sky is conga drum stretched tight for a bembe ceremony."

Vega's story belongs in the tradition of political literature and invites comparison with fiction by Franz Kafka (THE METAMORPHOSIS), Nadine Gordimer ("The Termitary"), and Langston Hughes ("Slave on the Block"). — R H S

VENEZIS, ELIAS. MYCENAE.

Greece

Introduction to Modern Greek Literature: An Anthology of Fiction, Drama, and Poetry. New York: Twayne, 1969. Translated by Mary P. Gianos.

Author: Elias Venezis, the pen name of Elias Mellowvenezis (1904–1973), was born in Aivali, Turkey, into a family that could be considered landed gentry. The lands they occupied had belonged to Greece since the days of ancient Troy. They were lands that, according to the Greek dream called the Megale (Grand) Idea, would one day be a part of a renewed Greek Empire. In 1922, that dream was shattered by what is called "The Asia Minor Disaster" or "The Catastrophe." Greeks who had settled in Turkey and Turks who had settled in Greece were uprooted and exchanged. One million Greeks and Turks died in the process. The eighteen-year-old Venezis was arrested before he could flee Turkey and placed in a labor battalion. His novel *Number 31328,* written after his release from captivity, is the recognized masterpiece of that period of Greek history.

In addition to novels, travel impressions, histories, and a play, Venezis wrote numerous literary and journalistic articles for Greek magazines and newspapers. He wrote in demotic Greek and is one of the most widely translated of modern Greek writers. At one time, he worked as an executive with the Bank of Greece, and he was the secretary–advisory director of the Greek National Theater.

Aeolian Soil and *Beyond the Aegean* are probably the best known of his works outside Greece. Stunning descriptions and narration, dreamlike atmosphere, and a lyric quality are usually hallmarks of his works, and, like so many twentieth-century Greek writers, Venezis shows repeatedly a reverence for the landscape and the heritage of Greece. In 1939, he received the Greek National Prize in Literature. MYCENAE was published in 1944. Venezis died in Athens in 1973. Along with Lilika Nakos and Elli Alexiou, Venezis was a member of the "Generation of the 1930s," a group of writers who broke from ethnography, the description of manners and morals of Greek folklore, to write about the human being within society. He is especially noted for his short stories, in which his characters often try to resolve conflicts between the demands of society and their own sense of justice and freedom.

Story: Originally published in a collection of short stories entitled *Winds* (1944), MYCENAE begins in Anatolia, Turkey. Its main character is a Greek noblewoman. Katerina Pallis, widowed right after the birth of her son, is determined to prepare the boy properly for manhood. To do so, she tells him not only about his father, but also about the gods of Olympus and the heroes of Greece. One of the stories she often relates is about how King Agamemnon left Queen Klytemnestra and went with other warriors to rescue Helen, Queen of Sparta. She tells him how the warriors had to wait and wait for a fair wind to sail to Troy, and how the soothsayers finally told Agamemnon that a young woman must be sacrificed if they were ever to be able to leave. The daughter of Agamemnon and Klytemnestra, named Iphigenia, then offered herself as that sacrifice, and, when it was done, the winds became favorable. The mother also told the boy how Agamemnon, when he returned from his triumph over Troy, was murdered by his queen, who wanted his kingdom. When her son was old enough, Pallis took him to Mycenae, where Agamemnon and Klytemnestra reigned, and to Agamemnon's tomb.

Years later, after her son dies in "The Catastrophe," Pallis revisits Agamemnon's tomb. This time she goes into the tomb of Klytemnestra as well. There she learns another version of the legend of Troy. A brutal king named Agamemnon, the story goes, learned from travelers of the many riches of Troy and decided that he must have them. He sent for warriors to join him, but none of the ships could sail until the wind became favorable. The soothsayers told him that he must sacrifice his daughter, Iphigenia, to appease the gods. Agamemnon sent word to Klytemnestra to send their daughter to him, that he had found a suitor for her. Iphigenia was sent by her mother only to be murdered on the beach by her father.

Katerina Pallis hears the heartbroken screams of Klytemnestra when she learned of her daughter's sacrifice, and she hears Klytemnestra's curses that filled the land. Finally, Pallis learns that Agamemnon was murdered by Klytemnestra years later not to inherit his kingdom, but rather in revenge for their daughter's death.

Comparison: The traditional rescue-Helen story of Troy is exceedingly well known, but if it needs reviewing, it can be found in the play *Agamemnon* by Aeschylus and in other works based on the Iphigenia story by Goethe, Racine, Kenneth Rexroth, and Walter Savage Landor. Pictures of the remains of Mycenae, including the acropolis, Lion's Gate, and royal tombs, may be found in such books as George E. Mylonas's *Mycenae and the Mycenaen Age* (Princeton University Press, 1966).

The great significance of this story by Venezis is that it presents, in a most readable form, the same story from an entirely different viewpoint. There is a good chance that Venezis's story comes closer to the truth than the legend of Troy as often related. In any case, the version Katerina Pallis hears in Klytemnestra's tomb is well known in Greece. Those who teach the old tales of Greece as though they were historically correct can benefit from understanding that many of them were politically motivated and that a deeper

knowledge of the Greek culture can come from alternate versions. Comparisons of these two versions can also be a springboard for research into how and why they came about.

MYCENAE is, on one level, a nostalgic story of the past and of the meaning of tradition. It may be compared with Alexander Solzhenitsyn's story ZAKHAR-THE-POUCH and with poems such as Giacomo Leopardi's "To Italy" and Alfred de Vigny's "The Sound of the Horn," which show a similar concern with the past.

On another level, MYCENAE is about Katerina's learning the true meaning of death through the loss of her son. At this level, the story compares well with such works as John Steinbeck's "The Gift" from *The Red Pony,* James Agee's *A Death in the Family,* Sherwood Anderson's "Death in the Woods," and Edwin Arlington Robinson's "Reuben Bright."

Richard Connell, in his story "The Most Dangerous Game," writes of a violence comparable to that in MYCENAE. A man falls from a ship, swims to a nearby island, and receives what he at first believes to be the traditional, hospitable welcome given shipwrecked people. Very soon, however, he finds himself being hunted by his host in a life and death contest. Another story of bizarre violence is Shirley Jackson's "The Lottery." Still another strange ritual of destruction is depicted in Graham Greene's "The Destructors," where boys completely destroy a man's home. — E M   and   R S

VERGA, GIOVANNI. PROPERTY.

Italy
Of Time and Place: Comparative World Literature in Translation. Glenview, IL: ScottForesman, 1976. Translated by D. H. Lawrence.

Author: Giovanni Verga (1840–1922) was born in Catania, Sicily. Verga abandoned his university studies there to turn to journalism and the writing of melodramatic, sentimental novels, which, while popular, are quite different from the works of what has been called his "mature" period. That period, beginning in 1874, saw the writing of stories, including PROPERTY in 1880, and novels dealing

with the struggle for existence of the Sicilian peasant. These stories of daily life, written in a realistic style quite different from that of his earlier work, typically show people as victims of circumstances that they are powerless to change and unable even to understand, making Verga a pioneer of *verismo,* the Italian version of naturalism. The best known of these mature works are the two novels *The House by the Medlar Tree* (1881) and *Mastro Don Gesualdo* (1888), which were to have formed parts of a trilogy dealing with the destruction of a Sicilian family of fishermen. The third novel, however, was never written. "Cavalleria Rusticana," written as a story in 1880, was recast as a play in 1884 and formed the basis of Mascagni's opera of that name.

Story: Though like a parable in its focus on the Midas theme of corruption wrought by financial success, PROPERTY is built up of precisely observed, very specific details not characteristic of parables. It opens with a lengthy description of extensive farmlands, orchards, and grazing herds of the Sicilian countryside, all owned by a certain Mazzarò, who, though born a Sicilian peasant, had been taken in his youth by the local baron "out of charity, naked and ignorant, to work on his fields." While working, he noticed the baron's inattention to the details of the work on his lands and discovered how easy it was to steal from him. Believing that "property doesn't belong to those that have got it, but to those that know how to acquire it," Mazzarò soon became single-minded in his acquisitiveness. As the story puts it, "in that way Mazzarò little by little became master of all the baron's possessions."

Although the townspeople admired his success, they had become dependent on him for their living, and he was a merciless taskmaster, always looking for a chance to acquire more wealth by demanding more work or cheating them of what little they had. Consequently, Mazzarò, with his growing wealth, became more and more isolated and, as he grew old, came to realize that even all the wealth he had acquired could not buy him renewed youth and vigor or protect him from death. "So that when they told him it was time to be turning away from his property and thinking of his soul, he rushed out into the courtyard like a madman, staggering, and went around killing his own ducks and turkeys, hitting them with his stick and screaming, 'You're my own property, you come along with me.'"

Comparison: In its theme of the corruption and isolation brought by wealth, PROPERTY can be compared to Dickens's *A Christmas Carol,* although the transformation of Scrooge at the end of that story has no counterpart here. Similarly, PROPERTY might be contrasted with O. Henry's "Gift of the Magi," which shows in a comparably parable-like fashion that unselfishness rather than graspingness leads to love and happiness. D. H. Lawrence's "The Rocking Horse Winner" demonstrates, in a more psychologically complex and profound manner, the same seemingly inevitable conflict between lasting happiness and love on the one hand and the single-minded pursuit of material wealth on the other.

In its focus on the inevitable operation of material laws on human destiny, PROPERTY might be compared with the works of such naturalistic writers as Theodore Dreiser, Frank Norris, James T. Farrell, and Richard Wright, although their focus is generally on the poor and the unsuccessful, as is Verga's in many cases, rather than on those who succeed only to find that their success is in reality a failure. — P T M

VILLIERS DE L'ISLE-ADAM. THE DESIRE TO BE A MAN.

France
French Stories and Tales. New York: Knopf, 1954. Translated by Pierre Schneider.

Author: Villiers de L'Isle-Adam, the pen name of Comte Jean Marie Mathias Philippe de August (1838–1889), was born in Saint-Brieuc, the descendant of a long line of Breton Catholic nobility. As a young man, he moved from the provinces to Paris, where he enjoyed a bohemian lifestyle. Yet he still devoted a considerable quantity of time to reading—Edgar Allan Poe was one of his favorite authors—and to his highly poetic, elegant writing. Unfortunately, his literary efforts produced little revenue, and he spent most of his adult life in penurious circumstances. Reflecting his proud heritage, he called himself "le prince ignoré." Much of his work contrasts an idealized world to stark reality. His plays and his fantastic tales, collected in *Contes Cruels* (1883) and *Nouveaux Contes Cruels* (1888), reflect his Romanticism. THE DESIRE TO BE A MAN was first published in 1882 and THE TORTURE BY HOPE in 1888. He is usually classified as a precursor of the French symbolist movement.

Story: A famous tragedian, Esprit Chaudval, upon reaching the age of fifty, realizes that he has never experienced any true emotions, only feigned them as an actor. Believing that passion, emotions, and real acts are what constitute a man, he decides to commit a heinous crime in order to suffer remorse, the one emotion he believes he can experience. He sets a huge fire that kills nearly a hundred people and renders many families homeless. Escaping to an isolated lighthouse, he hopes to be plagued by ghosts of regret and guilt. But "contrary to all his hopes and expectations, his conscience" gives "him no pangs." The old actor eventually dies, having felt "*nothing, absolutely nothing!*"

Comparison: In several works, there is a similar inverse relationship between the ability of performers to enact the passions of others and their ability to experience real emotion. A famous singer in the play *The Tenor* by Frank Wedekind is another who can-

not form deep emotional attachments. In Oscar Wilde's *The Picture of Dorian Gray,* Sibyl Vance, a lovely, talented young actress, finds herself unable to give a satisfactory performance once she has experienced real passion, her love for Dorian Gray. Matthew Arnold's poem "The Buried Life" treats the difficulty of expressing or even knowing true emotion.

Chaudval's calm, deliberate plotting of an atrocious crime resembles that of Raskolnikov in Dostoevski's *Crime and Punishment.* Yet the impoverished intellectual in this novel, believing himself an amoral superman, expects to feel no remorse. Even when his conscience eventually torments him into confessing, he does not feel sorry for his actions.

The painting *Self-Portrait* by Parmigianino could be used to illustrate the concentration on self that can lead to destructiveness. The subject is a man's image reflected in a convex mirror, an image distorted by the shape of the glass. Chaudval poses often in front of mirrors and windows, fascinated by his appearance.

The desire to "be a man" is a central theme in Richard Wright's short story "Almos' a Man." The leading character, Dave, a seventeen-year-old black teenager, has been belittled by his fellow field workers, oppressed by his white boss, and beaten by his father. Determined to prove himself a man that no one can "run over," he buys a gun. Like Chaudval, he looks unsuccessfully for objects and experiences that will guarantee his manhood. — M A F

VILLIERS DE L'ISLE-ADAM. THE TORTURE BY HOPE.

France
Isaac Asimov Presents the Best Horror and Supernatural of the 19th Century. New York: Beaufort Books, 1983.

Author: See THE DESIRE TO BE A MAN.

Story: Rabbi Aser Abarbanel, imprisoned during the Spanish Inquisition, is tortured for over a year but refuses to adjure his faith. One evening, the Grand Inquisitor announces that the next day the rabbi will be included in the auto-da-fé, a slow, painful death by

fire that he describes. That night, Abarbanel discovers that his cell door is unlocked. He cautiously crawls down the long, dark corridor, clinging to the wall in terror as others pass by. Finally, he reaches a door that opens on a garden. As he savors his first glimpse of freedom, he suddenly finds himself in the clasp of the Grand Inquisitor. He then realizes that *"all the phases of this fatal evening were only a prearranged torture, that of* HOPE.*"*

Comparison: "The Legend of the Grand Inquisitor" from Dostoevski's *The Brothers Karamazov* has a similar setting and general topic. The most obvious comparison is to Edgar Allan Poe's "The Pit and the Pendulum," although THE TORTURE BY HOPE is much shorter. Villiers even included an epigraph from Poe's tale: "Oh, for a voice to speak!" Both protagonists are prisoners of the Spanish Inquisition who have been tortured and sentenced to death. The atmosphere of mounting terror is similar. In Poe's tale, it is due to the physical dangers, especially the relentless slow descent of the razor-sharp pendulum over the victim's shackled body. In THE TORTURE BY HOPE, the agony is psychological in origin, induced by the rabbi's

intense fear of being captured as he inches his way along the dark corridor. The ironic twist at the end when he realizes that his supposed escape was just the ultimate torture is quite different from the rescue of the protagonist in Poe's story.

The deliberate shattering of the illusion of hope as a form of torture can also be found in much of the Holocaust literature centering on religious persecution. Kafka's IN THE PENAL COLONY, with its death machine, has a comparable macabre tone. And the anticipation of death is central in Sartre's THE WALL.

A fitting companion piece of art would be Edvard Munch's painting *The Scream.* This work depicts a person on a bridge with his hands over his ears and his mouth open, apparently screaming in anguish, while two shadowy figures in the background show no reaction. The despair and agony expressed parallel the rabbi's feelings upon his capture. — M A F

WELLER, ARCHIE. GOING HOME.

Australian Aborigine
Going Home. North Sydney, Australia: Allen & Unwin Pty, 1990.

Author: Archie Weller (1957–) is an Aboriginal of the Bibulman people. Born in Cranbrook, he was brought up on a farm in southwest Western Australia. His early years were isolated until his parents divorced when he was twelve, and he went with his mother to live in East Perth, in those days a semislum district inhabited by migrants, Aboriginals, and poor whites. His grandfather's love of books inspired him. His first story, "Dead Dingo," was published in 1977. His first novel, *The Day of the Dog,* was published in 1981 and details the cruelty and violence of Aboriginal life in inner-city Perth. Although the land has always been central to Aboriginal life, urban Aboriginals have lost this profound connection and, as Weller indicates, suffer the consequences. In 1986, Weller published a collection of short stories in an anthology entitled *Going Home,* "one of the most singular and impressive collections of contemporary stories to appear in Australia," according to *The Australian.* This anthology was the first book-length collection of short stories published by an Aboriginal writer. Weller also coedited an anthology of

Aboriginal writing, *Us Fellas* (1987). Two of his stories were produced for film, *Blackfellas* from *The Day of the Dog* and *Saturday Night, Saturday Morning* from *Going Home. Nidgera* ("children crying softly"), which he wrote for the Melbourne Workers Theatre, examines a Koori (Aboriginal) family's encounter with prejudice while looking for work. Weller is currently working on a science-fiction book that incorporates Aboriginal legends, particularly Aboriginal respect for the land, the old people, and humanity itself.

Story: Billy Woodward, who is half-Aboriginal, has denied his black heritage to live in a white world for the past five years. He is now returning home on his twenty-first birthday. He is doing so in a new car bought with proceeds from his first art exhibition. Successful in the white man's worlds of both sport and painting, Woodward thinks about the past as he drives down the highway toward home. He picks up Darcy Goodrich, a fellow Aboriginal, who updates him on his family, including the fact that

Woodward's father was killed by a hit-and-run driver several years back. The fact that he didn't know this about his own family disturbs him. When the two men stop to get liquor at a local bar and are hassled, Woodward realizes about himself, "Yet when it comes down to it all, he is just a black man." It doesn't make any difference to the prejudiced barman that he has "made it" in the white world. All he is judged by is the color of his skin.

Billy is not recognized by his own family until Darcy introduces him. He learns that his cousin Rennie's girl is pregnant, and he listens to his mom's reprimand that he was too good even to return for his father's funeral. Rennie and Billy's brother Carlton go to get more liquor for a party to celebrate Billy's birthday. The next morning, as Billy is returning from the waterhole he has been visiting to rekindle memories of his father, a police van pulls up. The police accuse Carlton and Billy of robbing the liquor store. Billy knows he is innocent, but he also knows the others are guilty. "Billy returns their gaze with the look of a cornered dingo who does not understand how he was trapped yet who knows he is about to die." Billy's going home to be with his "mob" costs him his life.

Comparison: Billy Woodward is clearly someone caught between two worlds: his Aboriginal heritage and the white world. Must he choose in which to live? To be successful, he feels he must choose the white world, not the world of the dilapidated "humpies" where his Aboriginal family lives. And he succeeds in that white world, but at what price?

Likewise, in James Baldwin's "Sonny's Blues," the elder brother succeeds in a white world and dissociates himself from his family and from his brother Sonny's world of drugs and alienation and music. Sonny's brother has become a teacher and sees himself in a better position than Sonny, just as Billy sees himself as better situated than his Aboriginal family. By accepting Sonny's music and understanding its importance to his brother's identity, the narrator begins to accept his own black heritage. In sharing his brother's guilt, Billy too accepts his heritage. Both understand what it means to be judged by skin color and what it means to be denied a "fair go" at being successful. It is this realization that brings them back from their "white" successful lives to rejoin the lives of the rest of their family.

Ann Petry's story "The Migrane Workers," set in New York State, captures the hopelessness of African Americans just as Weller's story captures that of Australian Aborigines. In Petry's story, Pedro, the truck stop owner, "decided that they were so accustomed to being pushed around that they accepted it as a normal part of their lives." In much the same way, Darcy Goodrich, Billy's friend, accepts that in order to be served in a white bar, he has to act servilely. When one of Petry's "migrane workers" jumps from the truck transporting him to the next job, the attendant asks, "Where'd you come from? . . . Where's your home?" The "migrane worker" answers, "'I don't know. I don't rightly know, boss.' He said it apologetically." Woodward doesn't know, either. He's caught in the in-between world, the shadows. — M J S

Yáñez, Mirta. WE BLACKS ALL DRINK COFFEE.

Cuba

Her True-True Name: An Anthology of Women's Writing from the Caribbean. Portsmouth, NH: Heinemann, 1990. Translated by Claudette Williams.

Author: Born in Havana, Cuba, in 1947, Mirta Yáñez has published poems, short stories, and a novel. She received a degree in Spanish language and literature from the University of Havana in 1970 and has taught Spanish-American literature. Her deep interest in cultural history is illustrated by her fiction and the time she served as director of the Department of Cultural Activities in the University Extension Service. She published a novel, *La Hora de los Mameyes,* in 1983. She has also published two short story collections: *Havana Es una Ciudad bien Grande* in 1980 and *Todos los Negros Tomamos Cafe* in 1976. WE BLACKS ALL DRINK COFFEE, from the latter collection of the same name, draws on Yáñez's experiences as a "brigadista," a member of the brigades of young Cubans who in the 1960s and 1970s did agricultural work. Yáñez worked on a coffee plantation in rural Cuba.

Story: Although WE BLACKS ALL DRINK COFFEE is a monologue, it seems to open in the middle of a conversation between a mother and daughter and has in it the familiar ingredients of generational conflict complicated by the particular issues of color and political activism. The unnamed narrator, the daughter, wants to become a "brigadista," a decision her mother both opposes and fears.

The fifteen-year-old's mother cites age as sufficient reason for her to stay at home. In the daughter's paraphrase, "She says that I don't even know how to wash my own clothes." Leaving would be selfish, certain death to her grandmother, claims the mother, and the country has "so many dangers," such as disease. The more compelling reasons emerge, however, as the story unfolds. This girl is the oldest and, in her mother's view, spoiled child of a respectable middle-class white family. The mother is concerned that the young girl will become pregnant. Worse, she might "even fall in love with a Negro, [the mother] says in a powerless rage." To this, the daughter hurls a challenge to white respectability: "who knows what kind of blood anyone has?"

With the young girl as narrator, the viewpoint is hers. She is sarcastic as she recalls her mother's accusations and claims (e.g., "The blood pressure of grandmothers and aunts can fall precipitously because of a 'brigadista' who picks coffee"). But regardless of tone, the point of departure is clear: the daughter believes her mother lives hopelessly far in the past. Clearly suggesting her mother's inability to keep up, the narrator muses, "How times change." She mocks what she believes is her mother's inexperience ("In the mountains where they pick coffee, or so she has heard, she has never seen it with her own eyes"). The daughter longs to escape from "this castle which is the protective shell of my family life" and live a life not only of adventure, but also of political value.

Comparison: This very brief story invites comparison with a range of "growing-up" stories. From *Catcher in the Rye* by J. D. Salinger to *Annie John* by Jamaica Kincaid, teenagers in literature, as in life, have decried the lack of understanding, feeling, and experience of their parents. In both of those works, the voice is also that of the young person. Doris Lessing's early work *Martha Quest* provides an interesting comparison because of the difficult political reality in which a young white girl comes of age in what was Rhodesia, now Zimbabwe.

Fiction with similar themes but with a viewpoint shifted to the mother includes "Everyday Use" by Alice Walker. In that story, the mother is also seen as old-fashioned and unenlightened, someone who cannot keep up with changing times. Though several years older, the daughter, Dee, like the narrator in WE BLACKS ALL DRINK COFFEE, believes that she understands the larger world and the political issues that matter more deeply than her mother ever could. An interesting counterpoint might be Tillie Olsen's "I Stand Here Ironing," because it shows the mother reflecting upon the impact her own hard life has had on her nearly grown daughter.

Comparisons on the basis of form might be made with other short fiction, such as "The Jilting of Granny Weatherall" by Katherine Anne Porter and "The Waltz" by Dorothy Parker, though the themes are dissimilar.   — R H S

YEHOSHUA, ABRAHAM B. FACING THE FOREST.

Israel
Three Days and the Child. Garden City, NY: Doubleday, 1970. Translated by Miriam Arad.

Author: Abraham B. Yehoshua (1937–), a fifth-generation Jerusalemite, studied philosophy and Hebrew literature at Hebrew University and became a high school teacher. After doctoral work in comparative literature at the University of Paris, he was appointed secretary of the World Union of Jewish

Students in Paris. His military experience included a stint in the agricultural-military unit of the Israel Defense Forces. Married and the father of a daughter, he has published numerous works, including short stories, novels, radio scripts, and a play. He has received many literary awards.

Story: "Another winter lost in fog. As usual he did nothing." This introduces a protagonist who is rootless, without conscience, self-absorbed, and living a life of dissipation. An "eternal student" who once had a bright idea or two, this man, now approaching thirty, dreams only of "solitude." He allows himself to become convinced that he might find solitude in summer employment as a "fire watcher," a forest scout.

He is sent to one of the larger forests, where he will be working with a laborer, an Arab. When he arrives, he finds the forest breathtakingly beautiful. His Arab assistant, who lives with his small daughter, had his tongue cut out during the war. "By one of them or one of us? Does it matter?" The narrator tries talking to the Arab, but the man does not understand Hebrew. At long last, he turns to his books, to his thesis on the subject of "The Crusades." The summer grows hot. He finds concentration difficult. By the middle of summer, he has covered only "the preface to a preface." Early in the summer, when hikers started small fires, he had worried about the safety of the forest. By the end of the summer, "he would welcome a little conflagration, a little local tumult."

The most interesting discovery of the summer is the fact that the forest he is guarding has been planted over the top of a ruined Arab village. In fact, one of the most visible ruins is that of the former home of his Arab companion. The fire watcher hears rumors that the Arab may be laying in a stock of kerosene. To this, as to everything else, he remains indifferent.

When the nights grow longer and the desert winds mingle with rain, the fire watcher packs his belongings for tomorrow's departure. The Arab has disappeared. The child sleeps. From his window, the ranger suddenly spies fire. Taking the child, leaving his other possessions behind, he heads down the road to safety.

At dawn, he returns to the window from which he had watched so patiently for fire. From there, "out of the smoke and haze, the ruined village appears before his eyes; born anew in its basic outlines as an abstract drawing, as all things past and buried. He smiles to himself, a thin smile." Arson is discovered. The smell of kerosene lingers with the smell of smoke and dew. The Arab reappears, and the questioning ensues, first of the fire watcher and then of the Arab. The hot day and persistent interrogation break him. He points to the Arab as the culprit. As the Arab is driven away, the narrator sees in his eyes "a gratified expression . . . a sense of achievement." There is no such sense of achievement for the narrator. He returns to the city, to the rootlessness and apathy he left behind.

Comparison: Israeli literature spans three thematic periods: the Diaspora to 1948, with its optimism upon gaining statehood; 1948 to the Six Day War, with its pioneering idealism; and 1969 to the present, with its difficulty in defining its character amid an increasingly hostile Arab populace. Because his work bridges all three periods, Yehoshua's writing offers a distinct view of the emerging Israeli character. As an example of third-period literature, FACING THE FOREST deals with the continuing Arab problem. The story illustrates an understanding of the Arab in an occupied land, just as Camus's THE GUEST perceives the plight of the native Algerian held captive by French conquerors.

Controlled by the same ennui found in T. S. Eliot's "Hollow Men," the protagonist drifts into his job as a fire watcher just as Conrad's Marlowe became a fresh water sailor in *Heart of Darkness.* Whereas Marlowe lied about Kurtz's final words, the fire watcher is forced to tell the truth about the Arab to save the young daughter. In "Six Feet of the Country" by Nadine Gordimer, the white overlords think nothing of lying to the black workers or even of carelessly discarding the remains of their dead. When lies are uncovered, the white conquerors make no attempt to rectify them. How to handle an indigenous captive population, as well as how to understand its plight, is illustrated in a number of stories and movies, not the least of which is *Dances with Wolves.* Thus, Yehoshua presents a picture of the Occupied as Luisa Valenzuela in I'M YOUR HORSE FOR THE NIGHT depicts the plight of Argentina's "Disappeared." — D V D

YIZHAR, S. HABAKUK.

Israel
Midnight Convoy and Other Stories. Jerusalem: Israel Universities Press, 1969.
Translated by Miriam Arad.

Author: S. Yizhar (1916–) belongs to the first generation of Israeli writers. Born in a family of writers, he taught in secondary school, fought in the 1948 War of Independence, and became a member of the Knesset until 1967, when he traveled extensively abroad. Considered the foremost writer of the Palmah period, Yizhar has written short stories, novellas, and novels. As a romantic with a deep attachment to his native wild landscape, he uses complex rhetoric in the style of Faulkner. His characters are Israeli youths torn between conflicting moral values within a dynamic situation. His stories have aroused protest because they suggest a controversial side to the War of Independence: the consequent corruption of the victor and the vanquished. A struggle within the hero's soul recurs in all his stories, suggesting the struggle for the high standard of morality popularly associated with the pioneering spirit.

Story: "I'm not at all certain this story won't be sad," warns the narrator at the opening of HABAKUK. Habakuk's real name is Jedidiah, but the boys call him Habakuk. The narrator is a young student who chances to see Habakuk carrying a violin and talks him into playing the only piece of classical music with which the narrator is familiar. Habakuk leads the boy down to his bare basement room and plays Beethoven's Violin Concerto. "I was absorbed," the narrator reports, "lost in this man and his playing, fascinated by the very reality of notes being produced before my eyes." Habakuk further surprises the boy by turning astrologer, drawing a circle and placing lines, curves, angles, and boxes within it, muttering to himself the whole time. "An astrologer," Habakuk calls himself. "Or prophet."

The boy "grew to be a regular visitor in the man's basement—the kingdom of music and stars." He shares his fascination with several friends, and they too are mesmerized by the music and intrigued by glimpses of the future. Habakuk tells the boys' fortunes and protects them from unfavorable predictions, including his knowledge of his own future: "he kept his lips firmly closed and never let fall a hint about that shell hitting him out of a clear sky, there beside the kibbutz dining-hall, on the lawn." Adding words to his music, he weaves magic. The prophet and Goethe and the Nazarene and even Beethoven himself move among them. He conjures pictures combining history and fantasy and faith and mysticism. In his hands, Bach's "Sonata for Unaccompanied Violin" becomes the story of humankind, moving from a peaceful beginning to rising terror. "The holocaust grows and spreads. . . . Even nature is relentless. There is no escape. . . . what was even yesterday the image of everything good and pure and valiant is now exposed in all its vanity and meanness, powerless to withstand the great test, the day of trial." Years later, the narrator wonders, "Did Bach really write all this? Or is Bach only in brackets and is it Habakuk come to prophesy on his own and as he played, lo, the Spirit of God was upon him?"

From the moment of profound emotion that follows the Bach Sonata, the story draws to a quick close. All the boys become members of the Haganah and commanders of the Palmah, each living under the shadow of his own stars. The shell falls on Habakuk. The narrator attends a Memorial Day service at a cemetery where the violinist lies. With a somber heart, he prays that Habakuk's spirit soars to a higher place, for the heaven he has come to know is empty. "What is demanded of us here?" he asks Habakuk. "What must we do? Where go?" In the end, he prays to his old friend: "Say, speak to us, be not silent, not now, speak. Thou that seest in the stars, thy companions hearken to thy voice."

Comparison: Habakuk's predictions hint of the Kabala. Word and music weave psalm and history within a cloud of mystery. Ambrose Bierce's "An Occurrence at Owl Creek Bridge," especially in its film version, offers that same sense of two different time frames within a misty enigma. Whereas "An Occurrence at Owl Creek Bridge" involves past and present, Julio Cortázar's NIGHT FACE UP projects the past into the present through the use of the flash forward. His story reveals youth sacrificed on the altar of social ritual. Unlike the reluctant participants in both Cortázar's NIGHT FACE UP and Shirley Jackson's "The Lottery," Yizhar's young men bond to pledge themselves to the commonweal through the shared experiences of the music maker.

Music likewise provides the only tangible evidence of a hidden reality within Luisa Valenzuela's I'M YOUR HORSE IN THE NIGHT. Enduring the degradation of a search, Valenzuela's narrator hears only the voice of her lover, whereas Yizhar's narrator hears the voices of his companions, whose sound resonates in the one who has experienced it in the stars. — D V D

ZOLA, ÉMILE. THE INUNDATION.

France
Literature of the Western World. New York: Macmillan, 1984. Translated by Edward Vizetelly.

Author: Émile Zola (1840–1902) was born in Paris, but spent most of his younger years in Aix, the setting for many of his novels and short stories. Returning to Paris at age eighteen, he worked as a literary critic and journalist before devoting his time to writing fiction, mainly novels in the long *Rougon-Macquart* series, *Nana* and *L'Assommoir* among them. The series was intended to be similar to Balzac's even longer *Human Comedy* series. Zola's philosophy of fiction was different from Balzac's, however, in that he took a clinical, "scientific" approach to the study of humanity and nature. His interest in the effects of heredity, environment, and social station on the lives of his characters led him away from Balzacian realism to literary naturalism, which he is commonly regarded as having founded. His death came as the result of accidental asphyxiation.

Story: The richest farmer in the Garonne River valley, seventy-year-old Louis Roubieu, is suddenly and for the first time in his life victimized by nature. A flood, greater than any in his memory, comes and gradually destroys all that was his: first his fields, then his livestock, then his friends and their homes. Eventually, the waters submerge the farmhouse in which he and his family live, forcing them to the roof. One by one, he sees his brother and sister, his son and wife, his grandchildren, even his great-grandchildren taken by the flood. His helplessness through it all slowly defeats him, and he feels his prosperity had been a lie. When he is at last res-

cued, in a dead faint and clinging to the top of the lone chimney in the region left above water, Roubieu wonders why he has been left to suffer, to witness around him the destruction of what once were two thousand homes and farms. None of his loved ones are recovered, but he is shown a picture of his granddaughter and her fiancé, dead, locked in a firm embrace. He weeps.

Comparison: THE INUNDATION, inspired by news of a devastating flood in the Garonne River valley, is in many important ways comparable to the Bible's Book of Job. Both Job and Louis Roubieu have happiness and wealth before experiencing dreadful losses. Other interesting comparisons include adaptations of the Book of Job, such as Horace Kallen's *The Tragedy of Job* and Archibald MacLeish's *J.B.*, both dramas.

The theme of human suffering additionally links THE INUNDATION to a host of other works, such as Aeschylus's *Prometheus Bound*, Sophocles's *Oedipus Rex*, and Euripides's *The Trojan Women*. Even works like Franz Kafka's *The Trial*, Fyodor Dostoevski's *Crime and Punishment*, and the medieval Icelandic *Saga of Hrafnkel* may be compared with THE INUNDATION for the way suffering has varying causes and effects.

Louis Roubieu, at age seventy, is initiated into the horrors of life. The story, in light of its initiation theme, may be compared with such works as Voltaire's *Candide*, Nathaniel West's *A Cool Million*, and J. D. Salinger's *Catcher in the Rye,* in which initiation is a calamitous sequence of events for the hero.

Further still, Louis Roubieu can be compared to the lone survivor in numerous flood myths from around the world. Like the other survivors, he clings atop an eminence and is witness to the devastation. Unlike many of them, however, he receives no warning, knows of no cause, and is not the progenitor of a new human race.

The landscape painters of the French—Alfred Sisley, Camile Pissarro, Honoré Daumier, Jean François Millet, and Theodore Rousseau—could provide an excellent visual counterpoint to THE INUNDATION. — R S

ZOLA, ÉMILE. NAÏS MICOULIN.

France
The World in Literature. Rev. ed. Glenview, IL: ScottForesman, 1967.

Author: See THE INUNDATION.

Story: M. Rostand, a wealthy attorney, owns a chateau on an estate at the seashore, where the Micoulins work as caretakers and where most of the story is set. While Frederic, Rostand's son, is away at college, largely wasting his parents' money gambling and carousing, the hardworking Naïs Micoulin becomes a very beautiful young woman. Her beauty captivates Frederic, and the two become secret lovers. They are discovered, however, by Naïs's father, who twice tries to kill young Rostand, and by Toine, a hunchback who is Naïs's colleague in a tile factory where she works. Micoulin is killed in a landslide above which Toine has been seen digging. Although Frederic and Naïs are now free to continue their love affair, the death of old Micoulin dampens Frederic's interest, and he leaves to try his luck with city girls. Some time later, he is informed that Naïs has lost her looks, has grown old in appearance "the way peasant girls do at a young age," and will be married to Toine, the hunchback. The story ends with Frederic, unconcerned at the news, celebrating his cutlet as "a breakfast of sunshine."

Comparison: While simple in outline, the story is rich in the kinds of detail favored by literary naturalists. Zola goes to great length to show the differences in station of Naïs and Frederic: she is a peasant who must work hard and has a father who beats her; he is rich, works very little, and has parents who pamper him. What is most important, Naïs is flattered by the attentions of someone of such high estate and is an easy conquest for Frederic.

The disillusionment that causes Naïs to lose her beauty is similar to that of Nana Bouilloux in Colette's THE LITTLE BOUILLOUX GIRL. Class distinctions destroy the romantic dreams of both characters. As a mainstream naturalistic story, NAÏS MICOULIN bears close resemblance to the works of other naturalists. The stereotyped situation wherein a wealthy man has sexual access to a woman of lower station is found in many of them: Thomas Hardy's *Tess of the d'Urbervilles,* Stephen Crane's *Maggie: A Girl of the Streets,* August Strindberg's *Countess Julie,* Theodore Dreiser's *Sister Carrie,* and Guy de Maupassant's "Clochette," among them. Naïs Micoulin herself, wronged and left to a bleak future, invites comparison with those heroines and a great many others, especially in the way in which they cope with having been wronged: Félicité in Gustave Flaubert's A SIMPLE HEART, Ántonia Shimerda in Willa Cather's *My Ántonia,* Ophelia in Shakespeare's *Hamlet,* Alice Adams in Booth Tarkington's *Alice Adams,* Medea in Euripides' *Medea,* even Cho-Cho San in Giacomo Puccini's *Madame Butterfly.*

The paintings of peasant life by Jean François Millet, *The Gleaners* among them, provide good visual accompaniment to NAÏS MICOULIN. — R S

INDEXES

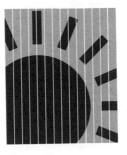

TITLE

We have included the following index for teachers searching for story annotations by title. See other indexes to search by country, theme, or English-language source.

CLOUD COVER CARIBBEAN
by Ana Lydia Vega
Puerto Rico

COCKROACHES
by Bruno Schulz
Poland

THE COLT
by Mikhail Sholokhov
Russia

THE CONJURER MADE OFF
WITH THE DISH
by Naguib Mahfouz
Egypt

THE DARLING
by Anton Chekhov
Russia

THE DAUGHTER
by H. I. E. Dhlomo
South Africa

THE DAY THE DANCERS CAME
by Bienvenido N. Santos
Philippines

THE DEATH OF IVÁN ILYICH
by Leo Tolstoy
Russia

THE DESIRE TO BE A MAN
by Villiers de L'Isle-Adam
France

A DEVOTED SON
by Anita Desai
India

DIARY OF A MADMAN
by Lu Xun
China

DISORDER AND EARLY SORROW
by Thomas Mann
Germany

THE DOCUMENT
by S. Y. Agnon
Israel

THE DREAM OF A RIDICULOUS
MAN
by Fyodor Dostoevski
Russia

END OF THE GAME
by Julio Cortázar
Argentina

THE ENEMY
by V. S. Naipaul
Trinidad

EPISODE IN MALAY CAMP
by Peter Abrahams
South Africa

FACING THE FOREST
by Abraham B. Yehoshua
Israel

THE FALL
by Alberto Moravia
Italy

THE FATE OF A MAN
by Mikhail Sholokhov
Russia

THE FATHER
by Björnstjerne Björnson
Norway

FATHER AND I
by Pär Lagerkvist
Sweden

FATHER'S HELP
by R. K. Narayan
India

THE FIGHTING CRICKET
by P'u Sung-Ling
China

A FISHER NEST
by Henrik Pontoppidan
Denmark

FLASHES IN THE NIGHT
by Aron Tamasi
Hungary

FRECKLES
by Fakir Baykurt
Turkey

FROM BEHIND THE VEIL
by Dhu'l Nun Ayyoub
Iraq

GAMES AT TWILIGHT
by Anita Desai
India

THE GARDEN OF FORKING
PATHS
by Jorge Luis Borges
Argentina

GIRLS AT WAR
by Chinua Achebe
Nigeria

GOING HOME
by Archie Weller
Australian Aborigine

LA GRANDE BRETÊCHE
by Honoré de Balzac
France

THE GRANDMOTHER
by K. Surangkhanang
Thailand

GRANDMOTHER TAKES CHARGE
by Lao She
China

THE GREAT BEYOND
by Cyprian Ekwensi
Nigeria

THE GUEST
by Albert Camus
France

HABAKUK
by S. Yizhar
Israel

HEAVEN IS NOT CLOSED
by Bessie Head
South Africa

THE MIRROR
by R. K. Narayan
India

MONUMENT
by Hebe Meleagrou
Greece

THE MOON ON THE WATER
by Kawabata Yasunari
Japan

MURKE'S COLLECTED SILENCES
by Heinrich Böll
Germany

MYCENAE
by Elias Venezis
Greece

MY LIFE WITH THE WAVE
by Octavio Paz
Mexico

NAEMA—WHEREABOUTS
UNKNOWN
by Mohammed Dib
Algeria

NAÏS MICOULIN
by Émile Zola
France

THE NAME
by Aharon Megged
Israel

THE NECKLACE
by Guy de Maupassant
France

THE NEW APARTMENT
by Heinz Huber
Germany

NIGHT FACE UP
by Julio Cortázar
Argentina

NOBODY WILL LAUGH
by Milan Kundera
Czech Republic

NO SWEETNESS HERE
by Ama Ata Aidoo
Ghana

THE OLD MAN AND THE SONG
by Milovan Djilas
Montenegro

THE OLD MAN OF USUMBURA
AND HIS MISERY
by Taban Lo Liyong
Uganda

ON A JOURNEY
by Slawomir Mrozek
Poland

ON MEETING MY 100 PERCENT
WOMAN ONE FINE APRIL
MORNING
by Murakami Haruki
Japan

THE OUTLAWS
by Selma Lagerlöf
Sweden

PAPER
by Catherine Lim
Singapore

PAPER BOAT
by Kundanika Kapadia
India

PAPER IS MONEY
by Razia Fasih Ahmad
Pakistan

THE PASHA'S DAUGHTER
by Naguib Mahfouz
Egypt

PASTORAL
by Tommaso Landolfi
Italy

PATRIOTISM
by Mishima Yukio
Japan

THE PHOTOGRAPHER'S MISSUS
by Colette
France

THE POET
by Hermann Hesse
Germany

POONEK
by Lim Beng Hap
Malaysia

THE PROCURATOR OF JUDEA
by Anatole France
France

PROPERTY
by Giovanni Verga
Italy

THE RETURN OF THE PRODI-
GAL SON
by André Gide
France

THE RIGHT HAND
by Alexander Solzhenitsyn
Russia

THE SAILOR BOY'S TALE
by Isak Dinesen
Denmark

THE SCYTHE
by Ivo Andric
Bosnia-Herzegovina

SEASIDE VILLAGE
by O Yong-su
Korea

SHADOW
by Hahn Moo-sook
Korea

A SIMPLE HEART
by Gustave Flaubert
France

THE SLAYING OF THE DRAGON
by Dino Buzzati
Italy

A SOLDIER'S EMBRACE
by Nadine Gordimer
South Africa

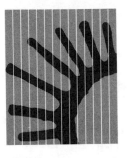

COUNTRY

We have included the following index for teachers searching for story annotations by country.
See other indexes to search by title, theme, or English-language source.

ALGERIA

Dib, Mohammed. NAEMA–WHEREABOUTS
   UNKNOWN

ARGENTINA

Borges, Jorge Luis. THE GARDEN OF FORKING
   PATHS
Cortázar, Julio. END OF THE GAME
Cortázar, Julio. NIGHT FACE UP
Valenzuela, Luisa. I'M YOUR HORSE IN THE NIGHT

AUSTRALIAN ABORIGINE

Weller, Archie. GOING HOME

BOSNIA-HERZEGOVINA

Andric, Ivo. THE SCYTHE
Andric, Ivo. A SUMMER IN THE SOUTH

BRAZIL

Amado, Jorge. HOW PORCIÚNCULA THE
   MULATTO GOT THE CORPSE OFF HIS BACK

CHILE

Allende, Isabel. TWO WORDS

CHINA

Feng Jicai. THE MAO BUTTON
Lao She. GRANDMOTHER TAKES CHARGE
Lu Xun. DIARY OF A MADMAN
P'u Sung-Ling. THE FIGHTING CRICKET

CUBA

Yáñez, Mirta. WE BLACKS ALL DRINK COFFEE

CZECH REPUBLIC

Kafka, Franz. A HUNGER ARTIST
Kafka, Franz. IN THE PENAL COLONY
Kafka, Franz. THE JUDGMENT
Kafka, Franz. THE METAMORPHOSIS
Kundera, Milan. NOBODY WILL LAUGH

DENMARK

Dinesen, Isak. THE SAILOR BOY'S TALE
Dinesen, Isak. SORROW-ACRE
Nexø, Martin Andersen. BIRDS OF PASSAGE
Pontoppidan, Henrik. A FISHER NEST

EGYPT

Idris, Youssef. THE CHEAPEST NIGHT'S
    ENTERTAINMENT
Mahfouz, Naguib. THE CONJURER MADE OFF
    WITH THE DISH
Mahfouz, Naguib. THE PASHA'S DAUGHTER
Rifaat, Alifa. ANOTHER EVENING AT THE CLUB
Rifaat, Alifa. AN INCIDENT IN THE GHOBASHI
    HOUSEHOLD
Rushdi, Rashad. ANGUISH

FRANCE

Aymé, Marcel. THE MAN WHO WALKED
    THROUGH WALLS
Balzac, Honoré de. THE ATHEIST'S MASS
Balzac, Honoré de. LA GRANDE BRETÊCHE
Camus, Albert. THE GUEST
Colette. THE LITTLE BOUILLOUX GIRL
Colette. THE PHOTOGRAPHER'S MISSUS
Daudet, Alphonse. THE LAST LESSON
Flaubert, Gustave. A SIMPLE HEART
France, Anatole. THE PROCURATOR OF JUDEA
Gide, André. THE RETURN OF THE PRODIGAL
    SON
Maupassant, Guy de. THE NECKLACE
Mérimée, Prosper. THE VENUS OF ILLE
Sand, George. THE MARQUISE
Sartre, Jean-Paul. THE WALL
Villiers de L'Isle-Adam. THE DESIRE TO BE A MAN
Villiers de L'Isle-Adam. THE TORTURE BY HOPE
Zola, Émile. THE INUNDATION
Zola, Émile. NAÏS MICOULIN

GERMANY

Aichinger, Ilse. THE BOUND MAN
Böll, Heinrich. MURKE'S COLLECTED SILENCES
Hesse, Hermann. THE POET
Heym, Georg. THE AUTOPSY
Hildesheimer, Wolfgang. A WORLD ENDS
Huber, Heinz. THE NEW APARTMENT
Lenz, Siegfried. THE LAUGHINGSTOCK
Mann, Thomas. DISORDER AND EARLY SORROW
Mann, Thomas. TONIO KRÖGER
Mann, Thomas. TRISTAN

GHANA

Aidoo, Ama Ata. NO SWEETNESS HERE
Dove-Danquah, Mabel. THE TORN VEIL

GREECE

Alexiou, Elli. THEY WERE ALL TO BE PITIED
Cicellis, Kay. BRIEF DIALOGUE
Haris, Petros. LIGHTS ON THE SEA
Meleagrou, Hebe. MONUMENT
Nakos, Lilika. THE BROKEN DOLL
Nakos, Lilika. HELENITSA
Papadiamantis, Alexandros. THE BEWITCHING OF
    THE AGA
Roufos, Rodis. THE CANDIDATE
Saranti, Galatea. SUNLIGHT
Theotokis, Konstantinos. VILLAGE LIFE
Venezis, Elias. MYCENAE

GUADELOUPE

Condé, Maryse. THREE WOMEN IN MANHATTAN

GUATEMALA

Asturias, Miguel. TATUANA'S TALE

HAITI

Danticat, Edwidge. CHILDREN OF THE SEA

HUNGARY

Tamasi, Aron. FLASHES IN THE NIGHT

ICELAND

Laxness, Haldor. LILY

INDIA

Desai, Anita. A DEVOTED SON
Desai, Anita. GAMES AT TWILIGHT
Kapadia, Kundanika. PAPER BOAT
Narayan, R. K. FATHER'S HELP
Narayan, R. K. A HORSE AND TWO GOATS
Narayan, R. K. THE MIRROR
Ray, Satyajit. ASHAMANJA BABU'S DOG
Sarang, Vilas. THE TERRORIST
Tagore, Rabindranath. KABULIWALLAH

PUERTO RICO

Vega, Ana Lydia. CLOUD COVER CARIBBEAN

RUSSIA

Andreyev, Leonid. LAZARUS
Chekhov, Anton. THE BET
Chekhov, Anton. THE DARLING
Chekhov, Anton. THE KISS
Dostoevski, Fyodor. THE DREAM OF A RIDICU-
    LOUS MAN
Dostoevski, Fyodor. THE HONEST THIEF
Dostoevski, Fyodor. WHITE NIGHTS
Sholokhov, Mikhail. THE COLT
Sholokhov, Mikhail. THE FATE OF A MAN
Solzhenitsyn, Alexander. MATRYONA'S HOME
Solzhenitsyn, Alexander. THE RIGHT HAND
Solzhenitsyn, Alexander. ZAKHAR-THE-POUCH
Tolstoy, Leo. THE DEATH OF IVÁN ILYICH
Tolstoy, Leo. HOW MUCH LAND DOES A MAN
    NEED
Turgenev, Ivan. YERMOLAY AND THE MILLER'S
    WIFE

SENEGAL

Diop, Birago. THE WAGES OF GOOD

SIERRA LEONE

Nicol, Abioseth. AS THE NIGHT THE DAY

SINGAPORE

Lim, Catherine. PAPER

SOUTH AFRICA

Abrahams, Peter. EPISODE IN MALAY CAMP
Dhlomo, H. I. E. THE DAUGHTER
Gordimer, Nadine. LITTLE WILLIE
Gordimer, Nadine. A SOLDIER'S EMBRACE
Head, Bessie. HEAVEN IS NOT CLOSED
La Guma, Alex. BLANKETS
Mphahlele, Es'kia. THE MASTER OF DOORNVLEI

SWEDEN

Lagerkvist, Pär. FATHER AND I
Lagerlöf, Selma. THE OUTLAWS
Siwertz, Sigfrid. IN SPITE OF EVERYTHING

THAILAND

Surangkhanang, K. THE GRANDMOTHER

TRINIDAD

Naipaul, V. S. B. WORDSWORTH
Naipaul, V. S. THE ENEMY

TURKEY

Baykurt, Fakir. FRECKLES
Cumali, Necati. IN GOD'S PLAINS
Izgü, Muzaffer. WANTED: A TOWN WITHOUT A
    CRAZY

UGANDA

Lo Liyong, Taban. THE OLD MAN OF USUMBURA
    AND HIS MISERY

VIETNAM

Nhat-Tien. AN UNSOUND SLEEP
Phiên Võ. THE KEY

ENGLISH-LANGUAGE SOURCE

We have included the following index for teachers searching for story annotations by English-language source. See other indexes to search by title, country, or theme.

The Charioteer: An Annual Review of Modern Greek Culture. No. 22–23. New York: Parnassos, Greek Cultural Society of New York, 1980/81.
Alexiou, Elli. THEY WERE ALL TO BE PITIED

The Children's Inferno: Stories of the Great Famine in Greece. Hollywood, CA: Gateway Books, 1946.
Nakos, Lilika. HELENITSA

Classics in World Literature. Glenview, IL: ScottForesman, 1989.
Tolstoy, Leo. HOW MUCH LAND DOES A MAN NEED

The Collector of Treasures. Portsmouth, NH: Heinemann, 1977.
Head, Bessie. HEAVEN IS NOT CLOSED

The Complete Fiction of Bruno Schulz. New York: Walker, 1989.
Schulz, Bruno. COCKROACHES

The Continental Edition of World Masterpieces. New York: Norton, 1986.
Tolstoy, Leo. THE DEATH OF IVÁN ILYICH

Continental Short Stories: The Modern Tradition. New York: Norton, 1968.
Aichinger, Ilse. THE BOUND MAN
Pavese, Cesare. SUICIDES

The Continental Short Story: An Existential Approach. New York: Odyssey Press, 1969.
Moravia, Alberto. THE FALL
Pirandello, Luigi. CINCI

Death in Midsummer and Other Stories. New York: New Directions, 1966.
Mishima Yukio. PATRIOTISM

Death in Venice and Seven Other Stories. New York: Vintage Books, 1936.
Mann, Thomas. DISORDER AND EARLY SORROW
Mann, Thomas. TRISTAN

A Doctor's Visit: Short Stories by Anton Chekhov. New York: Bantam, 1988.
Chekhov, Anton. THE KISS

Eighteen Texts: Writings by Contemporary Greek Authors. Cambridge: Harvard University Press, 1972.
Cicellis, Kay. BRIEF DIALOGUE
Roufos, Rodis. THE CANDIDATE

End of the Game and Other Stories. New York: Random House, 1967.
Cortázar, Julio. NIGHT FACE UP

English and Western Literature. New York: Macmillan, 1984.
Camus, Albert. THE GUEST

The Eye of the Heart: Short Stories from Latin America. New York: Bobbs-Merrill, 1973.
Amado, Jorge. HOW PORCIÚNCULA THE MULATTO GOT THE CORPSE OFF HIS BACK
Asturias, Miguel. TATUANA'S TALE
Cortázar, Julio. END OF THE GAME
Fuentes, Carlos. THE TWO ELENAS
Paz, Octavio. MY LIFE WITH THE WAVE

Fifty Great European Short Stories. New York: Bantam, 1971.
Björnson, Björnstjerne. THE FATHER

A Flag on the Island. London: Andre Deutsch, 1967.
Naipaul, V. S. THE ENEMY

Flowers of Fire: Twentieth Century Korean Stories. Honolulu: University of Hawaii Press, 1986.
Kiwon So. THE HEIR

Form in Fiction. New York: St. Martin's Press, 1974.
Calvino, Italo. ALL AT ONE POINT
Landolfi, Tommaso. PASTORAL

Franz Kafka: The Complete Stories. New York: Schocken, 1948.
Kafka, Franz. IN THE PENAL COLONY
Kafka, Franz. THE JUDGMENT
Kafka, Franz. THE METAMORPHOSIS

French Stories and Tales. New York: Knopf, 1954.
Villiers de L'Isle-Adam. THE DESIRE TO BE A MAN

French Stories/Contes Français: A Bantam Dual-Language Book. New York: Bantam, 1960.
Balzac, Honoré de. THE ATHEIST'S MASS

Friday's Footprint and Other Stories. New York: Viking, 1960.
Gordimer, Nadine. LITTLE WILLIE

Games at Twilight and Other Stories. London: Heinemann, 1978.
Desai, Anita. GAMES AT TWILIGHT

German Stories: Deutsche Novellen. New York: Bantam, 1946.
Hesse, Hermann. THE POET

Girls at War and Other Stories. Greenwich, CT: Fawcett, 1972.
Achebe, Chinua. GIRLS AT WAR
Achebe, Chinua. VENGEFUL CREDITOR

Going Home. North Sydney, Australia: Allen & Unwin Pty, 1990.
Weller, Archie. GOING HOME

Great German Short Stories. New York: Dell, 1960.
Heym, Georg. THE AUTOPSY

Great Modern European Short Stories. Greenwich, CT: Fawcett, 1967.
Böll, Heinrich. MURKE'S COLLECTED SILENCES
Hildesheimer, Wolfgang. A WORLD ENDS
Huber, Heinz. THE NEW APARTMENT

Great Stories by Nobel Prize Winners. New York: The Noonday Press, 1959.
Hamsun, Knut. THE CALL OF LIFE
Lagerlöf, Selma. THE OUTLAWS
Laxness, Haldor. LILY
Pontoppidan, Henrik. A FISHER NEST

Green Cane and Juicy Flotsam: Short Stories by Caribbean Women. New Brunswick, NJ: Rutgers University Press, 1991.
Condé, Maryse. THREE WOMEN IN MANHATTAN

Harper's Magazine. January 1947.
Aymé, Marcel. THE MAN WHO WALKED THROUGH WALLS

He Rau Aroha: A Hundred Leaves of Love. Auckland, New Zealand: Penguin, 1986.
Taylor, Apirana. THE CARVING

Her True-True Name: An Anthology of Women's Writing from the Caribbean. Portsmouth, NH: Heinemann, 1990.
Vega, Ana Lydia. CLOUD COVER CARIBBEAN
Yáñez, Mirta. WE BLACKS ALL DRINK COFFEE

H. I. E. Dhlomo: Collected Works. New York: Raven Press, 1985.
Dhlomo, H. I. E. THE DAUGHTER

Introduction to Literature: Stories. New York: Macmillan, 1963.
Sartre, Jean-Paul. THE WALL

Introduction to Literature: Stories. 3d ed. New York: Macmillan, 1980.
Mann, Thomas. TONIO KRÖGER

Introduction to Modern Greek Literature: An Anthology of Fiction, Drama, and Poetry. New York: Twayne, 1969.
Haris, Petros. LIGHTS ON THE SEA
Theotokis, Konstantinos. VILLAGE LIFE
Venezis, Elias. MYCENAE

Isaac Asimov Presents the Best Horror and Supernatural of the 19th Century. New York: Beaufort Books, 1983.
Villiers de L'Isle-Adam. THE TORTURE BY HOPE

Krik? Krak! New York: Soho Press, 1995.
Danticat, Edwidge. CHILDREN OF THE SEA

Labyrinths. New York: New Directions, 1962.
Borges, Jorge Luis. THE GARDEN OF FORKING PATHS

Laughable Loves. New York: Knopf, 1974.
Kundera, Milan. NOBODY WILL LAUGH

Life and Letters Today: An International Quarterly of Living Literature. Winter 1936.
Nakos, Lilika. THE BROKEN DOLL

Literature of the Western World. New York: Macmillan, 1984.
Flaubert, Gustave. A SIMPLE HEART
Zola, Émile. THE INUNDATION

Literature: The Human Experience. 3d ed. New York: St. Martin's Press, 1982.
Kafka, Franz. A HUNGER ARTIST
Moravia, Alberto. THE CHASE

Midnight Convoy and Other Stories. Jerusalem: Israel Universities Press, 1969.
Yizhar, S. HABAKUK

Modern African Prose. London: Heinemann, 1964.
Kariara, Jonathan. HER WARRIOR
Ngugi, James. THE MARTYR
Nicol, Abioseth. AS THE NIGHT THE DAY

Modern Arabic Short Stories. New York: Three Continents, 1976.
Idris, Youssef. THE CHEAPEST NIGHT'S ENTERTAINMENT
Mahfouz, Naguib. THE PASHA'S DAUGHTER

Modern Indian Short Stories. New Delhi: Indian Council for Cultural Relations, 1976.
Kapadia, Kundanika. PAPER BOAT

Modern Japanese Stories: An Anthology. Rutland, VT: Charles E. Tuttle, 1980.
Kawabata Yasunari. THE MOON ON THE WATER
Tanizaki Junichiro. TATTOO

Nobel Parade. Glenview, IL: ScottForesman, 1975.
Andric, Ivo. THE SCYTHE
Sholokhov, Mikhail. THE COLT
Sienkiewicz, Henryk. YANKO THE MUSICIAN

Nobel Prize Library: Giorgis Seferis, Mikhail Sholokhov, Henryk Sienkiewicz, Carl Spitteler. New York: Helvetica Press, 1971.
Sienkiewicz, Henryk. THE LIGHTHOUSE-KEEPER

Norton Anthology of World Masterpieces. New York: Norton, 1992.
Gide, André. THE RETURN OF THE PRODIGAL SON

Notes from Underground, "White Nights," "The Dream of a Ridiculous Man," and Selections from "The House of the Dead." New York: New American Library, 1961.
Dostoevski, Fyodor. THE DREAM OF A RIDICULOUS MAN
Dostoevski, Fyodor. WHITE NIGHTS

Of Time and Place: Comparative World Literature in Translation. Glenview, IL: ScottForesman, 1976.
Abrahams, Peter. EPISODE IN MALAY CAMP
Verga, Giovanni. PROPERTY

One World of Literature. Boston: Houghton Mifflin, 1993.
Dib, Mohammed. NAEMA—WHEREABOUTS UNKNOWN
Phiên Võ. THE KEY

Other Weapons. Hanover: Ediciones del Norte, 1985.
Valenzuela, Luisa. I'M YOUR HORSE IN THE NIGHT

Prentice Hall Literature World Masterpieces. Englewood Cliffs, NJ: Prentice Hall, 1991.
Chekhov, Anton. THE BET

Reading Modern Short Stories. Glenview, IL: ScottForesman, 1955.
Pirandello, Luigi. WAR

Restless City and Christmas Gold. London: Heinemann, 1975.
Ekwensi, Cyprian. THE GREAT BEYOND

Rōshomon and Other Stories by Akutagawa Ryūnosuke. Tokyo: Charles E. Tuttle, 1983.
Akutagawa Ryūnosuke. IN A GROVE

Russian and Eastern European Literature. Glenview, IL: ScottForesman, 1970.
Andric, Ivo. A SUMMER IN THE SOUTH
Djilas, Milovan. WAR
Mrozek, Slawomir. CHILDREN
Mrozek, Slawomir. ON A JOURNEY
Sholokhov, Mikhail. THE FATE OF A MAN
Solzhenitsyn, Alexander. MATRYONA'S HOME
Tamasi, Aron. FLASHES IN THE NIGHT

Secret Weavers. Fredonia, NY: White Pine Press, 1992.
Allende, Isabel. TWO WORDS

Selected Short Stories. London: Penguin, 1991.
Tagore, Rabindranath. KABULIWALLAH

A Walk in the Night and Other Stories. Evanston, IL: Northwestern University Press, 1967.
La Guma, Alex. BLANKETS

A Whole Loaf: Stories from Israel. New York: Vanguard Press, 1962.
Agnon, S. Y. A WHOLE LOAF

Winter's Tales. New York: Random House, 1942.
Dinesen, Isak. SORROW-ACRE

The World in Literature. Rev. ed. Glenview, IL: ScottForesman, 1967.
Balzac, Honoré de. LA GRANDE BRETÊCHE
Maupassant, Guy de. THE NECKLACE
Zola, Émile. NAÏS MICOULIN

A World of Great Stories. New York: Crown, 1947.
Dinesen, Isak. THE SAILOR BOY'S TALE
Nexø, Martin Andersen. BIRDS OF PASSAGE
Siwertz, Sigfrid. IN SPITE OF EVERYTHING

World Writers Today. Glenview, IL: ScottForesman, 1995.
Achebe, Chinua. THE VOTER
Ayyoub, Dhu'l Nun. FROM BEHIND THE VEIL
Desai, Anita. A DEVOTED SON
Feng Jicai. THE MAO BUTTON
Kawabata Yasunari. THE JAY
Lim, Catherine. PAPER
Mahfouz, Naguib. THE CONJURER MADE OFF WITH THE DISH
Murakami Haruki. ON MEETING MY 100 PER-CENT WOMAN ONE FINE APRIL MORNING
Naipaul, V. S. B. WORDSWORTH
Narayan, R. K. FATHER'S HELP
Ray, Satyajit. ASHAMANJA BABU'S DOG
Rifaat, Alifa. ANOTHER EVENING AT THE CLUB
Rifaat, Alifa. AN INCIDENT IN THE GHOBASHI HOUSEHOLD
Tanizaki Junichiro. THE THIEF

SUGGESTED COMPARISONS—THEMES

We have included the following index to help teachers identify stories with comparable themes.
Titles of works annotated in this text are capitalized wherever they appear.

AGE/AGING

Agnon, S. Y. THE DOCUMENT
Alexiou, Elli. THEY WERE ALL TO BE PITIED
Desai, Anita. A DEVOTED SON
Faulkner, William. "A Rose for Emily"
Flaubert, Gustave. A SIMPLE HEART
Joyce, James. "Clay"
Kafka, Franz. THE JUDGMENT
Laxness, Haldor. LILY
Mansfield, Katherine. "Miss Brill"
Megged, Aharon. THE NAME
Naipaul, V. S. B. WORDSWORTH
Nexø, Martin Andersen. BIRDS OF PASSAGE
Nhat-Tien. AN UNSOUND SLEEP
O'Connor, Flannery. "A Good Man Is Hard to Find"
Porter, Katherine Anne. "The Jilting of Granny
    Weatherall"
Saranti, Galatea. SUNLIGHT
Sienkiewicz, Henryk. THE LIGHTHOUSE-KEEPER
Solzhenitsyn, Alexander. THE RIGHT HAND
Steinbeck, John. "The Leader of the People"
Surangkhanang, K. THE GRANDMOTHER
Svevo, Italo. IN MY INDOLENCE
Theotokis, Konstantinos. VILLAGE LIFE
Welty, Eudora. "A Visit of Charity"

AGGRESSION/VIOLENCE

Akutagawa Ryūnosuke. IN A GROVE
Bierce, Ambrose. "An Occurrence at Owl Creek Bridge"

Connell, Richard. "The Most Dangerous Game"
Crane, Stephen. "The Bride Comes to Yellow Sky"
Cumali, Necati. IN GOD'S PLAINS
Dib, Mohammed. NAEMA—WHEREABOUTS
    UNKNOWN
Djilas, Milovan. WAR
Faulkner, William. "Barn Burning"
Faulkner, William. "The Bear"
Greene, Graham. "The Destructors"
Hemingway, Ernest. "The Killers"
Irving, Washington. "The Legend of Sleepy Hollow"
Jackson, Shirley. "The Lottery"
Ngugi, James. THE MARTYR
O'Connor, Flannery. "A Good Man Is Hard to Find"
O'Flaherty, Liam. "The Sniper"
Poe, Edgar Allan. "The Cask of Amontillado"
Poe, Edgar Allan. "The Tell-Tale Heart"
Pontoppidan, Henrik. A FISHER NEST
Steinbeck, John. "Flight"
Stockton, Frank. "The Lady, or the Tiger"
Stuart, Jesse. "Split Cherry Tree"
Theotokis, Konstantinos. VILLAGE LIFE
Venezis, Elias. MYCENAE
Villiers de L'Isle-Adam. THE DESIRE TO BE A MAN
Williams, William Carlos. "The Use of Force"

ALIENATION/ISOLATION/LONELINESS

Abrahams, Peter. EPISODE IN MALAY CAMP
Agnon, S. Y. THE DOCUMENT
Alexiou, Elli. THEY WERE ALL TO BE PITIED

Amado, Jorge. HOW PORCIÚNCULA THE MULATTO GOT THE CORPSE OFF HIS BACK

Anderson, Sherwood. "I'm a Fool"

Andreyev, Leonid. LAZARUS

Aymé, Marcel. THE MAN WHO WALKED THROUGH WALLS

Bowen, Elizabeth. "Tears, Idle Tears"

Camus, Albert. THE GUEST

Capote, Truman. "A Christmas Memory"

Cather, Willa. "Paul's Case"

Chekhov, Anton. THE BET

Conrad, Joseph. "Youth"

Desai, Anita. GAMES AT TWILIGHT

Dostoevski, Fyodor. THE DREAM OF A RIDICULOUS MAN

Dostoevski, Fyodor. WHITE NIGHTS

Faulkner, William. "Barn Burning"

Faulkner, William. "A Rose for Emily"

Flaubert, Gustave. A SIMPLE HEART

Gordimer, Nadine. A SOLDIER'S EMBRACE

Hahn Moo-sook. SHADOW

Hawthorne, Nathaniel. "The Minister's Black Veil"

Hawthorne, Nathaniel. "Young Goodman Brown"

Hemingway, Ernest. "The Killers"

Henry, O. "The Cop and the Anthem"

Irving, Washington. "The Legend of Sleepy Hollow"

Joyce, James. "Araby"

Joyce, James. "Clay"

Kafka, Franz. THE METAMORPHOSIS

Kariara, Jonathan. HER WARRIOR

Keyes, Daniel. "Flowers for Algernon"

Kundera, Milan. NOBODY WILL LAUGH

Lawrence, D. H. "The Rocking Horse Winner"

Laxness, Haldor. LILY

Lenz, Siegfried. THE LAUGHINGSTOCK

London, Jack. "To Build a Fire"

Lu Xun. DIARY OF A MADMAN

Mann, Thomas. TONIO KRÖGER

Mann, Thomas. TRISTAN

Mansfield, Katherine. "Miss Brill"

Megged, Aharon. THE NAME

Melville, Herman. "Bartleby the Scrivener"

O'Connor, Frank. "My Oedipus Complex"

Pavese, Cesare. SUICIDES

Phiên Võ. THE KEY

Pirandello, Luigi. CINCI

Poe, Edgar Allan. "The Fall of the House of Usher"

Poe, Edgar Allan. "The Tell-Tale Heart"

Salinger, J. D. "A Perfect Day for Bananafish"

Santos, Bienvenido N. THE DAY THE DANCERS CAME

Sarang, Vilas. THE TERRORIST

Sienkiewicz, Henryk. THE LIGHTHOUSE-KEEPER

Steinbeck, John. "The Chrysanthemums"

Steinbeck, John. "Flight"

Steinbeck, John. "The Leader of the People"

Stuart, Jesse. "Split Cherry Tree"

Thurber, James. "The Secret Life of Walter Mitty"

Tolstoy, Leo. THE DEATH OF IVÁN ILYICH

Verga, Giovanni. PROPERTY

Welty, Eudora. "A Visit of Charity"

Welty, Eudora. "Why I Live at the P.O."

Yehoshua, Abraham B. FACING THE FOREST

ARTIST'S PLACE IN SOCIETY

Aichinger, Ilse. THE BOUND MAN

Böll, Heinrich. MURKE'S COLLECTED SILENCES

Condé, Maryse. THREE WOMEN IN MANHATTAN

Gide, André. THE RETURN OF THE PRODIGAL SON

Greene, Graham. "The Destructors"

Hesse, Hermann. THE POET

James, Henry. "The Real Thing"

Joyce, James. "Araby"

Kafka, Franz. A HUNGER ARTIST

Mann, Thomas. TONIO KRÖGER

Mann, Thomas. TRISTAN

Mrozek, Slawomir. CHILDREN

Naipaul, V. S. B. WORDSWORTH

Paz, Octavio. MY LIFE WITH THE WAVE

Sand, George. THE MARQUISE

Sienkiewicz, Henryk. YANKO THE MUSICIAN

Tanizaki Junichiro. TATTOO

Yizhar, S. HABAKUK

CHILDHOOD/YOUTH

Achebe, Chinua. VENGEFUL CREDITOR

Anderson, Sherwood. "I'm a Fool"

Ayyoub, Dhu'l Nun. FROM BEHIND THE VEIL

Baykurt, Fakir. FRECKLES

Bowen, Elizabeth. "Tears, Idle Tears"

Capote, Truman. "A Christmas Memory"

Conrad, Joseph. "Youth"

Cortázar, Julio. END OF THE GAME

Borowski, Tadeusz. THE MAN WITH THE
PACKAGE
Bowen, Elizabeth. "Tears, Idle Tears"
Capote, Truman. "A Christmas Memory"
Cather, Willa. "Paul's Case"
Colette. THE PHOTOGRAPHER'S MISSUS
Connell, Richard. "The Most Dangerous Game"
Cortázar, Julio. NIGHT FACE UP
Crane, Stephen. "The Open Boat"
Djilas, Milovan. WAR
Ekwensi, Cyprian. THE GREAT BEYOND
Faulkner, William. "A Rose for Emily"
Flaubert, Gustave. A SIMPLE HEART
Hawthorne, Nathaniel. "The Minister's Black Veil"
Hayashi Fumiko. BONES
Hemingway, Ernest. "The Killers"
Heym, Georg. THE AUTOPSY
Jackson, Shirley. "The Lottery"
Jacobs, W. W. "The Monkey's Paw"
Joyce, James. "Clay"
Kafka, Franz. THE JUDGMENT
Kapadia, Kundanika. PAPER BOAT
Kariara, Jonathan. HER WARRIOR
Keyes, Daniel. "Flowers for Algernon"
La Guma, Alex. BLANKETS
Lawrence, D. H. "The Rocking Horse Winner"
London, Jack. "To Build a Fire"
Mansfield, Katherine. "The Garden Party"
Melville, Herman. "Bartleby the Scrivener"
Mishima Yukio. PATRIOTISM
Nakos, Lilika. HELENITSA
O'Connor, Flannery. "A Good Man Is Hard to Find"
O'Flaherty, Liam. "The Sniper"
Pavese, Cesare. SUICIDES
Pirandello, Luigi. CINCI
Pirandello, Luigi. WAR
Poe, Edgar Allan. "The Cask of Amontillado"
Poe, Edgar Allan. "The Fall of the House of Usher"
Poe, Edgar Allan. "The Tell-Tale Heart"
Porter, Katherine Anne. "The Jilting of Granny
Weatherall"
Salinger, J. D. "A Perfect Day for Bananafish"
Sartre, Jean-Paul. "The Wall"
Sholokhov, Mikhail. THE COLT
Steinbeck, John. "Flight"
Stockton, Frank. "The Lady, or the Tiger"
Tolstoy, Leo. THE DEATH OF IVÁN ILYICH
Verga, Giovanni. PROPERTY
Villiers de L'Isle-Adam. THE TORTURE BY HOPE

ENTRAPMENT

Agnon, S. Y. THE DOCUMENT
Balzac, Honoré de. LA GRANDE BRETÊCHE
Baykurt, Fakir. FRECKLES
Bierce, Ambrose. "An Occurrence at Owl Creek
Bridge"
Colette. THE PHOTOGRAPHER'S MISSUS
Connell, Richard. "The Most Dangerous Game"
Danticat, Edwidge. CHILDREN OF THE SEA
Hayashi Fumiko. BONES
Hemingway, Ernest. "The Killers"
Idris, Youssef. THE CHEAPEST NIGHT'S
ENTERTAINMENT
Jacobs, W. W. "The Monkey's Paw"
Kafka, Franz. THE METAMORPHOSIS
Mphahlele, Es'kia. THE MASTER OF DOORNVLEI
Poe, Edgar Allan. "The Cask of Amontillado"
Pontoppidan, Henrik. A FISHER NEST
Rifaat, Alifa. ANOTHER EVENING AT THE CLUB
Stockton, Frank. "The Lady, or the Tiger"
Turgenev, Ivan. YERMOLAY AND THE MILLER'S
WIFE
Twain, Mark. "The Celebrated Jumping Frog of
Calaveras County"
Villiers de L'Isle-Adam. THE TORTURE BY HOPE
Weller, Archie. GOING HOME

EPIPHANY

Faulkner, William. "The Bear"
Hemingway, Ernest. "The Killers"
Joyce, James. "Araby"
Mansfield, Katherine. "Miss Brill"
Steinbeck, John. "The Chrysanthemums"
Updike, John. "A & P"

ESCAPE

Aymé, Marcel. THE MAN WHO WALKED
THROUGH WALLS
Borowski, Tadeusz. THE MAN WITH THE
PACKAGE
Colette. THE PHOTOGRAPHER'S MISSUS
Crane, Stephen. "The Open Boat"
Danticat, Edwidge. CHILDREN OF THE SEA
Gide, André. THE RETURN OF THE PRODIGAL
SON
Hawthorne, Nathaniel. "Young Goodman Brown"

FRIENDSHIP

Balzac, Honoré de. THE ATHEIST'S MASS
Bowen, Elizabeth. "Tears, Idle Tears"
Camus, Albert. THE GUEST
Capote, Truman. "A Christmas Memory"
Crane, Stephen. "The Open Boat"
Dostoevski, Fyodor. AN HONEST THIEF
Harte, Bret. "Tennessee's Partner"
Head, Bessie. THE COLLECTOR OF TREASURES
Kapadia, Kundanika. PAPER BOAT
Keyes, Daniel. "Flowers for Algernon"
Lagerlöf, Selma. THE OUTLAWS
Melville, Herman. "Bartleby the Scrivener"
Naipaul, V. S. B. WORDSWORTH
Poe, Edgar Allan. "The Fall of the House of Usher"
Tagore, Rabindranath. KABULIWALLAH
Tanizaki Junichiro. THE THIEF

GRATITUDE OR INGRATITUDE

Borowski, Tadeusz. THE MAN WITH THE
 PACKAGE
Diop, Birago. THE WAGES OF GOOD
Dostoevski, Fyodor. THE HONEST THIEF
Faulkner, William. "Barn Burning"
Melville, Herman. "Bartleby the Scrivener"
Naipaul, V. S. B. WORDSWORTH
Solzhenitsyn, Alexander. THE RIGHT HAND
Steinbeck, John. "The Chrysanthemums"
Stuart, Jesse. "Split Cherry Tree"
Welty, Eudora. "A Visit of Charity"

GREED/SELFISHNESS

Achebe, Chinua. GIRLS AT WAR
Achebe, Chinua. VENGEFUL CREDITOR
Achebe, Chinua. THE VOTER
Capote, Truman. "A Christmas Memory"
Chekhov, Anton. THE BET
Feng Jicai. THE MAO BUTTON
Henry, O. "The Gift of the Magi"
Jacobs, W. W. "The Monkey's Paw"
Joyce, James. "Clay"
Lao She. GRANDMOTHER TAKES CHARGE
Lawrence, D. H. "The Rocking Horse Winner"
Lim, Catherine. PAPER
Lo Liyong, Taban. THE OLD MAN OF USUMBURA
 AND HIS MISERY

Tolstoy, Leo. HOW MUCH LAND DOES A MAN NEED
Twain, Mark. "The Man That Corrupted
 Hadleyburg"
Verga, Giovanni. PROPERTY
Welty, Eudora. "A Visit of Charity"

GUILT AND REPENTANCE

Bowen, Elizabeth. "Tears, Idle Tears"
Dostoevski, Fyodor. THE HONEST THIEF
Ekwensi, Cyprian. THE GREAT BEYOND
Hawthorne, Nathaniel. "The Minister's Black Veil"
Hawthorne, Nathaniel. "Young Goodman Brown"
Lagerlöf, Selma. THE OUTLAWS
Maupassant, Guy de. THE NECKLACE
Nicol, Abioseth. AS THE NIGHT THE DAY
Phiên Võ. THE KEY
Rifaat, Alifa. ANOTHER EVENING AT THE CLUB
Stevenson, Robert Louis. "Markheim"
Villiers de L'Isle-Adam. THE DESIRE TO BE A MAN

HERO AND ANTI-HERO

Agnon, S. Y. A WHOLE LOAF
Bierce, Ambrose. "An Occurrence at Owl Creek
 Bridge"
Buzzati, Dino. THE SLAYING OF THE DRAGON
Connell, Richard. "The Most Dangerous Game"
Crane, Stephen. "The Bride Comes to Yellow Sky"
Dib, Mohammed. NAEMA—WHEREABOUTS
 UNKNOWN
Djilas, Milovan. THE OLD MAN AND THE SONG
Faulkner, William. "Barn Burning"
Henry, O. "The Cop and the Anthem"
Irving, Washington. "The Legend of Sleepy Hollow"
Kariara, Jonathan. HER WARRIOR
Keyes, Daniel. "Flowers for Algernon"
Lenz, Siegfried. THE LAUGHINGSTOCK
London, Jack. "To Build a Fire"
Lu Xun. DIARY OF A MADMAN
Meleagrou, Hebe. MONUMENT
O'Flaherty, Liam. "The Sniper"
Roufos, Rodis. THE CANDIDATE
Sartre, Jean-Paul. THE WALL
Steinbeck, John. "Flight"
Steinbeck, John. "The Leader of the People"
Thurber, James. "The Secret Life of Walter Mitty"
Updike, John. "A & P"
Villiers de L'Isle-Adam. THE TORTURE BY HOPE

Mann, Thomas. TRISTAN
Mansfield, Katherine. "The Garden Party"
Mansfield, Katherine. "Miss Brill"
Ngugi, James. THE MARTYR
Nhat-Tien. AN UNSOUND SLEEP
Nicol, Abioseth. AS THE NIGHT THE DAY
O'Connor, Flannery. "A Good Man Is Hard to Find"
O'Flaherty, Liam. "The Sniper"
Phiên Vō. THE KEY
Rifaat, Alifa. AN INCIDENT IN THE GHOBASHI
    HOUSEHOLD
Roufos, Rodis. THE CANDIDATE
Solzhenitsyn, Alexander. THE RIGHT HAND
Steinbeck, John. "A Leader of the People"
Stockton, Frank. "The Lady, or the Tiger"
Stuart, Jesse. "Split Cherry Tree"
Theotokis, Konstantinos. VILLAGE LIFE
Updike, John. "A & P"
Valenzuela, Luisa. I'M YOUR HORSE IN THE
    NIGHT
Weller, Archie. GOING HOME
Welty, Eudora. "A Visit of Charity"
Zola, Émile. NAÏS MICOULIN

INITIATION/LOSS OF INNOCENCE

Achebe, Chinua. VENGEFUL CREDITOR
Anderson, Sherwood. "I'm a Fool"
Bowen, Elizabeth. "Tears, Idle Tears"
Calvino, Italo. ALL AT ONE POINT
Capote, Truman. "A Christmas Memory"
Cather, Willa. "Paul's Case"
Chekhov, Anton. THE KISS
Conrad, Joseph. "Youth"
Daudet, Alphonse. THE LAST LESSON
Dib, Mohammed. NAEMA—WHEREABOUTS
    UNKNOWN
Dinesen, Isak. THE SAILOR BOY'S TALE
Ellison, Ralph. "Battle Royal"
Faulkner, William. "Barn Burning"
Faulkner, William. "The Bear"
Gordimer, Nadine. LITTLE WILLIE
Hawthorne, Nathaniel. "Young Goodman Brown"
Hemingway, Ernest. "The Killers"
Joyce, James. "Araby"
Kapadia, Kundanika. PAPER BOAT
Keyes, Daniel. "Flowers for Algernon"
Lagerkvist, Pär. FATHER AND I
Lawrence, D. H. "The Rocking Horse Winner"

Lessing, Doris. "Through the Tunnel"
Mahfouz, Naguib. THE CONJURER MADE OFF
    WITH THE DISH
Mansfield, Katherine. "The Garden Party"
Moravia, Alberto. THE FALL
Mrozek, Slawomir. CHILDREN
Naipaul, V. S.   B. WORDSWORTH
Naipaul, V. S. THE ENEMY
O'Connor, Frank. "My Oedipus Complex"
Steinbeck, John. "The Chrysanthemums"
Steinbeck, John. "The Leader of the People"
Tanizaki Junichiro. TATTOO
Updike, John. "A & P"
Welty, Eudora. "A Visit of Charity"
Zola, Émile. THE INUNDATION
Zola, Émile. NAÏS MICOULIN

JEALOUSY

Balzac, Honoré de. LA GRANDE BRETÊCHE
Faulkner, William. "Barn Burning"
Faulkner, William. "A Rose for Emily"
Irving, Washington. "The Legend of Sleepy Hollow"
Moravia, Alberto. THE CHASE
Narayan, R. K. THE MIRROR
O'Connor, Frank. "My Oedipus Complex"
Paz, Octavio. MY LIFE WITH THE WAVE
Rushdi, Rashad. ANGUISH
Stockton, Frank. "The Lady, or the Tiger"
Welty, Eudora. "Why I Live at the P.O."

JUSTICE AND INJUSTICE

Aidoo, Ama Ata. NO SWEETNESS HERE
Akutagawa Ryūnosuke. IN A GROVE
Borowski, Tadeusz. THE MAN WITH THE
    PACKAGE
Chekhov, Anton. THE BET
Cubena. THE AFRICAN GRANNIE
Cumali, Necati. IN GOD'S PLAINS
Dinesen, Isak. SORROW-ACRE
Diop, Birago. THE WAGES OF GOOD
Faulkner, William. "Barn Burning"
Henry, O. "The Cop and the Anthem"
Jackson, Shirley. "The Lottery"
Mérimée, Prosper. THE VENUS OF ILLE
Nicol, Abioseth. AS THE NIGHT THE DAY
O'Connor, Flannery. "A Good Man Is Hard to Find"
Stockton, Frank. "The Lady, or the Tiger"

Narayan, R. K. THE MIRROR
Nexø, Martin Andersen. BIRDS OF PASSAGE
O'Connor, Frank. "My Oedipus Complex"
Pavese, Cesare. SUICIDES
Porter, Katherine Anne. "The Jilting of Granny
  Weatherall"
Rushdi, Rashad. ANGUISH
Salinger, J. D. "A Perfect Day for Bananafish"
Sand, George. THE MARQUISE
Siwertz, Sigfrid. IN SPITE OF EVERYTHING
Steinbeck, John. "The Chrysanthemums"
Steinbeck, John. "The Leader of the People"
Stockton, Frank. "The Lady, or the Tiger"
Svevo, Italo. IN MY INDOLENCE
Tanizaki Junichiro. TATTOO
Thurber, James. "The Secret Life of Walter Mitty"
Valenzuela, Luisa. I'M YOUR HORSE IN THE
  NIGHT
Welty, Eudora. "Why I Live at the P.O."

METAMORPHOSIS/TRANSFORMATION

Asturias, Miguel. TATUANA'S TALE
Aymé, Marcel. THE MAN WHO WALKED
  THROUGH WALLS
Hawthorne, Nathaniel. "The Minister's Black Veil"
Henry, O. "The Cop and the Anthem"
Irving, Washington. "The Legend of Sleepy Hollow"
Kafka, Franz. THE METAMORPHOSIS
Keyes, Daniel. "Flowers for Algernon"
Sand, George. THE MARQUISE
Schulz, Bruno. COCKROACHES
Taylor, Apirana. THE CARVING

NATIONALISM

Agnon, S. Y. A WHOLE LOAF
Bierce, Ambrose. "An Occurrence at Owl Creek
  Bridge"
Borowski, Tadeusz. THE MAN WITH THE
  PACKAGE
Camus, Albert. THE GUEST
Daudet, Alphonse. THE LAST LESSON
Dib, Mohammed. NAEMA—WHEREABOUTS
  UNKNOWN
Dinesen, Isak. SORROW-ACRE
Djilas, Milovan. THE OLD MAN AND THE SONG
Djilas, Milovan. WAR
Feng Jicai. THE MAO BUTTON

Greene, Graham. "The Destructors"
Hemingway, Ernest. "Old Man at the Bridge"
O'Connor, Frank. "My Oedipus Complex"
O'Flaherty, Liam. "The Sniper"
Papadiamantis, Alexandros. THE BEWITCHING OF
  THE AGA
Salinger, J. D. "A Perfect Day for Bananafish"
Solzhenitsyn, Alexander. ZAKHAR-THE-POUCH
Vega, Ana Lydia. CLOUD COVER CARIBBEAN
Yehoshua, Abraham B. FACING THE FOREST
Yizhar, S. HABAKUK

NATURE

Connell, Richard. "The Most Dangerous Game"
Conrad, Joseph. "Youth"
Crane, Stephen. "The Open Boat"
Faulkner, William. "The Bear"
Feng Jicai. THE MAO BUTTON
Huber, Heinz. THE NEW APARTMENT
Landolfi, Tommaso. PASTORAL
Lenz, Siegfried. THE LAUGHINGSTOCK
London, Jack. "To Build a Fire"
O Yong-su. SEASIDE VILLAGE
Steinbeck, John. "The Chrysanthemums"
Steinbeck, John. "Flight"
Twain, Mark. "The Celebrated Jumping Frog of
  Calaveras County"
Yehoshua, Abraham B. FACING THE FOREST
Zola, Émile. THE INUNDATION

OPPRESSION

Cicellis, Kay. BRIEF DIALOGUE
Colette. THE PHOTOGRAPHER'S MISSUS
Cumali, Necati. IN GOD'S PLAINS
Danticat, Edwidge. CHILDREN OF THE SEA
Daudet, Alphonse. THE LAST LESSON
Dib, Mohammed. NAEMA—WHEREABOUTS
  UNKNOWN
Haris, Petros. LIGHTS ON THE SEA
Head, Bessie. THE COLLECTOR OF TREASURES
Mphahlele, Es'kia. THE MASTER OF DOORNVLEI
Ngugi, James. THE MARTYR
Sienkiewicz, Henryk. YANKO THE MUSICIAN
Valenzuela, Luisa. I'M YOUR HORSE IN THE
  NIGHT
Villiers de L'Isle-Adam. THE TORTURE BY HOPE
Weller, Archie. GOING HOME

POLITICS AND THE INDIVIDUAL

Achebe, Chinua. GIRLS AT WAR
Achebe, Chinua. THE VOTER
Cubena. THE AFRICAN GRANNIE
Danticat, Edwidge. CHILDREN OF THE SEA
Mrozek, Slawomir. CHILDREN
Mrozek, Slawomir. ON A JOURNEY
Roufos, Rodis. THE CANDIDATE
Solzhenitsyn, Alexander. THE RIGHT HAND
Taylor, Apirana. THE CARVING
Vega, Ana Lydia. CLOUD COVER CARIBBEAN

POVERTY

Achebe, Chinua. GIRLS AT WAR
Ahmad, Razia Fasih. PAPER IS MONEY
Baykurt, Fakir. FRECKLES
Dostoevski, Fyodor. THE HONEST THIEF
Idris, Youssef. THE CHEAPEST NIGHT'S
    ENTERTAINMENT
La Guma, Alex. BLANKETS
Nakos, Lilika. HELENITSA
Narayan, R. K. A HORSE AND TWO GOATS
Nexø, Martin Andersen. BIRDS OF PASSAGE
Siddiqi, Shaukat. A MAN OF HONOR
Sienkiewicz, Henryk. YANKO THE MUSICIAN
Surangkhanang, K. THE GRANDMOTHER

PREJUDICE

Abrahams, Peter. EPISODE IN MALAY CAMP
Achebe, Chinua. VENGEFUL CREDITOR
Asturias, Miguel. TATUANA'S TALE
Borowski, Tadeusz. THE MAN WITH THE
    PACKAGE
Condé, Maryse. THREE WOMEN IN MANHATTAN
Cubena. THE AFRICAN GRANNIE
Dove-Danquah, Mabel. THE TORN VEIL
Gordimer, Nadine. LITTLE WILLIE
Grace, Patricia. A WAY OF TALKING
Melville, Herman. "Bartleby the Scrivener"
Mphahlele, Es'kia. THE MASTER OF DOORNVLEI
Nicol, Abioseth. AS THE NIGHT THE DAY
Stockton, Frank. "The Lady, or the Tiger"
Tagore, Rabindranath. KABULIWALLAH
Weller, Archie. GOING HOME
Williams, William Carlos. "The Use of Force"
Yehoshua, Abraham B. FACING THE FOREST
Zola, Émile. NAÏS MICOULIN

PRIDE

Björnson, Björnstjerne. THE FATHER
Capote, Truman. "A Christmas Memory"
Colette. THE LITTLE BOUILLOUX GIRL
Conrad, Joseph. "Youth"
Desai, Anita. GAMES AT TWILIGHT
Dove-Danquah, Mabel. THE TORN VEIL
Faulkner, William. "Barn Burning"
Faulkner, William. "A Rose for Emily"
Gordimer, Nadine. LITTLE WILLIE
Hemingway, Ernest. "The Killers"
James, Henry. "The Real Thing"
Joyce, James. "Clay"
Lenz, Siegfried. THE LAUGHINGSTOCK
Mansfield, Katherine. "Miss Brill"
Maupassant, Guy de. THE NECKLACE
Mphahlele, Es'kia. THE MASTER OF DOORNVLEI
Poe, Edgar Allan. "The Cask of Amontillado"
Rifaat, Alifa. ANOTHER EVENING AT THE CLUB
Rifaat, Alifa. AN INCIDENT IN THE GHOBASHI
    HOUSEHOLD
Siddiqi, Shaukat. A MAN OF HONOR
Steinbeck, John. "The Leader of the People"
Stuart, Jesse. "Split Cherry Tree"
Updike, John. "A & P"
Welty, Eudora. "Why I Live at the P.O."

RELIGION

Balzac, Honoré de. THE ATHEIST'S MASS
Ekwensi, Cyprian. THE GREAT BEYOND
France, Anatole. THE PROCURATOR OF JUDEA
Gide, André. THE RETURN OF THE PRODIGAL
    SON
Hawthorne, Nathaniel. "The Minister's Black Veil"
Hawthorne, Nathaniel. "Young Goodman Brown"
Head, Bessie. HEAVEN IS NOT CLOSED
Henry, O. "The Gift of the Magi"
Joyce, James. "Araby"
Joyce, James. "Clay"
Kariara, Jonathan. HER WARRIOR
Lagerlöf, Selma. THE OUTLAWS
O'Connor, Flannery. "A Good Man Is Hard to Find"
Tolstoy, Leo. THE DEATH OF IVÁN ILYICH
Villiers de L'Isle-Adam. THE TORTURE BY HOPE
Yizhar, S. HABAKUK

SACRIFICE AND SELF-SACRIFICE

Capote, Truman. "A Christmas Memory"
Crane, Stephen. "The Open Boat"
Dib, Mohammed. NAEMA—WHEREABOUTS
    UNKNOWN
Dinesen, Isak. SORROW-ACRE
Hawthorne, Nathaniel. "The Minister's Black Veil"
Hayashi Fumiko. BONES
Henry, O. "The Gift of the Magi"
Jackson, Shirley. "The Lottery"
Jacobs, W. W. "The Monkey's Paw"
Joyce, James. "Clay"
Kafka, Franz. A HUNGER ARTIST
Keyes, Daniel. "Flowers for Algernon"
Lawrence, D. H. "The Rocking Horse Winner"
Meleagrou, Hebe. MONUMENT
Mishima Yukio. PATRIOTISM
Nhat-Tien. AN UNSOUND SLEEP
Rifaat, Alifa. AN INCIDENT IN THE GHOBASHI
    HOUSEHOLD
Solzhenitsyn, Alexander. MATRYONA'S HOME
Stockton, Frank. "The Lady, or the Tiger"
Updike, John. "A & P"

SEARCH FOR IDENTITY

Abrahams, Peter. EPISODE IN MALAY CAMP
Cather, Willa. "Paul's Case"
Chekhov, Anton. THE DARLING
Condé, Maryse. THREE WOMEN IN MANHATTAN
Dinesen, Isak. THE SAILOR BOY'S TALE
Faulkner, William. "The Bear"
Gide, André. THE RETURN OF THE PRODIGAL
    SON
Hawthorne, Nathaniel. "The Minister's Black Veil"
Joyce, James. "Araby"
O Yong-su. SEASIDE VILLAGE
Sarang, Vilas. THE TERRORIST
Sartre, Jean-Paul. THE WALL
Taylor, Apirana. THE CARVING
Weller, Archie. GOING HOME

SEARCH FOR MEANING

Agnon, S. Y. THE DOCUMENT
Agnon, S. Y. A WHOLE LOAF
Aichinger, Ilse. THE BOUND MAN
Andreyev, Leonid. LAZARUS
Björnson, Björnstjerne. THE FATHER

Borges, Jorge Luis. THE GARDEN OF FORKING
    PATHS
Buzzati, Dino. THE SLAYING OF THE DRAGON
Dib, Mohammed. NAEMA—WHEREABOUTS
    UNKNOWN
Dostoevski, Fyodor. THE DREAM OF A RIDICU-
    LOUS MAN
Dostoevski, Fyodor. THE HONEST THIEF
Greene, Graham. "The Destructors"
Head, Bessie. HEAVEN IS NOT CLOSED
Hemingway, Ernest. "The Killers"
Hildesheimer, Wolfgang. A WORLD ENDS
Huber, Heinz. THE NEW APARTMENT
Izgü, Muzaffer. WANTED: A TOWN WITHOUT A
    CRAZY
Lim, Catherine. PAPER
Meleagrou, Hebe. MONUMENT
Melville, Herman. "Bartleby the Scrivener"
Nakos, Lilika. HELENITSA
Pirandello, Luigi. WAR
Saranti, Galatea. SUNLIGHT
Sartre, Jean-Paul. THE WALL
Tolstoy, Leo. THE DEATH OF IVÁN ILYICH
Yehoshua, Abraham B. FACING THE FOREST
Yizhar, S. HABAKUK
Zola, Émile. THE INUNDATION

SUPERSTITION/SUPERNATURAL

Achebe, Chinua. THE VOTER
Allende, Isabel. TWO WORDS
Andreyev, Leonid. LAZARUS
Andric, Ivo. A SUMMER IN THE SOUTH
Asturias, Miguel. TATUANA'S TALE
Benét, Stephen Vincent. "The Devil and Daniel
    Webster"
Dickens, Charles. "A Christmas Carol"
Dove-Danquah, Mabel. THE TORN VEIL
DuMaurier, Daphne. "The Blue Lenses"
Ekwensi, Cyprian. THE GREAT BEYOND
Hawthorne, Nathaniel. "Young Goodman Brown"
Irving, Washington. "The Legend of Sleepy Hollow"
Jacobs, W. W. "The Monkey's Paw"
Kariara, Jonathan. HER WARRIOR
Lawrence, D. H. "The Rocking Horse Winner"
Lim Beng Hap. POONEK
Mérimée, Prosper. THE VENUS OF ILLE
Narayan, R. K. THE MIRROR
Papadiamantis, Alexandros. THE BEWITCHING OF
    THE AGA

SUGGESTED COMPARISONS—LITERARY DEVICES

We have included the following index to help teachers identify stories that use similar literary devices. Titles of works annotated in this text are capitalized wherever they appear.

ALLEGORY/PARABLE

Buzzati, Dino. THE SLAYING OF THE DRAGON
Gide, André. THE RETURN OF THE PRODIGAL SON
Jackson, Shirley. "The Lottery"
Kafka, Franz. IN THE PENAL COLONY
Kafka, Franz. THE METAMORPHOSIS
Lenz, Siegfried. THE LAUGHINGSTOCK
Ray, Satyajit. ASHAMANJA BABU'S DOG
Tamasi, Aron. FLASHES IN THE NIGHT
Vega, Ana Lydia. CLOUD COVER CARIBBEAN

CHARACTER STUDY

Ahmad, Razia Fasih. PAPER IS MONEY
Alexiou, Elli. THEY WERE ALL TO BE PITIED
Balzac, Honoré de. THE ATHEIST'S MASS
Capote, Truman. "A Christmas Memory"
Cather, Willa. "Paul's Case"
Chekhov, Anton. THE DARLING
Colette. THE LITTLE BOUILLOUX GIRL
Dostoevski, Fyodor. THE HONEST THIEF
Faulkner, William. "A Rose for Emily"
Flaubert, Gustave. A SIMPLE HEART
Fuentes, Carlos. THE TWO ELENAS
Hawthorne, Nathaniel. "The Minister's Black Veil"
Hildesheimer, Wolfgang. A WORLD ENDS
Idris, Youssef. THE CHEAPEST NIGHT'S ENTERTAINMENT
Izgü, Muzaffer. WANTED: A TOWN WITHOUT A CRAZY
Joyce, James. "Clay"
Lao She. GRANDMOTHER TAKES CHARGE
Laxness, Haldor. LILY
Lenz, Siegfried. THE LAUGHINGSTOCK
Mahfouz, Naguib. THE CONJURER MADE OFF WITH THE DISH
Mahfouz, Naguib. THE PASHA'S DAUGHTER
Mansfield, Katherine. "The Garden Party"
Mansfield, Katherine. "Miss Brill"
Megged, Aharon. THE NAME
Melville, Herman. "Bartleby the Scrivener"
Naipaul, V. S. B. WORDSWORTH
Nexø, Martin Andersen. BIRDS OF PASSAGE
Nicol, Abioseth. AS THE NIGHT THE DAY
O'Connor, Flannery. "The Life You Save May Be Your Own"
Pirandello, Luigi. CINCI
Poe, Edgar Allan. "The Fall of the House of Usher"
Poe, Edgar Allan. "The Tell-Tale Heart"
Rushdi, Rashad. ANGUISH
Salinger, J. D. "A Perfect Day for Bananafish"
Santos, Bienvenido N. THE DAY THE DANCERS CAME
Sholokhov, Mikhail. THE FATE OF A MAN
Sienkiewicz, Henryk. THE LIGHTHOUSE-KEEPER
Sienkiewicz, Henryk. YANKO THE MUSICIAN
Solzhenitsyn, Alexander. MATRYONA'S HOME
Solzhenitsyn, Alexander. ZAKHAR-THE-POUCH

Steinbeck, John. "The Chrysanthemums"
Surangkhanang, K. THE GRANDMOTHER
Tamasi, Aron. FLASHES IN THE NIGHT
Theotokis, Konstantinos. VILLAGE LIFE
Tolstoy, Leo. HOW MUCH LAND DOES A MAN NEED
Welty, Eudora. "A Visit of Charity"
Welty, Eudora. "Why I Live at the P.O."
Yehoshua, Abraham B. FACING THE FOREST
Yizhar, S. HABAKUK

DIARY/JOURNAL/LETTERS

Danticat, Edwidge. CHILDREN OF THE SEA
Dib, Mohammed. NAEMA—WHEREABOUTS UNKNOWN
Keyes, Daniel. "Flowers for Algernon"
Landolfi, Tommaso. PASTORAL
Lu Xun. DIARY OF A MADMAN
Sarang, Vilas. THE TERRORIST

FANTASY

Agnon, S. Y. THE DOCUMENT
Allende, Isabel. TWO WORDS
Aymé, Marcel. THE MAN WHO WALKED THROUGH WALLS
Buzzati, Dino. THE SLAYING OF THE DRAGON
Landolfi, Tommaso. PASTORAL
Lawrence, D. H. "The Rocking Horse Winner"
Lo Liyong, Taban. THE OLD MAN OF USUMBURA AND HIS MISERY
Mérimée, Prosper. THE VENUS OF ILLE
Papadiamantis, Alexandros. THE BEWITCHING OF THE AGA
P'u Sung-Ling. THE FIGHTING CRICKET
Ray, Satyajit. ASHAMANJA BABU'S DOG
Sarang, Vilas. THE TERRORIST
Tanizaki Junichiro. TATTOO

FIRST PERSON

Ahmad, Razia Fasih. PAPER IS MONEY
Capote, Truman. "A Christmas Memory"
Conrad, Joseph. "Heart of Darkness"
Cortázar, Julio. END OF THE GAME
Grace, Patricia. A WAY OF TALKING
Joyce, James. "Araby"
Melville, Herman. "Bartleby the Scrivener"

Naipaul, V S. B. WORDSWORTH
Naipaul, V. S. THE ENEMY
O'Connor, Frank. "My Oedipus Complex"
Pavese, Cesare. SUICIDES
Phiên Võ. THE KEY
Poe, Edgar Allan. "The Cask of Amontillado"
Poe, Edgar Allan. "The Fall of the House of Usher"
Poe, Edgar Allan. "The Tell-Tale Heart"
Sarang, Vilas. THE TERRORIST
Sholokhov, Mikhail. THE FATE OF A MAN
Solzhenitsyn, Alexander. MATRYONA'S HOME
Solzhenitsyn, Alexander. ZAKHAR-THE-POUCH
Stuart, Jesse. "Split Cherry Tree"
Tanizaki Junichiro. THE THIEF
Thurber, James. "The Secret Life of Walter Mitty"
Turgenev, Ivan. YERMOLAY AND THE MILLER'S WIFE
Updike, John. "A & P"
Valenzuela, Luisa. I'M YOUR HORSE IN THE NIGHT
Welty, Eudora. "Why I Live at the P.O."
Williams, William Carlos. "The Use of Force"
Yizhar, S. HABAKUK

FRAME STORY

Balzac, Honoré de. LA GRANDE BRETÊCHE
Conrad, Joseph. "Heart of Darkness"
Conrad, Joseph. "Youth"
Dostoevski, Fyodor. THE DREAM OF A RIDICULOUS MAN
Dostoevski, Fyodor. THE HONEST THIEF
Kawabata Yasunari. THE JAY
La Guma, Alex. BLANKETS
Lu Xun. DIARY OF A MADMAN
Melville, Herman. "Bartleby the Scrivener"
Phiên Võ. THE KEY
Salinger, J. D. "For Esmé—with Love and Squalor"
Sand, George. THE MARQUISE
Sholokhov, Mikhail. THE FATE OF A MAN
Twain, Mark. "The Celebrated Jumping Frog of Calaveras County"

HORROR/GOTHICISM

Balzac, Honoré de. LA GRANDE BRETÊCHE
Heym, Georg. THE AUTOPSY
Kafka, Franz. IN THE PENAL COLONY
Kafka, Franz. THE METAMORPHOSIS
Kariara, Jonathan. HER WARRIOR

Landolfi, Tommaso. PASTORAL
Mérimée, Prosper. THE VENUS OF ILLE
Moravia, Alberto. THE CHASE
Moravia, Alberto. THE FALL
Poe, Edgar Allan. "The Cask of Amontillado"
Poe, Edgar Allan. "The Fall of the House of Usher"
Poe, Edgar Allan. "The Tell-Tale Heart"
Schulz, Bruno. COCKROACHES
Villiers de L'Isle-Adam. THE TORTURE BY HOPE

HUMOR

Achebe, Chinua. THE VOTER
Andric, Ivo. THE SCYTHE
Aymé, Marcel. THE MAN WHO WALKED
      THROUGH WALLS
Calvino, Italo. ALL AT ONE POINT
Crane, Stephen. "The Bride Comes to Yellow Sky"
Idris, Youssef. THE CHEAPEST NIGHT'S
      ENTERTAINMENT
Kundera, Milan. NOBODY WILL LAUGH
Lenz, Siegfried. THE LAUGHINGSTOCK
Mahfouz, Naguib. THE PASHA'S DAUGHTER
Mrozek, Slawomir. CHILDREN
Mrozek, Slawomir. ON A JOURNEY
Narayan, R. K. A HORSE AND TWO GOATS
Nexø, Martin Andersen. BIRDS OF PASSAGE
O'Connor, Frank. "My Oedipus Complex"
Thurber, James. "The Secret Life of Walter Mitty"
Twain, Mark. "The Celebrated Jumping Frog of
      Calaveras County"
Vega, Ana Lydia. CLOUD COVER CARIBBEAN
Welty, Eudora. "Why I Live at the P.O."

IRONY

Aidoo, Ama Ata. NO SWEETNESS HERE
Aymé, Marcel. THE MAN WHO WALKED
      THROUGH WALLS
Borowski, Tadeusz. THE MAN WITH THE
      PACKAGE
Camus, Albert. THE GUEST
Chekhov, Anton. THE BET
Daudet, Alphonse. THE LAST LESSON
Desai, Anita. A DEVOTED SON
Dhlomo, H. I. E. THE DAUGHTER
Feng Jicai. THE MAO BUTTON
Fuentes, Carlos. THE TWO ELENAS
Hamsun, Knut. THE CALL OF LIFE

Hildesheimer, Wolfgang. A WORLD ENDS
Kundera, Milan. NOBODY WILL LAUGH
Laxness, Haldor. LILY
Lenz, Siegfried. THE LAUGHINGSTOCK
Lo Liyong, Taban. THE OLD MAN OF USUMBURA
      AND HIS MISERY
Maupassant, Guy de. THE NECKLACE
Murakami Haruki. ON MEETING MY 100 PERCENT
      WOMAN ONE FINE APRIL MORNING
Sarang, Vilas. THE TERRORIST
Sartre, Jean-Paul. THE WALL
Solzhenitsyn, Alexander. MATRYONA'S HOME
Tolstoy, Leo. HOW MUCH LAND DOES A MAN
      NEED
Villiers de L'Isle-Adam. THE TORTURE BY HOPE

LOCAL COLOR

Achebe, Chinua. THE VOTER
Allende, Isabel. TWO WORDS
Amado, Jorge. HOW PORCIÚNCULA THE
      MULATTO GOT THE CORPSE OFF HIS BACK
Baykurt, Fakir. FRECKLES
Crane, Stephen. "The Bride Comes to Yellow Sky"
Djilas, Milovan. THE OLD MAN AND THE SONG
Djilas, Milovan. WAR
Idris, Youssef. THE CHEAPEST NIGHT'S
      ENTERTAINMENT
Izgü, Muzaffer. WANTED: A TOWN WITHOUT A
      CRAZY
Kariara, Jonathan. HER WARRIOR
Mahfouz, Naguib. THE CONJURER MADE OFF
      WITH THE DISH
Maupassant, Guy de. THE NECKLACE
Naipaul, V. S. B. WORDSWORTH
Naipaul, V. S. THE ENEMY
Narayan, R. K. A HORSE AND TWO GOATS
Nexø, Martin Andersen. BIRDS OF PASSAGE
Pontoppidan, Henrik. A FISHER NEST
Sarang, Vilas. THE TERRORIST
Sholokhov, Mikhail. THE COLT
Solzhenitsyn, Alexander. MATRYONA'S HOME
Steinbeck, John. "Flight"
Stuart, Jesse. "Split Cherry Tree"
Taylor, Apirana. THE CARVING
Twain, Mark. "The Celebrated Jumping Frog of
      Calaveras County"
Weller, Archie. GOING HOME

MONOLOGUE

Calvino, Italo. ALL AT ONE POINT
Pavese, Cesare. SUICIDES
Porter, Katherine Anne. "The Jilting of Granny Weatherall"
Rushdi, Rashad. ANGUISH
Svevo, Italo. IN MY INDOLENCE
Yáñez, Mirta. WE BLACKS ALL DRINK COFFEE

MYTHOLOGY/FOLKLORE/FABLE

Agnon, S. Y. A WHOLE LOAF
Asturias, Miguel. TATUANA'S TALE
Borges, Jorge Luis. THE GARDEN OF FORKING PATHS
Diop, Birago. THE WAGES OF GOOD
Hesse, Hermann. THE POET
Kafka, Franz. A HUNGER ARTIST
Kafka, Franz. THE METAMORPHOSIS
Melville, Herman. "Bartleby the Scrivener"
Mérimée, Prosper. THE VENUS OF ILLE
Mrozek, Slawomir. CHILDREN
Narayan, R. K. THE MIRROR
Taylor, Apirana. THE CARVING
Venezis, Elias. MYCENAE

NATURE AS LITERARY DEVICE

Aichinger, Ilse. THE BOUND MAN
Cumali, Necati. IN GOD'S PLAINS
Dinesen, Isak. THE SAILOR BOY'S TALE
Dinesen, Isak. SORROW-ACRE
Faulkner, William. "The Bear"
Huber, Heinz. THE NEW APARTMENT
Landolfi, Tommaso. PASTORAL
Lenz, Siegfried. THE LAUGHINGSTOCK
Moravia, Alberto. THE CHASE
Moravia, Alberto. THE FALL
Mphahlele, Es'kia. THE MASTER OF DOORNVLEI
O Yong-su. SEASIDE VILLAGE
Paz, Octavio. MY LIFE WITH THE WAVE
Pirandello, Luigi. CINCI
Sholokhov, Mikhail. THE COLT
Sholokhov, Mikhail. THE FATE OF A MAN
Sienkiewicz, Henryk. THE LIGHTHOUSE-KEEPER
Steinbeck, John. "The Red Pony"
Tamasi, Aron. FLASHES IN THE NIGHT

SATIRE

Aymé, Marcel. THE MAN WHO WALKED THROUGH WALLS
Feng Jicai. THE MAO BUTTON
Hildesheimer, Wolfgang. A WORLD ENDS
Huber, Heinz. THE NEW APARTMENT
Kundera, Milan. NOBODY WILL LAUGH
Lao She. GRANDMOTHER TAKES CHARGE
Lu Xun. DIARY OF A MADMAN
Mahfouz, Naguib. THE PASHA'S DAUGHTER
Mrozek, Slawomir. CHILDREN
Mrozek, Slawomir. ON A JOURNEY
P'u Sung-Ling. THE FIGHTING CRICKET
Ray, Satyajit. ASHAMANJA BABU'S DOG
Rushdi, Rashad. ANGUISH
Vega, Ana Lydia. CLOUD COVER CARIBBEAN
Welty, Eudora. "A Visit of Charity"

SLICE OF LIFE

Baykurt, Fakir. FRECKLES
Cicellis, Kay. BRIEF DIALOGUE
Cortázar, Julio. END OF THE GAME
Grace, Patricia. A WAY OF TALKING
Hemingway, Ernest. "The Killers"
Steinbeck, John. "The Chrysanthemums"
Theotokis, Konstantinos. VILLAGE LIFE
Tolstoy, Leo. HOW MUCH LAND DOES A MAN NEED
Updike, John. "A & P"
Weller, Archie. GOING HOME

SURPRISE ENDING

Bierce, Ambrose. "An Occurrence at Owl Creek Bridge"
Faulkner, William. "A Rose for Emily"
France, Anatole. THE PROCURATOR OF JUDEA
Fuentes, Carlos. THE TWO ELENAS
Hamsun, Knut. THE CALL OF LIFE
Henry, O. "The Cop and the Anthem"
Henry, O. "The Gift of the Magi"
Kundera, Milan. NOBODY WILL LAUGH
Maupassant, Guy de. THE NECKLACE
Ngugi, James. THE MARTYR
O'Flaherty, Liam. "The Sniper"
Paz, Octavio. MY LIFE WITH THE WAVE

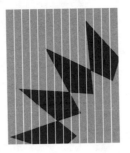

CROSS-REFERENCE

Finally, we have compiled a comprehensive index to the annotations in *Teaching the Short Story* to help teachers reference comparative material from virtually any starting point. Titles of works annotated in this text are capitalized wherever they appear.

A

"A & P" by John Updike

■ *see*

Chekhov, Anton. THE KISS
Rifaat, Alifa. AN INCIDENT IN THE GHOBASHI HOUSEHOLD

Abrahams, Peter. EPISODE IN MALAY CAMP

■ *compared with*

Camus, Albert. THE GUEST
Crane, Stephen. "The Open Boat"
Ellison, Ralph. *Invisible Man*
Stevenson, Robert Louis. "Markheim"
Thurber, James. "The Secret Life of Walter Mitty"

■ *also see*

Gordimer, Nadine. LITTLE WILLIE

Achebe, Chinua. GIRLS AT WAR

■ *compared with*

Head, Bessie. "The Collector of Treasures"

Achebe, Chinua. *Man of the People*

■ *see*

Achebe, Chinua. THE VOTER

Achebe, Chinua. *No Longer at Ease*

■ *see*

Achebe, Chinua. THE VOTER

Achebe, Chinua. *Things Fall Apart*

■ *see*

Grace, Patricia. A WAY OF TALKING
Head, Bessie. HEAVEN IS NOT CLOSED
Siddiqi, Shaukat. A MAN OF HONOR

Achebe, Chinua. VENGEFUL CREDITOR

■ *compared with*

Cather, Willa. "Paul's Case"
Ellison, Ralph. "Battle Royal"
Greene, Graham. "The Destructors"
Hawthorne, Nathaniel. *The Scarlet Letter*
Hawthorne, Nathaniel. "Young Goodman Brown"

■ *also see*

Gordimer, Nadine. LITTLE WILLIE
Kariara, Jonathan. HER WARRIOR
La Guma, Alex. BLANKETS

Achebe, Chinua. THE VOTER

■ *compared with*

Achebe, Chinua. *Man of the People*
Achebe, Chinua. *No Longer at Ease*
Ekwensi, Cyprian. *Jagua Nana*
Ibsen, Henrik. *An Enemy of the People*
Soyinka, Wole. *The Interpreter*
Twain, Mark. "The Man That Corrupted Hadleyburg"

Aeschylus. *Agamemnon*
- *see*
Venezis, Elias. MYCENAE

Aeschylus. *Prometheus Bound*
- *see*
Zola, Émile. THE INUNDATION

Aesop's Fables
- *see*
Diop, Birago. THE WAGES OF GOOD

THE AFRICAN GRANNIE by Cubena
- *compared with*
Wright, Richard. *Black Boy*

After the Fall by Arthur Miller
- *see*
Calvino, Italo. ALL AT ONE POINT
Moravia, Alberto. THE FALL

Against the Grain by J. K. Huysman
- *see*
Landolfi, Tommaso. PASTORAL

Agamemnon by Aeschylus
- *see*
Venezis, Elias. MYCENAE

Agee, James. *A Death in the Family*
- *see*
Björnson, Björnstjerne. THE FATHER
Venezis, Elias. MYCENAE

Agnon, S. Y. THE DOCUMENT
- *compared with*
Kafka, Franz. THE METAMORPHOSIS
Melville, Herman. "Bartleby the Scrivener"
Wolfe, Thomas. "For What Is Man?" from *You Can't Go Home Again*

Agnon, S. Y. A WHOLE LOAF
- *compared with*
Everyman
Ferre, Rosario. "The Youngest Doll"
Joyce, James. *Dubliners*
Kafka, Franz. A HUNGER ARTIST
MacLeish, Archibald. *J.B.*

Ahmad, Razia. PAPER IS MONEY
- *compared with*
"Hansel and Gretel"
Henry, O. "The Gift of the Magi"
"Jack and the Beanstalk"
Stella (film)
Stella Dallas (film)

Aichinger, Ilse. THE BOUND MAN
- *compared with*
Bacon, Francis. *Lying Figure* (painting)
Camus, Albert. *The Myth of Sisyphus*
Kafka, Franz. A HUNGER ARTIST
- *also see*
Kafka, Franz. A HUNGER ARTIST
Mann, Thomas. TRISTAN

Aidoo, Ama Ata. NO SWEETNESS HERE
- *compared with*
Selormey, Francis. *The Narrow Path*

Aiken, Conrad. "Silent Snow, Secret Snow"
- *see*
Lu Xun. DIARY OF A MADMAN
Mann, Thomas. TONIO KRÖGER

Akutagawa Ryūnosuke. IN A GROVE
- *compared with*
Narayan, R. K. THE MIRROR
Rose, Reginald. "Twelve Angry Men"

Albright, Ivan. *Into the World There Came a Soul Called Ida* (painting)
- *see*
Colette. THE LITTLE BOUILLOUX GIRL

Alexiou, Elli. THEY WERE ALL TO BE PITIED
- *compared with*
Cather, Willa. "A Wagner Matinee"
Faulkner, William. "Barn Burning"
Joyce, James. "Eveline"
Lawrence, D. H. "The Rocking Horse Winner"
Mason, Bobbie Ann. "Shiloh"
Olsen, Tillie. "I Stand Here Ironing"
Parker, Dorothy. "The Standard of Living"

Alice Adams by Booth Tarkington

■ *see*

Zola, Émile. NAÏS MICOULIN

ALL AT ONE POINT by Italo Calvino

■ *compared with*

Barth, John. "Night-Sea Journey"
Joyce, James. "Araby"
Miller, Arthur. *After the Fall*
Whitman, Walt. "Song of Myself"

Allende, Isabel. TWO WORDS

■ *compared with*

How the Garcia Girls Lost Their Accent (film)
Kafka, Franz. A HUNGER ARTIST
Like Water for Chocolate (film)

Aller-Retour by Marcel Aymé

■ *see*

Aymé, Marcel. THE MAN WHO WALKED
THROUGH WALLS

"Almos' a Man" by Richard Wright

■ *see*

Mahfouz, Naguib. THE CONJURER MADE OFF
WITH THE DISH
Villiers de L'Isle-Adam. THE DESIRE TO BE A MAN

Amado, Jorge. HOW PORCIÚNCULA THE MULAT-
TO GOT THE CORPSE OFF HIS BACK

■ *compared with*

Tutuola, Amos. *The Palm-Wine Drinkard*
Twain, Mark. "Baker's Blue-Jay Yarn"
Twain, Mark. "The Celebrated Jumping Frog of
Calaveras County"

Anderson, Sherwood. "Death in the Woods"

■ *see*

Flaubert, Gustave. A SIMPLE HEART
Venezis, Elias. MYCENAE

Anderson, Sherwood. "The Egg"

■ *see*

Maupassant, Guy de. THE NECKLACE

Anderson, Sherwood. "I'm a Fool"

■ *see*

Roufos, Rodis. THE CANDIDATE

Anderson, Sherwood. "I Want to Know Why"

■ *see*

Mann, Thomas. DISORDER AND EARLY SORROW
Moravia, Alberto. THE FALL

Anderson, Sherwood. *Winesburg, Ohio*

■ *see*

Idris, Youssef. THE CHEAPEST NIGHT'S
ENTERTAINMENT
Kawabata Yasunari. THE MOON ON THE WATER

Andreyev, Leonid. LAZARUS

■ *compared with*

Franklin, Benjamin. "The Ephemera"
Kafka, Franz. THE METAMORPHOSIS
Klaus, Annette Curtis. *Silver Kiss*
Melville, Herman. "Bartleby the Scrivener"
Shelley, Percy Bysshe. "Ozymandias"

Andric, Ivo. THE SCYTHE

■ *compared with*

Andric, Ivo. A SUMMER IN THE SOUTH
Maupassant, Guy de. "A Piece of String"
Sholokhov, Mikhail. THE COLT
Solzhenitsyn, Alexander. MATRYONA'S HOME
Solzhenitsyn, Alexander. ZAKHAR-THE-POUCH

■ *also see*

Andric, Ivo. A SUMMER IN THE SOUTH
Djilas, Milovan. THE OLD MAN AND THE SONG
Djilas, Milovan. WAR
Sienkiewicz, Henryk. THE LIGHTHOUSE-KEEPER
Solzhenitsyn, Alexander. MATRYONA'S HOME
Tamasi, Aron. FLASHES IN THE NIGHT

Andric, Ivo. A SUMMER IN THE SOUTH

■ *compared with*

Andric, Ivo. THE SCYTHE
DuMaurier, Daphne. "The Blue Lenses"
Hawthorne, Nathaniel. "The Artist of the
Beautiful"
James, Henry. *The Turn of the Screw*
Melville, Herman. "Bartleby the Scrivener"
Poe, Edgar Allan. "The Fall of the House of Usher"
Sholokhov, Mikhail. THE COLT
Sholokhov, Mikhail. THE FATE OF A MAN
Solzhenitsyn, Alexander. MATRYONA'S HOME
Stockton, Frank. "The Lady, or the Tiger"

Tamasi, Aron. FLASHES IN THE NIGHT

■ *also see*

Andric, Ivo. THE SCYTHE
Sienkiewicz, Henryk. THE LIGHTHOUSE-KEEPER
Tamasi, Aron. FLASHES IN THE NIGHT

ANGUISH by Rashad Rushdi

■ *compared with*

Barth, John. *Lost in the Funhouse*
Browning, Robert. "My Last Duchess"
Eliot, T. S. "The Love Song of J. Alfred Prufrock"

Animal Farm by George Orwell

■ *see*

Kafka, Franz. THE METAMORPHOSIS

Anna Karenina by Leo Tolstoy

■ *see*

Sand, George. THE MARQUISE
Tolstoy, Leo. THE DEATH OF IVÁN ILYICH

Annie John by Jamaica Kincaid

■ *see*

Yáñez, Mirta. WE BLACKS ALL DRINK COFFEE

ANOTHER EVENING AT THE CLUB by Alifa Rifaat

■ *compared with*

Faulkner, William. "A Rose for Emily"
Maupassant, Guy de. THE NECKLACE
Walker, Alice. *The Color Purple*

The Aphrodite at Cnidos by Praxiteles (painting)

■ *see*

Mérimée, Prosper. THE VENUS OF ILLE

Apollo and Phaethon myth

■ *see*

Lao She. GRANDMOTHER TAKES CHARGE
Lim Beng Hap. POONEK

The Apparition by Gustave Moreau (painting)

■ *see*

Hesse, Hermann. THE POET

Apuleius. *The Golden Ass*

■ *see*

Kafka, Franz. THE METAMORPHOSIS

Arabian Nights

■ *see*

Balzac, Honoré de. LA GRANDE BRETÊCHE

"Araby" by James Joyce

■ *see*

Baykurt, Fakir. FRECKLES
Calvino, Italo. ALL AT ONE POINT
Chekhov, Anton. THE KISS
Desai, Anita. GAMES AT TWILIGHT
Dib, Mohammed. NAEMA—WHEREABOUTS
   UNKNOWN
Djilas, Milovan. THE OLD MAN AND THE SONG
Kapadia, Kundanika. PAPER BOAT
Mahfouz, Naguib. THE CONJURER MADE OFF
   WITH THE DISH
Mann, Thomas. TONIO KRÖGER
Moravia, Alberto. THE FALL
Naipaul, V. S. B. WORDSWORTH

Arnold, Matthew. "The Buried Life"

■ *see*

Villiers de L'Isle-Adam. THE DESIRE TO BE A
   MAN

"The Artist of the Beautiful" by Nathaniel Hawthorne

■ *see*

Andric, Ivo. A SUMMER IN THE SOUTH

ASHAMANJA BABU'S DOG by Satyajit Ray

■ *compared with*

Dickens, Charles. *A Christmas Carol*
King Midas folktale
Lawrence, D. H. "The Rocking Horse Winner"
Lim, Catherine. PAPER

As I Lay Dying by William Faulkner

■ *see*

Cortázar, Julio. NIGHT FACE UP

AS THE NIGHT THE DAY by Abioseth Nicol

■ *compared with*

Dostoevski, Fyodor. *Crime and Punishment*
Ellison, Ralph. "Battle Royal"
Golding, William. *Lord of the Flies*
Hawthorne, Nathaniel. *The Scarlet Letter*
Jackson, Shirley. "The Lottery"

B

Tolstoy, Leo. THE DEATH OF IVÁN ILYICH

■ *also see*

Balzac, Honoré de. LA GRANDE BRETÊCHE

Balzac, Honoré de. *Cousin Bette*

■ *see*

Balzac, Honoré de. LA GRANDE BRETÊCHE

Balzac, Honoré de. LA GRANDE BRETÊCHE

■ *compared with*

Arabian Nights
Balzac, Honoré de. THE ATHEIST'S MASS
Balzac, Honoré de. *Cousin Bette*
Balzac, Honoré de. *Père Goriot*
Boccaccio, Giovanni. *Decameron*
Chaucer, Geoffrey. *Canterbury Tales*
Conrad, Joseph. *Heart of Darkness*
James, Henry. *The Turn of the Screw*
Melville, Herman. *Moby Dick*
Poe, Edgar Allan. "The Cask of Amontillado"
Poe, Edgar Allan. "The Fall of the House of Usher"

Balzac, Honoré de. *Père Goriot*

■ *see*

Balzac, Honoré de. LA GRANDE BRETÊCHE

Bambara, Toni Cade. "The Lesson"

■ *see*

Daudet, Alphonse. THE LAST LESSON

"Barbados" by Paul Marshall

■ *see*

Ayyoub, Dhu'l Nun. FROM BEHIND THE VEIL

"Barn Burning" by William Faulkner

■ *see*

Alexiou, Elli. THEY WERE ALL TO BE PITIED
Mahfouz, Naguib. THE CONJURER MADE OFF WITH THE DISH
Rifaat, Alifa. AN INCIDENT IN THE GHOBASHI HOUSEHOLD

Barrie, J. M. *Peter Pan*

■ *see*

Mahfouz, Naguib. THE CONJURER MADE OFF WITH THE DISH

Barth, John. *Lost in the Funhouse*

■ *see*

Rushdi, Rashad. ANGUISH

Barth, John. "Night-Sea Journey"

■ *see*

Calvino, Italo. ALL AT ONE POINT

"Bartleby the Scrivener" by Herman Melville

■ *see*

Agnon, S. Y. THE DOCUMENT
Andreyev, Leonid. LAZARUS
Andric, Ivo. A SUMMER IN THE SOUTH
Dostoevski, Fyodor. THE HONEST THIEF
Izgü, Muzaffer. WANTED: A TOWN WITHOUT A CRAZY
La Guma, Alex. BLANKETS
Mann, Thomas. TONIO KRÖGER
Mann, Thomas. TRISTAN
Pavese, Cesare. SUICIDES
Sholokhov, Mikhail. THE FATE OF A MAN

"Battle Royal" by Ralph Ellison

■ *see*

Achebe, Chinua. VENGEFUL CREDITOR
Dove-Danquah, Mabel. THE TORN VEIL
Gordimer, Nadine. LITTLE WILLIE
Nicol, Abioseth. AS THE NIGHT THE DAY

Baykurt, Fakir. FRECKLES

■ *compared with*

Gogol, Nikolai. "Taras Bulba"
Joyce, James. "Araby"

"The Bear" by William Faulkner

■ *see*

Sholokhov, Mikhail. THE COLT
Turgenev, Ivan. YERMOLAY AND THE MILLER'S WIFE

"The Beast in the Jungle" by Henry James

■ *see*

Moravia, Alberto. THE CHASE

Benét, Stephen Vincent. "The Blood of the Martyrs"

■ *see*

Mishima Yukio. PATRIOTISM

Benét, Stephen Vincent. "The Devil and Daniel Webster"

■ *see*

Dove-Danquah, Mabel. THE TORN VEIL
Solzhenitsyn, Alexander. ZAKHAR-THE-POUCH
Tolstoy, Leo. HOW MUCH LAND DOES A MAN NEED

Benét, Stephen Vincent. "A Tooth for Paul Revere"

■ *see*

Solzhenitsyn, Alexander. ZAKHAR-THE-POUCH

Benson, Sally. "The Overcoat"

■ *see*

Siddiqi, Shaukat. A MAN OF HONOR

THE BET by Anton Chekhov

■ *compared with*

Norris, Frank. *McTeague*
Tolstoy, Leo. HOW MUCH LAND DOES A MAN NEED
Wall Street (film)

THE BEWITCHING OF THE AGA by Alexandros Papadiamantis

■ *compared with*

Buck, Pearl. "The Old Demon"
Chopin, Kate. "The Story of an Hour"
Gilman, Charlotte Perkins. "The Yellow Wallpaper"
Munro, H. H. "The Open Window"
Thurber, James. "The Secret Life of Walter Mitty"
Wharton, Edith. "Roman Fever"

The Bible

■ *see*

Tolstoy, Leo. HOW MUCH LAND DOES A MAN NEED
Zola, Émile. THE INUNDATION

Bierce, Ambrose. "The Coup de Grace"

■ *see*

Sholokhov, Mikhail. THE COLT

Bierce, Ambrose. "An Occurrence at Owl Creek Bridge"

■ *see*

Heym, Georg. THE AUTOPSY
Meleagrou, Hebe. MONUMENT

Sholokhov, Mikhail. THE COLT
Yizhar, S. HABAKUK

The Big Glass by Marcel Duchamps (painting)

■ *see*

Kafka, Franz. IN THE PENAL COLONY

"Big Two-Hearted River" by Ernest Hemingway

■ *see*

Turgenev, Ivan. YERMOLAY AND THE MILLER'S WIFE

"Billy Budd" by Herman Melville

■ *see*

La Guma, Alex. BLANKETS

BIRDS OF PASSAGE by Martin Andersen Nexø

■ *compared with*

Bontemps, Arna. "A Summer Tragedy"

Björnson, Björnstjerne. THE FATHER

■ *compared with*

Agee, James. *A Death in the Family*
Djilas, Milovan. WAR
Guest, Judith. *Ordinary People*
Gunther, John. *Death Be Not Proud*
Pirandello, Luigi. WAR

Black Boy by Richard Wright

■ *see*

Cubena. THE AFRICAN GRANNIE
Kariara, Jonathan. HER WARRIOR
La Guma, Alex. BLANKETS

"The Black Cat" by Edgar Allan Poe

■ *see*

Dostoevski, Fyodor. THE DREAM OF A RIDICULOUS MAN

BLANKETS by Alex La Guma

■ *compared with*

Achebe, Chinua. VENGEFUL CREDITOR
Melville, Herman. "Bartleby the Scrivener"
Melville, Herman. "Billy Budd"
Porter, Katherine Anne. "The Jilting of Granny Weatherall"
Salinger, J. D. "For Esmé—with Love and Squalor"
Wright, Richard. *Black Boy*

227

Buzzati, Dino. THE SLAYING OF THE DRAGON
- ■ *compared with*

Crane, Stephen. "The Monster"
Jackson, Shirley. "The Lottery"
Jeffers, Robinson. "Original Sin"
Kafka, Franz. IN THE PENAL COLONY

B. WORDSWORTH by V. S. Naipaul
- ■ *compared with*

Cisneros, Sandra. "Sally"
Joyce, James. "Araby"
Wordsworth's short poems

C

Cage, John. *4'33* (piano composition)
- ■ *see*

Böll, Heinrich. MURKE'S COLLECTED SILENCES

THE CALL OF LIFE by Knut Hamsun
- ■ *compared with*

Chopin, Kate. "The Story of an Hour"

Calvino, Italo. ALL AT ONE POINT
- ■ *compared with*

Barth, John. "Night-Sea Journey"
Joyce, James. "Araby"
Miller, Arthur. *After the Fall*
Whitman, Walt. "Song of Myself"

Camus, Albert. THE GUEST
- ■ *compared with*

Camus, Albert. *The Stranger*
Kafka, Franz. A HUNGER ARTIST
Roth, Philip. "The Defender of the Faith"
Sartre, Jean-Paul. THE WALL
- ■ *also see*

Abrahams, Peter. EPISODE IN MALAY CAMP
Sartre, Jean-Paul. THE WALL
Yehoshua, Abraham B. FACING THE FOREST

Camus, Albert. *The Myth of Sisyphus*
- ■ *see*

Aichinger, Ilse. THE BOUND MAN
Tolstoy, Leo. THE DEATH OF IVÁN ILYICH

Camus, Albert. *The Stranger*
- ■ *see*

Camus, Albert. THE GUEST
Dostoevski, Fyodor. THE DREAM OF A
  RIDICULOUS MAN
Pirandello, Luigi. CINCI

THE CANDIDATE by Roufos Rodis
- ■ *compared with*

Anderson, Sherwood. "I'm a Fool"
Steinbeck, John. "The Chrysanthemums"

Candide by Voltaire
- ■ *see*

Zola, Émile. THE INUNDATION

Canterbury Tales by Geoffrey Chaucer
- ■ *see*

Balzac, Honoré de. LA GRANDE BRETÊCHE
Lo Liyong, Taban. THE OLD MAN OF USUMBURA
  AND HIS MISERY

Čapek, Karel. *War with the Newts*
- ■ *see*

Kafka, Franz. THE METAMORPHOSIS

Capote, Truman. "A Christmas Memory"
- ■ *see*

Nakos, Lilika. THE BROKEN DOLL

THE CARVING by Apirana Taylor

■ *compared with*

Gordimer, Nadine. "Home"
Thiong'o, Ngũgĩ wa. *Weep Not Child*

"The Cask of Amontillado" by Edgar Allan Poe

■ *see*

Balzac, Honoré de. LA GRANDE BRETÊCHE
Ngugi, James. THE MARTYR
Theotokis, Konstantinos. VILLAGE LIFE
Tolstoy, Leo. THE DEATH OF IVÁN ILYICH

The Castle by Franz Kafka

■ *see*

Kafka, Franz. THE JUDGMENT

"The Catbird Seat" by James Thurber

■ *see*

Theotokis, Konstantinos. VILLAGE LIFE

Catch-22 by Joseph Heller

■ *see*

Mahfouz, Naguib. THE PASHA'S DAUGHTER

A Catcher in the Rye by J. D. Salinger

■ *see*

Kiwon So. THE HEIR
Yáñez, Mirta. WE BLACKS ALL DRINK COFFEE
Zola, Émile. THE INUNDATION

Cather, Willa. *My Ántonia*

■ *see*

Zola, Émile. NAÏS MICOULIN

Cather, Willa. "Paul's Case"

■ *see*

Achebe, Chinua. VENGEFUL CREDITOR
Gordimer, Nadine. LITTLE WILLIE
Haris, Petros. LIGHTS ON THE SEA
Kafka, Franz. THE JUDGMENT
Kariara, Jonathan. HER WARRIOR
Lu Xun. DIARY OF A MADMAN
Ngugi, James. THE MARTYR

Cather, Willa. "A Wagner Matinee"

■ *see*

Alexiou, Elli. THEY WERE ALL TO BE PITIED
Santos, Bienvenido N. THE DAY THE DANCERS CAME

"The Celebrated Jumping Frog of Calaveras County" by Mark Twain

■ *see*

Amado, Jorge. HOW PORCIÚNCULA THE MULATTO GOT THE CORPSE OFF HIS BACK
Phiên Võ. THE KEY

Cephalus and Procris myth (from *The Metamorphoses* by Ovid)

■ *see*

Tanizaki Junichiro. THE THIEF

THE CHASE by Alberto Moravia

■ *compared with*

Eliot, T. S. "The Love Song of J. Alfred Prufrock"
Fitzgerald, F. Scott. *The Great Gatsby*
Hemingway, Ernest. "The Short Happy Life of Francis Macomber"
James, Henry. "The Beast in the Jungle"
Lawrence, D. H. "The Horse Dealer's Daughter"

Chaucer, Geoffrey. *Canterbury Tales*

■ *see*

Balzac, Honoré de. LA GRANDE BRETÊCHE
Lo Liyong, Taban. THE OLD MAN OF USUMBURA AND HIS MISERY

THE CHEAPEST NIGHT'S ENTERTAINMENT by Youssef Idris

■ *compared with*

Anderson, Sherwood. *Winesburg, Ohio*
Freemen, Mary Wilkins. "A Village Singer"
Garland, Hamlin. "Mrs. Ripley's Trip"
Hurston, Zora Neale. *The Eatonville Anthology*
Jewett, Sarah Orne. "The Town Poor"
O'Connor, Flannery. "The Life You Save May Be Your Own"
Singer, Isaac B. "Gimpel the Fool"
Welty, Eudora. "Petrified Man"
Welty, Eudora. "Why I Live at the P.O."

Chekhov, Anton. THE BET
- *compared with*

Norris, Frank. *McTeague*
Tolstoy, Leo. HOW MUCH LAND DOES A MAN NEED
Wall Street (film)

Chekhov, Anton. *The Cherry Orchard*
- *see*

Turgenev, Ivan. YERMOLAY AND THE MILLER'S WIFE

Chekhov, Anton. THE DARLING
- *compared with*

Flaubert, Gustave. *Madame Bovary*
García Márquez, Gabriel. *Love in the Time of Cholera*

Chekhov, Anton. "A Dreary Story"
- *see*

Tolstoy, Leo. THE DEATH OF IVÁN ILYICH

Chekhov, Anton. THE KISS
- *compared with*

Joyce, James. "Araby"
Updike, John. "A & P"
- *also see*

Hesse, Hermann. THE POET

The Cherry Orchard by Anton Chekhov
- *see*

Turgenev, Ivan. YERMOLAY AND THE MILLER'S WIFE

CHILDREN by Slawomir Mrozek
- *compared with*

Mrozek, Slawomir. ON A JOURNEY
Sienkiewicz, Henryk. YANKO THE MUSICIAN
- *also see*

Sienkiewicz, Henryk. YANKO THE MUSICIAN
Solzhenitsyn, Alexander. MATRYONA'S HOME
Solzhenitsyn, Alexander. THE RIGHT HAND

CHILDREN OF THE SEA by Edwidge Danticat
- *compared with*

Frank, Anne. *The Diary of Anne Frank*

Gaines, Ernest. *A Lesson Before Dying*
Hayden, Robert. "Middle Passage"
Keyes, Daniel. *Flowers for Algernon*
Walker, Alice. *The Color Purple*

Chopin, Kate. "The Story of an Hour"
- *see*

Hamsun, Knut. THE CALL OF LIFE
Papadiamantis, Alexandros. THE BEWITCHING OF THE AGA

Christ Before Pilate by Tintoretto (painting)
- *see*

France, Anatole. THE PROCURATOR OF JUDEA

A Christmas Carol by Charles Dickens
- *see*

Ekwensi, Cyprian. THE GREAT BEYOND
Ray, Satyajit. ASHAMANJA BABU'S DOG
Verga, Giovanni. PROPERTY

"Christmas Every Day" by Heinrich Böll
- *see*

Mann, Thomas. DISORDER AND EARLY SORROW

"A Christmas Memory" by Truman Capote
- *see*

Nakos, Lilika. THE BROKEN DOLL

"The Chrysanthemums" by John Steinbeck
- *see*

Roufos, Rodis. THE CANDIDATE
Tanizaki Junichiro. TATTOO

Cicellis, Kay. BRIEF DIALOGUE
- *compared with*

Hemingway, Ernest. "A Clean, Well-Lighted Place"
Hemingway, Ernest. "The Killers"

CINCI by Luigi Pirandello
- *compared with*

Camus, Albert. *The Stranger*
Crane, Stephen. "The Upturned Face"
Hemingway, Ernest. "The Short Happy Life of Francis Macomber"
Mishima Yukio. PATRIOTISM
Wright, Richard. *Native Son*

Condé, Maryse. THREE WOMEN IN MANHATTAN
- *compared with*

Cisneros, Sandra. *House on Mango Street*
Cisneros, Sandra. "Woman Hollering Creek"
Olsen, Tillie. "I Stand Here Ironing"
Silko, Leslie Marmon. "Lullaby"
Yamamoto, Hisaye. "Seventeen Syllables"

Confessions of Felix Krull: Confidence Man by Thomas Mann
- *see*

Sand, George. THE MARQUISE

THE CONJURER MADE OFF WITH THE DISH by Naguib Mahfouz
- *compared with*

Barrie, J. M. *Peter Pan*
Conrad, Joseph. "Youth"
Faulkner, William. "Barn Burning"
"Jack and the Beanstalk"
Joyce, James. "Araby"
Wright, Richard. "Almos' a Man"

Connell, Richard. "The Most Dangerous Game"
- *see*

Pontoppidan, Henrik. A FISHER NEST
Venezis, Elias. MYCENAE

Conrad, Joseph. *Heart of Darkness*
- *see*

Balzac, Honoré de. THE ATHEIST'S MASS
Balzac, Honoré de. LA GRANDE BRETÊCHE
Cortázar, Julio. NIGHT FACE UP
Kariara, Jonathan. HER WARRIOR
Sholokhov, Mikhail. THE FATE OF A MAN
Yehoshua, Abraham B. FACING THE FOREST

Conrad, Joseph. "The Secret Sharer"
- *see*

Kawabata Yasunari. THE MOON ON THE WATER

Conrad, Joseph. "Youth"
- *see*

Dostoevski, Fyodor. WHITE NIGHTS
Mahfouz, Naguib. THE CONJURER MADE OFF WITH THE DISH

Consuelo by George Sand
- *see*

Sand, George. THE MARQUISE

A Cool Million by Nathaniel West
- *see*

Zola, Émile. THE INUNDATION

Coover, Robert. "A Pedestrian Accident"
- *see*

Lu Xun. DIARY OF A MADMAN

Cortázar, Julio. END OF THE GAME
- *compared with*
Blow-up (film)
Rostand, Edmund. *Cyrano de Bergerac*

Cortázar, Julio. *Manual for Manuel*
- *see*

Valenzuela, Luisa. I'M YOUR HORSE IN THE NIGHT

Cortázar, Julio. NIGHT FACE UP
- *compared with*

Conrad, Joseph. *Heart of Darkness*
Faulkner, William. *As I Lay Dying*
Jackson, Shirley. "The Lottery"
Star Wars (film)
Yu-Lan Fung. *History of Chinese Philosophy*
- *also see*

Yizhar, S. HABAKUK

Countess Julie by August Strindberg
- *see*

Zola, Émile. NAÏS MICOULIN

"The Coup de Grace" by Ambrose Bierce
- *see*

Sholokhov, Mikhail. THE COLT

Cousin Bette by Honoré de Balzac
- *see*

Balzac, Honoré de. LA GRANDE BRETÊCHE

Crane, Stephen. "The Bride Comes to Yellow Sky"
- *see*

Phiên Võ. THE KEY

Crane, Stephen. "An Episode of War"

■ *see*

Dib, Mohammed. NAEMA—WHEREABOUTS UNKNOWN

Crane, Stephen. *Maggie: A Girl of the Streets*

■ *see*

Zola, Émile. NAÏS MICOULIN

Crane, Stephen. "The Monster"

■ *see*

Buzzati, Dino. THE SLAYING OF THE DRAGON

Crane, Stephen. "The Open Boat"

■ *see*

Abrahams, Peter. EPISODE IN MALAY CAMP
Nakos, Lilika. HELENITSA

Crane, Stephen. "The Upturned Face"

■ *see*

Pirandello, Luigi. CINCI

Crime and Punishment by Fyodor Dostoevski

■ *see*

Dostoevski, Fyodor. THE DREAM OF A RIDICULOUS MAN
Dostoevski, Fyodor. THE HONEST THIEF

Nicol, Abioseth. AS THE NIGHT THE DAY
Villiers de L'Isle-Adam. THE DESIRE TO BE A MAN
Zola, Émile. THE INUNDATION

Cubena. THE AFRICAN GRANNIE

■ *compared with*

Wright, Richard. *Black Boy*

Cumali, Necati. IN GOD'S PLAINS

■ *compared with*

Shelley, Mary. *Frankenstein*
Sholokhov, Mikhail. THE COLT
Sienkiewicz, Henryk. YANKO THE MUSICIAN
Tamasi, Aron. FLASHES IN THE NIGHT

Cupid, Venus, and Vulcan by Tintoretto (painting)

■ *see*

Mérimée, Prosper. THE VENUS OF ILLE

"A Curtain of Green" by Eudora Welty

■ *see*

Svevo, Italo. IN MY INDOLENCE

Cyrano de Bergerac by Edmund Rostand

■ *see*

Cortázar, Julio. THE END OF THE GAME

D

Daisy Miller by Henry James

■ *see*

Balzac, Honoré de. THE ATHEIST'S MASS

Dances with Wolves (film)

■ *see*

Yehoshua, Abraham B. FACING THE FOREST

Dante. *The Divine Comedy*

■ *see*

Dove-Danquah, Mabel. THE TORN VEIL

Danticat, Edwidge. CHILDREN OF THE SEA

■ *compared with*

Frank, Anne. *The Diary of Anne Frank*
Gaines, Ernest. *A Lesson Before Dying*
Hayden, Robert. "Middle Passage"
Keyes, Daniel. *Flowers for Algernon*
Walker, Alice. *The Color Purple*

Daphne and Apollo myth (from *The Metamorphoses* by Ovid)

■ *see*

Asturias, Miguel. TATUANA'S TALE
Murakami Haruki. ON MEETING MY 100 PERCENT WOMAN ONE FINE APRIL MORNING

THE DARLING by Anton Chekhov
- *compared with*

Flaubert, Gustave. *Madame Bovary*
García Márquez, Gabriel. *Love in the Time of Cholera*

Daudet, Alphonse. THE LAST LESSON
- *compared with*

Bambara, Toni Cade. "The Lesson"
Daudet, Alphonse. "The Siege of Berlin"
James, Henry. "The Pupil"
- *also see*

Narayan, R. K. FATHER'S HELP

Daudet, Alphonse. "The Siege of Berlin"
- *see*

Daudet, Alphonse. THE LAST LESSON

THE DAUGHTER by H. I. E. Dhlomo
- *compared with*

Sophocles. *Oedipus Rex*

THE DAY THE DANCERS CAME by Bienvenido N. Santos
- *compared with*

Cather, Willa. "A Wagner Matinee"
Hemingway, Ernest. "A Clean, Well-Lighted Place"
Kafka, Franz. THE METAMORPHOSIS
- *also see*

Murakami Haruki. ON MEETING MY 100 PER-CENT WOMAN ONE FINE APRIL MORNING

"The Dead" by James Joyce
- *see*

Heym, Georg. THE AUTOPSY
Pirandello, Luigi. WAR
Svevo, Italo. IN MY INDOLENCE

"Death and the Compass" by Jorge Luis Borges
- *see*

Borges, Jorge Luis. THE GARDEN OF FORKING PATHS

Death Be Not Proud by John Gunther
- *see*

Björnson, Björnstjerne. THE FATHER

A Death in the Family by James Agee
- *see*

Björnson, Björnstjerne. THE FATHER
Venezis, Elias. MYCENAE

"Death in the Woods" by Sherwood Anderson
- *see*

Flaubert, Gustave. A SIMPLE HEART
Venezis, Elias. MYCENAE

Death in Venice by Thomas Mann
- *see*

Mann, Thomas. TRISTAN

THE DEATH OF IVÁN ILYICH by Leo Tolstoy
- *compared with*

Böll, Heinrich. MURKE'S COLLECTED SILENCES
Camus, Albert. *The Myth of Sisyphus*
Chekhov, Anton. "A Dreary Story"
Eliot, T. S. "The Love Song of J. Alfred Prufrock"
Poe, Edgar Allan. "The Cask of Amontillado"
Sartre, Jean-Paul. *No Exit*
Tolstoy, Leo. *Anna Karenina*
Tolstoy, Leo. *Family Business*
Tolstoy, Leo. *Master and Man*
- *also see*

Balzac, Honoré de. THE ATHEIST'S MASS

"Death of the Hired Man" by Robert Frost
- *see*

Flaubert, Gustave. A SIMPLE HEART

Death Without Burial by Jean-Paul Sartre
- *see*

Sartre, Jean-Paul. THE WALL

Decameron by Giovanni Boccaccio
- *see*

Balzac, Honoré de. LA GRANDE BRETÊCHE

"The Defender of the Faith" by Philip Roth
- *see*

Camus, Albert. THE GUEST

Delvaux, Paul. *The Sleeping City* (painting)
- *see*

Landolfi, Tommaso. PASTORAL

Delvaux, Paul. *Venus Asleep* (painting)

- *see*

Hildesheimer, Wolfgang. A WORLD ENDS

Desai, Anita. A DEVOTED SON

- *compared with*

Lao She. GRANDMOTHER TAKES CHARGE
Surangkhanang, K. THE GRANDMOTHER

- *also see*

Kawabata Yasunari. THE JAY

Desai, Anita. GAMES AT TWILIGHT

- *compared with*

Joyce, James. "Araby"
Kafka, Franz. THE METAMORPHOSIS
Shakespeare, William. *Romeo and Juliet*

THE DESIRE TO BE A MAN by Villiers de L'Isle-Adam

- *compared with*

Arnold, Matthew. "The Buried Life"
Dostoevski, Fyodor. *Crime and Punishment*
Parmigianino. *Self-Portrait* (painting)
Wedekind, Frank. *The Tenor*
Wilde, Oscar. *The Picture of Dorian Gray*
Wright, Richard. "Almos' a Man"

"The Destructors" by Graham Greene

- *see*

Achebe, Chinua. VENGEFUL CREDITOR
Böll, Heinrich. MURKE'S COLLECTED SILENCES
Huber, Heinz. THE NEW APARTMENT
Venezis, Elias. MYCENAE

"The Devil and Daniel Webster" by Stephen Vincent Benét

- *see*

Dove-Danquah, Mabel. THE TORN VEIL
Solzhenitsyn, Alexander. ZAKHAR-THE-POUCH
Tolstoy, Leo. HOW MUCH LAND DOES A MAN NEED

"The Devil and Tom Walker" by Washington Irving

- *see*

Tolstoy, Leo. HOW MUCH LAND DOES A MAN NEED

A DEVOTED SON by Anita Desai

- *compared with*

Lao She. GRANDMOTHER TAKES CHARGE
Surangkhanang, K. THE GRANDMOTHER

- *also see*

Kawabata Yasunari. THE JAY

Dhlomo, H. I. E. THE DAUGHTER

- *compared with*

Sophocles. *Oedipus Rex*

"The Diamond Lens" by Fitz-James O'Brien

- *see*

Dostoevski, Fyodor. WHITE NIGHTS

"Diary of a Madman" by Nikolai Gogol

- *see*

Tanizaki Junichiro. THE THIEF

DIARY OF A MADMAN by Lu Xun

- *compared with*

Aiken, Conrad. "Silent Snow, Secret Snow"
Baldwin, James. "Previous Condition"
Cather, Willa. "Paul's Case"
Coover, Robert. "A Pedestrian Accident"

- *also see*

Tanizaki Junichiro. THE THIEF

The Diary of Anne Frank by Anne Frank

- *see*

Danticat, Edwidge. CHILDREN OF THE SEA

Dib, Mohammed. NAEMA—WHEREABOUTS UNKNOWN

- *compared with*

Crane, Stephen. "An Episode of War"
Dos Passos, John. *USA*
Joyce, James. "Araby"
Lessing, Doris. "Through the Tunnel"
Steinbeck, John. *The Grapes of Wrath*
Steinbeck, John. *In Dubious Battle*

Dickens, Charles. *A Christmas Carol*

- *see*

Ekwensi, Cyprian. THE GREAT BEYOND
Ray, Satyajit. ASHAMANJA BABU'S DOG
Verga, Giovanni. PROPERTY

Dickens, Charles. *A Tale of Two Cities*

- *see*

Fuentes, Carlos. THE TWO ELENAS

Dickinson, Emily. "There's a certain slant of light"

- *see*

Pirandello, Luigi. WAR

Dinesen, Isak. THE SAILOR BOY'S TALE

- *compared with*

Coleridge, Samuel Taylor. "The Rime of the Ancient Mariner"
Lessing, Doris. "A Sunrise on the Veld"
Orwell, George. "Shooting an Elephant"

Dinesen, Isak. SORROW-ACRE

- *compared with*

Gordimer, Nadine. "The Train from Rhodesia"
Sholokhov, Mikhail. THE COLT
Tamasi, Aron. FLASHES IN THE NIGHT

Diop, Birago. THE WAGES OF GOOD

- *compared with*

Aesop's fables
Fontaine's fables
Kafka's parables

DISORDER AND EARLY SORROW by Thomas Mann

- *compared with*

Anderson, Sherwood. "I Want to Know Why"
Böll, Heinrich. "Christmas Every Day"
Picasso, Pablo. *Bust of a Woman* (painting)
Updike, John. "Flight"

- *also see*

Huber, Heinz. THE NEW APARTMENT
Megged, Aharon. THE NAME

The Divine Comedy by Dante

- *see*

Dove-Danquah, Mabel. THE TORN VEIL

Djilas, Milovan. THE OLD MAN AND THE SONG

- *compared with*

Andric, Ivo. THE SCYTHE
Djilas, Milovan. WAR
Hemingway, Ernest. "The Killers"
Joyce, James. "Araby"
Steinbeck, John. "The Leader of the People"

- *also see*

Solzhenitsyn, Alexander. MATRYONA'S HOME

Djilas, Milovan. WAR

- *compared with*

Andric, Ivo. THE SCYTHE
Hemingway, Ernest. "Old Man at the Bridge"
Sholokhov, Mikhail. THE COLT
Sholokhov, Mikhail. THE FATE OF A MAN
Sienkiewicz, Henryk. YANKO THE MUSICIAN
Solzhenitsyn, Alexander. MATRYONA'S HOME
Solzhenitsyn, Alexander. THE RIGHT HAND

- *also see*

Björnson, Björnstjerne. THE FATHER
Djilas, Milovan. THE OLD MAN AND THE SONG
Sholokhov, Mikhail. THE COLT
Solzhenitsyn, Alexander. MATRYONA'S HOME
Solzhenitsyn, Alexander. THE RIGHT HAND

THE DOCUMENT by S. Y. Agnon

- *compared with*

Kafka, Franz. THE METAMORPHOSIS
Melville, Herman. "Bartleby the Scrivener"
Wolfe, Thomas. *You Can't Go Home Again*

"The Dog That Bit People" by James Thurber

- *see*

Turgenev, Ivan. YERMOLAY AND THE MILLER'S WIFE

A Doll's House by Henrik Ibsen

- *see*

Colette. THE PHOTOGRAPHER'S MISSUS

Don Giovanni by Wolfgang Amadeus Mozart (opera)

- *see*

Dove-Danquah, Mabel. THE TORN VEIL
Mérimée, Prosper. THE VENUS OF ILLE

Don Juan by Molière

- *see*

Mérimée, Prosper. THE VENUS OF ILLE

Dos Passos, John. *USA*

- *see*

Dib, Mohammed. NAEMA—WHEREABOUTS UNKNOWN

Dr. Faustus by Christopher Marlowe

■ *see*

Dove-Danquah, Mabel. THE TORN VEIL
Tolstoy, Leo. HOW MUCH LAND DOES A MAN
    NEED

Dubliners by James Joyce

■ *see*

Agnon, S. Y. A WHOLE LOAF

Duchamps, Marcel. *The Big Glass* (painting)

■ *see*

Kafka, Franz. IN THE PENAL COLONY

"The Duel" by Guy de Maupassant

■ *see*

Maupassant, Guy de. THE NECKLACE

DuMaurier, Daphne. "The Blue Lenses"

■ *see*

Andric, Ivo. A SUMMER IN THE SOUTH

Durrenmatt, Friedrich. "The Tunnel"

■ *see*

Sartre, Jean-Paul. THE WALL

E

The Eatonville Anthology by Zora Neale Hurston

■ *see*

Idris, Youssef. THE CHEAPEST NIGHT'S
    ENTERTAINMENT

Ed-Din, Abu Bakr Siraj. *The Book of Certainty*

■ *see*

Borges, Jorge Luis. THE GARDEN OF FORKING
    PATHS

"The Egg" by Sherwood Anderson

■ *see*

Maupassant, Guy de. THE NECKLACE

Ekwensi, Cyprian. THE GREAT BEYOND

■ *compared with*

Dickens, Charles. *A Christmas Carol*
Dove-Danquah, Mable. THE TORN VEIL
Faulkner, William. "A Rose for Emily"
Hawthorne, Nathaniel. *The Scarlet Letter*
Irving, Washington. "The Legend of Sleepy Hollow"
Stevenson, Robert Louis. "Markheim"

Ekwensi, Cyprian. *Jagua Nana*

■ *see*

Achebe, Chinua. THE VOTER

Eliot, T. S. "The Hollow Men"

■ *see*

Yehoshua, Abraham B. FACING THE FOREST

Eliot, T. S. "The Love Song of J. Alfred Prufrock"

■ *see*

Mann, Thomas. TRISTAN
Moravia, Alberto. THE CHASE
Rushdi, Rashad. ANGUISH
Tolstoy, Leo. THE DEATH OF IVÁN ILYICH

Ellison, Ralph. "Battle Royal"

■ *see*

Achebe, Chinua. VENGEFUL CREDITOR
Dove-Danquah, Mabel. THE TORN VEIL
Gordimer, Nadine. LITTLE WILLIE
Nicol, Abioseth. AS THE NIGHT THE DAY

Ellison, Ralph. *Invisible Man*

■ *see*

Abrahams, Peter. EPISODE IN MALAY CAMP
Borowski, Tadeusz. THE MAN WITH THE
    PACKAGE
Ngugi, James. THE MARTYR

Elmer Gantry by Sinclair Lewis

■ *see*

Fuentes, Carlos. THE TWO ELENAS

END OF THE GAME by Julio Cortázar

- *compared with*

Blow-up (film)
Rostand, Edmund. *Cyrano de Bergerac*

THE ENEMY by V. S. Naipaul

- *compared with*

Schulz, Bruno. COCKROACHES
Welty, Eudora. "Kin"
Welty, Eudora. "Why I Live at the P.O."

- *also see*

Schulz, Bruno. COCKROACHES

An Enemy of the People by Henrik Ibsen

- *see*

Achebe, Chinua. THE VOTER

"The Ephemera" by Benjamin Franklin

- *see*

Andreyev, Leonid. LAZARUS

EPISODE IN MALAY CAMP by Peter Abrahams

- *compared with*

Camus, Albert. "The Guest"
Crane, Stephen. "The Open Boat"
Ellison, Ralph. *Invisible Man*
Stevenson, Robert Louis. "Markheim"
Thurber, James. "The Secret Life of Walter Mitty"

- *also see*

Gordimer, Nadine. LITTLE WILLIE

"An Episode of War" by Stephen Crane

- *see*

Dib, Mohammed. NAEMA—WHEREABOUTS UNKNOWN

Ethan Frome by Edith Wharton

- *see*

Dostoevski, Fyodor. WHITE NIGHTS

Euripides. *Medea*

- *see*

Zola, Émile. NAÏS MICOULIN

Euripides. *The Trojan Women*

- *see*

Zola, Émile. THE INUNDATION

"Eveline" by James Joyce

- *see*

Alexiou, Elli. THEY WERE ALL TO BE PITIED

"Everyday Use" by Alice Walker

- *see*

Megged, Aharon. THE NAME
Yáñez, Mirta. WE BLACKS ALL DRINK COFFEE

Everyman

- *see*

Agnon, S. Y. A WHOLE LOAF

F

FACING THE FOREST by Abraham B. Yehoshua

- *compared with*

Camus, Albert. THE GUEST
Conrad, Joseph. *Heart of Darkness*
Dances with Wolves (film)
Eliot, T. S. "The Hollow Men"
Gordimer, Nadine. "Six Feet of the Country"
Valenzuela, Luisa. I'M YOUR HORSE IN THE NIGHT

THE FALL by Alberto Moravia

- *compared with*

Anderson, Sherwood. "I Want to Know Why"
Hawthorne, Nathaniel. "Young Goodman Brown"
Joyce, James. "Araby"
Miller, Arthur. *After the Fall*
Pirandello, Luigi. CINCI

"The Fall of the House of Usher" by Edgar Allan Poe
- *see*

Andric, Ivo. A SUMMER IN THE SOUTH
Balzac, Honoré de. LA GRANDE BRETÊCHE
Hildesheimer, Wolfgang. A WORLD ENDS
Mérimée, Prosper. THE VENUS OF ILLE

Family Business by Leo Tolstoy
- *see*

Tolstoy, Leo. THE DEATH OF IVÁN ILYICH

THE FATE OF A MAN by Mikhail Sholokhov
- *compared with*

Conrad, Joseph. *Heart of Darkness*
Melville, Herman. "Bartleby the Scrivener"
Sholokhov, Mikhail. THE COLT
Solzhenitsyn, Alexander. MATRYONA'S HOME
- *also see*

Andric, Ivo. A SUMMER IN THE SOUTH
Djilas, Milovan. WAR
Mrozek, Slawomir. ON A JOURNEY
Solzhenitsyn, Alexander. MATRYONA'S HOME
Solzhenitsyn, Alexander. ZAKHAR-THE-POUCH

THE FATHER by Björnstjerne Björnson
- *compared with*

Agee, James. *A Death in the Family*
Djilas, Milovan. WAR
Guest, Judith. *Ordinary People*
Gunther, John. *Death Be Not Proud*
Pirandello, Luigi. WAR

FATHER AND I by Pär Lagerkvist
- *compared with*

Lawrence, D. H. "The Rocking Horse Winner"
Mansfield, Katherine. "The Garden Party"

FATHER'S HELP by R. K. Narayan
- *compared with*

Daudet, Alphonse. THE LAST LESSON
Twain, Mark. *Tom Sawyer*

Faulkner, William. *As I Lay Dying*
- *see*

Cortázar, Julio. NIGHT FACE UP

Faulkner, William. "The Auction of the Spotted Horses"
- *see*

Mahfouz, Naguib. THE PASHA'S DAUGHTER

Faulkner, William. "Barn Burning"
- *see*

Alexiou, Elli. THEY WERE ALL TO BE PITIED
Mahfouz, Naguib. THE CONJURER MADE OFF WITH THE DISH
Rifaat, Alifa. AN INCIDENT IN THE GHOBASHI HOUSEHOLD

Faulkner, William. "The Bear"
- *see*

Sholokhov, Mikhail. THE COLT
Turgenev, Ivan. YERMOLAY AND THE MILLER'S WIFE

Faulkner, William. "A Rose for Emily"
- *see*

Colette. THE LITTLE BOUILLOUX GIRL
Ekwensi, Cyprian. THE GREAT BEYOND
Hayashi Fumiko. BONES
Hildesheimer, Wolfgang. A WORLD ENDS
Rifaat, Alifa. ANOTHER EVENING AT THE CLUB

Faust by Johann Goethe
- *see*

Tolstoy, Leo. HOW MUCH LAND DOES A MAN NEED

Feng Jicai. THE MAO BUTTON
- *compared with*
King Midas folktale

Ferre, Rosario. "The Youngest Doll"
- *see*

Agnon, S. Y. A WHOLE LOAF

THE FIGHTING CRICKET by P'u Sung-Ling
- *compared with*

Malamud, Bernard. "The Jewbird"
Swift, Jonathan. *Gulliver's Travels*

A FISHER NEST by Henrik Pontoppidan

- *compared with*

Connell, Richard. "The Most Dangerous Game"
Hartley, L. P. "The Island"
Jackson, Shirley. "The Lottery"
Russell, John. "The Price of the Head"

Fitzgerald, F. Scott. *The Great Gatsby*

- *see*

Balzac, Honoré de. THE ATHEIST'S MASS
Moravia, Alberto. THE CHASE

FLASHES IN THE NIGHT by Aron Tamasi

- *compared with*

Andric, Ivo. THE SCYTHE
Andric, Ivo. A SUMMER IN THE SOUTH
Sholokhov, Mikhail. THE COLT
Solzhenitsyn, Alexander. MATRYONA'S HOME

- *also see*

Andric, Ivo. A SUMMER IN THE SOUTH
Cumali, Necati. IN GOD'S PLAINS
Dinesen, Isak. SORROW-ACRE

Flaubert, Gustave. *Madame Bovary*

- *see*

Chekhov, Anton. THE DARLING
Colette. THE LITTLE BOUILLOUX GIRL
Colette. THE PHOTOGRAPHER'S MISSUS
Flaubert, Gustave. A SIMPLE HEART
Sand, George. THE MARQUISE

Flaubert, Gustave. A SIMPLE HEART

- *compared with*

Anderson, Sherwood. "Death in the Woods"
Flaubert, Gustave. *Madame Bovary*
Frost, Robert. "Death of the Hired Man"

- *also see*

Zola, Émile. NAÏS MICOULIN

"Flight" by John Updike

- *see*

Mann, Thomas. DISORDER AND EARLY SORROW

Flowers for Algernon by Daniel Keyes

- *see*

Danticat, Edwidge. CHILDREN OF THE SEA

"The Fog-Horn" by Ray Bradbury

- *see*

Sienkiewicz, Henryk. THE LIGHTHOUSE-KEEPER

Fontaine's fables

- *see*

Diop, Birago. THE WAGES OF GOOD

"For Esmé—with Love and Squalor" by J. D. Salinger

- *see*

La Guma, Alex. BLANKETS

"For What Is Man?" from *You Can't Go Home Again* by Thomas Wolfe

- *see*

Agnon, S. Y. THE DOCUMENT
Izgü, Muzaffer. WANTED: A TOWN WITHOUT A CRAZY

The Fountainhead by Ayn Rand

- *see*

Fuentes, Carlos. THE TWO ELENAS

4'33 by John Cage (piano composition)

- *see*

Böll, Heinrich. MURKE'S COLLECTED SILENCES

France, Anatole. THE PROCURATOR OF JUDEA

- *compared with*

Bulgakov, Mikhail. *The Master and Margarita*
Dostoevski, Fyodor. *The Brothers Karamazov*
Hardy, Thomas. "God Forgotten"
Tintoretto. *Christ Before Pilate* (painting)

Frank, Anne. *The Diary of Anne Frank*

- *see*

Danticat, Edwidge. CHILDREN OF THE SEA

Frankenstein by Mary Shelley

- *see*

Cumali, Necati. IN GOD'S PLAINS

Franklin, Benjamin. "The Ephemera"

- *see*

Andreyev, Leonid. LAZARUS

FRECKLES by Fakir Baykurt

- ■ *compared with*

Gogol, Nikolai. "Taras Bulba"
Joyce, James. "Araby"

Freemen, Mary Wilkins. "A Village Singer"

- ■ *see*

Idris, Youssef. THE CHEAPEST NIGHT'S
ENTERTAINMENT
Saranti, Galatea. SUNLIGHT

"Fresh Fish" by Siegfried Lenz

- ■ *see*

Narayan, R. K. A HORSE AND TWO GOATS

FROM BEHIND THE VEIL by Dhu'l Nun Ayyoub

- ■ *compared with*

Cisneros, Sandra. *House on Mango Street*
Hurston, Zora Neale. *Their Eyes Were Watching God*

Marshall, Paul. "Barbados"
Walker, Alice. *The Color Purple*

Frost, Robert. "Death of the Hired Man"

- ■ *see*

Flaubert, Gustave. A SIMPLE HEART

Fuentes, Carlos. THE TWO ELENAS

- ■ *compared with*

Dickens, Charles. *A Tale of Two Cities*
Hemingway, Ernest. *The Sun Also Rises*
Lewis, Sinclair. *Elmer Gantry*
Rand, Ayn. *The Fountainhead*

Furman, Laura. "Watch Time Fly"

- ■ *see*

Theotokis, Konstantinos. VILLAGE LIFE

G

Gaines, Ernest. *A Lesson Before Dying*

- ■ *see*

Danticat, Edwidge. CHILDREN OF THE SEA

GAMES AT TWILIGHT by Anita Desai

- ■ *compared with*

Joyce, James. "Araby"
Kafka, Franz. THE METAMORPHOSIS
Shakespeare, William. *Romeo and Juliet*

García Márquez, Gabriel. *Love in the Time of Cholera*

- ■ *see*

Chekhov, Anton. THE DARLING

THE GARDEN OF FORKING PATHS by Jorge Luis Borges

- ■ *compared with*

Borges, Jorge Luis. "Death and the Compass"
Borges, Jorge Luis. "The Library of Babel"
Borges, Jorge Luis. "The Lottery in Babylon"

Borges, Jorge Luis. "Theme of the Traitor and the Hero"
Ed-Din, Abu Bakr Siraj. *The Book of Certainty*
Pinter, Harold. *Old Times*
Pirandello, Luigi. *Six Characters in Search of an Author*

"The Garden Party" by Katherine Mansfield

- ■ *see*

Lagerkvist, Pär. FATHER AND I
Nakos, Lilika. THE BROKEN DOLL

Garland, Hamlin. "Mrs. Ripley's Trip"

- ■ *see*

Idris, Youssef. THE CHEAPEST NIGHT'S
ENTERTAINMENT

Géricault. *Severed Heads* (painting)

- ■ *see*

Heym, Georg. THE AUTOPSY

Goodbye, Columbus by Philip Roth
- ■ *see*

Mahfouz, Naguib. THE PASHA'S DAUGHTER

Gordimer, Nadine. "Home"
- ■ *see*

Taylor, Apirana. THE CARVING

Gordimer, Nadine. LITTLE WILLIE
- ■ *compared with*

Abrahams, Peter. EPISODE IN MALAY CAMP
Achebe, Chinua. VENGEFUL CREDITOR
Cather, Willa. "Paul's Case"
Dove-Danquah, Mabel. THE TORN VEIL
Ellison, Ralph. "Battle Royal"

Gordimer, Nadine. "Six Feet of the Country"
- ■ *see*

Yehoshua, Abraham B. FACING THE FOREST

Gordimer, Nadine. A SOLDIER'S EMBRACE
- ■ *compared with*

O'Connor, Flannery. "Revelation"

Gordimer, Nadine. "The Termitary"
- ■ *see*

Vega, Ana Lydia. CLOUD COVER CARIBBEAN

Gordimer, Nadine. "The Train from Rhodesia"
- ■ *see*

Dinesen, Isak. SORROW-ACRE
Haris, Petros. LIGHTS ON THE SEA

Gorky, Maxim. *The Lower Depths*
- ■ *see*

Sartre, Jean-Paul. THE WALL

Gorky, Maxim. "Twenty-Six Men and a Girl"
- ■ *see*

Sartre, Jean-Paul. THE WALL

Grace, Patricia. A WAY OF TALKING
- ■ *compared with*

Achebe, Chinua. *Things Fall Apart*
Bradbury, Ray. "August 2002: Night Meeting"
Heker, Liliana. "The Stolen Party"
Merrick, Elliott. "Without Words"

"A Grand Day in Schissomir" by Siegfried Lenz
- ■ *see*

Narayan, R. K. A HORSE AND TWO GOATS

LA GRANDE BRETÊCHE by Honoré de Balzac
- ■ *compared with*
Arabian Nights
Balzac, Honoré de. THE ATHEIST'S MASS
Balzac, Honoré de. *Cousin Bette*
Balzac, Honoré de. *Père Goriot*
Boccaccio, Giovanni. *Decameron*
Chaucer, Geoffrey. *Canterbury Tales*
Conrad, Joseph. *Heart of Darkness*
James, Henry. *The Turn of the Screw*
Melville, Herman. *Moby Dick*
Poe, Edgar Allan. "The Cask of Amontillado"
Poe, Edgar Allan. "The Fall of the House of Usher"

"Grandfather and Grandson" by Isaac B. Singer
- ■ *see*

Megged, Aharon. THE NAME

THE GRANDMOTHER by K. Surangkhanang
- ■ *compared with*

Hemingway, Ernest. *The Old Man and the Sea*
Mansfield, Katherine. "Miss Brill"
O'Connor, Flannery. "A Good Man Is Hard to Find"
- ■ *also see*

Desai, Anita. A DEVOTED SON
Nhat-Tien. AN UNSOUND SLEEP

GRANDMOTHER TAKES CHARGE by Lao She
- ■ *compared with*

Apollo and Phaethon myth
Kelley, William. "A Visit to Grandmother"
- ■ *also see*

Desai, Anita. A DEVOTED SON
Nhat-Tien. AN UNSOUND SLEEP

The Grapes of Wrath by John Steinbeck
- ■ *see*

Dib, Mohammed. NAEMA—WHEREABOUTS UNKNOWN

H

Haley, Alex. *Roots*
- ■ *see*

Mphahlele, Es'kia. THE MASTER OF DOORNVLEI

Hamlet by William Shakespeare
- ■ *see*

Zola, Émile. NAÏS MICOULIN

Hamsun, Knut. THE CALL OF LIFE
- ■ *compared with*

Chopin, Kate. "The Story of an Hour"

"Hansel and Gretel"
- ■ *see*

Ahmad, Razia. PAPER IS MONEY

Hardy, Thomas. "God Forgotten"
- ■ *see*

France, Anatole. THE PROCURATOR OF JUDEA

Hardy, Thomas. *Tess of the d'Urbervilles*
- ■ *see*

Zola, Émile. NAÏS MICOULIN

Haris, Petros. LIGHTS ON THE SEA
- ■ *compared with*

Cather, Willa. "Paul's Case"
Gordimer, Nadine. "The Train from Rhodesia"
Lessing, Doris. "A Woman on a Roof"

Harte, Bret. "Tennessee's Partner"
- ■ *see*

Balzac, Honoré de. THE ATHEIST'S MASS

Hartley, L. P. "The Island"
- ■ *see*

Pontoppidan, Henrik. A FISHER NEST

"Hautot and His Son" by Guy de Maupassant
- ■ *see*

Maupassant, Guy de. THE NECKLACE

Hawthorne, Nathaniel. "The Artist of the Beautiful"
- ■ *see*

Andric, Ivo. SUMMER IN THE SOUTH

Hawthorne, Nathaniel. "The Great Stone Face"
- ■ *see*

Hesse, Hermann. THE POET

Hawthorne, Nathaniel. "The Minister's Black Veil"
- ■ *see*

Balzac, Honoré de. THE ATHEIST'S MASS
Lagerlöf, Selma. THE OUTLAWS
Phiên Võ. THE KEY
Saranti, Galatea. SUNLIGHT

Hawthorne, Nathaniel. *The Scarlet Letter*
- ■ *see*

Achebe, Chinua. VENGEFUL CREDITOR
Ekwensi, Cyprian. THE GREAT BEYOND
Nicol, Abioseth. AS THE NIGHT THE DAY

Hawthorne, Nathaniel. "Wakefield"
- ■ *see*

Pavese, Cesare. SUICIDES

Hawthorne, Nathaniel. "Young Goodman Brown"
- ■ *see*

Achebe, Chinua. VENGEFUL CREDITOR
Dove-Danquah, Mabel. THE TORN VEIL
Hesse, Hermann. THE POET
Lagerlöf, Selma. THE OUTLAWS
Moravia, Alberto. THE FALL

Hayashi Fumiko. BONES
- ■ *compared with*

Butters, Dorothy Gilman. "Sorrow Rides a Fast Horse"
Faulkner, William. "A Rose for Emily"

Hayden, Robert. "Middle Passage"
- ■ *see*

Danticat, Edwidge. CHILDREN OF THE SEA

A Hazard of New Fortunes by William Dean Howells
- ■ *see*

Maupassant, Guy de. THE NECKLACE

Head, Bessie. "The Collector of Treasures"
- ■ *see*

Achebe, Chinua. GIRLS AT WAR

Head, Bessie. HEAVEN IS NOT CLOSED

  ■ *compared with*

  Achebe, Chinua. *Things Fall Apart*
  Douglass, Frederick. *The Life of Frederick Douglass, An Autobiography*
  Soyinka, Wole. *The Lion and the Jewel*

The Heart of a Dog by Mikhail Bulgakov

  ■ *see*

  Kafka, Franz. THE METAMORPHOSIS

Heart of Darkness by Joseph Conrad

  ■ *see*

  Balzac, Honoré de. THE ATHEIST'S MASS
  Balzac, Honoré de. LA GRANDE BRETÊCHE
  Cortázar, Julio. NIGHT FACE UP
  Kariara, Jonathan. HER WARRIOR
  Sholokhov, Mikhail. THE FATE OF A MAN
  Yehoshua, Abraham B. FACING THE FOREST

HEAVEN IS NOT CLOSED by Bessie Head

  ■ *compared with*

  Achebe, Chinua. *Things Fall Apart*
  Douglass, Frederick. *The Life of Frederick Douglass, An Autobiography*
  Soyinka, Wole. *The Lion and the Jewel*

Hedda Gabler by Henrik Ibsen

  ■ *see*

  Colette. THE PHOTOGRAPHER'S MISSUS
  Sand, George. THE MARQUISE

THE HEIR by Kiwon So

  ■ *compared with*

  Salinger, J. D. *A Catcher in the Rye*

Heker, Liliana. "The Stolen Party"

  ■ *see*

  Grace, Patricia. A WAY OF TALKING

HELENITSA by Lilika Nakos

  ■ *compared with*

  Crane, Stephen. "The Open Boat"
  Jewett, Sarah Orne. "Miss Tempy's Watchers"
  London, Jack. "To Build a Fire"

Heller, Joseph. *Catch-22*

  ■ *see*

  Mahfouz, Naguib. THE PASHA'S DAUGHTER

Hemingway, Ernest. "Big Two-Hearted River"

  ■ *see*

  Turgenev, Ivan. YERMOLAY AND THE MILLER'S WIFE

Hemingway, Ernest. "A Clean, Well-Lighted Place"

  ■ *see*

  Böll, Heinrich. MURKE'S COLLECTED SILENCES
  Cicellis, Kay. BRIEF DIALOGUE
  Pirandello, Luigi. WAR
  Santos, Bienvenido N. THE DAY THE DANCERS CAME

Hemingway, Ernest. *In Our Time*

  ■ *see*

  Mishima Yukio. PATRIOTISM

Hemingway, Ernest. "The Killers"

  ■ *see*

  Cicellis, Kay. BRIEF DIALOGUE
  Djilas, Milovan. THE OLD MAN AND THE SONG
  Tanizaki Junichiro. TATTOO

Hemingway, Ernest. *The Old Man and the Sea*

  ■ *see*

  Lenz, Siegfried. THE LAUGHINGSTOCK
  Surangkhanang, K. THE GRANDMOTHER

Hemingway, Ernest. "Old Man at the Bridge"

  ■ *see*

  Djilas, Milovan. WAR

Hemingway, Ernest. "The Short Happy Life of Francis Macomber"

  ■ *see*

  Moravia, Alberto. THE CHASE
  Nakos, Lilika. THE BROKEN DOLL
  Pirandello, Luigi. CINCI

Hemingway, Ernest. *The Sun Also Rises*

  ■ *see*

  Fuentes, Carlos. THE TWO ELENAS

Henry, O. "Gift of the Magi"

- *see*

Ahmad, Razia. PAPER IS MONEY
Maupassant, Guy de. THE NECKLACE
Rifaat, Alifa. AN INCIDENT IN THE GHOBASHI
    HOUSEHOLD
Verga, Giovanni. PROPERTY

HER WARRIOR by Jonathan Kariara

- *compared with*

Achebe, Chinua. VENGEFUL CREDITOR
Cather, Willa. "Paul's Case"
Conrad, Joseph. *Heart of Darkness*
Golding, William. *Lord of the Flies*
Mansfield, Katherine. "Miss Brill"
Poe, Edgar Allan. "The Masque of the Red Death"
Wright, Richard. *Black Boy*

Hesse, Hermann. "Piktor's Metamorphosis"

- *see*

Asturias, Miguel. TATUANA'S TALE

Hesse, Hermann. THE POET

- *compared with*

Chekhov, Anton. THE KISS
Hawthorne, Nathaniel. "The Great Stone Face"
Hawthorne, Nathaniel. "Young Goodman Brown"
Hoffmann, E. T. A. "The Golden Flower Pot"
James, Henry. "The Real Thing"
Mann, Thomas. *Joseph and His Brothers*
Mann, Thomas. TONIO KRÖGER
Mann, Thomas. TRISTAN
Moreau, Gustave. *The Apparition* (painting)

Heym, Georg. THE AUTOPSY

- *compared with*

Bierce, Ambrose. "An Occurrence at Owl Creek
    Bridge"
Géricault. *Severed Heads* (painting)
Joyce, James. "The Dead"

Hildesheimer, Wolfgang. A WORLD ENDS

- *compared with*

Delvaux, Paul. *Venus Asleep* (painting)
Faulkner, William. "A Rose for Emily"
Grosz, George. *Pillars of Society* (painting)
Poe, Edgar Allan. "The Fall of the House of Usher"

- *also see*

Huber, Heinz. THE NEW APARTMENT

Hilton, James. *Lost Horizon*

- *see*

Dostoevski, Fyodor. THE DREAM OF A
    RIDICULOUS MAN

History of Chinese Philosophy by Yu-Lan Fung

- *see*

Cortázar, Julio. NIGHT FACE UP

Hoffmann, E. T. A. "The Golden Flower Pot"

- *see*

Hesse, Hermann. THE POET

"The Hollow Men" by T. S. Eliot

- *see*

Yehoshua, Abraham B. FACING THE FOREST

"Home" by Nadine Gordimer

- *see*

Taylor, Apirana. THE CARVING

THE HONEST THIEF by Fyodor Dostoevski

- *compared with*

Dostoevski, Fyodor. *Crime and Punishment*
Dostoevski, Fyodor. WHITE NIGHTS
Kafka, Franz. THE METAMORPHOSIS
Melville, Herman. "Bartleby the Scrivener"

- *also see*

Balzac, Honoré de. THE ATHEIST'S MASS

A HORSE AND TWO GOATS by R. K. Narayan

- *compared with*

Bowles, Paul. "You Have Left Your Lotus Pods on
    the Bus"
Lenz, Siegfried. "Fresh Fish"
Lenz, Siegfried. "A Grand Day in Schissomir"

"The Horse Dealer's Daughter" by D. H. Lawrence

- *see*

Landolfi, Tommaso. PASTORAL
Moravia, Alberto. THE CHASE
Svevo, Italo. IN MY INDOLENCE

Ibsen, Henrik. *A Doll's House*

- *see*

Colette. THE PHOTOGRAPHER'S MISSUS

Ibsen, Henrik. *An Enemy of the People*

- *see*

Achebe, Chinua. THE VOTER

Ibsen, Henrik. *Hedda Gabler*

- *see*

Colette. THE PHOTOGRAPHER'S MISSUS
Sand, George. THE MARQUISE

Ibsen, Henrik. *Wild Duck*

- *see*

Sand, George. THE MARQUISE

Icarus myth

- *see*

Tanizaki Junichiro. TATTOO

Idris, Youssef. THE CHEAPEST NIGHT'S
ENTERTAINMENT

- *compared with*

Anderson, Sherwood. *Winesburg, Ohio*
Freemen, Mary Wilkins. "A Village Singer"
Garland, Hamlin. "Mrs. Ripley's Trip"
Hurston, Zora Neale. *The Eatonville Anthology*
Jewett, Sarah Orne. "The Town Poor"
O'Connor, Flannery. "The Life You Save May Be
    Your Own"
Singer, Isaac B. "Gimpel the Fool"
Welty, Eudora. "Petrified Man"
Welty, Eudora. "Why I Live at the P.O."

"If I Should Open My Mouth" by Paul Bowles

- *see*

Sarang, Vilas. THE TERRORIST

"I'm a Fool" by Sherwood Anderson

- *see*

Roufos, Rodis. THE CANDIDATE

I'M YOUR HORSE IN THE NIGHT by Luisa
    Valenzuela

- *compared with*

Cortázar, Julio. *Manual for Manuel*
Missing (film)
Official Story (film)

- *also see*

Yehoshua, Abraham B. FACING THE FOREST
Yizhar, S. HABAKUK

IN A GROVE by Akutagawa Ryūnosuke

- *compared with*

Narayan, R. K. THE MIRROR
Rose, Reginald. "Twelve Angry Men"

AN INCIDENT IN THE GHOBASHI HOUSEHOLD by
    Alifa Rifaat

- *compared with*

Faulkner, William. "Barn Burning"
Henry, O. "The Gift of the Magi"
Ju Dou (film)
Shikibu Murasaki. "The Lake Which Took People
    In" from *The Tale of Genji*
Updike, John. "A & P"

In Dubious Battle by John Steinbeck

- *see*

Dib, Mohammed. NAEMA—WHEREABOUTS
UNKNOWN

"The Infant Prodigy" by Thomas Mann

- *see*

Sienkiewicz, Henryk. YANKO THE MUSICIAN

IN GOD'S PLAINS by Necati Cumali

- *compared with*

Shelley, Mary. *Frankenstein*
Sholokhov, Mikhail. THE COLT
Sienkiewicz, Henryk. YANKO THE MUSICIAN
Tamasi, Aron. FLASHES IN THE NIGHT

Izgü, Muzaffer. WANTED: A TOWN WITHOUT A
    CRAZY
- *compared with*
Browning, Robert. "The Pied Piper of Hamelin"
Kafka, Franz. THE METAMORPHOSIS
Melville, Herman. "Bartleby the Scrivener"

Pocket Full of Miracles (film)
Thoreau, Henry David. "Where I Lived and What
    I Lived For" from *Walden*
Wolfe, Thomas. "For What Is Man?" from *You
    Can't Go Home Again*

J

"Jack and the Beanstalk"
- *see*
Ahmad, Razia. PAPER IS MONEY
Mahfouz, Naguib. THE CONJURER MADE OFF
    WITH THE DISH

Jackson, Shirley. "The Lottery"
- *see*
Buzzati, Dino. THE SLAYING OF THE DRAGON
Cortázar, Julio. NIGHT FACE UP
Dove-Danquah, Mabel. THE TORN VEIL
Kafka, Franz. IN THE PENAL COLONY
Nicol, Abioseth. AS THE NIGHT THE DAY
Pontoppidan, Henrik. A FISHER NEST
Venezis, Elias. MYCENAE
Yizhar, S. HABAKUK

Jacobs, W. W. "The Monkey's Paw"
- *see*
Lim, Catherine. PAPER
Narayan, R. K. THE MIRROR

Jagua Nana by Cyprian Ekwensi
- *see*
Achebe, Chinua. THE VOTER

James, Henry. "The Beast in the Jungle"
- *see*
Moravia, Alberto. THE CHASE

James, Henry. *Daisy Miller*
- *see*
Balzac, Honoré de. THE ATHEIST'S MASS

James, Henry. "The Pupil"
- *see*
Daudet, Alphonse. THE LAST LESSON

James, Henry. "The Real Thing"
- *see*
Hesse, Hermann. THE POET
Tanizaki Junichiro. TATTOO

James, Henry. *The Turn of the Screw*
- *see*
Andric, Ivo. A SUMMER IN THE SOUTH
Balzac, Honoré de. LA GRANDE BRETÈCHE

THE JAY by Kawabata Yasunari
- *compared with*
Desai, Anita. A DEVOTED SON

J.B. by Archibald MacLeish
- *see*
Agnon, S. Y. A WHOLE LOAF
Zola, Émile. THE INUNDATION

Jeffers, Robinson. "Original Sin"
- *see*
Buzzati, Dino. THE SLAYING OF THE DRAGON

K

KABULIWALLAH by Rabindranath Tagore

- *compared with*

Lawrence, D. H. "The Rocking Horse Winner"
Shakespeare, William. *Romeo and Juliet*
Twain, Mark. *Huckleberry Finn*
Welty, Eudora. "A Visit of Charity"

Kafka, Franz. *The Castle*

- *see*

Kafka, Franz. THE JUDGMENT

Kafka, Franz. A HUNGER ARTIST

- *compared with*

Aichinger, Ilse. THE BOUND MAN
Ionesco, Eugene. *Rhinoceros*
Le Guin, Ursula K. "The Ones Who Walk Away
    from Omelas"
Mann, Thomas. TRISTAN
O'Neill, Eugene. *The Hairy Ape*

- *also see*

Agnon, S. Y. A WHOLE LOAF
Aichinger, Ilse. THE BOUND MAN
Allende, Isabel. TWO WORDS
Camus, Albert. THE GUEST
Kafka, Franz. THE JUDGMENT
Kafka, Franz. THE METAMORPHOSIS
Mann, Thomas. TRISTAN

Kafka, Franz. IN THE PENAL COLONY

- *compared with*

Duchamps, Marcel. *The Big Glass* (painting)
Jackson, Shirley. "The Lottery"
Kafka, Franz. THE METAMORPHOSIS

- *also see*

Borowski, Tadeusz. THE MAN WITH THE
    PACKAGE
Buzzati, Dino. THE SLAYING OF THE DRAGON
Villiers de L'Isle-Adam. THE TORTURE BY HOPE

Kafka, Franz. THE JUDGMENT

- *compared with*

Cather, Willa. "Paul's Case"

Gide, André. THE RETURN OF THE PRODIGAL
    SON
Kafka, Franz. *The Castle*
Kafka, Franz. A HUNGER ARTIST
Kafka, Franz. THE METAMORPHOSIS
Kafka, Franz. *The Trial*
Mérimée, Prosper. "Mateo Falcone"

Kafka, Franz. THE METAMORPHOSIS

- *compared with*

Apuleius. *The Golden Ass*
Bulgakov, Mikhail. *The Heart of a Dog*
Čapek, Karel. *War with the Newts*
Ionesco, Eugene. *Rhinoceros*
Kafka, Franz. A HUNGER ARTIST
Kafka, Franz. *The Trial*
Orwell, George. *Animal Farm*
Ovid. *The Metamorphoses*

- *also see*

Agnon, S. Y. THE DOCUMENT
Andreyev, Leonid. LAZARUS
Asturias, Miguel. TATUANA'S TALE
Desai, Anita. GAMES AT TWILIGHT
Dostoevski, Fyodor. THE DREAM OF A
    RIDICULOUS MAN
Dostoevski, Fyodor. THE HONEST THIEF
Izgü, Muzaffer. WANTED: A TOWN WITHOUT A
    CRAZY
Kafka, Franz. IN THE PENAL COLONY
Kafka, Franz. THE JUDGMENT
Mann, Thomas. TONIO KRÖGER
Santos, Bienvenido N. THE DAY THE DANCERS
    CAME
Schulz, Bruno. COCKROACHES
Sienkiewicz, Henryk. THE LIGHTHOUSE-KEEPER
Vega, Ana Lydia. CLOUD COVERED CARIBBEAN

Kafka, Franz. *The Trial*

- *see*

Kafka, Franz. THE JUDGMENT
Kafka, Franz. THE METAMORPHOSIS
Zola, Émile. THE INUNDATION

Kafka's parables

■ *see*

Diop, Birago. THE WAGES OF GOOD

Kallen, Horace. *The Tragedy of Job*

■ *see*

Zola, Émile. THE INUNDATION

Kapadia, Kundanika. PAPER BOAT

■ *compared with*

Joyce, James. "Araby"
Lessing, Doris. "Through the Tunnel"

Kariara, Jonathan. HER WARRIOR

■ *compared with*

Achebe, Chinua. VENGEFUL CREDITOR
Cather, Willa. "Paul's Case"
Conrad, Joseph. *Heart of Darkness*
Golding, William. *Lord of the Flies*
Mansfield, Katherine. "Miss Brill"
Poe, Edgar Allan. "The Masque of the Red Death"
Wright, Richard. *Black Boy*

Kawabata Yasunari. THE JAY

■ *compared with*

Desai, Anita. A DEVOTED SON

Kawabata Yasunari. THE MOON ON THE WATER

■ *compared with*

Anderson, Sherwood. *Winesburg, Ohio*
Conrad, Joseph. "The Secret Sharer"
Narcissus myth
Wilde, Oscar. *The Picture of Dorian Gray*

Kelley, William. "A Visit to Grandmother"

■ *see*

Lao She. GRANDMOTHER TAKES CHARGE

THE KEY by Phiên Võ

■ *compared with*

Crane, Stephen. "The Bride Comes to Yellow Sky"
Hawthorne, Nathaniel. "The Minister's Black Veil"
Twain, Mark. "The Celebrated Jumping Frog of Calaveras County"

Keyes, Daniel. *Flowers for Algernon*

■ *see*

Danticat, Edwidge. CHILDREN OF THE SEA

"The Killers" by Ernest Hemingway

■ *see*

Cicellis, Kay. BRIEF DIALOGUE
Djilas, Milovan. THE OLD MAN AND THE SONG
Tanizaki Junichiro. TATTOO

"Kin" by Eudora Welty

■ *see*

Naipaul, V. S. THE ENEMY

Kincaid, Jamaica. *Annie John*

■ *see*

Yáñez, Mirta. WE BLACKS ALL DRINK COFFEE

King Midas folktale

■ *see*

Feng Jicai. THE MAO BUTTON
Ray, Satyajit. ASHAMANJA BABU'S DOG

Kipling, Rudyard. "The Man Who Would Be King"

■ *see*

Meleagrou, Hebe. MONUMENT

THE KISS by Anton Chekhov

■ *compared with*

Joyce, James. "Araby"
Updike, John. "A & P"

■ *also see*

Hesse, Hermann. THE POET

Kiwon So. THE HEIR

■ *compared with*

Salinger, J. D. *A Catcher in the Rye*

Klaus, Annette Curtis. *Silver Kiss*

■ *see*

Andreyev, Leonid. LAZARUS

Kosinski, Jerzy. *The Painted Bird*

■ *see*

Borowski, Tadeusz. THE MAN WITH THE PACKAGE

L

"The Lady, or the Tiger" by Frank Stockton

- *see*

Andric, Ivo. A SUMMER IN THE SOUTH

Lagerkvist, Pär. FATHER AND I

- *compared with*

Lawrence, D. H. "The Rocking Horse Winner"
Mansfield, Katherine. "The Garden Party"

Lagerlöf, Selma. THE OUTLAWS

- *compared with*

Hawthorne, Nathaniel. "The Minister's Black Veil"
Hawthorne, Nathaniel. "Young Goodman Brown"

La Guma, Alex. BLANKETS

- *compared with*

Achebe, Chinua. VENGEFUL CREDITOR
Melville, Herman. "Bartleby the Scrivener"
Melville, Herman. "Billy Budd"
Porter, Katherine Anne. "The Jilting of Granny
  Weatherall"
Salinger, J. D. "For Esmé—with Love and Squalor"
Wright, Richard. *Black Boy*

"The Lake Which Took People In" from *The Tale of
  Genji* by Shikibu Murasaki

- *see*

Rifaat, Alifa. AN INCIDENT IN THE GHOBASHI
HOUSEHOLD

Landolfi, Tommaso. PASTORAL

- *compared with*

Delvaux, Paul. *The Sleeping City* (painting)
Huysman, J. K. *Against the Grain*
Lawrence, D. H. "The Horse Dealer's Daughter"
Magritte, René. *The Red Model* (painting)

Lao She. GRANDMOTHER TAKES CHARGE

- *compared with*

Apollo and Phaethon myth
Kelley, William. "A Visit to Grandmother"

- *also see*

Desai, Anita. A DEVOTED SON
Nhat-Tien. AN UNSOUND SLEEP

THE LAST LESSON by Alphonse Daudet

- *compared with*

Bambara, Toni Cade. "The Lesson"
Daudet, Alphonse. "The Siege of Berlin"
James, Henry. "The Pupil"

- *also see*

Narayan, R. K. FATHER'S HELP

THE LAUGHINGSTOCK by Siegfried Lenz

- *compared with*

Hemingway, Ernest. *The Old Man and the Sea*

Lawrence, D. H. "The Horse Dealer's Daughter"

- *see*

Landolfi, Tommaso. PASTORAL
Moravia, Alberto. THE CHASE
Svevo, Italo. IN MY INDOLENCE

Lawrence, D. H. "The Island"

- *see*

Sienkiewicz, Henryk. THE LIGHTHOUSE-KEEPER

Lawrence, D. H. "The Rocking Horse Winner"

- *see*

Alexiou, Elli. THEY WERE ALL TO BE PITIED
Lagerkvist, Pär. FATHER AND I
Lim, Catherine. PAPER
Ray, Satyajit. ASHAMANJA BABU'S DOG
Tagore, Rabindranath. KABULIWALLAH
Verga, Giovanni. PROPERTY

Laxness, Haldor. LILY

- *compared with*

Sillitoe, Alan. "Uncle Ernest" from *The Loneliness
  of the Long Distance Runner*

LAZARUS by Leonid Andreyev

- *compared with*

Franklin, Benjamin. "The Ephemera"
Kafka, Franz. THE METAMORPHOSIS
Klaus, Annette Curtis. *Silver Kiss*
Melville, Herman. "Bartleby the Scrivener"
Shelley, Percy Bysshe. "Ozymandias"

"The Lottery" by Shirley Jackson

■ *see*

Buzzati, Dino. THE SLAYING OF THE DRAGON
Cortázar, Julio. NIGHT FACE UP
Dove-Danquah, Mabel. THE TORN VEIL
Kafka, Franz. IN THE PENAL COLONY
Nicol, Abioseth. AS THE NIGHT THE DAY
Pontoppidan, Henrik. A FISHER NEST
Venezis, Elias. MYCENAE
Yizhar, S. HABAKUK

"The Lottery in Babylon" by Jorge Luis Borges

■ *see*

Borges, Jorge Luis. THE GARDEN OF FORKING PATHS

Love in the Time of Cholera by Gabriel García Márquez

■ *see*

Chekhov, Anton. THE DARLING

"The Love Song of J. Alfred Prufrock" by T. S. Eliot

■ *see*

Mann, Thomas. TRISTAN
Moravia, Alberto. THE CHASE
Rushdi, Rashad. ANGUISH
Tolstoy, Leo. THE DEATH OF IVÁN ILYICH

The Lower Depths by Maxim Gorky

■ *see*

Sartre, Jean-Paul. THE WALL

"Lullaby" by Leslie Marmon Silko

■ *see*

Condé, Maryse. THREE WOMEN IN MANHATTAN

Lu Xun. DIARY OF A MADMAN

■ *compared with*

Aiken, Conrad. "Silent Snow, Secret Snow"
Baldwin, James. "Previous Condition"
Cather, Willa. "Paul's Case"
Coover, Robert. "A Pedestrian Accident"

■ *also see*

Tanizaki Junichiro. THE THIEF

Lying Figure by Francis Bacon (painting)

■ *see*

Aichinger, Ilse. THE BOUND MAN

M

MacLeish, Archibald. *J. B.*

■ *see*

Agnon, S. Y. A WHOLE LOAF
Zola, Émile. THE INUNDATION

Madame Bovary by Gustave Flaubert

■ *see*

Chekhov, Anton. THE DARLING
Colette. THE LITTLE BOUILLOUX GIRL
Colette. THE PHOTOGRAPHER'S MISSUS
Flaubert, Gustave. A SIMPLE HEART
Sand, George. THE MARQUISE

Madame Butterfly by Giacomo Puccini

■ *see*

Zola, Émile. NAÏS MICOULIN

Maggie: A Girl of the Streets by Stephen Crane

■ *see*

Zola, Émile. NAÏS MICOULIN

"The Magic Barrel" by Bernard Malamud

■ *see*

Mahfouz, Naguib. THE PASHA'S DAUGHTER

Magritte, René. *The Red Model* (painting)
- *see*

Landolfi, Tommaso. PASTORAL

Mahfouz, Naguib. THE CONJURER MADE OFF
  WITH THE DISH
- *compared with*

Barrie, J. M. *Peter Pan*
Conrad, Joseph. "Youth"
Faulkner, William. "Barn Burning"
"Jack and the Beanstalk"
Joyce, James. "Araby"
Wright, Richard. "Almos' a Man"

Mahfouz, Naguib. THE PASHA'S DAUGHTER
- *compared with*

Faulkner, William. "The Auction of the Spotted
  Horses"
Heller, Joseph. *Catch-22*
Malamud, Bernard. "The Magic Barrel"
Roth, Philip. *Goodbye, Columbus*

Malamud, Bernard. "The Jewbird"
- *see*

P'u Sung-Ling. THE FIGHTING CRICKET

Malamud, Bernard. "The Magic Barrel"
- *see*

Mahfouz, Naguib. THE PASHA'S DAUGHTER

Mann, Thomas. *Buddenbrooks*
- *see*

Mann, Thomas. TRISTAN

Mann, Thomas. *Confessions of Felix Krull:
  Confidence Man*
- *see*

Sand, George. THE MARQUISE

Mann, Thomas. *Death in Venice*
- *see*

Mann, Thomas. TRISTAN

Mann, Thomas. DISORDER AND EARLY SORROW
- *compared with*

Anderson, Sherwood. "I Want to Know Why"
Böll, Heinrich. "Christmas Every Day"
Picasso, Pablo. *Bust of a Woman* (painting)
Updike, John. "Flight"

- *also see*

Huber, Heinz. THE NEW APARTMENT
Megged, Aharon. THE NAME

Mann, Thomas. "The Infant Prodigy"
- *see*

Sienkiewicz, Henryk. YANKO THE MUSICIAN

Mann, Thomas. *Joseph and His Brothers*
- *see*

Hesse, Hermann. THE POET

Mann, Thomas. "Tobias Mindernickel"
- *see*

Sienkiewicz, Henryk. THE LIGHTHOUSE-KEEPER

Mann, Thomas. TONIO KRÖGER
- *compared with*

Aiken, Conrad. "Silent Snow, Secret Snow"
Joyce, James. "Araby"
Kafka, Franz. THE METAMORPHOSIS
Melville, Herman. "Bartleby the Scrivener"

- *also see*

Hesse, Hermann. THE POET
Mann, Thomas. TRISTAN

Mann, Thomas. TRISTAN
- *compared with*

Aichinger, Ilse. THE BOUND MAN
Eliot, T. S. "The Love Song of J. Alfred Prufrock"
Kafka, Franz. A HUNGER ARTIST
Mann, Thomas. *Buddenbrooks*
Mann, Thomas. *Death in Venice*
Mann, Thomas. TONIO KRÖGER
Melville, Herman. "Bartleby the Scrivener"
Thurber, James. "The Secret Life of Walter Mitty"
Wagner, Richard. "Liebestod" from *Tristan and
  Isolde* (aria)

- *also see*

Hesse, Hermann. THE POET
Kafka, Franz. A HUNGER ARTIST

A MAN OF HONOR by Shaukat Siddiqi
- *compared with*

Achebe, Chinua. *Things Fall Apart*
Benson, Sally. "The Overcoat"
Maupassant, Guy de. THE NECKLACE.

Master and Man by Leo Tolstoy
- *see*

Tolstoy, Leo. THE DEATH OF IVÁN ILYICH

The Master and Margarita by Mikhail Bulgakov
- *see*

France, Anatole. THE PROCURATOR OF JUDEA

THE MASTER OF DOORNVLEI by Es'kia Mphahlele
- *compared with*

Douglass, Frederick. *The Life of Frederick Douglass, An Autobiography*
Haley, Alex. *Roots*
Wright, Richard. *Native Son*

"Mateo Falcone" by Prosper Mérimée
- *see*

Kafka, Franz. THE JUDGMENT

MATRYONA'S HOME by Alexander Solzhenitsyn
- *compared with*

Andric, Ivo. THE SCYTHE
Djilas, Milovan. THE OLD MAN AND THE SONG
Djilas, Milovan. WAR
Mrozek, Slawomir. CHILDREN
Mrozek, Slawomir. ON A JOURNEY
Sholokhov, Mikhail. THE COLT
Sholokhov, Mikhail. THE FATE OF A MAN
Sienkiewicz, Henryk. YANKO THE MUSICIAN
Solzhenitsyn, Alexander. THE RIGHT HAND
Solzhenitsyn, Alexander. ZAKHAR-THE-POUCH
- *also see*

Andric, Ivo. THE SCYTHE
Andric, Ivo. A SUMMER IN THE SOUTH
Djilas, Milovan. WAR
Mrozek, Slawomir. ON A JOURNEY
Sholokhov, Mikhail. THE FATE OF A MAN
Solzhenitsyn, Alexander. THE RIGHT HAND
Solzhenitsyn, Alexander. ZAKHAR-THE-POUCH
Tamasi, Aron. FLASHES IN THE NIGHT

Maugham, Somerset. *Of Human Bondage*
- *see*

Siwertz, Sigfrid. IN SPITE OF EVERYTHING

Maupassant, Guy de. "Clochette"
- *see*

Maupassant, Guy de. THE NECKLACE
Zola, Émile. NAÏS MICOULIN

Maupassant, Guy de. "The Duel"
- *see*

Maupassant, Guy de. THE NECKLACE

Maupassant, Guy de. "Hautot and His Son"
- *see*

Maupassant, Guy de. THE NECKLACE

Maupassant, Guy de. "Minuet"
- *see*

Maupassant, Guy de. THE NECKLACE

Maupassant, Guy de. THE NECKLACE
- *compared with*

Anderson, Sherwood. "The Egg"
Henry, O. "The Gift of the Magi"
Howells, William Dean. *A Hazard of New Fortunes*
Maupassant, Guy de. "Clochette"
Maupassant, Guy de. "The Duel"
Maupassant, Guy de. "Hautot and His Son"
Maupassant, Guy de. "Minuet"
Maupassant, Guy de. "A Piece of String"
- *also see*

Rifaat, Alifa. ANOTHER EVENING AT THE CLUB
Siddiqi, Shaukat. A MAN OF HONOR

Maupassant, Guy de. "A Piece of String"
- *see*

Andric, Ivo. THE SCYTHE
Maupassant, Guy de. THE NECKLACE

McTeague by Frank Norris
- *see*

Chekhov, Anton. THE BET

Medea by Euripides
- *see*

Zola, Émile. NAÏS MICOULIN

Megged, Aharon. THE NAME
- *compared with*

Huber, Heinz. THE NEW APARTMENT
Mann, Thomas. DISORDER AND EARLY SORROW
Singer, Isaac B. "Grandfather and Grandson"
Singer, Isaac B. "The Old Man"
Walker, Alice. "Everyday Use"

"Middle Passage" by Robert Hayden
- *see*

Danticat, Edwidge. CHILDREN OF THE SEA

"The Migrane Workers" by Ann Petry
- *see*

Weller, Archie. GOING HOME

Miller, Arthur. *After the Fall*
- *see*

Calvino, Italo. ALL AT ONE POINT
Moravia, Alberto. THE FALL

Millet, Jean François. *The Gleaners* (painting)
- *see*

Zola, Émile. NAÏS MICOULIN

"The Minister's Black Veil" by Nathaniel Hawthorne
- *see*

Balzac, Honoré de. THE ATHEIST'S MASS
Lagerlöf, Selma. THE OUTLAWS
Phiên Vō. THE KEY
Saranti, Galatea. SUNLIGHT

"Minuet" by Guy de Maupassant
- *see*

Maupassant, Guy de. THE NECKLACE

THE MIRROR by R. K. Narayan
- *compared with*

Jacobs, W. W. "The Monkey's Paw"
Ovid. *The Metamorphoses*
- *also see*

Akutagawa Ryūnosuke. IN A GROVE
Tanizaki Junichiro. THE THIEF

Mishima Yukio. PATRIOTISM
- *compared with*

Benét, Stephen Vincent. "The Blood of the Martyrs"
Hemingway, Ernest. *In Our Time*
- *also see*

Pirandello, Luigi. CINCI

Mishima Yukio. *The Sound of Waves*
- *see*

O Yong-su. SEASIDE VILLAGE

"Miss Brill" by Katherine Mansfield
- *see*

Kariara, Jonathan. HER WARRIOR
Ngugi, James. THE MARTYR
Surangkhanang, K. THE GRANDMOTHER

Missing (film)
- *see*

Valenzuela, Luisa. I'M YOUR HORSE IN THE NIGHT

"Miss Tempy's Watchers" by Sarah Orne Jewett
- *see*

Nakos, Lilika. HELENITSA

Moby Dick by Herman Melville
- *see*

Balzac, Honoré de. LA GRANDE BRETÊCHE
Pirandello, Luigi. WAR

"A Modest Proposal" by Jonathan Swift
- *see*

Mrozek, Slawomir. ON A JOURNEY

Molière. *Don Juan*
- *see*

Mérimée, Prosper. THE VENUS OF ILLE

"The Monkey's Paw" by W. W. Jacobs
- *see*

Lim, Catherine. PAPER
Narayan, R. K. THE MIRROR

"The Monster" by Stephen Crane
- *see*

Buzzati, Dino. THE SLAYING OF THE DRAGON

MONUMENT by Hebe Meleagrou
- *compared with*

Bierce, Ambrose. "An Occurrence at Owl Creek Bridge"
Kipling, Rudyard. "The Man Who Would Be King"
Venezis, Elias. MYCENAE

MURKE'S COLLECTED SILENCES by Heinrich Böll

- *compared with*

Cage, John. *4'33* (piano composition)
Greene, Graham. "The Destructors"
Hemingway, Ernest. "A Clean, Well-Lighted Place"

- *also see*

Tolstoy, Leo. THE DEATH OF IVÁN ILYICH

My Ántonia by Willa Cather

- *see*

Zola, Émile. NAÏS MICOULIN

MYCENAE by Elias Venezis

- *compared with*

Aeschylus. *Agamemnon*
Agee, James. *A Death in the Family*
Anderson, Sherwood. "Death in the Woods"
Connell, Richard. "The Most Dangerous Game"
Greene, Graham. "The Destructors"
Jackson, Shirley. "The Lottery"

Leopardi, Giacomo. "To Italy"
Robinson, Edward Arlington. "Reuben Bright"
Solzhenitsyn, Alexander. ZAKHAR-THE-POUCH
Steinbeck, John. *The Red Pony*
Vigny, Alfred de. "The Sound of the Horn"

- *also see*

Meleagrou, Hebe. MONUMENT

"My Last Duchess" by Robert Browning

- *see*

Rushdi, Rashad. ANGUISH

MY LIFE WITH THE WAVE by Octavio Paz

- *compared with*

Silverstein, Shel. "The Giving Tree"

The Myth of Sisyphus by Albert Camus

- *see*

Aichinger, Ilse. THE BOUND MAN
Tolstoy, Leo. THE DEATH OF IVÁN ILYICH

N

NAEMA—WHEREABOUTS UNKNOWN by
  Mohammed Dib

- *compared with*

Crane, Stephen. "An Episode of War"
Dos Passos, John. *USA*
Joyce, James. "Araby"
Lessing, Doris. "Through the Tunnel"
Steinbeck, John. *The Grapes of Wrath*
Steinbeck, John. *In Dubious Battle*

Naipaul, V. S. B. WORDSWORTH

- *compared with*

Cisneros, Sandra. "Sally"
Joyce, James. "Araby"
Wordsworth's short poems

Naipaul, V. S. THE ENEMY

- *compared with*

Schulz, Bruno. COCKROACHES
Welty, Eudora. "Kin"
Welty, Eudora. "Why I Live at the P.O."

- *also see*

Schulz, Bruno. COCKROACHES

NAÏS MICOULIN by Émile Zola

- *compared with*

Cather, Willa. *My Ántonia*
Crane, Stephen. *Maggie: A Girl of the Streets*
Dreiser, Theodore. *Sister Carrie*
Euripides. *Medea*
Flaubert, Gustave. A SIMPLE HEART
Hardy, Thomas. *Tess of the d'Urbervilles*
Maupassant, Guy de. "Clochette"
Millet, Jean François. *The Gleaners* (painting)
Puccini, Giacomo. *Madame Butterfly* (opera)
Shakespeare, William. *Hamlet*
Strindberg, August. *Countess Julie*
Tarkington, Booth. *Alice Adams*

- *also see*

Colette. THE LITTLE BOUILLOUX GIRL

Nhat-Tien. AN UNSOUND SLEEP
- ■ *compared with*

Lao She. GRANDMOTHER TAKES CHARGE
Surangkhanang, K. THE GRANDMOTHER

Nicol, Abioseth. AS THE NIGHT THE DAY
- ■ *compared with*

Dostoevski, Fyodor. *Crime and Punishment*
Ellison, Ralph. "Battle Royal"
Golding, William. *Lord of the Flies*
Hawthorne, Nathaniel. *The Scarlet Letter*
Jackson, Shirley. "The Lottery"

NIGHT FACE UP by Julio Cortázar
- ■ *compared with*

Conrad, Joseph. *Heart of Darkness*
Faulkner, William. *As I Lay Dying*
Jackson, Shirley. "The Lottery"
Star Wars (film)
Yu-Lan Fung. *History of Chinese Philosophy*
- ■ *also see*

Yizhar, S. HABAKUK

"Night-Sea Journey" by John Barth
- ■ *see*

Calvino, Italo. ALL AT ONE POINT

No Exit by Jean-Paul Sartre
- ■ *see*

Sartre, Jean-Paul. THE WALL
Tolstoy, Leo. THE DEATH OF IVÁN ILYICH

No Longer at Ease by Chinua Achebe
- ■ *see*

Achebe, Chinua. THE VOTER

Norris, Frank. *McTeague*
- ■ *see*

Chekhov, Anton. THE BET

NO SWEETNESS HERE by Ama Ata Aidoo
- ■ *compared with*
Selormey, Francis. *The Narrow Path*

Notes from Underground by Fyodor Dostoevski
- ■ *see*

Sarang, Vilas. THE TERRORIST

O

O Yong-su. SEASIDE VILLAGE
- ■ *compared with*
Mishima Yukio. *The Sound of Waves*

O'Brien, Fitz-James. "The Diamond Lens"
- ■ *see*

Dostoevski, Fyodor. WHITE NIGHTS

"An Occurrence at Owl Creek Bridge" by Ambrose
Bierce
- ■ *see*

Heym, Georg. THE AUTOPSY
Meleagrou, Hebe. MONUMENT
Sholokhov, Mikhail. THE COLT
Yizhar, S. HABAKUK

O'Connor, Flannery. "A Good Man Is Hard to Find"
- ■ *see*

Surangkhanang, K. THE GRANDMOTHER

O'Connor, Flannery. "The Life You Save May Be
Your Own"
- ■ *see*

Idris, Youssef. THE CHEAPEST NIGHT'S
ENTERTAINMENT

O'Connor, Flannery. "Revelation"
- ■ *see*

Gordimer, Nadine. A SOLDIER'S EMBRACE

"The Open Window" by H. H. Munro
- *see*

Papadiamantis, Alexandros. THE BEWITCHING OF THE AGA

Ordinary People by Judith Guest
- *see*

Björnson, Björnstjerne. THE FATHER

"Original Sin" by Robinson Jeffers
- *see*

Buzzati, Dino. THE SLAYING OF THE DRAGON

Orwell, George. *Animal Farm*
- *see*

Kafka, Franz. THE METAMORPHOSIS

Orwell, George. "Shooting an Elephant"
- *see*

Dinesen, Isak. THE SAILOR BOY'S TALE

THE OUTLAWS by Selma Lagerlöf
- *compared with*

Hawthorne, Nathaniel. "The Minister's Black Veil"
Hawthorne, Nathaniel. "Young Goodman Brown"

"The Outstation" by Somerset Maugham
- *see*

Venezis, Elias. MYCENAE

"The Overcoat" by Sally Benson
- *see*

Siddiqi, Shaukat. A MAN OF HONOR

Ovid. *The Metamorphoses*
- *see*

Asturias, Miguel. TATUANA'S TALE
Kafka, Franz. THE METAMORPHOSIS
Murakami Haruki. ON MEETING MY 100 PERCENT WOMAN ONE FINE APRIL MORNING
Narayan, R. K. THE MIRROR
Tanizaki Junichiro. THE THIEF

"Ozymandias" by Percy Bysshe Shelley
- *see*

Andreyev, Leonid. LAZARUS

P

The Painted Bird by Jerzy Kosinski
- *see*

Borowski, Tadeusz. THE MAN WITH THE PACKAGE

The Palm-Wine Drinkard by Amos Tutuola
- *see*

Amado, Jorge. HOW PORCIÚNCULA THE MULATTO GOT THE CORPSE OFF HIS BACK

Papadiamantis, Alexandros. THE BEWITCHING OF THE AGA
- *compared with*

Buck, Pearl. "The Old Demon"

Chopin, Kate. "The Story of an Hour"
Gilman, Charlotte Perkins. "The Yellow Wallpaper"
Munro, H. H. "The Open Window"
Thurber, James. "The Secret Life of Walter Mitty"
Wharton, Edith. "Roman Fever"

PAPER by Catherine Lim
- *compared with*

Jacobs, W. W. "The Monkey's Paw"
Lawrence, D. H. "The Rocking Horse Winner"
Thurber, James. "The Secret Life of Walter Mitty"
- *also see*

Ray, Satyajit. ASHAMANJA BABU'S DOG

PAPER BOAT by Kundanika Kapadia

■ *compared with*

Joyce, James. "Araby"
Lessing, Doris. "Through the Tunnel"

PAPER IS MONEY by Razia Ahmad

■ *compared with*

"Hansel and Gretel"
Henry, O. "The Gift of the Magi"
"Jack and the Beanstalk"
Stella (film)
Stella Dallas (film)

Parker, Dorothy. "The Standard of Living"

■ *see*

Alexiou, Elli. THEY WERE ALL TO BE PITIED

Parker, Dorothy. "The Waltz"

■ *see*

Yáñez, Mirta. WE BLACKS ALL DRINK COFFEE

Parmigianino. *Self-Portrait* (painting)

■ *see*

Villiers de L'Isle-Adam. THE DESIRE TO BE A MAN

THE PASHA'S DAUGHTER by Naguib Mahfouz

■ *compared with*

Faulkner, William. "The Auction of the Spotted Horses"
Heller, Joseph. *Catch-22*
Malamud, Bernard. "The Magic Barrel"
Roth, Philip. *Goodbye, Columbus*

PASTORAL by Tommaso Landolfi

■ *compared with*

Delvaux, Paul. *The Sleeping City* (painting)
Huysman, J. K. *Against the Grain*
Lawrence, D. H. "The Horse Dealer's Daughter"
Magritte, René. *The Red Model* (painting)

PATRIOTISM by Mishima Yukio

■ *compared with*

Benét, Stephen Vincent. "The Blood of the Martyrs"
Hemingway, Ernest. *In Our Time*

■ *also see*

Pirandello, Luigi. CINCI

"Paul's Case" by Willa Cather

■ *see*

Achebe, Chinua. VENGEFUL CREDITOR
Gordimer, Nadine. LITTLE WILLIE
Haris, Petros. LIGHTS ON THE SEA
Kafka, Franz. THE JUDGMENT
Kariara, Jonathan. HER WARRIOR
Lu Xun. DIARY OF A MADMAN
Ngugi, James. THE MARTYR

Pavese, Cesare. SUICIDES

■ *compared with*

Gilman, Charlotte Perkins. "The Yellow Wallpaper"
Hawthorne, Nathaniel. "Wakefield"
Lessing, Doris. "To Room Nineteen"
Melville, Herman. "Bartleby the Scrivener"
Wright, Richard. "The Man Who Lived Underground"

Paz, Octavio. MY LIFE WITH THE WAVE

■ *compared with*

Silverstein, Shel. "The Giving Tree"

"A Pedestrian Accident" by Robert Coover

■ *see*

Lu Xun. DIARY OF A MADMAN

Père Goriot by Honoré de Balzac

■ *see*

Balzac, Honoré de. LA GRANDE BRETÊCHE

Peter Pan by J. M. Barrie

■ *see*

Mahfouz, Naguib. THE CONJURER MADE OFF WITH THE DISH

"Petrified Man" by Eudora Welty

■ *see*

Idris, Youssef. THE CHEAPEST NIGHT'S ENTERTAINMENT

Petry, Ann. "The Migrane Workers"

■ *see*

Weller, Archie. GOING HOME

Phiên Võ. THE KEY

- *compared with*

Crane, Stephen. "The Bride Comes to Yellow Sky"
Hawthorne, Nathaniel. "The Minister's Black Veil"
Twain, Mark. "The Celebrated Jumping Frog of Calaveras County"

THE PHOTOGRAPHER'S MISSUS by Colette

- *compared with*

Flaubert, Gustave. *Madame Bovary*
Gilman, Charlotte Perkins. "The Yellow Wallpaper"
Ibsen, Henrik. *A Doll's House*
Ibsen, Henrik. *Hedda Gabler*
Lessing, Doris. *A Proper Marriage*

Picasso, Pablo. *Bust of a Woman* (painting)

- *see*

Mann, Thomas. DISORDER AND EARLY SORROW

The Picture of Dorian Gray by Oscar Wilde

- *see*

Kawabata Yasunari. THE MOON ON THE WATER
Tolstoy, Leo. HOW MUCH LAND DOES A MAN NEED
Villiers de L'Isle-Adam. THE DESIRE TO BE A MAN

"A Piece of String" by Guy de Maupassant

- *see*

Andric, Ivo. THE SCYTHE
Maupassant, Guy de. THE NECKLACE

"The Pied Piper of Hamelin" by Robert Browning

- *see*

Izgü, Muzaffer. WANTED: A TOWN WITHOUT A CRAZY

"Piktor's Metamorphosis" by Hermann Hesse

- *see*

Asturias, Miguel. TATUANA'S TALE

Pillars of Society by George Grosz (painting)

- *see*

Hildesheimer, Wolfgang. A WORLD ENDS

Pinter, Harold. *Old Times*

- *see*

Borges, Jorge Luis. THE GARDEN OF FORKING PATHS

Pirandello, Luigi. CINCI

- *compared with*

Camus, Albert. *The Stranger*
Crane, Stephen. "The Upturned Face"
Hemingway, Ernest. "The Short Happy Life of Francis Macomber"
Mishima Yukio. PATRIOTISM
Wright, Richard. *Native Son*

- *also see*

Moravia, Alberto. THE FALL
Pirandello, Luigi. WAR

Pirandello, Luigi. *Six Characters in Search of an Author*

- *see*

Borges, Jorge Luis. THE GARDEN OF FORKING PATHS

Pirandello, Luigi. WAR

- *compared with*

Dickinson, Emily. "There's a certain slant of light"
Hemingway, Ernest. "A Clean, Well-Lighted Place"
Joyce, James. "The Dead"
Melville, Herman. "The Whiteness of the Whale" from *Moby Dick*
Pirandello, Luigi. CINCI
Sartre, Jean-Paul. THE WALL

- *also see*

Björnson, Björnstjerne. THE FATHER

"The Pit and the Pendulum" by Edgar Allan Poe

- *see*

Villiers de L'Isle-Adam. THE TORTURE BY HOPE

Pocket Full of Miracles (film)

- *see*

Izgü, Muzaffer. WANTED: A TOWN WITHOUT A CRAZY

Poe, Edgar Allan. "The Black Cat"

- *see*

Dostoevski, Fyodor. THE DREAM OF A RIDICULOUS MAN

Poe, Edgar Allan. "The Cask of Amontillado"

- *see*

Balzac, Honoré de. LA GRANDE BRETÊCHE

Puccini, Giacomo. *Madame Butterfly* (opera)
- ■ *see*

Zola, Émile. NAÏS MICOULIN

"The Pupil" by Henry James
- ■ *see*

Daudet, Alphonse. THE LAST LESSON

Pushkin, Alexander. *The Stone Guest*
- ■ *see*

Mérimée, Prosper. THE VENUS OF ILLE

Pygmalion and Galatea by W. S. Gilbert
- ■ *see*

Mérimée, Prosper. THE VENUS OF ILLE

R

Rand, Ayn. *The Fountainhead*
- ■ *see*

Fuentes, Carlos. THE TWO ELENAS

Ray, Satyajit. ASHAMANJA BABU'S DOG
- ■ *compared with*

Dickens, Charles. *A Christmas Carol*
King Midas folktale
Lawrence, D. H. "The Rocking Horse Winner"
Lim, Catherine. PAPER

"The Real Thing" by Henry James
- ■ *see*

Hesse, Hermann. THE POET
Tanizaki Junichiro. TATTOO

The Red Model by René Magritte (painting)
- ■ *see*

Landolfi, Tommaso. PASTORAL

The Red Pony by John Steinbeck
- ■ *see*

Sholokhov, Mikhail. THE COLT
Venezis, Elias. MYCENAE

THE RETURN OF THE PRODIGAL SON by André Gide
- ■ *compared with*

Greuze, Jean Baptiste. *The Return of the Prodigal Son* (painting)
Joyce, James. *A Portrait of the Artist as a Young Man*

Sullivan, Arthur. *The Return of the Prodigal Son* (oratorio)
Welty, Eudora. "Why I Live at the P.O."
Wolfe, Thomas. *Look Homeward, Angel*
- ■ *also see*

Kafka, Franz. THE JUDGMENT

The Return of the Prodigal Son by Jean Baptiste Greuze (painting)
- ■ *see*

Gide, André. THE RETURN OF THE PRODIGAL SON

The Return of the Prodigal Son by Arthur Sullivan (oratorio)
- ■ *see*

Gide, André. THE RETURN OF THE PRODIGAL SON

"Reuben Bright" by Edward Arlington Robinson
- ■ *see*

Venezis, Elias. MYCENAE

"Revelation" by Flannery O'Connor
- ■ *see*

Gordimer, Nadine. A SOLDIER'S EMBRACE

Rhinoceros by Eugene Ionesco
- ■ *see*

Aymé, Marcel. THE MAN WHO WALKED THROUGH WALLS
Kafka, Franz. A HUNGER ARTIST
Kafka, Franz. THE METAMORPHOSIS

Roth, Philip. *Goodbye, Columbus*

■ *see*

Mahfouz, Naguib. THE PASHA'S DAUGHTER

Roufos, Rodis. THE CANDIDATE

■ *compared with*

Anderson, Sherwood. "I'm a Fool"
Steinbeck, John. "The Chrysanthemums"

Rushdi, Rashad. ANGUISH

■ *compared with*

Barth, John. *Lost in the Funhouse*
Browning, Robert. "My Last Duchess"
Eliot, T. S. "The Love Song of J. Alfred Prufrock"

Russell, John. "The Price of the Head"

■ *see*

Pontoppidan, Henrik. A FISHER NEST

S

Saga of Hrafnkel

■ *see*

Zola, Émile. THE INUNDATION

THE SAILOR BOY'S TALE by Isak Dinesen

■ *compared with*

Coleridge, Samuel Taylor. "The Rime of the Ancient Mariner"
Lessing, Doris. "A Sunrise on the Veld"
Orwell, George. "Shooting an Elephant"

"Saint Emmanuel the Good Martyr" by Miguel Unamuno

■ *see*

Sartre, Jean-Paul. THE WALL

Salinger, J. D. *A Catcher in the Rye*

■ *see*

Kiwon So. THE HEIR
Yáñez, Mirta. WE BLACKS ALL DRINK COFFEE
Zola, Émile. THE INUNDATION

Salinger, J. D. "For Esmé—with Love and Squalor"

■ *see*

La Guma, Alex. BLANKETS

"Sally" by Sandra Cisneros

■ *see*

Naipaul, V. S. B. WORDSWORTH

Sand, George. *Consuelo*

■ *see*

Sand, George. THE MARQUISE

Sand, George. THE MARQUISE

■ *compared with*

Flaubert, Gustave. *Madame Bovary*
Ibsen, Henrik. *Hedda Gabler*
Ibsen, Henrik. *Wild Duck*
Mann, Thomas. *Confessions of Felix Krull: Confidence Man*
Sand, George. *Consuelo*
Tolstoy, Leo. *Anna Karenina*

Santos, Bienvenido N. THE DAY THE DANCERS CAME

■ *compared with*

Cather, Willa. "A Wagner Matinee"
Hemingway, Ernest. "A Clean, Well-Lighted Place"
Kafka, Franz. THE METAMORPHOSIS

■ *also see*

Murakami Haruki. ON MEETING MY 100 PERCENT WOMAN ONE FINE APRIL MORNING

Sarang, Vilas. THE TERRORIST

■ *compared with*

Bowles, Paul. "If I Should Open My Mouth"
Dostoevski, Fyodor. *Notes from Underground*
Thurber, James. "The Secret Life of Walter Mitty"

"The Siege of Berlin" by Alphonse Daudet

■ *see*

Daudet, Alphonse. THE LAST LESSON

Sienkiewicz, Henryk. THE LIGHTHOUSE-KEEPER

■ *compared with*

Andric, Ivo. THE SCYTHE
Andric, Ivo. A SUMMER IN THE SOUTH
Bradbury, Ray. "The Fog-Horn"
Kafka, Franz. THE METAMORPHOSIS
Lawrence, D. H. "The Island"
Mann, Thomas. "Tobias Mindernickel"
Solzhenitsyn, Alexander. THE RIGHT HAND

Sienkiewicz, Henryk. YANKO THE MUSICIAN

■ *compared with*

Mann, Thomas. "The Infant Prodigy"
Mrozek, Slawomir. CHILDREN

■ *also see*

Cumali, Necati. IN GOD'S PLAINS
Djilas, Milovan. WAR
Mrozek, Slawomir. CHILDREN
Solzhenitsyn, Alexander. MATRYONA'S HOME
Solzhenitsyn, Alexander. THE RIGHT HAND

"Silent Snow, Secret Snow" by Conrad Aiken

■ *see*

Lu Xun. DIARY OF A MADMAN
Mann, Thomas. TONIO KRÖGER

Silko, Leslie Marmon. "Lullaby"

■ *see*

Condé, Maryse. THREE WOMEN IN
MANHATTAN

Sillitoe, Alan. "Uncle Ernest" from *The Loneliness of
the Long Distance Runner*

■ *see*

Laxness, Haldor. LILY

Silver Kiss. Annette Curtis Klause

■ *see*

Andreyev, Leonid. LAZARUS

Silverstein, Shel. "The Giving Tree"

■ *see*

Paz, Octavio. MY LIFE WITH THE WAVE

A SIMPLE HEART by Gustave Flaubert

■ *compared with*

Anderson, Sherwood. "Death in the Woods"
Flaubert, Gustave. *Madame Bovary*
Frost, Robert. "Death of the Hired Man"

■ *also see*

Zola, Émile. NAÏS MICOULIN

Sinclair, Upton. *The Jungle*

■ *see*

Dostoevski, Fyodor. THE DREAM OF A
RIDICULOUS MAN

Singer, Isaac B. "Gimpel the Fool"

■ *see*

Idris, Youssef. THE CHEAPEST NIGHT'S
ENTERTAINMENT

Singer, Isaac B. "Grandfather and Grandson"

■ *see*

Megged, Aharon. THE NAME

Singer, Isaac B. "The Old Man"

■ *see*

Megged, Aharon. THE NAME

Sister Carrie by Theodore Dreiser

■ *see*

Zola, Émile. NAÏS MICOULIN

Siwertz, Sigfrid. IN SPITE OF EVERYTHING

■ *compared with*

Brontë, Emily. *Wuthering Heights*
Maugham, Somerset. *Of Human Bondage*

Six Characters in Search of an Author by Luigi
Pirandello

■ *see*

Borges, Jorge Luis. THE GARDEN OF FORKING
PATHS

"Six Feet of the Country" by Nadine Gordimer

■ *see*

Yehoshua, Abraham B. FACING THE FOREST

"Slave on the Block" by Langston Hughes

■ *see*

Vega, Ana Lydia. CLOUD COVERED CARIBBEAN

THE SLAYING OF THE DRAGON by Dino Buzzati

- *compared with*

Crane, Stephen. "The Monster"
Jackson, Shirley. "The Lottery"
Jeffers, Robinson. "Original Sin"
Kafka, Franz. IN THE PENAL COLONY

The Sleeping City by Paul Delvaux (painting)

- *see*

Landolfi, Tommaso. PASTORAL

A SOLDIER'S EMBRACE by Nadine Gordimer

- *compared with*

O'Connor, Flannery. "Revelation"

Solzhenitsyn, Alexander. MATRYONA'S HOME

- *compared with*

Andric, Ivo. THE SCYTHE
Djilas, Milovan. THE OLD MAN AND THE SONG
Djilas, Milovan. WAR
Mrozek, Slawomir. CHILDREN
Mrozek, Slawomir. ON A JOURNEY
Sholokhov, Mikhail. THE COLT
Sholokhov, Mikhail. THE FATE OF A MAN
Sienkiewicz, Henryk. YANKO THE MUSICIAN
Solzhenitsyn, Alexander. THE RIGHT HAND
Solzhenitsyn, Alexander. ZAKHAR-THE-POUCH

- *also see*

Andric, Ivo. THE SCYTHE
Andric, Ivo. A SUMMER IN THE SOUTH
Djilas, Milovan. WAR
Mrozek, Slawomir. ON A JOURNEY
Sholokhov, Mikhail. THE FATE OF A MAN
Solzhenitsyn, Alexander. THE RIGHT HAND
Solzhenitsyn, Alexander. ZAKHAR-THE-POUCH
Tamasi, Aron. FLASHES IN THE NIGHT

Solzhenitsyn, Alexander. THE RIGHT HAND

- *compared with*

Djilas, Milovan. WAR
Mrozek, Slawomir. CHILDREN
Sienkiewicz, Henryk. YANKO THE MUSICIAN
Solzhenitsyn, Alexander. MATRYONA'S HOME
Solzhenitsyn, Alexander. ZAKHAR-THE-POUCH

- *also see*

Djilas, Milovan. WAR
Mrozek, Slawomir. ON A JOURNEY

Sienkiewicz, Henryk. THE LIGHTHOUSE-KEEPER
Solzhenitsyn, Alexander. MATRYONA'S HOME
Solzhenitsyn, Alexander. ZAKHAR-THE-POUCH

Solzhenitsyn, Alexander. ZAKHAR-THE-POUCH

- *compared with*

Benét, Stephen Vincent. "The Devil and Daniel Webster"
Benét, Stephen Vincent. "A Tooth for Paul Revere"
Sholokhov, Mikhail. THE COLT
Sholokhov, Mikhail. THE FATE OF A MAN
Solzhenitsyn, Alexander. MATRYONA'S HOME
Solzhenitsyn, Alexander. THE RIGHT HAND
Turgenev, Ivan. *Hunting Sketches*

- *also see*

Andric, Ivo. THE SCYTHE
Mrozek, Slawomir. ON A JOURNEY
Solzhenitsyn, Alexander. MATRYONA'S HOME
Solzhenitsyn, Alexander. THE RIGHT HAND
Venezis, Elias. MYCENAE

"Song of Myself" by Walt Whitman

- *see*

Calvino, Italo. ALL AT ONE POINT

"Sonny's Blues" by James Baldwin

- *see*

Weller, Archie. GOING HOME

Sophie's Choice by William Styron

- *see*

Borowski, Tadeusz. THE MAN WITH THE PACKAGE

Sophocles. *Oedipus Rex*

- *see*

Dhlomo, H. I. E. THE DAUGHTER
Zola, Émile. THE INUNDATION

SORROW-ACRE by Isak Dinesen

- *compared with*

Gordimer, Nadine. "The Train from Rhodesia"
Sholokhov, Mikhail. THE COLT
Tamasi, Aron. FLASHES IN THE NIGHT

T

Tagore, Rabindranath. KABULIWALLAH

- **compared with**

Lawrence, D. H. "The Rocking Horse Winner"
Shakespeare, William. *Romeo and Juliet*
Twain, Mark. *Huckleberry Finn*
Welty, Eudora. "A Visit of Charity"

The Tale of Genji by Shikibu Murasaki

- **see**

Rifaat, Alifa. AN INCIDENT IN THE GHOBASHI HOUSEHOLD

A Tale of Two Cities by Charles Dickens

- **see**

Fuentes, Carlos. THE TWO ELENAS

Tamasi, Aron. FLASHES IN THE NIGHT

- **compared with**

Andric, Ivo. THE SCYTHE
Andric, Ivo. A SUMMER IN THE SOUTH
Sholokhov, Mikhail. THE COLT
Solzhenitsyn, Alexander. MATRYONA'S HOME

- **also see**

Andric, Ivo. A SUMMER IN THE SOUTH
Cumali, Necati. IN GOD'S PLAINS
Dinesen, Isak. SORROW-ACRE

Tanizaki Junichiro. TATTOO

- **compared with**

Borges, Jorge Luis. "Secret Miracle"
Hemingway, Ernest. "The Killers"
Icarus myth
James, Henry. "The Real Thing"
Steinbeck, John. "The Chrysanthemums"

Tanizaki Junichiro. THE THIEF

- **compared with**

Cephalus and Procris myth (from Ovid's *The Metamorphoses*)
Gogol, Nikolai. "Diary of a Madman"
Lu Xun. DIARY OF A MADMAN
Narayan, R. K. THE MIRROR

"Taras Bulba" by Nikolai Gogol

- **see**

Baykurt, Fakir. FRECKLES

Tarkington, Booth. *Alice Adams*

- **see**

Zola, Émile. NAÏS MICOULIN

TATTOO by Tanizaki Junichiro

- **compared with**

Borges, Jorge Luis. "Secret Miracle"
Hemingway, Ernest. "The Killers"
Icarus myth
James, Henry. "The Real Thing"
Steinbeck, John. "The Chrysanthemums"

TATUANA'S TALE by Miguel Asturias

- **compared with**

Daphne and Apollo myth (from Ovid's *The Metamorphoses*)
Hesse, Hermann. "Piktor's Metamorphosis"
Kafka, Franz. THE METAMORPHOSIS

Taylor, Apirana. THE CARVING

- **compared with**

Gordimer, Nadine. "Home"
Thiong'o, Ngũgĩ wa. *Weep Not Child*

"The Tell-Tale Heart" by Edgar Allan Poe

- **see**

Dostoevski, Fyodor. THE DREAM OF A RIDICULOUS MAN

"Tennessee's Partner" by Bret Harte

- **see**

Balzac, Honoré de. THE ATHEIST'S MASS

The Tenor by Frank Wedekind

- **see**

Villiers de L'Isle-Adam. THE DESIRE TO BE A MAN

"The Termitary" by Nadine Gordimer

- **see**

Vega, Ana Lydia. CLOUD COVER CARIBBEAN

U

V

Verga, Giovanni. PROPERTY

■ *compared with*

Dickens, Charles. *A Christmas Carol*
Henry, O. "Gift of the Magi"
Lawrence, D. H. "The Rocking Horse Winner"

Vigny, Alfred de. "The Sound of the Horn"

■ *see*

Venezis, Elias. MYCENAE

VILLAGE LIFE by Konstantinos Theotokis

■ *compared with*

Furman, Laura. "Watch Time Fly"
Glaspell, Susan. "A Jury of Her Peers"
Poe, Edgar Allan. "The Cask of Amontillado"
Thurber, James. "The Catbird Seat"
Welty, Eudora. "Why I Live at the P.O."

"A Village Singer" by Mary Wilkins Freemen

■ *see*

Idris, Youssef. THE CHEAPEST NIGHT'S
   ENTERTAINMENT
Saranti, Galatea. SUNLIGHT

Villiers de L'Isle-Adam. THE DESIRE TO BE A MAN

■ *compared with*

Arnold, Matthew. "The Buried Life"
Dostoevski, Fyodor. *Crime and Punishment*
Parmigianino. *Self-Portrait* (painting)
Wedekind, Frank. *The Tenor*
Wilde, Oscar. *The Picture of Dorian Gray*
Wright, Richard. "Almos' a Man"

Villiers de L'Isle-Adam. THE TORTURE BY HOPE

■ *compared with*

Dostoevski, Fyodor. *The Brothers Karamazov*
Kafka, Franz. IN THE PENAL COLONY
Munch, Edvard. *The Scream* (painting)
Poe, Edgar Allan. "The Pit and the Pendulum"
Sartre, Jean-Paul. THE WALL

"A Visit of Charity" by Eudora Welty

■ *see*

Tagore, Rabindranath. KABULIWALLAH

"A Visit to Grandmother" by William Kelley

■ *see*

Lao She. GRANDMOTHER TAKES CHARGE

Voltaire. *Candide*

■ *see*

Zola, Émile. THE INUNDATION

THE VOTER by Chinua Achebe

■ *compared with*

Achebe, Chinua. *Man of the People*
Achebe, Chinua. *No Longer at Ease*
Ekwensi, Cyprian. *Jagua Nana*
Ibsen, Henrik. *An Enemy of the People*
Soyinka, Wole. *The Interpreter*
Twain, Mark. "The Man That Corrupted
   Hadleyburg"

W

THE WAGES OF GOOD by Birago Diop

■ *compared with*

Aesop's fables
Fontaine's fables
Kafka's parables

Wagner, Richard. "Liebestod" from *Tristan and
   Isolde* (aria)

■ *see*

Mann, Thomas. TRISTAN

y

YERMOLAY AND THE MILLER'S WIFE by Ivan
Turgenev

■ *compared with*

Chekhov, Anton. *The Cherry Orchard*
Faulkner, William. "The Bear"
Hemingway, Ernest. "Big Two-Hearted River"
Thurber, James. "The Dog That Bit People"
Walker, Alice. *The Color Purple*

Yizhar, S. HABAKUK

■ *compared with*

Bierce, Ambrose. "An Occurrence at Owl Creek
Bridge"
Cortázar, Julio. NIGHT FACE UP
Jackson, Shirley. "The Lottery"
Valenzuela, Luisa. I'M YOUR HORSE IN THE
NIGHT

You Can't Go Home Again by Thomas Wolfe

■ *see*

Agnon, S. Y. THE DOCUMENT
Izgü, Muzaffer. WANTED: A TOWN WITHOUT A
CRAZY

"You Have Left Your Lotus Pods on the Bus" by Paul
Bowles

■ *see*

Narayan, R. K. A HORSE AND TWO GOATS

"The Youngest Doll" by Rosario Ferre

■ *see*

Agnon, S. Y. A WHOLE LOAF

"Young Goodman Brown" by Nathaniel Hawthorne

■ *see*

Achebe, Chinua. VENGEFUL CREDITOR
Dove-Danquah, Mabel. THE TORN VEIL
Hesse, Hermann. THE POET
Lagerlöf, Selma. THE OUTLAWS
Moravia, Alberto. THE FALL

"Youth" by Joseph Conrad

■ *see*

Dostoevski, Fyodor. WHITE NIGHTS
Mahfouz, Naguib. THE CONJURER MADE OFF
WITH THE DISH

Yu-Lan Fung. *History of Chinese Philosophy*

■ *see*

Cortázar, Julio. NIGHT FACE UP

Z

ZAKHAR-THE-POUCH by Alexander Solzhenitsyn

■ *compared with*

Benét, Stephen Vincent. "The Devil and Daniel
Webster"
Benét, Stephen Vincent. "A Tooth for Paul
Revere"
Sholokhov, Mikhail. THE COLT
Sholokhov, Mikhail. THE FATE OF A MAN
Solzhenitsyn, Alexander. MATRYONA'S HOME
Solzhenitsyn, Alexander. THE RIGHT HAND
Turgenev, Ivan. *Hunting Sketches*

■ *also see*

Andric, Ivo. THE SCYTHE
Mrozek, Slawomir. ON A JOURNEY
Solzhenitsyn, Alexander. MATRYONA'S HOME
Solzhenitsyn, Alexander. THE RIGHT HAND
Venezis, Elias. MYCENAE

Bonnie H. Neumann (BHN) has been professor of English at the University of Wisconsin–Platteville and dean of undergraduate studies at San Diego State University. A graduate of the University of Wisconsin, the Writers Workshop at the University of Iowa, and the University of New Mexico, she has published books on Mary Wollstonecraft Shelley and Robert Smith Surtees and coedited *Literature from the World.* She is currently dean of arts and sciences at East Stroudsburg University of Pennsylvania. She is past chair of the NCTE Committee on World and Comparative Literature and has served on that committee for more than fifteen years.

(HMM) received a B.A. from Monmouth University, an M.A. ty, and a Ph.D. from Rutgers University. Now retired, she was at Ocean Township High School in Oakhurst, New Jersey, for s served as author or editor for nineteen ScottForesman lit- cluding *Of Time and Place, Teutonic Literature, Russian ture,* and *Classics in World Literature.* She has been a ee on World and Comparative Literature from 1967 to s as chair and associate chair of that committee. Dr. educational matters.

CONTRIBUTORS

James DeMuth (JDM), now deceased, was associate professor of English and director of American studies at the University of Wisconsin–River Falls. He received a B.A. in English from Carleton College and an M.A. and Ph.D. in American studies from the University of Minnesota. His publications include the book *Small Town America* and articles in *The Library Chronicle* and *Studies in American Humor.*

Mary Alice Fite (MAF) currently holds the John V. Chapman Distinguished Chair of English at The Columbus School for Girls in Columbus, Ohio. A long-standing member of the NCTE Committee on World and Comparative Literature, she has made numerous presentations at NCTE national conventions and at conferences of the Ohio Association of Independent Schools. She is coauthor of *Classics in World Literature.*

Daphne Grabovoi (DG) has taught high school English and journalism in the Clark County School District in Las Vegas for twenty-five years. She has been involved in the Advanced Placement English program in addition to being an adjunct faculty member at the Community College of Southern Nevada for the past fifteen years. She received her B.A. in English literature from the University of Washington and an M.A. in English education from the University of Nevada at Las Vegas.

Judith A. Granese (JAG) received both a B.A. and an M.A. in English from New York's St. John's University. During her eighteen years at Valley High School in Las Vegas, Nevada, she has implemented a Latin program, taught English, and served as English department chair. She has served as president of the Southern Nevada Teachers of English and treasurer of the Nevada State Council of Teachers of English. In 1993, she received the Reader's Digest American Hero in Education Award.

Hobart Jarrett (HJ), Ph.D., is professor emeritus of English of Brooklyn College of the City University of New York. A Shakespeare and humanities scholar, he received presidential medals from two presidents of Brooklyn College and a special citation from CUNY for excellence in teaching. He was the first CUNY professor to conduct a live seminar on cable television. An activist, he was chief negotiator for the opening of the eating facilities that the sit-ins had won in Greensboro, North Carolina.

Myrtle J. Jones (MJJ), retired assistant professor of English, Clark Atlanta University, Atlanta, Georgia, is a native of Rome, Georgia. She received her B.A. from Clark University and her M.A. from New York University. She is coauthor of *England in Literature,* a textbook for high school students, and author of the unit on black African literature in NCTE's *Guide to World Literature.*

Paul G. Lankford (PGL) is English department chair at Green Run High School in Virginia Beach, Virginia. A graduate of the College of William and Mary and Old Dominion University, he was City and State English Teacher of the Year in 1982 and Regional Teacher of the Year in 1991. A former chair and present member of the NCTE Committee on World and Comparative Literature, Mr. Lankford is coauthor of *Classics in World Literature.*

May Lee (ML) was born in China, but spent her childhood in India, Taiwan, and Japan and has lived, studied, and taught primarily in the United States. Educated Western but raised Asian, she was challenged early to integrate international and multicultural elements into her personal experience. Her quest to develop and make sense of a global perspective has continued through her years of teaching world literature and philosophy, her work in film, her pursuit of a doctoral degree in integral st with a concentration in East-West psyche

Peter T. Markman (PTM), professor of English at Fullerton College in California for thirty-one years, holds a B.A. from the University of Texas and an M.A. from Claremont Graduate School, where he worked toward the Ph.D. supported by a Woodrow Wilson Fellowship. He teaches writing, the literature of the United States, literary analysis, and mythology. His publications, coauthored with his wife, include *10 Steps in Writing the Research Paper, Masks of the Spirit: Image and Metaphor in Mesoamerica,* and *The Flayed God: The Mythology of Mesoamerica.*

Roberta Hoffman Markman (RHM) has been professor of comparative literature and comparative mythology at California State University, Long Beach, since 1968. She holds a B.A. from Hunter College, an M.A. from Columbia University, and a Ph.D. from Occidental/Claremont Colleges. In 1983, she was chosen as outstanding professor for the California State University system. She has chaired the NCTE Committee on World and Comparative Literature and has coauthored, with her husband, *10 Steps in Writing the Research Paper, Masks of the Spirit: Image and Metaphor in Mesoamerica,* and *The Flayed God: The Mythology of Mesoamerica.*

Elizabeth Max (EM) is professor emerita of English education, Oklahoma State University. She holds a B.S. from Texas Woman's University, a master's degree from the University of North Texas, and an Ed.D. from Oklahoma State University. Her interest in Greek literature, pursued during sabbatical research in Greece, stems from undergraduate theater study. Author of numerous journal articles and reviews, Dr. Max is a founding member of the National Women's Studies Association.

Breon Mitchell (BM) is director of the Wells Scholars Program at Indiana University, where he is professor of comparative literature and Germanic studies. He is author of *James Joyce and the German Novel* and has published widely on modern European and American literature. He has also translated contemporary German novels and short story collections by such authors as Heinrich Böll, Siegfried Lenz, and Franz Kafka.

Renée H. Shea (RHS), associate professor of English at the University of the District of Columbia, directs the M.A. program in composition and rhetoric. A contributing editor to *Belles Lettres, A Review of Books by Women,* she has published interviews with Lee Smith, Michelle Cliff, Edwidge Danticat, and Sandra Cisneros. She holds a doctorate from the University of Pennsylvania in writing assessment and works with test design for the College Board, American Council on Education, Law School Admission Service, and U.S. Chamber of Commerce.

Ron Smith (RS), emeritus professor of English, Utah State University, is author of *Mythologies of the World: A Guide to Sources; A Guide to Post-Classical Works of Art, Literature, and Music Based on Myths of the Greeks and Romans;* and numerous articles in academic journals and popular periodicals. He has been a program participant at more than forty national, regional, and international conventions and was elected to the executive committee of the Conference on College Composition and Communication.

Marilyn J. Strelau (MJS) teaches English at Simsbury High School in Connecticut, where she has established a multicultural literature course. She has developed and taught a similar course at Central Connecticut State University. She frequently leads teacher workshops on multicultural issues. She holds a B.A. from Valparaiso University and an M.A. in African literature from the University of Denver.

Donald Van Dyke (DVD) has taught for thirty-four years at Glenbrook North High School in Northbrook, Illinois. He holds an M.A. in classical studies and has taught Latin, English, and humanities to all levels of students.

Clifton Warren (CW) received his B.A. and M.A. in history and English at the University of Richmond and his Ph.D. in comparative literature and letters from Indiana University, where he was associate editor of *Folio.* A well-known book and film critic for newspapers, TV, and radio, Dr. Warren's critical articles have appeared in *The Cyclopedia of World Authors* and *The Encyclopedia of 20th Century Literature.* He is currently dean of the college of liberal arts at the University of Central Oklahoma.